Discover
Kaua'i

Experience the best
of Kaua'i

This edition written and researched by
Sara Benson

Contents

Contents

Discover Kaua'i

Po'ipu & the South Shore   155

Waimea Canyon & the Westside   193

In Focus

Survival Guide

This Is Kaua'i

Tropical paradise – if ever there was an idea with a powerful grip on the mind, this would be it. And if ever there was a place to match, it is the Garden Island of Kaua'i. The emerald pinnacles of the Na Pali Coast, the painted walls of Waimea Canyon, the misty mountains of Hanalei and the sunny beaches of Po'ipu radiate outward from the ancient cone of Mt Wai'ale'ale, all of which is surrounded by a cornucopia of flamboyant marine life. These elements forge a magical union that sets this island apart from the world and, indeed, produce the giddy feeling of having risen above it.

With an astonishing list of outdoor adventures, Kaua'i will puncture your resort bubble.

Here you can soar over tropical valleys, zip through treetops on a cable, paddle to inaccessible beaches and float with sea turtles in azure bays. Each new experience is a special, often unforgettable, way of interacting with the island.

Kaua'i inspires more inward explorations, too.

The values of the ancient Hawaiians are alive and well here, rooted in mountains, waves, clouds and a holistic understanding of the natural world. You will encounter this in simple ways, such as when someone gives you directions *mauka* (toward the mountains) or *makai* (toward the sea). On a deeper level, this traditional culture is built on moderation, balance, fairness and unity, producing a gentle pace of life, strong families and legendary hospitality.

You can't help admiring the way that Kaua'i has preserved itself in the face of the 21st century.

Here, no town surpasses 10,000 people. By law, no building is taller than a coconut tree, and it is impossible to circumnavigate the coast by car. When a multimillion-dollar ferry arrived to begin service to neighboring islands, Kaua'i residents, concerned over environmental and other issues, blocked its path. It never returned. Visitors do.

Hanakapi'ai Falls (p151)

> **"**
> The values of the ancient Hawaiians are alive and well here.
> **"**

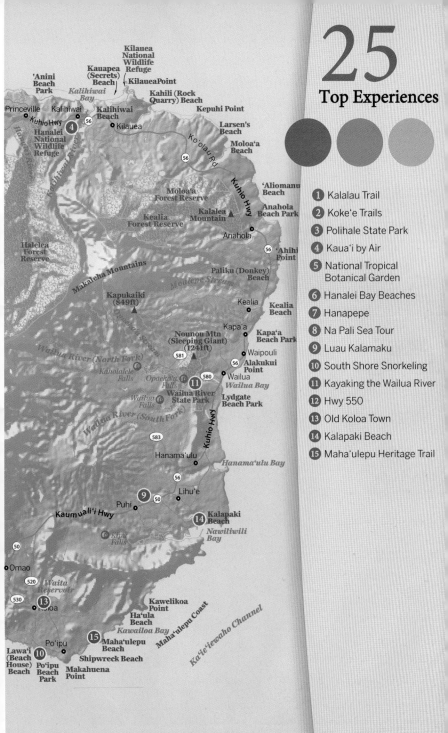

25
Top Experiences

15 Kaua'i's Top Experiences

Kalalau Trail

Rugged, elevated and celebrated, this Na Pali Coast trail (p149) will lead you as far as you're willing to go (well, up to 11 miles). The most trodden portion, to Hanakapi'ai Beach, is an adventure in itself. Bolder trekkers continue up the valley to Hanakapi'ai Falls, where a refreshing 300ft waterfall awaits. The boldest of the bold walk until there is no more walking and arrive at – oohs and aahs – Kalalau Valley, where your exhausted self enters, and your purest self exits. Na Pali Coast (p148), as seen from the Kalalau Trail

Koke'e Trails

Trekking Koke'e's Nu'alolo Trail or the Awa'awapuhi Trail (p231) is enough to satisfy the most demanding trailblazer. Strenuous climbs with hair-raising drops are rewarded with breathtaking views. There's also a long boardwalk through the Alaka'i Swamp, a misty primordial bog and birdwatcher's paradise at the very top of the park. View of the Na Pali Coast from the Nu'alolo Trail (p231)

Polihale State Park

A spiritual beach (p223) that, in essence, is Polihale. The ancient Hawaiians thought so, and nothing has changed. The broad and endless sands, the vast Pacific and the dramatic beginnings of the mighty Na Pali cliffs bring the eternal to Earth here. There are a number of great beaches on Kaua'i, but none of them inspire reflection in quite the same way, making this the perfect spot to relax and reflect after a long hike or a busy trip. Suitably, it's at the end of a long and bumpy road.

Kaua'i by Air

There's nothing like seeing Kaua'i by air (p295). Twisting through verdant tropical valleys, landing at remote waterfalls, hovering inside a volcanic crater and soaring like a bird over gorgeous coastline are all open to you, depending on your chariot. Choices include the universally popular helicopter tour (with the doors off, if you dare) or an open-cockpit biplane. Helicopter tour of the Na Pali Coast (p45)

CARIN JOE/GETTY IMAGES ©

4

The Best...
Hikes

KALALAU TRAIL
Epic views from a global favorite. (p149)

NOUNOU MOUNTAIN TRAILS
The best perch from which to view the Coconut Coast. (p75)

MAHA'ULEPU HERITAGE TRAIL
Four miles of wet 'n' wild coastline, with paleontology thrown in for free. (p174)

ALAKA'I SWAMP TRAIL
A boardwalk through a primordial bog, with bird-watching galore. (p235)

NU'ALOLO CLIFFS TRAIL
The vertiginous link between two other classic trails. Just don't look down. (p232)

National Tropical Botanical Garden

5

You don't need a green thumb to enjoy the Garden Island's awesome gardens, as the National Tropical Botanical Garden (p179) reveals. At its flagship Allerton Garden (p172) in Po'ipu, you'll find one man's Shangri La – landscape art that manages to improve on Mother Nature. In contrast, the vast and unmanicured McBryde Garden lies next door. Then there's the North Shore's Limahuli Garden (p144), nestled mid-valley in Ha'ena's dramatic topography. Look! An Eden for everyone.

Limahuli Garden (p144)

SUNGJIN AHN PHOTOGRAPHY/GETTY IMAGES ©

The Best...
Beaches

HANALEI BAY
Plenty of waves and 2 miles of sand to call your own. (p126)

HA'ULA BEACH
Wild. Remote. Wonderful. (p172)

KALAPAKI BEACH
Learn to surf at a Hawaii classic. (p38)

POLIHALE STATE PARK
Some beaches tan your body; this one expands your spirit. (p223)

PO'IPU BEACH PARK
The family-friendly option, with snorkeling benefits. (p168)

6 Hanalei Bay Beaches

Arguably the nicest in the universe, the beaches of crescent-shaped Hanalei Bay (p126) have something for pleasure seekers of all types. While go-getters can bodyboard, kayak, fish off the pier, take surf-lessons or test their skills at one of several timeless surf breaks (best in winter), easygoers can amble along 2 miles of golden sand. Home to world-class surfers and starlets alike, this global icon manages to stay low-key at all times, if not define what that means. Hanalei Beach Park (p129)

ANN CECIL/GETTY IMAGES ©

Hanapepe

Every Friday is Art Night (p207) in the historic Westside town of Hanapepe (p203), when galleries open late and the main street is awash with people hankering for art and a good time. This Old West lookalike is worth a trip on any day; just make sure you stop by Talk Story Bookstore (p210), the USA's westernmost bookstore, and the Taro Ko Chips Factory (p208) for a crunchy, island-grown snack. Craft gallery, Hanapepe

Na Pali Sea Tour

The sight of the primordial Na Pali Coast rising out of the sea, with its knife-edge pinnacles and alluring valleys, is the gripping stage for multiple ocean adventures (p286). For high-octane thrills, zip around sea caves in a raft (inflatable boat), before landing at Nu'alolo Kai (p199), an ancient Hawaiian settlement only just this side of paradise. Prefer more luxury? Sail a far-steadier catamaran without spilling your drink. If that's not enough, seek out your inner Iron Man on a 17-mile sea kayak journey (p287).

Luau Kalamaku

Admit it. Ever since you watched *The Brady Bunch* enjoying a Hawaiian luau, you've wanted to try one yourself. Today, luau shows are a well-oiled machine, serving hundreds of visitors nightly with a buffet feast and Polynesian revue. Luau Kalamaku (p53) turns the same old show into crowd-pleasing dinner theater, with dancers, flashy leotards and pyrotechnics adding a dash of Cirque du Soleil. The central stage play describes one family's epic voyage to Hawaii, culminating in a dramatic Samoan fire dance. Just don't forget to eat your roasted pig.

9

The Best...
Ocean Adventures

NA PALI KAYAK TRIP
Because you *can* exercise in paradise. (p286)

HANALEI SURF LESSONS
Get bitten by the surf bug (and nothing else) in the enchanting Hanalei Bay. (p131)

NA PALI RAFT TRIP
Got your sea legs? Then you're ready to rock 'n' roll. (p286)

DIVING NI'IHAU
They say it's the best diving in the state! (p216)

SNORKELING PO'IPU
Marine treasures for everyone, regardless of ability. (p175)

South Shore Snorkeling

The South Shore is the Sunset Strip of snorkeling (p176), with one great site after another popping up as you drive down the coast, providing access for everyone, from newbies to Aquaman. Prepare to be amazed by the diverse and spectacular marine life that hugs the shore here: sea turtles, dolphins and monk seals are common, while beautiful tropical fish are everywhere. Beginners head to Po'ipu Beach Park (p168); experts to Koloa Landing (p170). Waters off Po'ipu (p168)

10

The Best...
Views

KE'E BEACH
Magical mountains on one side; a multihued sunset on the other. (p148)

ST REGIS PRINCEVILLE
From the bluff or the patio, take in Hanalei to Bali Hai. (p122)

SEAVIEW TERRACE
A South Seas panorama unfolds from the Grand Hyatt in Po'ipu. (p186)

WAIMEA CANYON LOOKOUT
The Grand Canyon? Here? You're forgiven the confusion. (p225)

KALALAU LOOKOUT
Even better than the postcard. Or the movies. (p230)

Kayaking the Wailua River

11

Once home to ancient Hawaiian royalty, Kaua'i's largest tropical river (p67) still holds the same mystique and allure that have drawn generations up and down these sacred waters. Encounter several ancient heiau (religious sites), come ashore for a short trek to a 'secret' waterfall, swim endlessly, and dry out in the sun as you paddle down the river (p72). Though experienced kayakers may opt to go it alone (cheaper), several companies offer guided tours that open up the unique history of this waterway, making for a richer journey. All experience levels are invited – kids too.

Hwy 550

The island's greatest drive (p225), this long ascent takes you from one end of Waimea Canyon – aptly called the Grand Canyon of the Pacific – to another. And yet you're only halfway there. Next comes Koke'e State Park, whose lookouts are the stuff of postcards, never mind numerous Hollywood films. Along the way you can stretch your legs with a number of short hikes, enough to whet your appetite for some legendary trails. Where else can you find a single road that encompasses as much as this?

12

ROBERT GLUSIC/GETTY IMAGES ©

Old Koloa Town

Take a historic main street full of quaint plantation cottages from the time of Big Sugar, refill them with shops and restaurants catering to the modern visitor, and you get charming Old Koloa Town (p160), a pragmatic blend of Old Hawaii and new. Visitors, drop your walking maps. All you have to do here is stroll from one end to the other, sampling along the way. And when it comes to the Koloa Fish Market or Sueoka Snack Shop (p165), sampling is the order of the day.

Shopfronts, Koloa

ANN CECIL/GETTY IMAGES ©

Kalapaki Beach

Kaua'i's version of Waikiki Beach is a lot smaller than its cousin, but performs the same function: if you want to learn to surf, this is a great place to start (p38). If you want to people watch with a tropical drink in your hand, Duke's Barefoot Bar (p53) is a great place to end. The beach lines the turn of a U-shaped bay and is a hive of activity, fueled by the Marriott behind. Kick off your vacation with a sidewalk stroll along this Hawaii classic.

Mahaʻulepu Heritage Trail

If variety is the spice of life, then Mahaʻulepu is one hot coastline. This trail (p174) takes you from the popular beaches of Poʻipu to a wild stretch of land, full of secluded coves, snorkeling reefs and dramatic sea cliffs. It's a 4-mile PhD in geology, too, culminating in the fascinating Makauwahi Sinkhole (p175), where you enter the Land of the Lost. Don't worry, you'll find your way back – if you want to.

15

The Best...
Dining

JOSSELIN'S TAPAS BAR & GRILL
The foodie superstar in Poʻipu. (p184)

BARACUDA TAPAS & WINE
Chic and trendy meets low-key Hanalei. (p138)

BEACH HOUSE RESTAURANT
There is only one iconic oceanfront restaurant in Poʻipu – and this is it. (p185)

KOLOA FISH MARKET
Your one-stop shop for fresh *poke*, mixed with only-in-Hawaii flavors. (p165)

KAUAʻI COMMUNITY MARKET
Taste down-on-the-farm goodness with local food vendors galore every Saturday in Lihuʻe. (p49)

Kaua'i's Top Itineraries

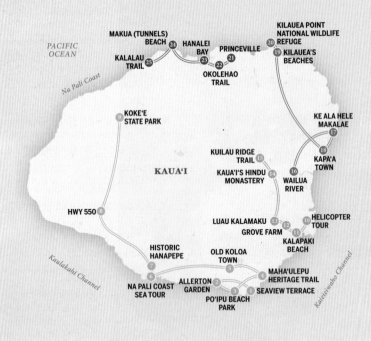

PACIFIC OCEAN

MAKUA (TUNNELS) BEACH 24
HANALEI BAY
KALALAU TRAIL 25
KILAUEA POINT NATIONAL WILDLIFE REFUGE 20
23 **PRINCEVILLE** 21
KILAUEA'S BEACHES 19
22
OKOLEHAO TRAIL

Na Pali Coast

KOKE'E STATE PARK 9

KE ALA HELE MAKALAE 17

18

KUILAU RIDGE TRAIL 15
KAPA'A TOWN

KAUA'I

KAUA'I'S HINDU MONASTERY 14
16 **WAILUA RIVER**

HWY 550 8

LUAU KALAMAKU 13
12 10 **HELICOPTER TOUR**
GROVE FARM
11
KALAPAKI BEACH

HISTORIC HANAPEPE
OLD KOLOA TOWN
7
6 5
NA PALI COAST SEA TOUR
ALLERTON GARDEN 2
4 **MAHA'ULEPU HERITAGE TRAIL**
3 1 **SEAVIEW TERRACE**
PO'IPU BEACH PARK

Kaulakahi Channel

Kaiei'eiwaho Channel

● **Po'ipu to Koke'e State Park** Four days

● **Lihu'e to Wailua** Two days

● **Wailua to Kilauea** Two days

● **Princeville to Na Pali Coast State Park** Two days

Po'ipu to Koke'e State Park

Po'ipu Beach Park (p168)

VAUGHN GREG/GETTY IMAGES ©

1 Seaview Terrace (p186)

Start your first day right at this espresso bar dwarfed by a panoramic view.

2 Allerton Garden (p172)

Enjoy an early tour at this idyllic work of landscape art.

3 Po'ipu Beach Park (p168)

Spend the afternoon at this local favorite, great for kids. Don't forget your snorkel.

4 Maha'ulepu Heritage Trail (p174)

On day two, stretch those morning legs on this wild and beautiful coastal hike. Stop by the **Makauwahi Sinkhole** for a bit of reflection on the past 10,000 years.

5 Old Koloa Town (p160)

End the day with a relaxing stroll along this quaint main street of shops and restaurants.

6 Na Pali Coast Sea Tour (p286)

Day three. Whether you bash around by raft or blow around by catamaran, don't miss the Na Pali from the sea. Take the early tour.

7 Historic Hanapepe (p203)

Got a paintbrush in your holster? This outpost of the Old West is like a huge art colony, which buzzes on Friday's Art Night.

8 Hwy 550 (p225)

First, the 'Grand Canyon of the Pacific', then the Na Pali views: for day four it's hard to beat this road to nowhere.

9 Koke'e State Park (p229)

Choose a trail and go.

THIS LEG: 60 MILES

2 DAYS

Luau Kalamaku (p53)

COURTESY OF LUAU KALAMAKU ©

10 **Helicopter Tour** (p45)

A busy day five begins early, with a perennial favorite. Circle the island, ducking into valleys, searching out waterfalls, and hovering in the crater of Mt Waiʻaleʻale.

11 **Kalapaki Beach** (p38)

One glance at this Hawaii classic and you'll expect to see the Duke catching the next wave. Spend your lunch money at Kalapaki Beach Hut.

12 **Grove Farm** (p39)

To understand old Hawaii in the age of Big Sugar, come to this utterly authentic plantation house, once home to Lihuʻe's greatest sugar baron, for the afternoon tour.

13 **Luau Kalamaku** (p53)

End the day with this contemporary take on the old-time luau and some first-rate show biz underneath a big top. Don't focus too much on your *kalua* (earth oven) pig: you may miss the blazing fire dance.

14 **Kauaʻi's Hindu Monastery** (p67)

Day six is all about relaxing. Begin with a long spiritual check-in at these 458 meticulously landscaped acres, where Eastern religion meets the Garden Island: the perfect marriage?

15 **Kuilau Ridge Trail** (p73)

Short but sweet, this mile-long hike links many verdant nooks together. Be sure to bring something to nibble on: the lookout has a covered picnic table perfect for contemplating the 80 different shades of green before you.

➡ THIS LEG: 15 MILES

Wailua to Kilauea

Wailua River (p67)

ANN CECIL/GETTY IMAGES ©

16 **Wailua River** (p67)

Day seven starts with a paddle adventure up the scenic Wailua River. Whether you join a tour group or blaze your own wake, venture up this sacred waterway to view several ancient heiau (temples) and explore a hidden waterfall by foot.

17 **Ke Ala Hele Makalae** (p87)

Not enough exercise? This gentle bike path stretches from the south end of Kapa'a Beach Park past Paliku (Donkey) Beach to the north, encompassing the Coconut Coast's many ocean vistas.

18 **Kapa'a Town** (p86)

Now cool down from the action by perusing the shops and eateries in the Eastside's most charming commercial hub. For a quick but worthy bite, stop by **Mermaids** (p92) and order the ahi (tuna)

nori wrap with a Thai tea to accompany. For the vegan crowd, walk around the back to **Rainbow Living Foods** (p92).

19 **Kilauea's Beaches** (p106)

As an introduction to the North Shore, day eight begins either at **Kahili (Rock Quarry) Beach** or **Kauapea (Secrets) Beach**. Take a quick dip, plant your body in the sand, repeat as necessary.

20 **Kilauea Point National Wildlife Refuge** (p108)

An early 20th-century lighthouse, a never-ending view and a plethora of land-, air- and water-based species make exploring this peninsula an intriguing afternoon. Don't forget your picnic.

● ●
➔ THIS LEG: 20 MILES

Hanalei Beach Park (p129)

LINDA CHING/GETTY IMAGES ©

21 Princeville (p117)

Day nine. Wake early and beat the crowds at either the **Prince Course** or **Makai Golf Club**, both designed by Robert Trent Jones Jr. If no one's a golf enthusiast, a morning trot on one of **Princeville Ranch Stables'** beautiful mares is a worthy substitution.

22 Okolehao Trail (p133)

Before entering the near-addictive Hanalei Bay, catch a glimpse from 1250ft high.

23 Hanalei Bay (p126)

There's 2 miles of beach to choose from here and you can't go wrong on any of it. For surf voyeurism or active participation, focus on **Waiʻoli (Pine Trees)**. For the most family-friendly zone, set up day camp by **Hanalei Pier**, where lifeguards keep a watchful eye.

24 Makua (Tunnels) Beach (p143)

Your last day begins with a choice: either snorkeling this classic spot, or strolling eastward around Shell Point, where you can start your collection of cowries, mulberry drupes and Hebrew cones. Or do both. In any case, come early to get a good parking spot and beat the midday trade winds.

25 Kalalau Trail (p149)

Where the road ends is where the real adventure begins, the **Na Pali Coast**. If you don't want to bite off more than you can chew, opt for the 4-mile round-trip hike to **Hanakapiʻai Beach**. This provides more than enough visual grandeur to keep your heart pumping.

➡ THIS LEG: 14 MILES

Get Inspired

📖 Books

○ **Star Mana** (Ken Carlson; 1997) Reveals how today's Hawaiian healing arts transform Kaua'i's flowers and gemstones into spiritual medicine.

○ **Mark Twain in Hawaii: Roughing It in the Sandwich Islands** (Mark Twain; 1866) Pre-fame Twain's colorful musings about his journey through the Hawaiian Islands in the 1860s.

○ **A Kaua'i Reader: The Exotic Literary Heritage of the Garden Island** (ed Chris Cook; 1999) A collection of stories covering the gamut from *menehune* (little people) legends to big-wave surfing.

🎥 Films

○ **South Pacific** (1958) Rossano Brazzi and Mitzi Gaynor tempt love and fate in the film that put Kaua'i on the Hollywood map.

○ **The Descendants** (2011) George Clooney finds his soul on Kaua'i.

○ **Hawaii** (1966) The fictional account of a New England missionary's journey to convert Hawaiians to Christianity.

🎵 Music

○ **Beautiful Rainbow** (1997) Born and raised on Kaua'i, Larry Rivera has composed over 100 songs en route to becoming a local music legend.

○ **Acoustic Soul** (1996) Singer-songwriter John Cruz cut his teeth on the mainland and returned to Hawaii to celebrate his heritage in song.

○ **Alone in IZ World** (2001) A posthumous collection of tunes from the legendary vocalist and ukulele player Israel Kamakawiwo'ole.

🌐 Websites

○ **Kaua'i Festivals** (www.kauaifestivals. com) The most up-to-date festival listings. For many events on Kaua'i, it's cheaper to buy tickets in advance.

○ **Kaua'i Historical Society** (http:// kauaihistoricalsociety. org) The point of access for numerous resources on Kaua'i's history.

○ **Hawaiian Language Center** (www.olelo. hawaii.edu) Easy lessons on learning the Hawaiian language, and playable recordings of Hawaiian cultural education radio spots.

🕐 Short on time?

This list will give you instant insight into Kaua'i.

Read *The Separate Kingdom* (1984) Edward Joesting's well-researched and colorfully woven account of Kaua'i's history.

Watch *Taylor Camp* (2009) Robert C Stone's documentary about life on the North Shore in the '60s and '70s.

Listen *Legends of Hawaiian Slack Key Guitar* (2007) Grammy Award–winning collection of open-tuned melodies brimming with nostalgia for Hawaii's history.

Log on Kauai Explorer (www. kauaiexplorer.com) Outdoors info and ocean safety with handy Q&A forums.

Kaua'i mountains

Kaua'i Month by Month

Top Events

⊛ **Waimea Town Celebration**
February

⊛ **Prince Kuhio Celebration**
March

⊛ **Eo e Emalani I Alaka'i**
October

⊛ **Coconut Festival** October

⊛ **Hawaiian Slack Key Guitar Festival** November

February

⊛ **Waimea Town Celebration**
Waimea Town comes alive during this event in mid-February, with lei making competitions, food, craft and game booths, a canoe race, rodeo events and good old-fashioned family fun (p218).

March

High surf season winds down on the North Shore, though wind and rain can still taunt.

⊛ **Prince Kuhio Celebration of the Arts**
Two weeks of festivities on the South Shore honor of Prince Jonah Kuhio Kalanianaole, known for his efforts to revitalize Hawaiian culture during his lifetime. Events include hula, an outrigger canoe race, an international spearfishing tournament and a rodeo, as well as Hawaiian entertainment and cultural demonstrations (p178).

April

✕ **Spring Gourmet Gala**
Some of Hawaii's most highly regarded chefs present pairings of food-and-wine that would impress even the snobbiest of gourmands at this fundraiser for Kaua'i Community College's culinary arts program.

May

⊛ **May Day Lei Contest**
Simple strings of *plumeria* (frangipani) are mere child's play next to the floral masterpieces entered in the annual Kaua'i Museum lei contest (p47), held in early May.

(left) *Poke with Hawaiian seaweed*
ANN CECIL/GETTY IMAGES ©

June

Taste of Hawaii
Known as the 'Ultimate Brunch Sunday' this casual affair held on the first Sunday of June showcases local chefs, gourmet food booths and no-holds-barred sampling (p76).

July

High surf starts on the South Shore, while the whole island generally sees consistent sunshine.

Koloa Plantation Days
This family-friendly, nine-day festival (p163) in late July celebrates the plantation history of the South Shore. Come watch rodeos and outrigger canoe races, partake in guided walks or scope out the crafts fair.

August

Heiva I Kaua'i Ia Orana Tahiti
Watch dance troupes from around Hawaii and as far away as Japan gather in Kapa'a for Tahitian drumming and dancing competitions (p88).

September

The summer crowds dissipate and ideal weather conditions usually prevail.

Kaua'i Composer's Contest & Concert
Encouraging the island's up-and-coming talent to show their skills in categories such as Hawaiian, Contemporary Hawaiian and Youth, this signature event of the

Kaua'i Mokihana Festival (p47) is held in mid to late September.

October

Coconut Festival
Join in and learn all one might ever need to know about coconuts. This two-day cultural festival (p89) held in Kapa'a in early October offers entertainment, exhibits, games, contests and cooking demonstrations all revolving around *niu*.

Eo e Emalani I Alaka'i
Held at Koke'e State Park in early October, this one-day festival (p233) of hula and Hawaiian music commemorates Queen Emma's 19th-century journey to Alaka'i Swamp.

November

High surf arrives in the north and heavy rain marks the 'unofficial' start of winter.

Hawaiian Slack Key Guitar Festival
Watch masters of the Hawaiian slack key guitar (*ki-ho'alu*) blend styles (and strings) for this event (p48) at the Aqua Kauai Beach Resort in mid-November.

December

The whales have arrived and are ready to be watched by the holiday crowds .

Kalo Festival
At a historic fishpond on Hanalei Bay, learn all about the Hawaiian 'staff of life,' taro. Food vendors, live music and traditional Hawaiian games make it fun for families (p134).

Need to Know

Currency
US dollar ($)

Language
English and Hawaiian

Visas
Generally not needed for Canadians or citizens of Visa Waiver Program (VWP) countries for stays of up to 90 days with ESTA pre-approval.

Money
ATMs widely available. Credit cards usually required for reservations. Traveler's checks (US dollars) rarely accepted.

Cell Phones
The only foreign phones that will work are GSM multiband models. Buy prepaid SIM cards locally.

Wi-Fi
Common at most accommodations. Top-end hotels typically charge daily fees. Free at some libraries and coffee shops.

Internet Access
Internet cafes are rare ($6 to $12 per hour). Public libraries have free computer terminals (non-resident library card $10).

Tipping
Typically 18–20% for restaurant waitstaff; 10–15% for taxi drivers; 15–20% for bartenders; $2 per bag at the airport or hotels.

When to Go

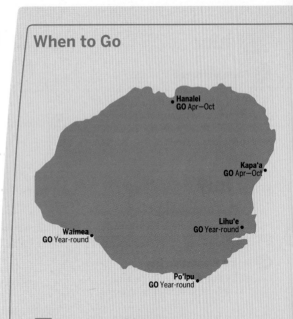

Hanalei
GO Apr–Oct

Kapa'a
GO Apr–Oct

Lihu'e
GO Year-round

Waimea
GO Year-round

Po'ipu
GO Year-round

■ Tropical climate, wet & dry seasons

High Season
(Dec–Mar, Jun–Aug)
○ Rates increase dramatically at hotels and resorts.
○ Winter brings rain, whale-watching and bigger surf on the North Shore.
○ Sunny July and August are busy.

Shoulder
(Apr & May)
○ Heavy rains slow down, but don't disappear.
○ Ocean surf is calmer.
○ Look for online specials and cheap airfares.

Low Season
(Sep–Nov)
○ Calm waters before winter.
○ More vacancies and lower rates at accommodations.
○ Typically dry and pleasant in September, sometimes into October.

Advance Planning

○ **Three months before** Decide which region's attractions and climate match your interests. Search for internet deals on flights, cars, accommodations.

○ **One month before** Secure reservations for popular activities, such as sailing or snorkeling cruises, helicopter tours and popular top-end restaurants .

○ **One week before** Check the weather and surf report, confirm car-rental and hotel reservations and start a seven-day countdown on your Facebook status.

Your Daily Budget

Budget Less than $100
- Campsite per night: $3–30
- Take-out plate lunch: $5–12
- One-way bus ride: $2

Midrange $100–250
- Hotel room, condo or B&B: $100–250
- Rental car(excluding insurance and gas): per day/week: $35/150
- Meals at midrange restaurants

Top End More than $250
- Beach resort hotel room: from $250
- Three-course meal with a cocktail in a top restaurant: $75–120
- Guided outdoor adventure tour or boat cruise: $80-200

Exchange Rates

Australia	A$1	$0.81
Canada	C$1	$0.86
Euro	€1	$1.22
Japan	¥100	$1.20
New Zealand	NZ$1	$0.77
UK	UK£1	$1.56

For current exchange rates see www.xe.com.

What to Bring

- **Driver's license** Needed to rent a car.
- **Hands-free device** Talking or texting on a handheld phone while driving is illegal.
- **Hiking shoes** Highly recommended for the Na Pali Coast, Waimea Canyon and Koke'e State Park.
- **UV-protection sunglasses** For ocean glare and highway driving.
- **Passport or photo ID (with date of birth)** Good idea if you want that mai tai at sunset.
- **Snorkeling gear** Easy to rent, but if picky about fit/quality, bring your own.
- **Sunscreen and hat** This is the tropics. Protect your face and body.

Arriving on Kaua'i

Lihu'e Airport

Car Rental companies located close to the airport with customary shuttle service.

Kaua'i Bus Limited airport runs ($2).

Taxi Usually available curbside during the day; call ahead if arriving at night.

For more information see p57.

Getting Around

- **Rental Car** Recommended unless you're on a very tight budget. Well-maintained highway provides access to most of the island. Free parking widely available.
- **Bus** Goes through all major towns; limited runs, especially on weekends.
- **Bike** Good option if staying in one town, but not for island-wide exploring. If on the Eastside or North Shore expect some rain.
- **Taxi** Flag-down fee is $3 plus $3 per mile. Plan on calling for a taxi.

Sleeping

- **B&Bs and Inns** Homes or small lodgings that are generally reliable and personable. Fruit and pastries typically served for breakfast.
- **Condominiums** Individually owned units clustered together. Ideal for independent types preferring amenities like a full kitchen.
- **Hotels and Resorts** Wide range of rates but generally pricier. High-end resorts typically have nicer pool and beach areas.
- **Vacation Rentals** Usually an entire house for a family or a party of several people to share, or sometimes just a studio apartment or suite for couples.

Be Forewarned

- **Rental car break-ins** Don't leave valuables in the car, especially at remote parking locations like beaches or trailheads.
- **Rain and floods** They don't call it one of the wettest spots on Earth for nothing. Close windows when parking and learn how to put up your convertible or Jeep top quickly.

Lihuʻe

Welcome to the capital of Kauaʻi, and a dose of Hawaiian reality.

At one end, a Walmart; at the other, postcard-perfect Kalapaki Beach. Jarring, perhaps, but undeniably authentic.

Lihuʻe's melting pot of tourism and local business comes with some practical advantages. The commercial center is strip-mall plain, but a welcome source of (relatively) inexpensive shops and restaurants, as well as the launchpad for a variety of island adventures.

Likewise, the long coastline mixes the island's international airport and main harbor with amenity-packed resorts and hotels. Sprinkle in two fascinating plantation-era historical sites, a cute museum, and some first-class golf courses, and you'll end up wondering how this modest town of 6500 manages it all. In fact, once you get used to it, this spunky hybrid has an appeal all its own.

Kalapaki Beach (p38)

Lihuʻe Highlights

Kalapaki Beach

This Kauaʻi classic melds natural beauty with loads of fun for the whole family. Take a dip or surfing lesson right at the beach (p38), which sees some glorious sunrises. After a full day in the sun, grab happy hour drinks and noshes at ocean-view Duke's Barefoot Bar. Souvenir shopping is big here, too – just take a stroll around Anchor Cove Shopping Center.

Kauaʻi Museum

Inside a beautiful lava-rock building on a busy corner of Rice St in downtown Lihuʻe, this historically minded treasure trove (p39) will teach you all about the unique history of the Garden Isle, beginning with ancient Hawaiians up through the end of the sugar-plantation era. Show up on Lei Day (May 1) for lei-making workshops, live Hawaiian music and more.

Helicopter Tour

3

The one vacation video everyone back home will want to see – including you – is of your aerial flight (p45) over Kaua'i's stunning scenery, made famous by countless Hollywood movies. Buzz over the soaring cliffs of the Na Pali Coast, Mt Wai'ale'ale's rain-soaked crater and the 'Grand Canyon of the Pacific.' For those who don't mind a rougher ride, opt for a thrilling doors-off helicopter tour. Na Pali Coast

4

Grove Farm

A time machine back to the era of Big Sugar, this authentically restored 19th-century plantation property (p39) is like a large-scale still life. Call at least a week in advance to sign up for a lovingly guided tour, which includes tea service on the lanai of the main house, whose interior is filled with antiques that nostalgically evoke a bygone era.

5

Luau Kalamaku

The island's best luau (p53) successfully combines the traditional and the contemporary. This unusual theater-in-the-round ups the ante with hip-shaking Tahitian and Samoan fire dancing, pyrotechnics and an epic story of one family's journey across the Pacific to Hawaii. The buffet food rates above average, featuring a whole pig unearthed from an *imu* (traditional Hawaiian underground oven).

Lihuʻe Itineraries

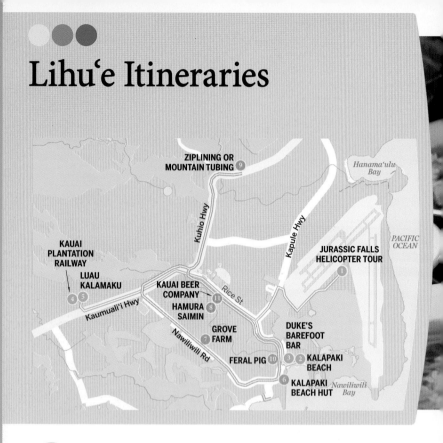

ZIPLINING OR
MOUNTAIN TUBING ⑨

Hanamaʻulu Bay

Kuhio Hwy

Kapule Hwy

PACIFIC OCEAN

KAUAI
PLANTATION
RAILWAY

JURASSIC FALLS
HELICOPTER TOUR ①

LUAU
KALAMAKU

④⑤

KAUAI BEER
COMPANY ⑪

Rice St

Kaumualiʻi Hwy

HAMURA
SAIMIN ⑧

DUKE'S
BAREFOOT
BAR

GROVE
FARM ⑦

Nawiliwili Rd

KALAPAKI
BEACH

FERAL PIG ⑩ ③ ②

KALAPAKI
BEACH HUT ⑥

Nawiliwili Bay

JURASSIC FALLS TO LUAU KALAMAKU
DAY ONE

Jump-start your Kauaʻi experience with an early-morning flight through paradisiacal valleys and a landing at an awesome waterfall on a ① **Jurassic Falls Helicopter Tour**.

Afterwards, spend the bulk of the day on ② **Kalapaki Beach** on a classic stretch of Hawaii coast, with water sports galore to choose from. For some easy surfing, rent a paddle board from Kalapaki Beach Boys. Stroll the palatial open-air corridors of the Kauaʻi Marriott resort, or walk the breakwater in Nawiliwili Bay for a look at the island's main harbor. A must for lunch, ③ **Duke's Barefoot Bar** has a lively beachfront bar and quick-fix kitchen. It's the beachfront hangout, with people-watching galore, sinful tropical drinks and live music at night.

In the afternoon, get a quick overview of local history as you chug along on a ④ **Kauaʻi Plantation Railway** through the fields and meet the local farm animals – a winner with children. Tickets can be combined with ⑤ **Luau Kalamaku** (check-in at 5pm). Cross a Hawaiian luau with polished dinner theater and you get Lihuʻe's best nighttime entertainment. Be sure to wander the grounds of Kilohana Plantation first, and try a shot of spiced rum at Koloa Rum Company.

KALAPAKI BEACH HUT TO KAUAI BEER COMPANY
DAY TWO

Start day two right, with breakfast at
6 Kalapaki Beach Hut. Try the *loco moco*
(two fried eggs, hamburger patty, rice and
gravy) for a bit of regional flavor.

It doesn't get any more authentic than
the Wilcox family home, **7 Grove Farm**,
which has managed to remain untouched
for decades. For the thoughtful traveler, this
is island history at its very best. Be sure to
book ahead.

In the afternoon, steaming bowls of
noodle soup might seem incongruous
for lunch in tropical heat, but saimin is an
island tradition – and a blast from the past.
8 Hamura Saimin is famous for it.

After eating, choose between
9 ziplining or mountain tubing for your
afternoon adventure. We prefer Just Live
for ziplines, whizzing through the forest
canopy, while Kaua'i Backcountry has a
lock on mountain tubing.

Later, unwind in town at **10 Feral Pig**.
This popular sports bar not only has Hawaii
beers on tap, but also dishes up a secret
off-menu burger topped with pork belly.
From here, head to the **11 Kauai Beer
Company**. Rub elbows with young, fun
locals at this downtown brewpub.

Noodle dishes at Hamura Saimin (p50)

LINDA CHING/GETTY IMAGES ©

Discover Lihu'e

History

Lihu'e's modern history is steeped in sugar. In 1849 German settlers established the first local sugarcane plantation, which struggled until the development of irrigation in 1856. Thereafter, profitability grew, attracting entrepreneur George Wilcox from Hanalei, who founded what would become the area's largest plantation, Grove Farm. Lihu'e's sugar mill (still standing south of town along Kaumuali'i Hwy) was once Kaua'i's largest.

Lihu'e's mill closed in 2000, ending more than a century of operation. But by then Lihu'e had already morphed into a very different animal. The Lihu'e you see today is almost entirely a creation of the past half-century. As tourism has replaced the sugar economy, Lihu'e has had the good fortune of hosting both the island's biggest airport and its major seaport, Nawiliwili Harbor. The result is Kaua'i's second-largest town and its commercial center. When it comes to trade, exporting sugar has now been replaced by the importation of most of the necessities of life – including sugar, if you can believe that.

🏖 Beaches

Kalapaki Beach   Beach

(Map p40; 🚹) This sandy beach and sheltered bay is tucked between a marina and the mountains. It's overlooked by the Marriott resort facing Kalapaki Bay and by an enviable collection of houses atop a rocky ridge to the east. Its easy-access location and versatility make it popular with families. Calmer waters toward the east are good for swimming, although a sandy bottom makes for poor snorkeling. Swells to the west draw bodyboarders and both novice and intermediate surfers.

For surfers, it's an easy paddle out of about 50yd to the reef, and there's no pounding shore break to get through. Most go right for a mellow, predictable wave, but there are more aggressive lefts, too.

Wailua Falls (p39)

Detour:
Lihu'e's Hidden Beaches

Kaua'i Lagoons Golf Club harbors two adjacent (and commonly confused) beaches that are fun to seek out if you have time.

To find **Ninini Beach** (Map p40), either enter the Marriott off Rice St and take a left after the first bridge, or enter Kaua'i Lagoons off Ahukini Rd and proceed straight along Ninini Point St all the way past the airport. In either case you'll end up at a car park, past a 'Coastline Access' sign. Cross the shrubbery to the golf course, take the path to the fifth hole, and follow the cliff edge until you see a path going down. The little beach below is very secluded, with just enough sand for a picnic.

Running Waters Beach (Map p40) is visible down the coast. From the car park, walk on the asphalt toward the shore, turn right around the buildings, and head cross-country toward the gazebo, which harbors a public outdoor cold-water shower. The small beach below has even less sand than Ninini Point Beach, but is popular with bodyboarders for its dynamic cross-current action. Swimmers take care.

From either beach you can see the 86ft tall **Ninini Point Lighthouse** (Map p40), marking the northern entrance to Nawiliwili Bay. Access is via the dirt road on the left just before the car park. Views are excellent from here, but the wind, trash, rough road, and jets screaming overhead make Ninini Beach the better picnic spot.

◉ Sights

Wailua Falls   Waterfall
(Ma'alo Rd) Made famous in the opening credits of *Fantasy Island,* these falls appear at a distance. When they are in full bloom and misting the surrounding tropical foliage, it's a fantastic photo op. While officially listed as 80ft, the falls have been repeatedly measured to have a far greater drop. Heed the sign that warns: 'Slippery rocks at top of falls. People have been killed.' Many have fallen while trying to scramble down the steep path beyond.

To get here from Lihu'e, follow Kuhio Hwy (Hwy 56) north. Turn left onto Ma'alo Rd (Hwy 583), which ends at the falls after 4 miles. Expect crowds and difficult parking.

Grove Farm   Historic Site
(Map p40; ☎808-245-3202; www.grovefarm. org; 4050 Nawiliwili Rd; 2hr tour adult/child 5-12yr $20/10; ⊙tours 10am & 1pm Mon, Wed

& Thu, by reservation only) History buffs adore this plantation museum, but kids may grow restless. Grove Farm once ranked among the most productive sugar companies on Kaua'i. George Wilcox, the Hilo-born son of Protestant missionaries, acquired the farm in 1864. The main house feels suspended in time, with rocking chairs sitting still on a covered porch and untouched books lining the library's shelves.

Call a week or more in advance to join a small-group tour, which includes cookies and mint tea served on the lanai.

Kaua'i Museum   Museum
(Map p44; ☎808-245-6931; www.kauaimuseum. org; 4428 Rice St; adult/child $10/2; ⊙10am-5pm Mon-Sat, tours 10:30am Tue-Fri) ✐ The island's largest museum is set in two buildings – one of which was built with lava rock in 1960. Come here for a quick grounding in Kaua'i's history and ecology, and in Hawaiian history and culture in

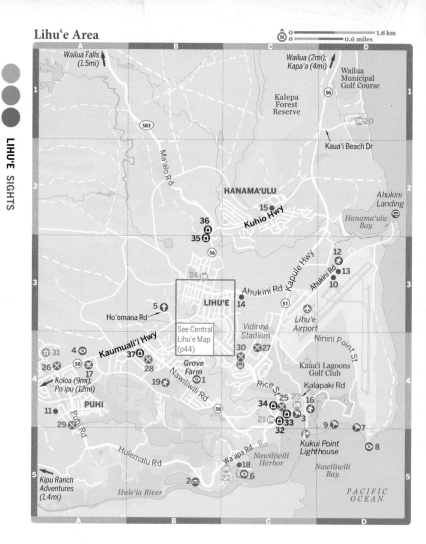

LIHU'E SIGHTS

general, which you'll gain especially if you take a free guided tour. A smattering of Asian art is also on display.

Admission is discounted on the first Saturday of the month.

Kilohana Plantation   Historic Site

(Map p40; ☎ 808-245-5608; www.kilo-hanakauai.com; 3-2087 Kaumuali'i Hwy; admission free, attraction prices vary; ⏰ 10:30am-9pm Mon-Sat, to 3pm Sun) FREE If you're curious about how Kaua'i's powerful

sugar barons lived, visit this historic plantation estate turned shopping complex, which also hosts a luau show (p53), the Kauai Plantation Railway (p45) and the Koloa Rum Company (p55). Plantation owner Gaylord Wilcox built the main house in 1936. Inside the 16,000-sq-ft Tudor-style mansion, antique-filled rooms and ornate carpets on hardwood floors lead past cases of poi pounders, koa bowls and other Hawaiiana to gallery shops.

Lihuʻe Area

Alekoko (Menehune) Fishpond Overlook   Viewpoint
(Map p40; Hulemalu Rd) This roadside overlook offers an oft-photographed vista of the Huleʻia Valley, where the Huleʻia River winds beneath a ring of verdant peaks. The river is walled off at one bend to form a 39-acre *loko wai* (freshwater fishpond). Local legend attributes construction to *menehune,* the 'little people' of Hawaiian mythology. The best time to visit is just before sunset. It's about 0.5 miles west of the entrance to Nawiliwili Harbor. ·

On the north side of the river lies the 240-acre Huleʻia National Wildlife Refuge, a breeding ground for endemic waterfowl. The refuge is closed to the public, except for guided kayaking tours.

Lihuʻe Lutheran Church   Church
(Map p40; 4602 Hoʻomana Rd; ☉daily, services 8am & 10:30am Sun) Hawaii's oldest Lutheran church is a quaint clapboard house, with an incongruously slanted floor that resembles a ship's deck and a balcony akin to a captain's bridge. The building is actually a faithful 1983 reconstruction of the 1885 original (built by German immigrants) leveled by Hurricane ʻIwa. It's located just off Kaumualiʻi Hwy (Hwy 50).

Island Insights

Constructed perhaps nearly 1000 years ago, the Alekoko fishpond's 900ft lava wall, now covered by a line of mangrove trees, created an ingenious fish trap. Small holes allowed young fish to enter the pond but prevented them from escaping when grown. The privately owned pond was productive with mullet until 1824, but is no longer in use. This is one of the finest examples of ancient Hawaiian aquaculture remaining, and has been on the National Register of Historic Places since 1973.

Activities

Just Live
Adventure Tour

(Map p40; ☑808-482-1295; www.justlive. org; Anchor Cove Shopping Center, 3416 Rice St; zipline tours $79-125; ⏰tours daily, by reservation only) This outfit stands above the rest – literally – by offering Kaua'i's only canopy-based zipping, meaning you never touch ground after your first zip. The 3½-hour tour includes seven ziplines and four bridge crossings, or there's a scaled-down 'Wikiwiki' zip tour. The 'Eco-Adventure' adds a climbing wall, a 100ft rappeling tower and a heart-stopping monster swing.

Participants must be at least nine years old and weigh between 70lb and 250lb.

Island Adventures
Adventure Tour

(Map p40; ☑808-246-6333; www.islandadventureskauai.com; Da Life, 3500 Rice St; tours incl lunch adult/child 6-12yr $180/157; ⏰tours 8am Mon-Wed & Sat, 11am Fri, by reservation only) Jump on a 5½-hour tour into Hule'ia National Wildlife Refuge, where you'll paddle 2.5 miles in, hike to two waterfalls on private land, learn how to wet rappel up to 60ft down the side of a waterfall, and take a lazy swim followed by a picnic lunch.

Kaua'i Backcountry Adventures
Adventure Tour

(Map p40; ☑808-245-2506, 888-270-0555; www.kauaibackcountry.com; 3-4131 Kuhio Hwy; 3hr tubing/zipline tours incl lunch $102/130; ⏰tours hourly 8am-2pm, by reservation only; 👪) This 3½-hour zipline tour features seven lines, which are elevated as high as 200ft above the ground and run as far as 900ft (almost three football fields). Afterward, you can refuel with a picnic lunch at the swimming pond. The family-friendly tubing tour (for ages five and up) floats through an old sugar plantation's ditch-and-tunnel irrigation system.

Zipliners must be at least 12 years old and weigh between 100lb and 250lb.

Outfitters Kauai
Adventure Tour

(Map p40; ☑888-742-9887, 808-742-9667; www.outfitterskauai.com; Outfitters Kayak Shack, Nawiliwili Small Boat Harbor, 2494 Niumalu Rd; zipline tours adult/child 7-14yr from $116/106, 5hr SUP tours incl lunch adult/child 12-14yr $126/96; ⏰by reservation only; 👪) Multi-activity tours at Kipu Ranch just outside town combine tandem ziplines with aerial bridges, hiking, and kayaking the Hule'ia River; the weight limit for zipliners is 250lb. Unique stand up paddle surfing (SUP) river tours include short hikes, swimming and a motorized canoe ride back upstream.

Captain Don's Sportfishing
Fishing, Cruise

(Map p40; ☑808-639-3012; www.captaindonsfishing.com; Nawiliwili Small Boat Harbor, 2494 Niumalu Rd; half-/full-day shared charters per person $140/250, 2/4hr private charters for up to 6 passengers from $325/600; ⏰by reservation only) One of the many fishing charters departing from Nawiliwili Small Boat Harbor, Captain Don's gives guests creative freedom to design their own trip (fishing, whale-watching, snorkeling, a Na Pali Coast cruise) on the 34ft *June*

Louise. Captain Don has decades of experience on Kaua'i's waters.

Kauai Beach Boys · Water Sports
(Map p40; ☎808-246-6333; www.kauaibeach boys.com; 3610 Rice St; 1hr sailboat cruises/lessons $39/140, 90min surfing or SUP lessons $75; ⏱8am-6pm, lesson hours vary) On Kalapaki Beach, this concession stand rents snorkel gear, surfboards and stand up paddle surfing (SUP) sets at reasonable prices, with 90-minute surfing and SUP lessons given several times daily. Call ahead for sailing lessons or to book a sailboat cruise on the bay.

Aloha Kaua'i Tours · Adventure Tour
(Map p40; ☎808-245-6400, 800-452-8113; www.alohakauaitours.com; 1702 Haleukana St; half-day tours adult/child 5-12yr $80/63) Aloha Kaua'i Tours specializes in 4WD trips on backroads, including a half-day trip (minimum four people, weekdays only) that rumbles through the gate used in filming *Jurassic Park* and ends with a 3-mile round-trip hike to a waterfall pool fed by a stream from mighty Mt Wai'ale'ale. Remember to book at least 24 hours in advance.

Kipu Ranch Adventures · Adventure Tour
(Map p162; ☎808-246-9288; www.kiputours. com; Kipu Rd; tours adult/child from $125/94; ⏱daily tour hours vary, by reservation only) This outfit's most popular all-terrain vehicle (ATV) tour takes you on a three-hour scenic journey around a private ranch used for filiming *Raiders of the Lost Ark* and *The Descendants*. The four-hour tour includes a short hike to a waterfall for swimming and a picnic lunch.

The Wilcox Legacy

From Wilcox Memorial Hospital to Gaylord's Restaurant, the face of Lihu'e is still deeply intertwined with the Wilcox family and its famous enterprise, Grove Farm Company.

The story begins in the latter part of the 19th century, when the family patriarch, George Wilcox of Hanalei, moved to Lihu'e and founded Grove Farm, just as the sugar business was beginning its long ascent. Wilcox was an innovative entrepreneur who developed new means of irrigation, planting and cultivation. He also became a power player in Hawaii politics, a community leader, and a philanthropist. During his long stewardship, from 1870 to 1933, Grove Farm Company flourished. It continued to grow after his nephew Gaylord Wilcox took over the reins. By 1950, the Wilcox family was one of Kaua'i's largest landowners, with approximately 22,000 acres. The family was also highly influential in many areas of local life, including pioneering a home ownership program for workers, and donating the land for Kaua'i Community College. In 1974, sugar operations ceased, and cane lands were leased to neighboring plantations. Grove Farm Company then diversified into land development, management and licensing.

In 2000, Grove Farm Company was sold to Steve Case, of AOL fame. He has since purchased another 18,000 acres, making the company nearly twice as large as it was at the height of the sugar business. Interestingly, Case's father once worked as an accountant for Grove Farm Company.

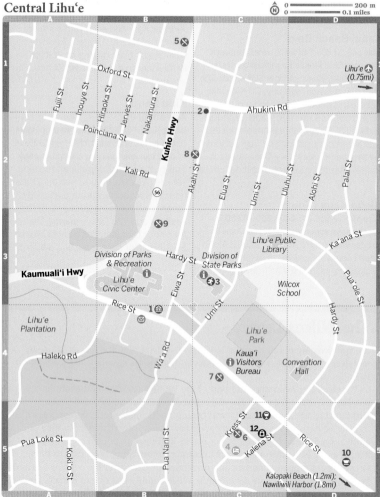

Kauai Lagoons Golf Club   Golf

(Map p40; ☎808-241-6000, 800-634-6400; 3351 Ho'olaule'a Way, Kaua'i Marriott Resort; green fees incl cart rental $135-205) Designed by Jack Nicklaus, the recently redone 18-hole, par-72 Kiele Course is tucked into the mountains by the coast. Book tee times up to 90 days in advance; discounts are offered to hotel guests. Club and shoe rentals available.

Puakea Golf Course   Golf

(Map p40; ☎808-245-8756, 866-773-5554; www.puakeagolf.com; 4150 Nuhou St; green fees incl cart rental $35-99) The lush cliffs of Mt Ha'upu serve as a backdrop to this Robin Nelson–designed public course. Club rentals are available. Aim to book tee times up to three months in advance.

LIHU'E ACTIVITIES

Central Lihu'e

Kauai Ohana YMCA   Swimming
(Map p40; ☎808-246-9090; www.ymcaofkauai. org; 4477 Nuhou St; day pass member/nonmember $5/10; ⊙5:30am-9am & 11am-7pm Mon-Fri, 10am-5:30pm Sat & Sun) Lap swimmers, get your fix at this open-air, Olympic-sized pool. A small weights/cardio workout room is also available, but towels and padlocks for lockers aren't provided. US mainland YMCA members should bring their card from home.

⊙ Tours

**Kauai Plantation
Railway**   Guided Tour
(Map p40; ☎808-245-7245; www.kilohanakauai. com; Kilohana Plantation, 3-2087 Kaumuali'i Hwy; 40min train rides adult/child 3-12yr $18/14, 4hr train & walking tours $75/60; ⊙hourly departures 10am-2pm, guided tours 9:30am Mon-Fri; ⊞) If you crave a bit of history and agricultural education, hop on this vintage-style train for a scenic 40-minute ride through a working plantation. The four-hour train and walking tour combo will get you into the fields and orchards, where you can pluck tropical fruit straight from the tree and feed the sheep, goats and wild pigs. Luau packages are also available.

HELICOPTER & BIPLANE

Most helicopter tours fly from Lihu'e Airport. Book ahead online for major discounts.

AirVentures Hawaii   Scenic Flights
(Map p40; ☎808-651-0679, 866-464-7864; www.kauaiairtour.com; Lihu'e Airport, 3651 Ahukini Rd; 1hr tours $245; ⊙tours Mon-Fri, by reservation only) When it comes to fixed-wing aircraft, there's nothing like an open-cockpit biplane. This outfit's gorgeous YMF-5 Super can seat two people up front. Visibility may not be the same as by helicopter, but the roar of the engine and the wind makes for a memorable experience. You'll even get to don an old-fashioned cloth aviator's hat and goggles.

Island Helicopters   Scenic Flights
(Map p40; ☎808-245-8588, 800-829-8588; www.islandhelicopters.com; 50/75min tours $297/371) Pilots with this long-running helicopter tour company have perfect safety records, and they only fly AStar helicopters, equipped with floor-to-ceiling windows. The 'Jurassic Falls' tour includes an exclusive 25-minute landing at 350ft-high Manawaiopuna Falls, hidden deep in Hanapepe Valley.

Kipu Falls

Once famous for its cliff jump and rope swing involving slippery rocks and water contaminated by leptospirosis, these falls are no longer legally accessible, let alone advisable to explore. Several tourists have been seriously injured or died here.

Family Outings

- Kalapaki Beach (p38)
- Kauai Plantation Railway (p45)
- Kaua'i Backcountry Adventures (p42) tubing tour
- Captain Don's Sportfishing (p42) snorkeling or whale-watching cruise
- Kauai Ohana YMCA (p45) swimming pool

Mauna Loa Helicopters
Scenic Flights

(Map p40; ☎808-652-3148; www.helicopter-tours-kauai.com; Harbor Mall, 3501 Rice St; 1hr tours from $275) Highly qualified pilots don't skimp on full 60-minute private tours for up to three passengers. Small groups allow for more-personalized interaction between pilot and passengers.

You can choose to have the doors on or off, and all seats are window seats.

Safari Helicopters
Scenic Flights

(Map p44; ☎808-246-0136, 800-326-3356; www.safarihelicopters.com; 3225 Akahi St; 60/90min tours $229/279) Flies AStar helicopters on the standard circle-island tour. The longer 'ecotour' includes a 40-minute stop at Robinson Ranch's wildlife refuge overlooking Okolele Canyon.

Jack Harter Helicopters
Scenic Flights

(Map p40; ☎808-245-3774, 888-245-2001; www.helicopters-kauai.com; 4231 Ahukini Rd; 60-65min tours $269) This pioneering outfit (operating since 1962) offers a standard enclosed, six-passenger AStar or a doors-off, four-passenger Hughes 500 helicopter. Longer doors-on tours are also offered.

Blue Hawaiian Helicopters
Scenic Flights

(Map p40; ☎808-245-5800, 800-745-2583; www.bluehawaiian.com/kauai/tours; 3651

Kaua'i Museum (p39)

Ahukini Rd; 55min tours $240) Flies high-end Eco-Star choppers, offering more space, glass and comfort, with less noise due to quiet, enclosed tail rotors. You can grab a souvenir DVD of your flight for an extra $25.

⚡ Festivals & Events

For the most up-to-date festivals listings, see www.kauaifestivals.com.

May Day Lei Contest   Cultural
(www.kauaimuseum.org; 🕑May) Established in 1981, the Kaua'i Museum's annual lei contest in early May brings out legendary floral art, with do-it-yourself workshops, live music and an auction.

**Fourth of July
Concert in the Sky**   Cultural
(www.kauaihospice.org; adult/child $15/7; 🕑4 Jul) Enjoy island food, live entertainment and the grand finale fireworks show set to music at Vidinha Stadium.

**Kaua'i County
Farm Bureau Fair**   Fair
(www.kauaifarmfair.org; 🕑Aug) Old-fashioned family fun happens at Vidinha Stadium in late August. The fair brings carnival rides and games, livestock shows, a petting zoo, hula performances and lots of local food.

**Kaua'i Composers
Contest & Concert**   Music
(www.maliefoundation.org/composers; 🕑Sep) 🌿 The signature event of the Kaua'i Mokihana Festival, this musical competition showcases homegrown musical talent in mid- to late September.

**Kaua'i Mokihana
Festival Hula
Competition**   Cultural, Dance
(📞808-822-2166; www.maliefoundation.org; 🕑Sep) 🌿 Three days of serious hula competitions are staged at the Aqua Kauai Beach Resort in mid- to late September. Both *kahiko* (ancient) and *'auana* (modern) styles enchant.

Local Knowledge

NAME: CURT LOFSTEDT

OCCUPATION: PRESIDENT AND DIRECTOR OF OPERATIONS, ISLAND HELICOPTERS

Why go on a helicopter tour of the island? Seventy percent of Kaua'i is either private land or inaccessible. So the only way to see it is by air. Helicopters are perfect for that. We can enter Mt Wai'ale'ale's crater and park in mid-air.

What is the typical tour route? You circumnavigate the island in an hour, enough time to see everything.

How safe is it? A modern helicopter, like an AStar, is a $2 million, FAA-certified machine. If there is a problem, it is typically pilot error.

What is the best time to go? An early morning flight is a good start to the day. The air is crisp. It's also nice after it has rained and the waterfalls are full. But anytime is good.

How do you choose between tour companies? You have to look at the aircraft, the cost, and the tour. Do you want a doors-off tour? Do you want to land someplace special? Be careful using the activities desk at your hotel, as they only work with certain companies.

Can you request a seat? You can, but there's only one front window seat, and passengers need to be spread out by weight.

Anything else to keep in mind? It's important that you schedule your helicopter flight early in your trip here. Some visitors miss out because they wait until the last minute.

Island Insights

There are two Wilcox family homes that you can visit today, both situated on roughly 100-acre estates. Grove Farm Homestead (p39) is the original house of George Wilcox, and a beacon of understatement. In contrast, Gaylord Wilcox's home at Kilohana Plantation (p40) is a 16,000-sq-ft Tudor mansion, once the most expensive home on Kaua'i.

The homes also occupy opposite ends of the tourism spectrum. Grove Farm is utterly authentic, to an astonishing degree. It is as if nothing has changed in decades – because it hasn't. If you want to enter old Hawaii, then this is your first stop, and a fascinating experience.

Kilohana Plantation, on the other hand, has largely been created for tourists (the Wilcox estate was never actually a plantation). Part of the original mansion has been turned into a restaurant, Gaylord's (p52). The train is not from Hawaii, but Alaska; the tracks were laid by current employees. The enormous luau pavilion was financed by Norwegian Cruise Line, which deposits hundreds of passengers there every week. The Koloa Rum was recently created from scratch. The end result is more of a well-done theme park than a historic site. Having said that, you can certainly enjoy both of these destinations equally well, but it will just be for entirely different reasons.

Garden Island Range & Food Festival
Food

(www.kauaifoodfestival.com; adult/child $35/18; ☺Nov) This annual foodie gathering at Kilohana Plantation in mid-November spotlights local chefs, as well as the farmers and ranchers who provide their Kaua'i-grown ingredients. Future dates and the location of this festival are subject to change.

Hawaiian Slack Key Guitar Festival
Music

(www.slackkeyfestival.com; ☺Nov) This opportunity to see master slack key guitarists is not to be missed. It's usually staged at the Aqua Kauai Beach Resort in mid-November.

Lights on Rice Parade
Parade

(www.lightsonrice.org; ☺Dec) A charming parade of illuminated floats takes over Rice St on the first Friday evening of December.

🛏 Sleeping

Lihu'e has one big beachfront resort and a smattering of hotels, inns and motels. For the best deals on private vacation rentals, search online at **Vacation Rentals By Owner** (www.vrbo.com) or **Airbnb** (www.airbnb.com). To talk to a live person, contact **Kaua'i Vacation Rentals** (Map p40; ☎808-245-8841, 800-367-5025; www.kauaivacation-rentals.com; 3-3311 Kuhio Hwy), one of the island's best rental agents.

Kaua'i Palms Hotel
Motel $

(Map p44; ☎808-246-0908; www.kauaipalms-hotel.com; 2931 Kalena St; r from $79; ☺office 7am-9pm; @ 🛜) One of two motels in central Lihu'e, this is easily the more appealing. Inside a two-story, open-air building, the 28 rooms are small but tidy, with refrigerators and cable TV. Air-con and kitchenettes cost extra. It's at the end of an industrial road downtown.

Aqua Kaua'i Beach Resort
Resort $$

(Map p40; ☎808-954-7419, 866-536-7976; www.kauaibeachresorthawaii.com; 4331 Kaua'i Beach Dr; r from $105; ❄🐾📶🏊) Set on its own thin ribbon of sand (no swimming), this sprawling resort sports 350 renovated boutique-on-a-budget rooms, four pools, nightly lounge entertainment and a full-service spa. You'll pay more for a room with a view. It's just north of town and the airport.

Garden Island Inn
Hotel $$

(Map p40; ☎808-245-7227, 800-648-0154; www.gardenislandinn.com; 3445 Wilcox Rd; r from $105; ❄📶🏊) This two-story hotel across the street from Kalapaki Beach holds its own for value and friendliness. Rooms are bright but kitschy, with murals splashed on the walls, tropical bamboo and wood furnishings, and kitchenettes. Free beach gear and DVDs to borrow.

Kaua'i Inn
Hotel $$

(Map p40; ☎808-245-9000, 800-808-2330; www.kauai-inn.com; 2430 Hulemalu Rd; r from $100; ❄@📶🏊) This large inn, just west of the harbor, offers a simple home base away from traffic and crowds. The 48 plain rooms each have a refrigerator and microwave. Ground-floor rooms come with back porches; those on the 2nd-floor are larger, but sans lanai.

Kaua'i Marriott
Resort $$$

(Map p40; ☎808-245-5050, 800-220-2925; www.marriott.com; 3610 Rice St; r from $279; ❄📶🏊) Anyone looking for a classic Hawaii resort experience won't be disappointed here. The hotel has Kalapaki Beach, a top golf club, the island's liveliest oceanfront restau-rant and a gargantuan pool for all-day entertainment. Hawaiian artifacts are displayed along the gleaming corridors. Room decor and amenities are contemporary chain-hotel standard; oceanfront units are worth it for the lanai views.

🍴 Eating

Kaua'i Community Market
Market $

(Map p40; ☎808-855-5429; www.kauaicommunitymarket.org; Kauai Community College, 3-1901 Kaumuali'i Hwy; ⏰9:30am-1pm Sat; 🅿🚻) 🍴 One of the island's biggest and best farmers markets, in partnership with the Kaua'i County Farm Bureau, brings a bonanza of locally grown, often organic fruits and vegetables; free-range eggs and local dairy cheeses; island-grown coffee and flowers; hand-harvested honey and sea salts; Hawaiian plate lunches and poi; and fresh smoothies, juices, popsicles and baked goods. Don't miss it!

Donkeys, Kilohana Plantation (p40)
LINDA CHING/GETTY IMAGES ©

Island Insights

If you see an enormous cruise ship in Nawiliwili Harbor, it's probably the *Pride of America*, which docks every Thursday for one night. Commissioned in 2005, the *Pride* was the first new cruise ship to be built in the US in nearly 50 years. It's one of the largest ships owned by Norwegian Cruise Line – at 920.3ft long and displacing more than 80,000 tons, it stands so tall in the water that it seems to defy the laws of buoyancy. On-board amenities include 14 restaurants, nine bars and lounges, a fitness center and spa, sports courts, a theater, two swimming pools, a kids club and much more.

Cruising at a swift 22 knots, the *Pride* carries up to 2186 passengers and 917 crew members on a seven-night inter-island journey with stops in Honolulu on O'ahu, Kahului on Maui, and Kona and Hilo on the Big Island. Fares start around $899 per person based on double occupancy. For more details, contact **Norwegian Cruise Line** (NCL; ☎877-397-1504; www.ncl.com).

Hamura Saimin Hawaiian $

(Map p44; ☎808-245-3271; 2956 Kress St; dishes $3-8; ⊙10am-10:30pm Mon-Thu, to midnight Fri & Sat, to 9:30pm Sun; 🖐) An island institution, Hamura is a hole-in-the-wall specializing in homemade saimin (local-style noodle soup). At lunchtime, expect crowds slurping noodles elbow-to-elbow at retro, U-shaped lunch counters. Save room for the other (and much more beloved) specialty, *liliko'i* chiffon pie.

Right Slice Bakery $

(Map p40; ☎808-212-8320; www.rightslice.com; Puhi Industrial Park, 1543 Haleukana St; slices from $5; ⊙11am-6pm Mon-Sat) The amazing pie vendor who graces farmers markets across the island has a commercial bake-shop. Order an hour ahead for your savory pot pie baked fresh, or swipe a sweet pie – blueberry piña colada, anyone? – by the slice or whole.

Kalapaki Beach Hut American $

(Map p40; ☎808-246-6330; www.kalapaki beachhut.com; 3474 Rice St; mains $7-10; ⊙7am-8pm; 🖐) This rubbah-slippah spot raises the bar for beach-shack cuisine. Order 100% Kaua'i grass-fed beef burgers with taro fries, catch-of-the-day fish sandwiches or gravy-licious *loco moco*, with fresh coconuts or shave ice to top it all off.

Lihu'e Farmers Markets Market $

Lihu'e has two small farmers markets each week: **Kukui Grove Center Farmers Market** (Map p40; www.kukuigrovecenter.com; 3-2600 Kamuali'i Hwy; ⊙3pm Mon; 🖈🖐) 🍴 in the Kmart parking lot at the Kukui Grove Center and **Kaua'i Sunshine Market** (Map p40; www. kauai.gov; Ho'olako St; ⊙3pm Fri; 🖈🖐) 🍴 at the Vidinha Stadium parking lot.

Pho Kauai Vietnamese $

(Map p44; ☎808-245-9858; Rice Shopping Center, 4303 Rice St; mains $7-12; ⊙10am-9pm Mon-Sat) Hidden in a strip mall, this no-frills Vietnamese noodle shop serves steaming bowls of decent *pho* (noodle soup). Choose from meat or vegetable toppings, such as beef brisket, grilled shrimp, snow peas or eggplant.

Tip Top Cafe Diner $

(Map p44; 3173 Akahi St; mains $6-12; ⊙6:30am-2pm Tue-Sun; 🖐) The stark white building might give you pause, but inside, this retro diner teems with locals filling up on good, ol'-fashioned eats. The main draws are its famous banana-macnut pancakes, oxtail soup and *loco moco*.

Fish Express
Seafood $

(Map p44; 📞808-245-9918; 3343 Kuhio Hwy; mains $7-12; 🕐10am-6pm Mon-Sat, grill until 3pm) Fish lovers, this is almost a no-brainer. Order chilled deli items, from fresh ahi *poke* to green seaweed salad, or try a plate lunch of blackened ahi (yellowfin tuna) with guava-basil sauce or a gourmet *bentō* (Japanese boxed meal). Get there early before the best *poke* runs out.

Times Supermarket
Supermarket $

(Map p40; www.timessupermarkets.com; Kukui Grove Center, 3-2600 Kaumuali'i Hwy; 🕐6am-11pm) Swing by this grocery store, which sells to-go salads, sandwiches, plate lunches and sushi. It has a smoothie bar and a *poke* (cubed raw fish mixed with *shōyu*, sesame oil, salt, chili pepper, *'inamona* or other condiments) station with 30 varieties made fresh daily.

Vim 'n Vigor
Health Food $

(Map p44; 📞808-245-9053; 3-3122 Kuhio Hwy; sandwiches around $6; 🕐9am-7pm Mon-Fri, to 5pm Sat; 🍴) Stocks healthy snacks, bulk staples and gluten-free and dairy-free products, but not much produce. Vegetarian and vegan sandwiches sell out fast.

Feral Pig
Pub Food $$

(Map p40; 📞808-246-1100; www.theferalpig-kauai.com; Harbor Mall, 3501 Rice St; mains $8-15; 🕐7:30am-9pm Wed-Mon) Across from Kalapaki Beach, this sports bar with a strong local following keeps Hawaii-brewed beers on tap and in bottles. Breakfasts and 'beermosas' are popular, but let's be honest: it's the massive namesake burger of island-raised beef topped with a slab of pork belly that wins. It's not on the menu, so ask for it.

Smiley's Local Grinds
Hawaiian $$

(Map p40; 📞808-245-4772; 4100 Rice St; meals $8-15; 🕐10:30am-1:30pm & 5-8:30pm Mon-Sat) Every workaday island town has its locals' favorite plate-lunch kitchen. 'Mini' plates will leave you stuffed with crispy pork katsu (cutlets), Korean-spiced chicken, Hawaiian *kalua* pig or even *laulau* (bundle made of pork or chicken and salted butterfish, wrapped in taro and *ti* leaves

Kiele Course, Kauai Lagoons Golf Club (p44)

CARL SHANEF/GETTY IMAGES ©

The Duke

When you're kicking back with your tropical drink at Duke's Barefoot Bar, you may just wonder – who was Duke anyway?

Duke Paoa Kahinu Mokoe Hulikohola Kahanamoku (1890–1968) is one of Hawaii's most famous sons. In his richly varied life, he was a five-time Olympic medalist in swimming, a Hollywood actor (his film and TV credits include *Mister Roberts*), the sheriff of Honolulu for almost 30 years and the first famous beachboy, as well as being the man credited with spreading surfing to Australia. Duke was also a legitimate hero: in 1925, he used his surfboard to effect the incredible rescue of eight men from a fishing vessel that had capsized in heavy surf off Newport Beach, California; 17 others died. Duke was not really royalty, however, his name notwithstanding. He was named after his father, who was himself named after the Duke of Edinburgh, Scotland. Over the years, however, he earned many honorary titles, including 'the Father of Surfing.'

For all his successes and international travels, Duke never forgot where he came from. He was always a traditional Hawaiian, speaking the language as much as he could, even preferring a longboard carved from koa wood. When he died of a heart attack in 1968, at the age of 77, his ashes were scattered at sea in front of Waikiki Beach.

and steamed). Contrary to the name, service can be curt.

Sweet Marie's Hawaii Bakery $$

(Map p40; ☎808-823-0227; www.sweet-marieshawaii.com; 3-4251 Kuhio Hwy; items from $2, mains $11-15; ⊙8am-2pm Tue-Sat) A gluten-free bakery operating out of a cute storefront delivers macaroons, cookies, brownies and a host of muffins and cakes, as well as a few breakfast and lunch dishes.

Gaylord's Hawaii Regional Cuisine $$$

(Map p40; ☎808-245-9593; www.kilohanakauai.com; Kilohana Plantation, 3-2087 Kaumuali'i Hwy; mains lunch $12-18, dinner $26-36, Sun brunch buffet adult/child 5-12yr $30/15; ⊙11am-2:30pm & 5-9pm Mon-Sat, 9am-2pm Sun) There is no doubt that the historic Wilcox home at Kilohana Plantation provides a handsome setting, particularly on the veranda. Amid manicured lawns and white tablecloths

in an open-air dining room, you can daydream as you fork into a local field greens salad, sesame-seared ahi with tempura avocado or banana-coconut cream pie. Sunday's brunch buffet has a Bloody Mary bar. Make reservations.

Duke's Fusion $$$

(Map p40; ☎808-246-9599; www.dukeskauai.com; Kaua'i Marriott, 3610 Rice St; mains bar $11-17, restaurant $23-34; ⊙restaurant 5-10pm, bar from 11am; P) You won't find an evening spot more fun and lively than Duke's, which offers a classic view of Kalapaki Beach. The steak-and-seafood menu is none too innovative, but fish tacos served in the downstairs Barefoot Bar are a fave, especially on cheaper 'Taco Tuesdays.' Hula Pie, a mound of macnut (macadamia nut) ice cream in a chocolate-cookie crust, satisfies a touristy crowd. Complimentary valet parking.

🍷 Drinking

Kauai Beer Company · Brewery
(Map p44; 📞808-245-2337; www.kauaibeer.com; 4265 Rice St; 🕐3-8pm Wed-Sat) Kaua'i's only microbrewery has a convivial bar downtown, where everyone kicks back with a honeyed IPAloha 2.0, a Lihu'e Lager or a rotating seasonal or nitrogenated brew. Some nights food trucks pull up right outside, while other nights the kitchen is open, serving pub grub such as poutine, Bavarian pretzels and taro avocado *poke*.

Hā Coffee Bar · Cafe
(Map p44; www.hacoffeebar.com; 4180 Rice St; 🕐6:30am-5pm Mon-Sat; 📶) Coffee hipsterdom has hit Kaua'i at this airy, high-ceilinged cafe, where retro island travel prints and local art hang on the walls. Locally baked maple macnut cinnamon rolls, focaccia sandwiches, gluten-free treats and teas round out the menu.

Duke's Barefoot Bar · Bar
(Map p40; www.dukeskauai.com; Kaua'i Marriott, 3610 Rice St; 🕐11am-11pm) For a convivial, Waikiki-style tropical bar with live music every night, hurry and grab a beachside table before the nonstop evening queue. Happy hour runs from 4pm to 6pm daily.

⭐ Entertainment

Luau Kalamaku · Luau
(Map p40; 📞877-622-1780; www.luaukalamaku.com; Kilohana Plantation, 3-2087 Kaumuali'i Hwy; adult/child 5-11yr/youth 12-16yr $100/40/60; 🕐5-8:30pm Tue & Fri; 👪) Skip the same-old commercial luau and catch this dinner theater-in-the-round with a dash of Cirque du Soleil (think lithe dancers, flashy leotards and pyrotechnics) thrown in. The stage play about one family's epic voyage to Hawaii features hula and Tahitian dancing, and showstopping, nail-biting Samoan fire

Gaylord's

ANN CECIL/GETTY IMAGES ©

dancing. The buffet dinner is above aver-age, despite the audience size (maxi-mum 1000 people).

Kaua'i Concert Association
Live Music

(808-245-7464; www.kauai-concert.org; tickets from $25) Stages the annual Red Clay Jazz Festivals and classical, jazz and world-music concerts at the **Kaua'i Community College (KCC) Performing Arts Center** (Map p40; 245-8311; http://kauai.hawaii.edu/pac; 3-1901 Kaumuali'i Hwy), where past performers include Berklee College of Music and the Harlem String Quartet.

Kukui Grove Cinema 4
Cinema

(Map p40; 808-245-5055; www.kukuigrove-cinema.com; 4368 Kukui Grove St; tickets $6-9;) Standard fourplex shows mainstream first-run Hollywood movies.

🔒 Shopping

Lihu'e's biggest mall is the aging, open-air **Kukui Grove Center** (Map p40; 808-245-7784; www.kukuigrovecenter.com; 3-2600 Kaumuali'i Hwy; 9:30am-7pm Mon-Thu & Sat, to 9pm Fri, 10am-6pm Sun;), home to department stores, sporting-goods and electronics shops, banks and more. Near Nawiliwili Harbor, the busy, low-slung **Anchor Cove Shopping Center** (Map p40; 3416 Rice St) and emptier two-story **Harbor Mall** (Map p40; 808-245-6255; www.harbormall.net; 3501 Rice St) draw mainly tourists from cruise ships and the nearby Marriott.

Edith King Wilcox Gift Shop & Bookstore
Books, Gifts

(Map p44; 808-246-2470; www.kauaimuseum.org; Kaua'i Museum, 4428 Rice St; 10am-5pm Mon-Sat) The Kaua'i Museum's gem of a gift shop carries a variety of genuine

Hawaiian crafts, such as Ni'ihau shell jewelry, koa woodwork and *lauhala* (a type of traditional Hawaiian leaf weaving) hats, along with collectible contemporary artworks and plenty of Hawaiiana books. Enter the shop, free of charge, through the museum lobby.

Koloa Rum Company   Drink

(Map p40; ☎808-246-8900; www.koloarum. com; Kilohana Plantation, 3-2087 Kaumuali'i Hwy; ☉store 9:30am-5pm Mon, Wed & Sat, to 9pm Tue & Fri, to 6:30pm Thu, to 3pm Sun, tasting room 10am-3:30pm Mon, Wed & Sat, to 7:30pm Tue & Fri, to 5pm Thu, to 2pm Sun) Kaua'i's own rum label is a relatively new brand, which means it doesn't have a fine aged rum yet, but its dark and spiced versions win awards. Learn how to mix a classic mai tai during a free rum tasting, starting every 30 minutes daily.

Koa Store   Gifts, Souvenirs

(Map p40; ☎808-245-4871, 800-838-9264; www.thekoastore.com; 3-3601 Kuhio Hwy; ☉10am-6pm) 🖉 Other galleries carry high-end masterpieces, but here you'll find more affordable and functional pieces, such as picture frames and jewelry boxes. Many items come in three grades, from the basic straight-grain koa to premium 'curly' koa. All woodcraft are genuine – they're not the cheap fakes sold at tourist traps. There's another location in Koloa.

Flowers Forever   Gifts

(Map p44; ☎808-245-4717, 800-646-7579; www.flowersforeverhawaii.com; 2679 Kalena St; ☉8am-5pm Mon-Thu, to 6pm Fri, to 4pm Sat) Voted 'Best Kaua'i Flower Shop' for 12 years running, Forever Flowers strings

Superferry Non Grata

In August 2007, when the Hawaii Superferry sailed toward Nawiliwili Harbor for its first arrival, there was a dramatic stand-off as some 300 Kaua'i protesters blocked its entry. Three-dozen people even swam into the gargantuan ferry's path, shouting, 'Go home, go home!' Ultimately, service to Maui (but not to Kaua'i) was launched in December 2007, but the whole enterprise was indefinitely terminated in March 2009, when the Hawai'i Supreme Court deemed Superferry's environmental impact statement (EIS) invalid.

Why was opposition to the ferry so furious? Actually, the opponents themselves were not 'anti-ferry' but, rather, anti-Superferry. They wanted smaller, passenger-only, publicly owned and slower-moving boats. Their main concerns were nighttime collisions with whales, worsened traffic on Neighbor Islands, the spread of environmental pests, and plundering of natural resources by nonresidents. Indeed, during the Superferry's brief run between O'ahu and Maui, some passengers were caught taking home 'opihi (a prized edible limpet), crustaceans, algae, rocks, coral and massive quantities of reef fish.

That said, not all locals were opposed. In fact, many locals (especially O'ahu residents) viewed the Superferry as a convenient way to visit friends and family on Neighbor Islands. They also cited the need for an alternate, fuel-efficient mode of transportation other than planes between the islands (though the enormous vessels were actually gas guzzlers).

For a compelling (if overwhelmingly detailed) account, read *The Superferry Chronicles* by Koohan Palk and Jerry Mander, which also analyzes the ferry's ties to US military and commercial interests.

together a multitude of flower, maile, *ti*-leaf and more unusual specialty lei. It will ship tropical flowers, plants and lei to the mainland, too.

Kapaia Stitchery Arts & Crafts
(Map p40; www.kapaia-stitchery.com; 3-3551 Kuhio Hwy; ⏰9am-5pm Mon-Sat) A quilter's heaven, this longtime shop features countless tropical-print cotton fabrics, plus island-made patterns and kits. Stop here also for handmade gifts and apparel, including children's clothing and aloha shirts.

Clayworks Arts & Crafts
(Map p40; ☎808-246-2529; www.clayworks atkilohana.com; Kilohana Plantation, 3-2087 Kaumuali'i Hwy; ⏰10am-6pm Mon-Fri, 11am-2pm Sat & Sun) A hidden pottery studio and gallery overflows with colorful vases, mugs, bowls and tiles. Potters also offer tutelage at the throwing wheel, and you'll get to take home your *raku*-fired, glazed masterpiece. Call ahead for lessons.

Tropic Isle Music & Gifts Souvenirs, Music
(Map p40; www.tropicislemusic.com; Anchor Cove Shopping Center, 3416 Rice St; ⏰10am-8pm) This tiny shop is crammed with a huge selection of Hawaiiana books, CDs, DVDs, bath and body products, home decor, island-made foodstuffs – you name it.

Here you can avoid mistakenly buying mass-produced knockoffs imported from Asia.

Da Life *Outdoor Equipment*
(Map p40; ☏808-246-6333; www.livedalife.com; 3500 Rice St; ⏰9am-5pm Mon-Fri, 10am-4pm Sat & Sun) This outdoor outfitter and booking agent's retail shop is stuffed with sports gear for all manner of land and sea adventures on Kaua'i. And if you forgot to pack it, Da Life probably stocks it.

Longs Drugs *Souvenirs, Food*
(Map p40; ☏808-245-8871; www.cvs.com; Kukui Grove Center, 3-2600 Kaumuali'i Hwy; ⏰7am-10pm) So much more than a drugstore, Longs is an inexpensive place to shop for a wide selection of Hawaii-made products, from children's books to macnuts and crack-seed candy.

ℹ Information

Emergency
Police, Fire & Ambulance (☏911)

Police Station (☏808-241-1638; www.kauai.gov; 3990 Kaana St) For nonemergencies and incident reporting.

Medical Services
Kaua'i Urgent Care (☏808-245-1532; www.wilcoxhealth.org; 4484 Pahe'e St; ⏰8am-7pm Mon-Fri, to 4pm Sat & Sun) Walk-in clinic for nonemergencies.

Longs Drugs (☏808-245-8871; Kukui Grove Center, 3-2600 Kaumuali'i Hwy; ⏰store 7am-10pm, pharmacy to 9pm Mon-Fri, to 6pm Sat & Sun) Full-service pharmacy.

Wilcox Memorial Hospital (☏808-245-1100; www.wilcoxhealth.org; 3-3420 Kuhio Hwy) Kaua'i's only major hospital has a 24-hour emergency room.

Money
American Savings Bank (☏808-246-8844; www.asbhawaii.com; Kukui Grove Center, 3-2600 Kaumuali'i Hwy) Convenient shopping-mall branch with a 24-hour ATM.

Bank of Hawaii (☏808-245-6761; www.boh.com; 4455 Rice St) Downtown bank with a 24-hour ATM.

Duke's (p52)

Post

Lihu'e Post Office (Map p44; ☏808-245-1628; www.usps.com; 4441 Rice St; ☺8am-4pm Mon-Fri, 9am-1pm Sat) Kaua'i's main post office.

Tourist Information

Kaua'i Visitors Bureau (Map p44; ☏808-245-3971, 800-262-1400; www.gohawaii.com/kauai; Suite 101, 4334 Rice St; ☺8am-4:30pm Mon-Fri) Comprehensive web resources for visitors, with free vacation-planning kits downloadable online.

❶ Getting There & Away

Air

Lihu'e Airport (LIH; Map p40; ☏808-274-3800; www.hawaii.gov/lih; 3901 Mokulele Loop, Lihu'e) Only 2 miles from downtown, this small airport handles all commercial interisland, US mainland and Canada flights.

Boat

The only commercial passenger vessels docking on Kaua'i at Lihu'e's Nawiliwili Harbor are cruise ships, mainly Norwegian Cruise Line (p50) and **Princess Cruises** (☏800-774-6237; www.princess.com).

Bus

Kaua'i Bus (Map p40; ☏808-246-8110; www.kauai.gov; 3220 Ho'olako St, Lihu'e; one-way fare adult/senior & child 7-18yr $2/1) As the hub for Kaua'i Bus, Lihu'e has service to all major island regions, including Hanalei, the Eastside and the Westside. Most routes run hourly or so on weekdays, with limited service on Saturdays, Sundays and holidays. Check the website for current schedules.

Car & Motorcycle

Kauai Car & Scooter Rental (☏808-245-7177; www.kauaimopedrentals.com; 3148 Oihana St; ☺8am-5pm) Locally owned agency rents older economy-size island cars from $25 per day, and scooters or mopeds from $35 per day, with additional taxes and fees. Younger drivers (over 21 years) and debit cardholders welcome. Book in advance; free airport pickups available.

Kaua'i Harley-Davidson (☏808-212-9469, 808-212-9495, 888-690-6233; www.kauaiharley.com; 3-1878 Kaumuali'i Hwy; ☺8am-5pm) It'll cost up to $200 per day, plus a $1000 minimum security deposit, but if you want a hog in paradise, you've got one.

Nawiliwili Harbor (p38)

ℹ Getting Around

To/From the Airport

To pick up rental cars, check in at agency booths outside the baggage-claim area, then catch a shuttle bus to the agency's parking lot. Or go straight to the rental-car lot, where there may be less of a queue.

Taxicabs are little used because most visitors rent cars, but you'll usually find them waiting curbside outside the baggage-claim area. If not, use the courtesy phones to call one. Average airport fares include Lihu'e ($9 to $13), Po'ipu ($42 to $53) and Princeville ($89 to $119).

Bus

Kaua'i Bus serves Lihu'e with a shuttle that runs hourly from about 6am until 9pm. Stops include Kukui Grove Center, Lihu'e Airport (no large backpacks or luggage allowed), Vidinha Stadium and Wilcox Memorial Hospital. There's also a lunchtime shuttle within central Lihu'e that runs at 15-minute intervals between approximately 10:30am and 2pm.

Car & Motorcycle

Most businesses have free parking lots for customers. Metered street parking is pretty easy to find.

Island Insights

Train fans, listen up. Between the late 1880s and early 1900s, Kaua'i relied on railroads for the running of the sugar business. Workers would catch the morning train out to the fields and spend the day moving cars loaded with cut cane to the mills, or moving bags of processed sugar to the nearest ship landing. None of the trains were meant for passenger use. Grove Farm owns four of these historic plantation steam locomotives. Three have been restored to full operation, and one is fired up every second Thursday of the month for a short ride.

Kapaʻa &
the Eastside

A combination of ancient history and modern convenience, this stretch of paradise once called *Kawaihau* (ice water) now has a warm buzz all its own.

With Kuhio Hwy as its coastal artery, Nounou Mountain ('Sleeping Giant') dividing the resort-laden 'Coconut Coast' from the quiet upcountry pasturelands, and the Wailua River making everything else seem like an echo, there's more than one face to the island's most populated region.

Once home to coconut groves, plantation towns, and *aliʻi* (high royalty) setting sail on the Pacific Ocean, today's Eastside is a budget traveler's best friend. Beachside resorts, crafty souvenirs, numerous eateries and cafes, and most any land or water-based activity you could desire are all within minutes of each other. Unless of course you find yourself in the 'Kapaʻa Crawl,' a tropical version of rush hour.

Wailua River (p67)
ANN CECIL/GETTY IMAGES ©

Kapaʻa & the Eastside Highlights

Lydgate Beach Park

Kid-friendly and safe, popular and scenic Lydgate Beach Park (p66) has not one, but two massive playgrounds for kids, plus outdoor showers, lifeguards, picnic tables and pavilions, and ample lounging and snorkeling opportunities. For timid swimmers, two pools are protected by a breakwater. Or just come for a relaxing walk down this long, long mane of blond sand.

② Ke Ala Hele Makalae

As a new day breaks, watch the sun say aloha in style as it appears over the Pacific beside this coastal path (p87). Paved for walkers, runners and cyclists, Ke Ala Hele Makalae will someday connect Lihuʻe with Anahola. For now the 5 miles already open between Kapaʻa Beach Park and Paliku (Donkey) Beach invite you to rent a beach cruiser and coast along.

Wailua River Kayaking

STEVEN GREAVES/GETTY IMAGES ©

Sacred to ancient Hawaiians, the Wailua River Valley was the birthplace of kings and the abode of *ali'i* (high royalty) and kahuna (priests) among centuries-old heiau (stone temples). The best way to experience the mystical natural beauty of Kaua'i's premier river (p67) today is by paddling a kayak, stopping to hike to a waterfall where you can swim (and wash off all that sweat) before floating back downstream.

LINDA CHING/GETTY IMAGES ©

Nounou Mountain

At times breath-stealing, the picturesque views from the 'Sleeping Giant' are worth the trek (p75). You'll have to climb more than 1000ft by taking one of the three approach routes in order to earn sweeping views of Kaua'i's lush Eastside, with its rivers, valleys, mountains and beaches. Bring a walking stick and plenty of water. This hike is best done during dry weather.

Kaua'i's Hindu Monastery

Serenity abounds in this domain, which may be the island's oddest and most unexpected sight. Almost like a forest sanctuary, the main temple (p67) sits surrounded by bountiful gardens high above the Wailua River. Intricate stone sculptures and a 700lb, 3ft-high quartz crystal *shivalingam* (representation of the god Shiva) are impressive. Visitors are welcome, but you'll need to dress modestly or borrow a sarong.

63

Kapaʻa & the Eastside Itineraries

ANAHOLA
BEACH PARK ⑪

PACIFIC
OCEAN

KEALIA BEACH
③

② KE ALA HELE MAKALAE
① JAVA KAI

KEAHUA
ARBORETUM ⑥

⑦ KAMOA UKELELE COMPANY

NOUNOU
MOUNTAIN

⑩ PAPAYA'S NATURAL FOODS
⑬
⑫ TIKI TACOS

KAUAʻI'S HINDU
MONASTERY ⑨

⑯⑮ KINTARO
⑧ ④ TREES LOUNGE
KILAUEA FISH MARKET

WAILUA RIVER
KAYAKING ⑤ ⑭
LYDGATE
BEACH PARK

2 DAYS

10 MILES

DAYS ONE & TWO

Enjoy your first morning at ①**Java Kai** coffeehouse, open early. Kick back with gourmet coffee, pastries and free wi-fi. Then, before the noon heat, cruise the coastal path, ②**Ke Ala Hele Makalae**, on a bike (or go for a walk or run). In the afternoon, surfers and sunbathers should head to ③**Kealia Beach** for formidable waves and a fierce tan (remember sunblock!).

Later, head to ④**Trees Lounge**, a hidden jazz, blues, rock and martini bar, for happy-hour madness and late-night crooners.

Start day two with some ⑤**Wailua River Kayaking**, on an invigorating kayak tour up the only navigable river in the Hawaiian

Islands. Your sweat will be rewarded by a waterfall swim. Pack some picnic foods and head to ⑥**Keahua Arboretum** in Wailua's refreshingly lush upcountry, where tall trees and a babbling brook couldn't be more picturesque.

Head back into town and stop by ⑦**Kamoa Ukulele Company**, the friendliest ukulele store on the island, and tempt yourself into a new hobby. Next, reward all your recreational endeavors with an early dinner of grilled Hawaiian fish with island greens, fresh *poke* or a giant ahi wrap at the ⑧**Kilauea Fish Market**. Get takeout and head over to the beach.

26 MILES

DAYS THREE & FOUR

On your third day, visit the grounds of a magnificent 9 **Hindu monastery**, where the tropical foliage surpasses most parks and a massive stone temple is under construction. Next, stop in at the island's long-time go-to health-food store, 10 **Papaya's Natural Foods**, for takeout lunch fixings. Then choose a beach spot and spread a *goza* (straw mat) for an impromptu picnic.

Most visitors miss rural 11 **Anahola Beach Park**, frequented by neighborhood residents. It's a sweet spot for swimming (and surfing), but respect the locals.

For dinner, visit roadside taco shop 12 **Tiki Tacos** and dig into a 'Surfing Pig'

taco, piled high with fish, *kalua* pig and cabbage.

Welcome the morning of day four by climbing the 'Sleeping Giant' – 13 **Nounou Mountain** – from any one of its three approaches. Expect a steep, sweaty hike, rewarded with panoramic views.

Finish your stay with a leisurely afternoon at kid-pleasing 14 **Lydgate Beach Park**. If you want to dine among the locals, head out early to phenomenally popular Japanese restaurant, 15 **Kintaro**, specializing in teppanyaki.

Antique buoy, Kealia Beach (p96)
LINDA CHING/GETTY IMAGES ©

Discover Kapaʻa & the Eastside

Wailua

Once the capital of Kauaʻi and one of the two most desired places for high royalty to live in ancient Hawaii, Wailua has a sacred history. Fresh water, fertile land, and easy ocean access for sustenance, recreation and travel were among numerous offerings this blessed area bestowed upon its inhabitants. The area at the mouth of the Wailua River was called Wailua Nui A Hoano ('great sacred Wailua').

As the modern world discovered the islands and industry became a priority, the area was known for its production of sugar cane, rice and pineapples. As well, it essentially became a thriving coconut factory, with groves lining the coast from Wailua north to Kapaʻa. The present-day result of this is the abundance of coconut trees that remain and its alliterative moniker – the 'Coconut Coast.'

Wailua's shore has plentiful oceanfront condos offering a 24/7 soundtrack of waves, and in the upcountry, B&Bs and vacation rentals abound in and among the rolling pasturelands, where residents are able to enjoy the quiet life while still being only a downhill stroll to the ocean.

🏃 Beaches

Lydgate Beach Park Beach (Map p70; www.kamalani.org; 🚼) A narrow stretch of windswept blond sand strewn with driftwood can entertain restless kids of all ages, all afternoon. There's generally safe swimming to be found in two pools inside a protected breakwater, and beginner snorkeling, too. Other amenities include two big playgrounds, game-sized soccer fields, a paved recreational path, picnic tables and pavilions, restrooms, outdoor showers, drinking water and lifeguards.

To get here, turn *makai* (seaward) on Kuhio Hwy between mile markers 5 and 6.

At the park's northern end, multifeatured **Kamalani Playground** is a massive 16,000-sq-ft wooden castle with swings, a volcano slide, mirror mazes, an epic suspension bridge and other kid-pleasing contraptions.

Lydgate Beach Park
MATTHEW MICAH WRIGHT/GETTY IMAGES ©

The Sacred Wailua River

To ancient Hawaiians, the Wailua River was among the most sacred places across the islands. The river basin, near its mouth, was one of the island's two royal centers (the other was Waimea) and home to the high chiefs. Here you can find the remains of many important heiau (ancient stone temples), now together designated a national historic landmark.

Hikina Akala Heiau (Rising of the Sun Temple) sits south of the Wailua River mouth, which is today the north end of Lydgate Beach Park. In its heyday, the long, narrow temple (built around AD 1300) was aligned directly north to south, but only a few remaining boulders outline its original massive shape. Neighboring **Hauola Pu'uhonua** (meaning 'the place of refuge of the dew of life') is marked by a bronze plaque. Ancient Hawaiian kapu (taboo) breakers were assured safety from persecution if they made it inside.

Believed to be the oldest *luakini* (temple dedicated to the war god Ku, often a place for human sacrifice) on the island, **Holoholoku Heiau** is located a quarter-mile up Kuamo'o Rd on the left. The whole area was royal property: toward the west, against the flat-backed birthstone marked by a plaque reading **Pohaku Ho'ohanau** (Royal Birthstone), queens gave birth to future kings. Only a male child born here could become king of Kaua'i.

Bear in mind, unmarked Hawaiian heiau might not catch your eye. Although they were originally imposing stone structures, most now lie in ruins, covered with scrub. But they are still considered powerful vortices of mana (spiritual essence) and should be treated with respect.

Beware of the open ocean beyond the protected pool – it can be rough and dangerous, with strong currents, huge waves, sharp coral and slippery rocks.

◉ Sights

Take a virtual tour of the Wailua Heritage Trail (www.wailuaheritagetrail.org) for an overview of historical sights and natural attractions, with a downloadable map.

Kaua'i's Hindu Monastery
Hindu Temple

(Map p68; ☎808-822-3012, 888-735-1619; www.himalayanacademy.com; 107 Kaholalele Rd; ☺9am-noon, inner gate open after 10:30am) FREE Serious pilgrims and curious sightseers are welcome at this Hindu monastery, set in 363 acres of verdant forest above the Wailua River. Amid bountiful gardens, the Kadavul Temple, Ganesha and Nandi statues, and other structures are all devoted to the god Shiva. While visitors can access a limited area on their own daily, free guided tours are offered once a week – call or check the website for details. Modest dress required: no shorts, T-shirts, tank tops or short dresses.

The **Kadavul Temple** contains a rare single-pointed quartz crystal, a 50-million-year-old, six-sided *shiva lingam* stone that weighs 700lb and stands over 3ft tall. In the temple (which visitors may not enter except to attend a 9am daily worship service), monks have performed a *puja* (prayer ritual) every three hours around the clock since the temple was established in 1973.

If you're not dressed properly, you can borrow sarongs to cover up with at the entrance.

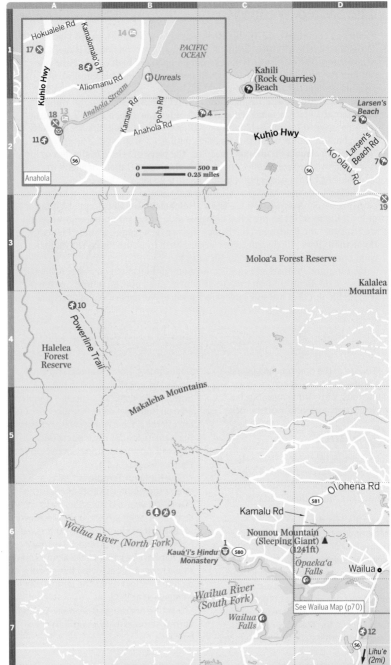

A   B   C   D

Inset map (Anahola):

Hokualele Rd

Kamalomalo'o Pl

14

PACIFIC OCEAN

17 ✕
8 ✚

'Aliomanu Rd

11 Unreals

Kuhio Hwy

Anahola Stream

Kamane Rd

Poha Rd

Anahola Rd

18 13
11 ✚

56

0 ————— 500 m
0 ————— 0.25 miles

Anahola

4

Main map:

Kahili (Rock Quarries) Beach

Larsen's Beach
2

Kuhio Hwy

Ko'olau Rd

Larsen's Beach Rd

7

56

19 ✕

Moloa'a Forest Reserve

Kalalea Mountain

10 ✚

Powerline Trail

Halelea Forest Reserve

Makaleha Mountains

O'ohena Rd

581

Kamalu Rd

6 ✚✚ 9

Wailua River (North Fork)

Nounou Mountain (Sleeping Giant) ▲ (1241ft)

Kaua'i's Hindu Monastery
1
580

'Opaeka'a Falls

Wailua

See Wailua Map (p70)

Wailua River (South Fork)

Wailua Falls

12

56

Lihu'e (2mi)

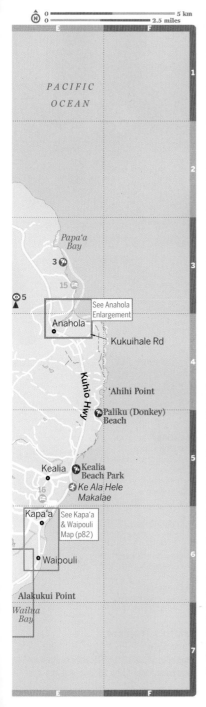

Eastside

'Opaeka'a Falls Lookout   Viewpoint

(Map p70) While not a showstopper, these 150ft-high waterfalls make for an easy roadside stop, less than 2 miles up Kumao'o Rd. For the best photographs, go in the morning. Don't be tempted to try trailblazing to the base of the falls. These steep cliffs are perilous and have caused fatalities. Cross the road for a fantastic photo op of the Wailua River.

Kamokila Hawaiian Village   Cultural Center

(Map p70; ☎ 808-823-0559; www.villagekauai. com; 5443 Kuamo'o Rd; village admission adult/ child 3-12yr $5/3, outrigger canoe tours adult/ child $30/20; ☺9am-5pm; ☷) While not a must-see, this is a pleasant diversion, es-pecially for kids. Along the Wailua River, the four-acre site includes reproductions of traditional Hawaiian structures amid thriving gardens of guava, mango and banana trees. Kamokila also offers canoe rentals and guided **outrigger canoe tours**, leaving hourly, which include pad-dling, hiking and waterfall swimming.

Wailua

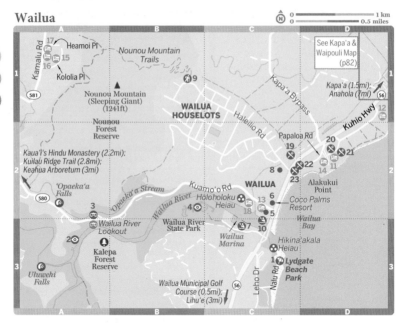

Wailua

⊙ Don't Miss Sights

Turn south from Kuamo'o Rd, opposite 'Opaeka'a Falls. The half-mile road leading to the village is steep and narrow.

Smith's Tropical Paradise
Gardens

(Map p70; ☎808-821-6895; www.smithskauai.com; adult/child 3-12yr $6/3; ⏱8:30am-4pm;

[img]) Other gardens might have fancier landscaping, but you can't beat Smith's for value. Take a leisurely stroll along a mile-long loop trail past a serene pond, grassy lawns and island-themed gardens. The setting can seem Disney-esque, with an Easter Island *moai* statue replica, but it's appealingly unpretentious.

Keahua Arboretum   Park

(Map p68) FREE Sitting prettily at the top of Kuamo'o Rd, this arboretum has grassy fields, a gurgling stream and groves of rainbow eucalyptus and other towering trees. Locals come here to picnic and to swim in the freshwater stream and pools, but beware the water is infected with leptospira bacteria.

Activities

Wailua Municipal
Golf Course   Golf

(Map p68; [tel]808-241-6666; www.kauai.gov/golf; 3-5350 Kuhio Hwy; nonresident green fees $48-60) This 18-hole, par-72 course, designed by former head pro Toyo Shirai, is one of Hawaii's top-ranked municipal golf courses. Plan ahead because morning tee times are sometimes reserved a week in advance. After 2pm, the green fee drops by half and it's first-come, first-served. Cart and club rentals available.

Kaua'i Cultural Center   Course

(Map p70; [tel]808-651-0682; www.kauaicultural center.com; Coconut Marketplace, 4-484 Kuhio Hwy; 1hr class from $5; [img]) [icon] Inside a shopping mall, this tiny community center is run by Leilani Rivera Low, a respected *kumu* hula (hula teacher). Take a beginner's hula, Tahitian dance or ukulele lesson, or learn how to make a *ti*-leaf skirt or flower lei. Call a day ahead to reserve a spot or drop by to ask about walk-in space.

Check the website for a schedule of upcoming classes, workshops and events.

Kauai Water Ski Co   Water Sports

(Map p70; [tel]808-822-3574, 808-639-2829; www.kauaiwaterskiandsurf.com; Kinipopo Shopping Village, 4-356 Kuhio Hwy; per 30/60min $75/140; [clock]9am-5pm Mon-Fri, to noon Sat) Hawaii's only non-ocean water-skiing happens on the Wailua River. Rates are per trip, not per person (maximum

Wooden canoe, Smith's Tropical Paradise

RITA ARIYOSHI/GETTY IMAGES ©

Cacao: Hawaii's Next Big Bean?

The world's chocolate comes mainly from West Africa, Brazil, Ecuador, Malaysia and Indonesia. But Kaua'i's humid tropical climate and regular rain allows the prized cacao bean to grow here, too. It's among the specialty crops that local-agriculture proponents are touting for Hawaii's next generation of farmers. Learn more about diversified agriculture and cacao growing at **Steelgrass Farm** (🖉 808-821-1857; www.steelgrass.org; 3hr tour adult/child under 12yr $60/free; ⊙ 9am-noon Mon, Wed & Fri; 🚼), which offers a unique chocolate farm tour that includes a tasting of single-estate dark chocolate bars produced around the world, including the Big Island's Original Hawaiian Chocolate Factory and O'ahu's Waialua Estate.

Their other crops are timber bamboo and vanilla, but the 8-acre farm features hundreds of flourishing tropical species, which you'll also see on the tour. It's a fantastic introduction if you're curious to see what thrives on Kaua'i, from avocados and citrus to soursop and sapodilla.

The owners, Will and Emily Lydgate, are the great-grandchildren of Kaua'i minister and community leader John Mortimer Lydgate, namesake of Lydgate Beach Park. The property was not an inheritance, as 'JM' had no desire to acquire land or profit from the sugar industry. With this thriving example of a 'teaching farm' – meant to experiment with workable crops – the Lydgates are trying to encourage a shift away from the monocrops and sheer capital outlays of industrial agriculture toward small-scale farming and diversified crops instead. Call ahead if you'd like to visit.

number of riders varies by skill level; beginners welcome), and include water-skiing or wakeboarding equipment and a professional instructor as your driver. Reservations required.

Powerline Trail Mountain Biking

(Map p68) While this trail (which covers more than 11 miles between Wailua and Princeville) is used mainly by hunters, it's a decent ride for die-hard mountain bikers. Hikers might find the trek too long, too exposed and, especially toward the north end, too monotonous. Beware of steep drop-offs hidden in dense foliage, and expect to slog through mud and puddly ruts.

The southern trailhead is at the end of Kuamo'o Rd. Beyond the Keahua Arboretum parking lot, you must cross water – not recommended with a standard car, especially in rainy weather.

KAYAKING

Majestic and calm, the Wailua River spans 20 miles, fed by two streams originating on Mt Wai'ale'ale. It's the only navigable river across the Hawaiian Islands, and kayaking the Wailua has become a tourist must-do. Fortunately, the paddle is a do-able 5 miles for all ages and fitness levels. Tours usually don't pass the Fern Grotto, and instead take the river's north fork, which leads to a mile-long hike through dense forest to **Uluwehi Falls** ('Secret Falls'), a 100ft waterfall. The hike scrambles over rocks and roots, and if muddy it will probably cause some slippin' and slidin'. Tip: wear sturdy, washable, nonslip watersports sandals.

Most tours last four to five hours and depart in the morning or early afternoon (call for exact check-in times). The maximum group size is 12, with paddlers going out in double kayaks. The pricier tours include lunch, but on budget tours you can store your own food in coolers and waterproof bags. Bring a hat, sunscreen and insect repellent.

Experienced paddlers might want to rent individual kayaks and go out on their own. Prices vary wildly. Note that not all tour companies are also licensed to rent individual kayaks. No kayak tours or rentals are allowed on Sundays.

Of the following companies, Kayak Kaua'i is big and established, with many other tour offerings. But the recommended little guys Kayak Wailua and Ali'i Kayaks & Water Sports offer better value for this basic tour. You can also rent kayaks from Wailua Kayak Adventures in Kapa'a, though you'll have to transport them on your rental car to the river.

Kayak Wailua
Kayaking, Hiking

(Map p70; 📞808-822-3388; www.kayakwailua. com; 4565 Haleilio Rd; 4½hr tours $50) This small, family-owned company specializes in Wailua River tours. It keeps its boats and equipment in tip-top shape, shuttles you to the marina launch site, and provides dry bags for your belongings and a nylon cooler for your own food.

Ali'i Kayaks & Water Sports
Kayaking, Hiking

(Map p70; 📞808-241-7700, 877-246-2544; www. aliikayaks.com; 174 Wailua Rd; kayak tours $40, SUP rental per 2hr/day $30/45, SUP lessons $60) Right on the Wailua River, this outfitter specializes in kayak-and-hike tours. You can also experience the river another way by stand up paddle surfing (SUP). No kayak rentals.

Kayak Kaua'i
Kayaking

(Map p70; 📞808-826-9844, 800-437-3507; www.kayakkauai.com; Wailua River Marina; double kayak rental per day $64, 4½hr tours $60-85) Reputable island-wide operator offering Wailua River tours and kayak rentals (small surcharge for dry bags and coolers). If you're renting, you'll have to transport the kayak a short distance atop your car.

Wailua Kayak & Canoe
Kayaking, Hiking

(Map p70; 📞808-821-1188; www.wailuariver kayaking.com; 169 Wailua Rd; single/double kayak rental $50/85, tours $65-90; 🚻) Located at the boat ramp on the north bank of the Wailua River, this outfit is very convenient for individual rentals (no need to transport the kayak), but service is minimal and prices have skyrocketed.

HIKING

Most Eastside hiking trails ascend into Kaua'i's tropical-jungle interior. Expect humidity, red dirt (or mud) and slippery patches after rains. Hiking safety needs to be taken seriously here.

Kuilau Ridge & Moalepe Trails
Hiking

(Map p68) Just more than 2 miles long each way, the Kuilau Ridge Trail is recommended for its sheer beauty: emerald valleys, dewy bushes, thick ferns and glimpses of misty Mt Wai'ale'ale in the distance. After 1 mile, you'll reach a grassy clearing with a picnic table. Continue

Island Insights

Take a look at Nounou Mountain. What do you see?

Islanders see the Sleeping Giant. According to legend, an amicable giant fell asleep on the hillside after gorging at a luau. His *menehune* ('little people') friends tried to rouse him by throwing stones. But the stones bounced from his full belly into his open mouth and lodged in his throat. He died in his sleep and turned into rock.

Now he rests, stretched with his head in Wailua and his feet in Kapa'a. At an elevation of almost 1250ft, the giant's forehead is the highest point on the ridge.

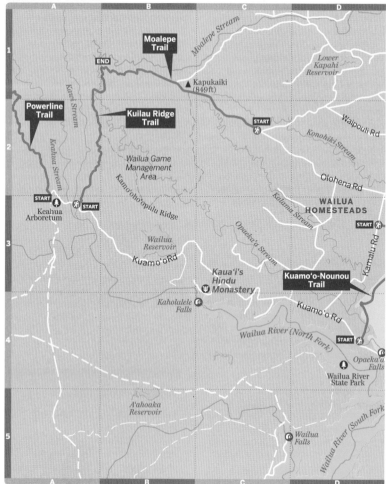

north on descending switchbacks until you meet the mountain-view Moalepe Trail (2.25 miles one-way).

Both of these moderate hikes are among the most visually rewarding on Kaua'i. Remember, the trails don't complete a circuit so you must retrace your steps (8.5 miles round-trip). You might want to skip the final mile of the outbound leg, which crosses the treeless pastureland of Wailua Game Management Area.

The Kuilau Ridge Trail starts at a marked trailhead on the right just before Kuamo'o Rd crosses the stream at the Keahua Arboretum, 4 miles above the junction of Kuamo'o Rd and Kamalu Rd. The Moalepe Trail trailhead is at the end of Olohena Rd in the Wailua Homesteads neighborhood.

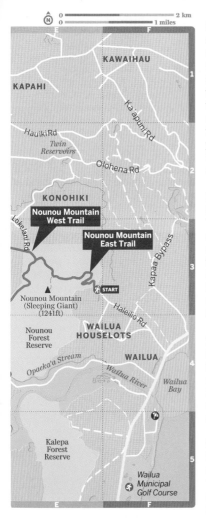

Most visitors prefer the exposed **Nounou East Trail** because it offers sweeping views of the ocean and distant mountains. The well-maintained trail is moderately strenuous and steep, with switchbacks almost to the ridge. At the three-way junction near the top, take the left fork, which leads to the summit, marked by a picnic shelter. Now atop the giant's chest, only his head prevents you from getting a 360-degree view. Climbing further is extremely risky and not recommended.

Do this hike early in the morning, when it's relatively cool and you can witness daylight spreading across the valley. The hard-packed dirt trail is exceedingly slippery when wet; look for a walking stick, which hikers sometimes leave near the trailhead. The trail starts at a parking lot a mile up Haleilio Rd in the Wailua Homesteads neighborhood. When the road curves left, look for telephone pole 38 with the trailhead sign.

The **Nounou West Trail** ascends faster, but it's better if you prefer a cooler, shadier forest trail. There are two ways to access the trailhead: from Kamalu Rd, near telephone pole 11, or from the end of Lokelani Rd, off Kamalu Rd. Walk through a metal gate signed as a forestry right-of-way.

The **Kuamo'o-Nounou Trail** runs through groves of trees planted in the 1930s by the Civilian Conservation Corps; it connects with the Nounou West Trail. Marked by a brown-and-yellow Na Ala Hele sign, the trailhead is right on Kuamo'o Rd between mile markers 2 and 3.

Nounou Mountain Trail   Hiking
(Map p74) Climbing Nounou Mountain (Sleeping Giant), you'll ascend over 1000ft for panoramic views of Kaua'i's Eastside. Approach the mountain on the Nounou East Trail (2 miles), on the Nounou West Trail (1.5 miles) or from the south on the Kuamo'o-Nounou Trail (2 miles). The trails meet near the center (all distances given are one-way).

Kaua'i Nature Tours   Hiking
(☎808-742-8305, 888-233-8365; www.kauai-naturetours.com; tours adult/child 7-12yr from $130/105) For guided hikes, the gold standard is geoscientist Chuck Blay's company, which offers a full-day tour – snacks, drinks and transportation included. Guided hikes also hit the North Shore's Na Pali Coast, Po'ipu, and Waimea Canyon and Koke'e State Parks.

Tours

Smith's Motor Boat Service
Boat Tour

(Map p70; 808-821-6892; www.smithskauai.com; Wailua Marina; 80min tour adult/child $20/10; departures 9:30am, 11am, 2pm & 3:30pm) If you're curious to see the once legendary Fern Grotto, this covered boat ride is hokey but homespun. Bear in mind that since heavy rains and rockslides in 2006, visitors cannot enter the grotto – which looks a bit parched, frankly – but must stay on the wooden platform quite a distance from the shallow cave.

Festivals & Events

Taste of Hawaii
Food

(www.tasteofhawaii.com) On the first Sunday in June, the Rotary Club of Kapa'a hosts the 'Ultimate Sunday Brunch' at Smith's Tropical Paradise, where you can indulge in gourmet samples by 40 chefs from around Hawaii. Dance it off to more than 10 live-music acts. For discounts, buy tickets online in advance.

Sleeping

Many condos, B&Bs and inns require a three-night minimum stay and charge a one-time cleaning fee. Some are located inland in residential areas, rather than by the coast. For condos, we list the contact information for the agency managing the majority of units, but also check with other local booking agencies and VRBO (www.vrbo.com) online.

Rosewood Kaua'i
Inn $

(Map p70; 808-822-5216; www.rosewoodkauai.com; 872 Kamalu Rd; r with shared bath $75-85;) Budget travelers will be spoiled by these meticulously tidy, if small, private rooms, each with bunk beds or a king-sized loft bed, a built-in kitchenette and lots of light. Bathrooms and a gazebo-enclosed outdoor shower are all shared. Expect a cleaning fee ($45).

For a step up, inquire about Rosewood's cottages, vacation homes and condo rentals.

Mt Wai'ale'ale (p78)

MICHAEL UTECH/GETTY IMAGES ©

KAPA'A & THE EASTSIDE WAILUA

The Mysterious Blue Hole

How close can you get to Mt Wai'ale'ale by foot? If you can find the Blue Hole, you're there. It's not a 'hole' per se, but a pool fed by a pretty stream and waterfall.

To get here, take Kuamo'o Rd up to Keahua Arboretum. Unless you're driving a 4WD, you should park in the lot and hike in. The unpaved road is head-jarringly rough, and the mud can engulf ordinary cars. Either way, head left onto Wailua Forest Management Rd. After less than 1.5 miles, you'll reach a junction; turn right (a gate blocks the left direction). Go straight for about 2 miles. Along the way, you'll pass an otherworldly forest of false staghorn, guava, eucalyptus and native mamane and ohia. The dense foliage introduces you to a rainbow of greens, from deep evergreen to eye-popping chartreuse.

You will then reach a locked yellow gate; it is meant to keep out cars, but the state allows foot traffic (be warned: lots of mud). From here you must slosh about 0.75 miles till you reach the dammed stream, which is the north fork of Wailua River. The stream rises and falls depending on the season and rainfall. Occasionally it is deep enough for kids to swim.

Blue Hole is a quiet, secluded spot, not a tourist destination by a long shot. To avoid getting stuck or lost, join Aloha Kaua'i Tours (p43) for a half-day tour that includes rain gear, walking sticks and snacks.

Sleeping Giant Cottage   Cottage $

(Map p70; ☎505-401-4403; www.wanek.com/sleepinggiant; 5979 Heamoi Pl; 1-bedroom cottage $99; ☎) Surrounded by tropical foliage and open-air lanai, this plantation-style bungalow makes a private and spacious retreat. It's pleasantly appointed with hardwood floors, a full kitchen, washer/dryer, a king-sized bed, BBQ grills and a huge screened patio facing a backyard garden. There's free beach gear to borrow. Cleaning fee $50.

Surf & Ski Cottage   Cottage $

(Map p70; ☎808-822-3574; www.kauaiwaterskiandsurf.com/cottage; Ohana St; cottage per night/week $85/550; ☎) Suitable for solos or couples looking for something serene but convenient, this tastefully decorated studio features a more-than-functional kitchenette, a queen bed and a Hawaiian palapa with a waterproof thatched roof. It's located a few steps from the Wailua River and has a private kayak launch.

Lani Keha   Cottage $

(Map p70; ☎808-822-1605; www.lanikeha.com; 848 Kamalu Rd; s/d from $55/65; ☎) Solo travelers and sociable types will appreciate the low-key, communal atmosphere at this simple guesthouse. It's nothing fancy, just three rooms with lauhala-mat flooring, king or twin beds and well-worn but clean furnishings. The shared kitchen is stocked with breakfast fixings. It doesn't always rent rooms, so call ahead. No credit cards.

Fern Grotto Inn   Inn $$

(Map p70; ☎808-821-9836; www.ferngrottoinn.com; 4561 Kuamo'o Rd; cottages $135-195, 3-bedroom house $250; ❄☎) Charmingly retro yet remodeled, these early 20th-century plantation-style cottages vary in size. All have hardwood floors, tasteful furnishings and a kitchen or kitchenette. A prime location near the Wailua River dock reduces the need to drive, and there is a kayak and bikes to borrow. Friendly owners go

The Source: Mt Wai'ale'ale

Nicknamed the Rain Machine, Mt Wai'ale'ale (translated as 'rippling water' or 'overflowing water') averages over 450 inches of rainfall annually. With a yearly record of 683 inches in 1982, it's widely regarded as one of the wettest places on earth. Its steep cliffs cause moist air to rise rapidly and focus rainfall in one area. Believed by ancient Hawaiians to be occupied by the god Kane, it's located in the center of the island, representing Kaua'i's *piko* (navel). It's the source of the Wailua, Hanalei and Waimea Rivers, as well as almost every visible waterfall on the island.

the extra mile to ensure guests' comfort. Cleaning fee $75 to $125.

Kauai Shores
Hotel $$
(Map p70; ☎808-822-4951, 866-970-4169; www.kauaishoreshotel.com; 420 Papaloa Rd; r $85-240; ❄@🛜☀) Recently renovated by Hawaii's boutique-hotel chain Aqua, this coastal property has tidy little rooms splashed with sunny modern panache. The mandatory 'hospitality fee' ($15 plus tax per night) covers continental breakfast, morning yoga and DVDs, video games, and beach chairs and towels for borrowing.

Courtyard by Marriott Kauai at Coconut Beach
Hotel $$
(Map p70; ☎808-822-3455, 877-997-6667; www.marriotthawaii.com; 650 Aleka Loop; r $110-290; ❄@🛜☀) This polished, 300-plus-room beachside hotel has been fully renovated, from a soaring lobby full of plush seating to an ocean-view pool. Business-class suites pamper guests with deep soaking tubs and kitch-

enettes. More than half of the regular rooms have cinnamon-wood plantation shutters opening onto private lanai. The mandatory resort fee ($20 per night) covers parking and two mai tais.

Aston Islander on the Beach
Hotel $$
(Map p70; ☎808-822-7417, 877-977-6667; www.astonislander.com; 440 Aleka Pl; r $175-230; ❄🛜☀) It's not a resort, so don't expect too many frills. Yet the rooms inside these low-rise beachfront buildings are contemporary and upscale, with teak furnishings, granite countertops, flat-screen TVs, microwaves and mini fridges. A mandatory amenity fee ($18 plus tax per night) covers parking plus DVD and video-game rentals. Deep discounts often available online.

Eating

For loads more options, head just a couple of miles north to Waipouli or Kapa'a.

Coconut Marketplace
Fast Food $
(Map p70; www.coconutmarketplace.com; 4-484 Kuhio Hwy; snacks from $2, mains $6-12) A tiny farmers market is held at this mall on Tuesday and Thursday mornings from 9am until noon. Outside of this, you'll find a few snack bars, fish-and-chips and burger stands, and ice-cream and shave ice stalls here (hours vary).

Kilauea Fish Market
Seafood $$
(Map p70; ☎808-822-3474; 440 Aleka Pl; mains $9-19; ⏰11am-8pm Mon-Sat; 🍴) Bringing their time-tested skills and recipes down from the original North Shore location, this kitchen makes *broke da mout* (delicious) ahi wraps, fresh *poke,* grilled fish plates, salads with local greens, and more. Get takeout for a picnic on the beach.

Monico's Taqueria
Mexican $$
(Map p70; ☎808-822-4300; www.monicostaqueria.com; Kinipopo Shopping Village, 4-356 Kuhio Hwy; mains $12-15; ⏰11am-3pm & 5-9pm Tue-Sun) Everything made by this Oaxaca-born chef tastes fresh and authentic, from

stuffed burritos and fish taco plates to the freshly made chips, salsa and sauces. It's worth the wait.

Hukilau Lanai   Hawaii Regional Cuisine $$

(Map p70; ☏808-822-0600; www.hukilaukauai. com; Kaua'i Coast Resort at the Beachboy, 520 Aleka Loop; mains $18-32; ⏱5-9pm Tue-Sun; 🚹) An upgrade from the typical T-shirt-casual joint, this laid-back spot hosts live music nightly. Although the menu doesn't always live up to its promise, it showcases top local ingredients, from Kilauea goat's cheese to Kailani Farms greens. Book a table for before 5:45pm if you want to try the early-bird happy hour tasting menu ($32; with wine pairings $50).

Caffè Coco   Fusion $$

(Map p70; ☏808-822-7990; www.restauranteur. com/caffecoco; 4-369 Kuhio Hwy; mains $13-21; ⏱11am-2pm Tue-Fri, 5-9pm Tue-Sun; 🍴) At this rustic little hideaway, Asian, Middle Eastern and other 'exotic' flavors infuse into healthful dishes to delight the *Yoga Journal* crowd. Moroccan-spiced ahi is a standout, served with banana chutney rice and a curried veggie samosa. There's

live music nightly in the garden, where voracious mosquitoes attack.

Kintaro   Japanese $$

(Map p70; ☏808-822-3341; 4-370 Kuhio Hwy; small plates $3-15, mains $12-26; ⏱5:30-9:30pm Mon-Sat) Night after night, this locals' favorite sushi bar packs 'em in, despite high prices and slowed-down service. From thick slices of sashimi to tempura combos, the dishes shine in quantity, but only glimmer in quality. The house specialty is sizzling *teppanyaki* service, with chefs showing off at table-side grills. Make reservations.

⭐ Entertainment

Life in Wailua thrives while the sun is shining. As with most of Kaua'i, the sun's setting is a symbolic signal to get tired and call it a day. As a result, there's not much more than a fleeting pulse of nightlife to be found around these parts.

Coconut Marketplace Hula Show   Hula, Music

(Map p70; ☏808-822-3641; www.coconutmar-ketplace.com; Coconut Marketplace, 4-484 Kuhio

Ganesha statue, Kaua'i's Hindu Monastery (p67)

What Ever Happened to Coco Palms?

Old-timers might recall Coco Palms Resort as Hollywood's go-to wedding site during the 1950s and '60s. Built in 1953, it was Kaua'i's first resort, and its romantic lagoons, gardens, thatched cottages, torch-lit paths and coconut groves epitomized tropical paradise. The highest-profile onscreen wedding here was when Elvis Presley wed Joan Blackman in the 1961 film *Blue Hawaii*.

At its height, the Coco Palms was a playground for Hollywood's leading males and their lithe ingenues, and the trendiest mainland couples came here to get hitched. But it was also an Old Hawaii kind of place where guests knew hotel staff on a first-name basis and returned year after year.

In 1992, Hurricane 'Iniki demolished the then-393-room hotel, which sat in benign neglect for years. In early 2006, a new owner announced a $220 million plan to resurrect Coco Palms as a condo-hotel, but plans fell through. By fall 2007, the 18-acre property was back on the market, where it has pretty much remained since.

The site remains abandoned except for **guided walking tours** (346-2048; www.cocopalmstour.com; 4-241 Kuhio Hwy; 2hr tour $20; usually 2pm Mon-Thu) and weddings performed by **Larry Rivera** (larryrivera@hawaiian.net). Rivera, a local musician and celebrity who made his career at Coco Palms, re-creates elaborate *Blue Hawaii* fantasy weddings on the grounds, which he and a tiny team of lifetime Coco Palms employees maintain with TLC.

To read more about this historic resort, see www.coco-palms.com, an unofficial website created by its fans.

Hwy; admission free; usually 5pm Wed & 1pm Sat;) While touristy, the Coconut Marketplace's free hula show is nevertheless fun and features Leilani Rivera Low and her hula *halau* (school). She's the daughter of famous Coco Palms entertainer Larry Rivera, who occasionally performs Hawaiian music here and talks story at the mall's Kaua'i Cultural Center (p71).

Smith's Garden Luau   Luau
(Map p70; 808-821-6895; www.smithskauai.com; Smith's Tropical Paradise, Wailua Marina; adult/child 7-13yr/child 3-6yr $88/30/19; 4:45pm or 5pm Mon, Wed & Fri;) It's a Kaua'i institution, attracting droves of tourists yet run with aloha spirit by four generations at the family's riverside gardens. Surprisingly, the highlight is the buffet food, including a roasted pig unearthed from an *imu* (underground oven). The multicultural Polynesian show of Hawaiian hula, Tahitian drum dances and Samoan fire dancing is less than exciting.

Trees Lounge   Live Music
(Map p70; 808-823-0600; www.treeslounge kauai.com; 440 Aleka Pl; 5-11pm Mon-Sat) For those seeking a live-music fix, this venue hosts two happy hours most nights. Headliner acts range from melt-your-face-off rock to mellow acoustic, jazz and traditional Hawaiian sounds. Occasionally a DJ spins. It's behind the Coconut Marketplace.

🛍 Shopping

Mint & Sea   Clothing
(Map p70; 808-822-7946; www.facebook.com/mintandsea; 4-369 Kuhio Hwy; 10am-4pm Mon-Thu, to 6pm Fri & Sat) This fresh-faced, breezy women's boutique is stocked with goodies for women who've outgrown the teenage surfer-chick look. Drapey knit tops, tropical-print shorts, knitted tanks and platform sandals are chic and affordable.

ℹ️ Information

Longs Drugs (📞808-822-4918; www.cvs.com; 645 Aleka Loop; ⏰store 7am-10pm daily, pharmacy 8am-9pm Mon-Fri, 9am-5pm Sat & Sun) Pharmacy has an ATM and also sells beach gear, snacks, drinks and souvenirs.

ℹ️ Getting There & Away

Don't look for a town center. Most attractions are scattered along coastal Kuhio Hwy (Hwy 56) or Kuamo'o Rd (Hwy 580) heading *mauka* (inland). Driving north, Kapa'a Bypass runs from the Coconut Plantation to beyond Kapa'a, completely skipping the traffic jams of Waipouli and Kapa'a.

Waipouli

Waipouli ('dark water') and its gentle lagoons used to serve as a departure point for ancient Hawaiians setting sail for Tahiti and other reaches of Polynesia. Snug between Wailua and Kapa'a, Waipouli today is less a town than a cluster of restaurants and supermarkets, plus a drugstore and other basic businesses. But don't let the strip-mall setting fool you. Here you'll find the island's best health-food store, a meadery and a few other gems. It's a convenient place to stock up and grab a bite.

🏃 Activities

Bear in mind that rentals are here, but the actual activities are elsewhere.

Ambrose's Kapuna Surf Gallery
Surfing, SUP

(Map p82; 📞808-822-3926; www.ambrosecurry.com; 770 Kuhio Hwy; per hour $40; ⏰by reservation only) Don't miss the chance to meet surf guru Ambrose

Curry, who offers to 'take people surfing' (or stand up paddling), not to 'give surf lessons.' If you're baffled, then you have much to learn from this longtime surfer-philosopher. Originally from California, Curry has lived on Kaua'i since 1968 and is also an artist and board shaper.

Yoga House
Yoga

(Map p82; 📞808-823-9642; www.bikramyogakapaa.com; 4-885 Kuhio Hwy; drop-in class $17) Come find your yogic bliss in this super-heated studio. Classes are offered daily, so there's plenty of opportunity to get centered. To build some serious *prana*, get the all-you-can-bend-in-a-week deal ($55). Go online for current schedules.

Kauai Cycle
Bicycle Rental

(Map p82; 📞808-821-2115; www.kauaicycle.com; 4-934 Kuhio Hwy; rental per day from $20; ⏰9am-6pm Mon-Fri, to 4pm Sat) Kauai Cycle sells, services and rents all kinds of models – cruisers, hybrids, and road and mountain bikes – that are maintained by experienced cyclists, who

Holoholoku Heiau (p67)
DANITA DELIMONT/GETTY IMAGES ©

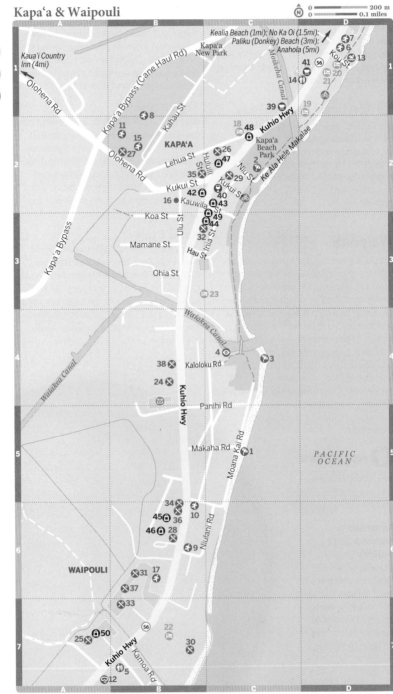

200 m
0.1 miles

Kauaʻi Country Inn (4mi)

Olohena Rd

Kealia Beach (1mi): No Ka Oi (1.5mi);
Paliku (Donkey) Beach (3mi);
Anahola (5mi)

Kapaʻa New Park

Moikeha Canal

Kapaʻa Bypass (Cane Haul Rd)

Kahau St

KAPAʻA

Lehua St

Olohena Rd

Kapaʻa Bypass

Kukui St

Koa St

Mamane St

Hau St

Ohia St

Waikaea Canal

Kalaloku Rd

Kuhio Hwy

Panihi Rd

Makaha Rd

Moana Kai Rd

WAIPOULI

Kuhio Hwy

Kamoa Rd

Niulani Rd

Kapaʻa Beach Park

Ke Ala Hele Makalae

Kuhio Hwy

Niu St

Kukui St

Kauwila St

Inia St

Ulu St

PACIFIC
OCEAN

Kapaʻa & Waipouli

also do repairs. Rental prices include a helmet and lock.

Snorkel Bob's   Snorkeling, Surfing
(Map p82; ☎808-823-9433; www.snorkelbob. com; 4-734 Kuhio Hwy; snorkel-set rental per week adult/child under 13yr from $25/22, wetsuit/bodyboard rental per week from $20/26; ☺8am-5pm) The cool thing about this place is that if you're island-hopping you can rent snorkel gear on Kauaʻi and return it on the Big Island, Oʻahu or Maui.

🛏 Sleeping

Waipouli is sandwiched between Wailua and Kapaʻa, both with plenty more lodging options.

Outrigger Waipouli Beach Resort & Spa   Resort $$
(Map p82; ☎808-822-6000, 800-688-7444; www.outriggerwaipouli.com; 4-820 Kuhio Hwy; studio/1-/2-bedroom condo from $165/225/275; ❄@🛜🏊) The surrounding strip malls and traffic belie the Outrigger's cachet as the Eastside's fanciest condo complex. Units are law-firm handsome with big flat-screen TVs, kitchenettes or full kitchens, and washer-dryers. There's no swim-mable beach, but a saltwater 'river pool' and sand-bottom hot tubs compensate somewhat. Outrigger represents nearly half of the almost 200 rental units, but also check www.vrbo.com.

🍴 Eating & Drinking

Tiki Tacos
Mexican $

(Map p82; 📞808-823-8226; www.facebook.com/tikitacos; Waipouli Complex, 4-961 Kuhio Hwy; mains $5-8; ⏱11am-8:30pm) Riding the wave of an island-wide taco craze, this laid-back place with a reggae soundtrack offers authentic *taqueria* gravitas right down to the house-made tortillas. Tacos come with chicken, fish, chorizo, shrimp, beef, pork, spicy vegetables or tofu, and they're piled high with island-grown cabbage, *queso fresco* (fresh cheese), sour cream and onion. Our fave? The 'surfing pig' taco with pork and fish.

Papaya's Natural Foods
Health Food $

(Map p82; 📞808-823-0190; www.papayasnaturalfoods.com; Kauai Village, 4-831 Kuhio Hwy; ⏱8am-8pm Mon-Sat, 10am-5pm Sun, cafe closes 1hr earlier; 🔧) 🌿 Kaua'i's biggest health-food store carries local and organic produce, plus other island specialties such as Kilauea honey and goat's cheese. Deli fixings and the salad bar make for a quick, healthy meal, while the cafe grills taro burgers, blends fresh fruit smoothies and sells shots of Hawaiian *noni* (a type of mulberry with smelly yellow fruit used medicinally) juice.

Shrimp Station
Seafood $

(Map p82; 📞808-821-0192; 4-985 Kuhio Hwy; dishes $8-14; ⏱11am-8:30pm Sun-Wed, to 9pm Thu-Sat; 👶) This offshoot of Waimea's original Shrimp Station serves recipes that have stayed in the family. With seasonings such as garlic, Cajun and Thai on their shrimp tacos, burgers and plate meals, it's hard to shoot and miss here. Some claim it has the 'best coconut shrimp on the planet.' Whaddya know?

Tropical Dreams
Ice Cream $

(Map p82; www.tropicaldreamsicecream.com; 4-831 Kuhio Hwy; snacks from $4; ⏱noon-9pm Sun-Thu, to 10pm Fri & Sat) A tiny taste of ice-cream heaven, this only-in-Hawaii chain rotates through scores of premium flavors crafted almost entirely from Hawaii-harvested ingredients. It does soft serve as well as old-fashioned scoops. Cash only.

Kadavul Temple (p67)

LINDA CHING/GETTY IMAGES ©

Island Insights

The intoxicatingly graceful movements of hula dancing have not always been practiced solely by those with two X chromosomes. Prior to Western contact, *kane* (men) performed hula, until early 19th-century Christian missionaries discouraged its practice altogether. Today, a slow-growing revival of *kane* hula has taken shape, with much credit given to local *kumu* (teachers).

Foodland
Supermarket $

(Map p82; ☎808-822-7271; www.foodland.com; Waipouli Town Center, 4-771 Kuhio Hwy; ◷6am-11pm) Groceries stocked here include local produce and artisanal foods, as well as select gourmet and health-conscious brands. Scoop up some fresh *poke* from the deli.

Safeway
Supermarket $

(Map p82; ☎808-822-2464; www.safeway.com; Kaua'i Village, 4-831 Kuhio Hwy; ◷store 24hr, pharmacy 8am-8pm Mon-Fri, 9am-6pm Sat & Sun) Caters to mainland tourists through familiar national brands and an American-style deli, bakery, pizza station and sushi bar.

Oasis on the Beach
Hawaii Regional Cuisine $$

(Map p82; ☎808-822-9332; www.oasiskauai.com; Outrigger Waipouli Beach Resort, 4-820 Kuhio Hwy; mains lunch & brunch $11-18, dinner $15-35; ◷11:30am-9pm Mon-Sat, 10am-9pm Sun) This is truly on the beach, like the name says, with unmatched ocean views, a romantic atmosphere and sophisticated cuisine featuring star local ingredients. It's perfect for sharing elevated fusion dishes or hitting up one of Kaua'i's better happy hours (4pm to 6pm daily). Sunday brunch spikes the *loco moco* (dish of rice, fried egg and hamburger patty topped with gravy or other condiments) with cognac and the eggs Benedict with Sriracha sauce.

Kaua'i Pasta
Italian $$

(Map p82; ☎808-822-7447; www.kauaipasta.com; 4-939b Kuhio Hwy; mains $12-24; ◷11am-9pm, lounge to midnight Mon-Sat, to 10pm Sun; ⊞) Your ticket to surprisingly good Italian food is this strip-mall bistro. Colorful salads meld peppery arugula, creamy goat's cheese and sweet tomatoes, while hot focaccia sandwiches, classic homemade pastas and spinach-artichoke dip pass muster even with finicky foodies. Gluten-free menu available.

🔒 Shopping

Waipouli's two pedestrian shopping malls are **Waipouli Town Center** (4-771 Kuhio Hwy) and **Kaua'i Village** (4-831 Kuhio Hwy).

Nani Moon Meadery & Tasting Room
Drink

(Map p82; ☎808-651-2453; www.nanimoon-mead.com; 4-939 Kuhio Hwy; ◷noon-5pm Tue-Sat) ✦ Nani Moon makes and pours tropical honey wine, which is arguably the oldest alcoholic beverage on earth – humans have been drinking it for 6000 years or more. It crafts a half-dozen flavors of mead using only locally sourced ingredients, including tropical fruit and ginger. Most are surprisingly dry, food-forward and 'best enjoyed under moonlight.'

Moloa'a Bay Coffee
Food & Drink

(Map p82; ☎808-821-8100; www.moloaabay-coffee.com; 943 Kipuni Way; ◷8am-noon Mon-Fri) If you miss sampling this North Shore estate-grown coffee at Kaua'i's top farmers markets, stop by the retail shop on weekday mornings to taste the hand-picked, small-batch roasted brews. Unusually, it also makes flavored teas from dried coffee-fruit husks.

Marta's Boat — Clothing, Jewelry
(Map p82; 808-822-3926; www.martasboat.com; 4-770 Kuhio Hwy; 10am-6pm Mon-Sat) This unique boutique delights 'princesses of all ages' with original block and screen prints on silks and other soft and flowing fabrics, and some funky, fab jewelry. A quirky art-love philosophy is at work in this jewel box. Expect big-city prices.

ℹ Information

There are ATMs inside Foodland (p85) in Waipouli Town Center and, just a minute north, inside Safeway (p85) in the Kaua'i Village shopping center, where you'll find free wi-fi at Starbucks.

Kapa'a

The only walkable town on the Eastside, Kapa'a is a charmer. The eclectic population of old timers, new transplants, nouveau hippies and tourists coexist smoothly. Sushi bars and boutique shops mingle with Bikram yoga and coffee bars. A paved recreational path runs along the part-sandy, part-rocky coast, the island's best vantage for sunrises. Kapa'a's downfall: it sits right along the highway. Try crossing the road during rush hours! (Really, be careful.)

🏖 Beaches

Kapa'a Beach Park — Beach
(Map p82; pool 808-822-3842; park dawn-dusk, pool 7:30am-3:45pm Tue-Fri, 10am-4:30pm Sat, noon-4:30pm Sun;) From the highway, you'd think that Kapa'a is beach-less. But along the coast is a mile-long ribbon of beach that's very low-key. While the whole area is officially a county park called Kapa'a Beach Park, that name is commonly used only for the northern end, where there's a grassy field, picnic tables and a public **swimming pool**. The best sandy area is at the south end, informally called **Lihi Beach**, where you'll find locals hanging out and talking story.

Further to the south is **Fujii Beach**, nicknamed 'Baby Beach' because an offshore reef creates a shallow, placid pool of water that's perfect for toddlers. Located in a modest neighborhood that attracts few tourists, this is a real locals' beach, so be respectful.

A good starting point for the paved coastal path is the footbridge just north of Lihi Beach. To get there, turn *makai* (seaward) on Panihi Rd from the Kuhio Hwy.

🏃 Activities

Kapa'a Beach Shop — Water Sports, Cycling
(Map p82; www.kapaabeachshop.com; 4-1592 Kuhio Hwy; rental bike per day $5-15, snorkel set per day/week $6/12, boogie board $7/20, surfboard $20/50; 8am-6pm Sun-Fri;) Located along the coastal path, this shop has loads of affordable

'Opaeka'a Falls (p69)

Kapaʻa's Coastal Path

The Eastside's newest road is not meant for cars. **Ke Ala Hele Makalae** ('the Path that Goes by the Coast') is a paved shared-use path reserved for pedestrians, cyclists and other non-motorized modes of transportation. Also known as the Kauai Path (www.kauaipath.org) or Kapaʻa Bike Path, it has jump-started locals into daily fitness: walking, jogging, cycling, rollerblading and, perhaps, forgoing the local habit of driving everywhere.

In Kapaʻa, the path currently starts at Lihi Boat Ramp at the south end of Kapaʻa Beach Park and ends just past Paliku (Donkey) Beach at Ahihi Point, a 5-mile stretch. But this constitutes only a small piece of the ambitious plan, which calls for the path to eventually extend over 16 miles all the way from Lihuʻe's Nawiliwili Harbor to Anahola Beach Park.

While a loud minority has complained about pouring concrete along the coast, most appreciate the easy-access path. Sunrise walks are brilliant but, for an added kick, rent a cruiser bike in Kapaʻa or Waipouli.

rental options, including cruiser, hybrid comfort and kids' bikes, snorkel and beach gear, boogie boards, surfboards, scuba equipment and even fishing poles. The helpful owners will gladly point enthusiasts in the right direction for whatever adventure they seek, and they also guide shore dives.

Online reservations available.

Coconut Coasters
Bicycle Rental

(Map p82; ☎808-822-7368; www.coconut coasters.com; 4-1586 Kuhio Hwy; bike rental per day from $20; ⏰9am-4pm Mon & Sun, to 6pm Tue-Sat;) Conveniently located in the heart of Kapaʻa town, this outfit rents beach cruiser bikes, tandem bicycles, hybrid comfort bikes, kids' bikes and tow trailers. The shop, which also does repairs, is right by the bike path.

Wailua Kayak Adventures
Kayaking, Hiking

(Map p82; ☎808-822-5795, 808-639-6332; www.kauaiwailuakayak.com; 1345 Ulu St; single/ double kayak rental per day $25/50, 4½hr tours $50-85) Offers good-value individual kayak rentals, but you'll have to transport kayaks to Wailua River yourself on top of your car. Budget-friendly guided kayak tours

include generous snacks at your paddle-and-hike waterfall destination.

Seasport Divers
Diving, Water Sports

(Map p82; ☎808-823-9222, 800-685-5889; www.seasportdivers.com; 4-976 Kuhio Hwy; dives $90-235) Eastside waters are less protected by reefs and choppier due to easterly onshore winds, so diving and snorkeling are very limited here. Still, this small branch of a Poʻipu-based outfit rents diving and snorkeling gear, boogie boards and surfboards, and offers seasonal dive trips to the North Shore.

Hawaiian Style Fishing
Fishing

(Map p82; ☎808-635-7335; www.hawaiianstyle-fishing.com; Kalokolu Rd; 4hr trips per person $140, half-/full-day private charter $600/1050) Join gregarious Captain Terry, who shares the catch with you. Shared and private charters (six-passenger maximum) depart from Lihi Boat Ramp at the end of Kaloloku Rd. Book a week or more in advance.

Tamba Surf Company
Surfing

(Map p82; ☎808-823-6942; www.tambasurf company.com; 4-1543 Kuhio Hwy; bodyboard/ surfboard rental per day from $10/25; ⏰9am-5pm

Below: Playing *ipu* (gourd instruments); **Right:** Kamokila Hawaiian Village (p69)

Mon-Sat) Along with board rentals, this small shop with local attitude sells surf clothing, and new and used boards. Surf fans may recognize the name as seen on the boards, hats and T-shirts of many pro surfers, past and present, who hail from Kaua'i.

Kapa'a
New Park   Tennis, Skateboarding
(Map p82; www.kauai.gov; 4536 Olehana Rd) You'll find free **tennis courts**, soccer and baseball fields, and a **skateboarding park** here.

Tours
Kapa'a Town
Walking Tour   Walking Tour
(☎808-822-1651, 808-245-3373; www.kauai historicalsociety.org; 90min tours adult/child $20/10; ☺by reservation only) Knowledge-able local guides will point out landmarks, describe the history of Kapa'a's sugar-

and pineapple-plantation days and, best of all, tell stories and answer questions. Advance reservations required.

Festivals & Events
Kapa'a Art Walk   Art, Cultural
On the first Saturday of every month from 5pm to 8pm, town businesses open their doors in celebration, showcasing island artists, live music and food. Locals and visitors alike come together in high spirits, and after-parties often keep going past 9pm. Parking is crowded, so arrive early or expect to walk into town. Bring cash.

Heiva I Kaua'i
Ia Orana Tahiti   Dance, Cultural
(www.heivaikauai.com; 🚻) 🏊 In early August, dance troupes from as far away as Tahiti, Japan and the US mainland join groups from around Hawaii at Kapa'a Beach Park for this Tahitian dancing and drumming competition.

Garden Isle Artisan Fair Art, Music
(www.gardenislandarts.org) Held three times
each year in mid-March (in Po'ipu) and
in mid-August and mid-November (in
Kapa'a), this fair brings out handcrafted
items, live Hawaiian music and local
food.

Coconut Festival Food, Cultural
(www.kbakauai.org; 🚻) Celebrate all things
coconut at this free two-day festival
at Kapa'a Beach Park. Held the first
weekend in October, it brings coconut-
pie-eating contests, a coconut cook-off,
cooking demonstrations, live music,
hula dancing, Polynesian crafts and local
food.

🛌 Sleeping

If you're seeking accommodations right
in town, pickings are slim. Kapa'a has
only one hotel, one timeshare resort and
two hostels. Almost all B&Bs and inns are
situated way beyond walking distance.
That said, driving *mauka* to residential

neighborhoods leads through picturesque pastures with sweeping views.
Remember to ask about minimum-night
requirements and cleaning fees.

Honuea Hostel Hostel $
(Map p82; 📞808-823-6142; www.kauaihostel.
com; 4532 Lehua St; dm from $30, r with
shared/private bath from $65/70; 🛜) Despite
lax management, this is the better of
Kapa'a's two hostels. Semiprivate rooms
located off mural-painted dorms share
bathrooms. Private rooms have access
to the communal kitchen and TV room
after hours, as well as private bathrooms.
Borrow snorkel gear and kayaks for free.
Check-in is after 1pm, but you can drop
off your bags anytime after 11am.

**Kauai Beach
House Hostel** Hostel $
(Map p82; 📞808-652-8162; www.kauaibeach
house.net; 4-1552 Kuhio Hwy; dm/r with shared
bath from $33/75; 🛜) Not the cleanest
of hostels, what with the ramshackle
bunks and courtyard, and the pervasive

hippy vibe. Private rooms tend to be better maintained than dorms, but they also share bathrooms. On the plus side, there's a communal kitchen and the hostel is lazily located right on the beach.

Kaua'i Country Inn — Inn $$

(☎808-821-0207; www.kauaicountryinn.com; 6440 Olohena Rd; ste incl breakfast from $169; ⏰office 8am-11am Mon-Fri, 9am-10:30pm Sat & Sun; @🛜) With gleaming hardwood floors and upscale furnishings, this inn is one class act. Four spacious suites each have cable TV, a DVD player, a computer and a kitchen or kitchenette. The inland location (read: 10-minute drive to the beach) lends itself to serene surroundings and breezy nights. Complimentary continental breakfast provided. Cleaning fee $35 (waived with four-night minimum stay).

No Ka Oi — Apartment $$

(Map p68; ☎808-651-1055, 808-822-0223; www.vrbo.com/125884; 4691 Pelehu Rd; studio apt $120; ❄🛜) Wake up to sunshine in this California king-bedded studio with a full kitchen and a wraparound lanai overlooking Kapa'a and the distant coast. Avid

surfers themselves, your hosts know all the local beaches and surf breaks, and lend boogie boards and beach gear for free. There's a three-night minimum stay; weekly and monthly discounts available. Cleaning fee $75.

Hotel Coral Reef — Hotel $$

(Map p82; ☎808-822-4481, 800-843-4659; www.hotelcoralreefresort.com; 4-1516 Kuhio Hwy; r/ste from $125/175; ❄🛜🏊) Kapa'a's sole hotel has one major advantage: an ocean-front location. True, it's a basic hotel, but it's also a stone's throw from the ocean and a short stroll into town. Quality-wise, you get what you pay for, with the budget rooms covering the basics and the pricier rooms affecting mock luxury. Book online for discounts.

Pono Kai Resort — Resort $$

(Map p82; ☎808-822-9831; www.ponokairesort.com; 4-1250 Kuhio Hwy; studio/1-/2-bedroom condo from $125/155/179; @🛜🏊) An aging three-star condo complex dominates the middle stretch of Kapa'a beach. The units are not especially well maintained, offering outdated bathrooms and electronics, but they're spacious. Outside there

Keahua Aboretum (p71)

LINDA CHING/GETTY IMAGES ©

are BBQ grills, shuffleboard and tennis courts. Cleaning and reservation fees, which vary by rental agency, typically total more than $150.

✕ Eating

Roadside restaurants abound, none terrible, some terribly touristy.

Kapa'a Farmers Market   Market $

(Map p82; www.kauaigrown.org; Kapa'a New Town Park, Kahau Rd & Olohena Rd; ☺3-5pm Wed; 🖍🚻) 🌿 One of the island's biggest and best-attended farmers markets, this weekly outdoor gathering is the spot to pick up local produce such as mangoes, star fruit, ginger and even fresh coconuts. Many of the vendors own organic North Shore farms.

Pono Market   Deli, Market $

(Map p82; 🖉808-822-4581; 4-1300 Kuhio Hwy; meals $6-12; ☺6am-6pm Mon-Fri, to 4pm Sat) Line up for local *grinds* (food) at this longtime hole-in-the-wall serving generous plate lunches, homemade sushi rolls, spicy ahi *poke* bowls, savory seafood delicacies such as smoked marlin, and traditional Hawaiian dishes including pork *laulau*. Bite into *manju* (Japanese sweet bean-paste-filled pastries) for dessert.

Coconut Cup Juice Bar & Cafe   Health Food $

(Map p82; 🖉808-823-8630; www.coconutcupjuicebar.com; Hotel Coral Reef, 4-1516 Kuhio Hwy; items $3-10; ☺8am-5pm; 🖍) Almost hidden, this roadside kitchen (slowly) makes big ol' sandwiches, salads and smoothies. Wash down your 'Pineapple Express' veggie wrap or island-style Waldorf salad with a passion-fruit smoothie or a green shot of kale juice.

Hoku Foods   Health Food $

(Map p82; 🖉808-821-1500; www.hokufoods.com; 4585 Lehua St; ☺10am-6pm; 🖍) 🌿 This small backstreet grocery store is ideal for health-conscious types who seek a wide assortment of organic, gluten-free and raw foods. Stocks locally

What do you do on your days off? Wait, you own two businesses, do you have days off? Whatever – I have a whole Saturday off, and every evening. I like to get outside. The Eastside has the coolest hikes, Sleeping Giant and the Kuilau Ridge Trail. If you go up the backside of the 'Giant,' it's pretty shady and scenic. And I'm training to swim to Kalalau Valley, so almost every evening I swim behind Pono Kai Resort.

How about nightlife? Where's the action around here? The first Saturday of every month is the Kapa'a Art Walk. There's also music every night at Tree's Lounge. And anytime there's a full moon, well, you can make your own fun.

What's an off-the-beaten-path spot that might be an unexpected delight? Baby Beach, also called Fujii's, behind the Chevron Station, is a great place to eat lunch. You can park under the trees and watch the waves and little kids playing while you eat.

Any must-sees or must-dos? Drive the whole island in a day, to experience the diversity that is Kaua'i. Eat fresh fish; it probably came out of the water that day.

Any tips on how travelers can most enjoy what Kaua'i has to offer? Yes! Stop looking at the clock. Wake up when you wake up, eat when hungry, sleep when sleepy. You'll find the rhythm of the island. The sunshine dictates your actions, you'll see.

grown produce and convenient snacks and drinks for hiking or the beach.

Big Save
Supermarket **$**

(Map p82; ☎808-822-4971; www.timessuper
markets.com; Kapa'a Shopping Center, 4-1105
Kuhio Hwy; ⊙6am-11pm) Great for self-
caterers, this local supermarket chain
has a deli that mixes up fresh *poke*. It also
stocks more locally grown produce and
Hawaii-made food products than any of
its competition.

Verde
Mexican, Fusion **$$**

(Map p82; ☎808-821-1400; www.verdehawaii.
com; Kapa'a Shopping Center, 4-1101 Kuhio Hwy;
mains $9-17; ⊙11am-9pm; 🚗) Chef Joshua
Stevens' Mexican, New Mexican and
California-style cooking might take what-
ever fish tacos you've been eating back
home and put them to shame. Be sure to
save room for the sopaipillas drizzled with
honey or the cinammon churro fries for
dessert. Excellent cocktails.

Mermaids Cafe
Fusion **$$**

(Map p82; ☎808-821-2026; www.mermaidskauai.
com; 4-1384 Kuhio Hwy; mains $10-14; ⊙11am-
9pm; 🖋) 'No shirt, no shoes, no worry' is
the slogan at this walk-up counter that
makes humongous burritos, wraps and

Asian-style curry and stir-fry plates. Get
the ahi nori wrap with brown rice and
wasabi cream sauce, and you'll return
every day thereafter to repeat the experience – maybe adding a coconut-milk Thai
ice tea. One bummer: cleanliness isn't
necessarily a priority in the kitchen.

Sushi Bushido
Japanese **$$**

(Map p82; ☎808-822-0664; www.sushibushido.
com; 4504 Kukui St; mains $13-28; ⊙4-9pm
Mon-Thu, to 9:30pm Fri, 5-9:30pm Sat, to 9pm
Sun) This locals' favorite sushi stop sets
up in a funky corner of the Dragon Build-
ing. It has pop art on the walls and serves
imaginative fusion sushi, such as the
yellowtail 'lollipop' roll drizzled with sweet
sauce. Prices are high, portions small and
waits excruciatingly long, but the social
atmosphere and extensive sake list make
it a fun night out.

Rainbow Living
Foods
Health Food **$$**

(Map p82; ☎808-821-9759; www.rainbowliving
foods.com; 4-1384 Kuhio Hwy; mains $12-14;
⊙10am-5pm Mon-Fri, to 3pm Sat; 🖋) 🍃
Absolutely everything is vegan, organic,

Wailua Municipal Golf Course (p71)

SHANEFF CARL/GETTY IMAGES ©

Detour:
Paliku (Donkey) Beach

Once unofficially known as a nude site, this beach is secluded and scenic, but rarely swimmable. It's a rugged place to escape the highway and cars, with rocks scattered at the water's edge, windswept ironwood trees, and *naupaka* and *'ilima* flowers adding dashes of color.

Summer swells might be manageable, but stay ashore if you're an inexperienced ocean swimmer. From October to May dangerous rip currents and a powerful shore break take over; stick to sunbathing or sunrise beach strolls.

The beach is accessible in two ways. You can cycle or walk the coastal path and turn *makai* (toward the ocean). Or you can drive the Kuhio Hwy to a parking lot about halfway between mile markers 11 and 12. Look for the small brown parking and hiking sign. Restrooms are open at the parking lot.

The beach-access path cuts through a 300-acre planned community called Kealia Kai (www.kealiakai.com). Note that public nudity is illegal in Hawaii, and the Kealia Kai developer has cracked down (no pun intended) on folks baring all.

raw and both gluten- and dairy-free. Portions can be too limited for the price, but Rainbow's integrity – utilizing local organic farms and serving an abundance of superfoods with inventive preparations – helps justify the expense. The entrance is around back, off Inia St.

Drinking

Java Kai
Cafe

(Map p82; ☏808-823-6887; www.javakaihawaii.com; 4-1384 Kuhio Hwy; ⏰6am-10pm Mon-Sat, to 6pm Sun; 📶) 🌿 Always busy, this Kaua'i-based micro-roastery is best for grabbing a cup of joe or a fruit smoothie to go. The muffins, scones, banana bread and coconut-macnut sticky rolls are baked fresh, and the salads are tossed with Kailani Farms greens. Another highlight is the selection of Blair Estate shade-grown organic coffee, grown just a few minutes up the road.

Small Town Coffee Co
Cafe

(Map p82; www.smalltowncoffee.com; ⏰6am-4pm) This indie coffeehouse brews organic, fair-trade coffee for the hippie-boho crowd, which also enjoys fresh kombucha and chai tea. Good tunes perpetually play at their temporary location, a big red bus in the former Kojima's parking lot.

Olympic Cafe
Bar

(Map p82; ☏808-822-5825; www.olympic-cafekauai.com; 4-1354 Kuhio Hwy; ⏰6am-9pm Sun-Thu, to 10pm Fri & Sat) People pack into this spacious 2nd-floor sports bar to enjoy perched views of the Coconut Coast's reefs. With a full bar, copious draft beers and decent island-style bar food, it's a popular place to grab a drink, especially during happy hour.

Art Cafe Hemingway
Cafe

(Map p82; www.art-cafe-hemingway.com; 4-1495 Kuhio Hwy; ⏰8am-2pm & 6-9pm Wed-Sun; 📶) This quaint cafe offers all the caffeine and croissants you crave downstairs, while putting on local art exhibitions upstairs.

Shopping

Kuhio Hwy is chock-full of beach-wear boutiques and assorted vintage and antiques shops worth a browse.

Hawaiian Healing Hands

In the late 1970s, Angeline Kaihalanaopuna Hopkins Locey moved back to Hawaii after years of living in California. Back in her native land, Angeline, who is three-quarters Native Hawaiian and grew up on O'ahu, experienced a cultural homecoming as well as a geographical one. She embraced Hawaiian healing, studied with *lomilomi kumu* (traditional Hawaiian massage teacher) Margret Machado on the Big Island, and in the mid-1980s established a homestead in Anahola, where she began to share her gift of therapeutic touch with the community. Over the years 'Auntie Angeline,' now in her late 70s, became a local icon, and today her son Michael and granddaughter Malia carry on her legacy.

Angeline's Mu'olaulani (Map p68; ☎808-822-3235; www.angelineslomikauai.com; Kamalomalo'o Pl; massage treatments $160; ⏱9am-2pm Mon-Fri, by appointment only) is an authentic introduction to Hawaiian healing practices and remains untouristy and frequented mainly by locals. Don't expect plush towels, glossy marble floors or an endless menu of face and nail pamperings. A trip to Angeline's is more like visiting a friend's bungalow, with an outdoor shower, wooden-plank deck, massage tables separated by curtains, and simple sarongs for covering up. Treatments include a steam, a sea salt–clay scrub and a Hawaiian *oli* (chant).

As an expression of *ho'okipa* (hospitality), the Loceys invite guests to stay and sip a drink on the patio after the treatment. The facilities (including showers and sauna) are unisex, but the staff is glad to provide same-sex facilities upon request. Advance reservations are a must; last appointment at noon.

Kamoa Ukulele Company   Music
(Map p82; Larry's Music; ☎808-652-9999; www.kamoaukulelecompany.com; 4-1310 Kuhio Hwy; ⏱11am-4pm Mon-Fri, to 2pm Sat) 🍴 This high-quality uke dealer offers starters for under $100 and vintage and high-end ukes costing $1000 to $5000. All come with the manufacturer's warranty. Inquire with any questions about ukuleles and expect a warm and thorough response from the musically talented folks doing the sales.

Orchid Alley Kauai   Flowers
(Map p82; ☎808-822-0486; www.orchidalleykauai.com; 4-1383 Kuhio Hwy; ⏱10am-5pm Mon-Sat) A certified orchid nursery that even grows its own award-winning hybrid plants. It'll ship whatever you buy back to the mainland for you, or pack it for you to take on the plane. Take deep breaths of the scented air as you browse.

Hula Girl   Clothing, Gifts
(Map p82; ☎808-822-1950; 4-1340 Kuhio Hwy; ⏱9am-6pm Mon-Sat, 10am-5:30pm Sun) This family-run shop is a standout for contemporary Hawaiiana clothing and gifts – shirts, dresses, jewelry, souvenirs and more. Aloha-shirt aficionados can find a wide selection of quality, name-brand shirts here. Feel the silky-soft Tori Richard line or admire the retro looks of the Paradise Found label.

Vicky's Fabrics   Handicrafts, Souvenirs
(Map p82; ☎808-822-1746; www.vickysfabrics.com; 4-1326 Kuhio Hwy; ⏱9am-5pm Mon-Sat) Established in the early 1980s, this simple storefront stocks a wide selection of Hawaiian, Japanese and batik print fabrics for quilters and crafters. Longtime owner and seamstress Vicky also sells some handmade Hawaiian quilts and bags.

Garden Isle
Bath & Body
Beauty, Gifts

(Map p82; ☎808-639-6351; www.garden-islebathandbody.com; 4-1353 Kuhio Hwy; ⏰9am-5pm Mon-Sat) Hurting from a beach sunburn? Don't sweat it. Swing by this family-run shop to sample island-made aloe lotions or the coconut-macadamia nut body butter, which even some Hollywood stars swear by.

Root
Clothing

(Map p82; ☎808-823-1277; 4-1435 Kuhio Hwy; ⏰9am-7pm Mon-Sat, noon-5:30pm Sun) Caters to women looking for hip, contemporary fashions including svelte bikinis, flowing maxi dresses, yoga threads, flowery beach hats and jewelry. Second location in Hanalei.

Blue House Booksellers
Books

Attached to Small Town Coffee Co (p93). What better way to browse for a new beach read in this book-nook than with a fresh cup of java in hand?

ℹ Information

First Hawaiian Bank (☎808-822-4966; www.fhb.com; 4-1366 Kuhio Hwy; ⏰8:30am-4pm Mon-Thu, to 6pm Fri) Has a 24-hour ATM.

Kapa'a Post Office (Map p82; ☎808-822-0093; www.usps.com; 4-1101 Kuhio Hwy; ⏰9am-4pm Mon-Fri, to 1pm Sat)

Samuel Mahelona Memorial Hospital (☎808-822-4961; www.smmh.hhsc.org; 4800 Kawaihau Rd) Basic 24-hour emergency care. Serious cases are transferred to Lihu'e's Wilcox Memorial Hospital (p57).

ℹ Getting There & Around

Kapa'a is located 8 miles north of the Lihue airport. To avoid the paralyzing Kapa'a to Wailua crawl, take the Kapa'a Bypass Rd. Note that except in the heart of Kapa'a, you will definitely need a car.

Kaua'i Bus (p58) runs north and south through Kapa'a once an hour from 6am to 7pm on weekdays (limited weekend service). To be the most enviro-friendly, rent a bike from Kapa'a Beach Shop (p86) or Coconut Coasters (p87) and cruise at your own pace.

Cycling along Ke Ala Hele Makalae (p87)

LINDA CHING/GETTY IMAGES ©

Kealia Beach

Blessed with a wild, near-pristine location, a laid-back vibe and easy access via car or the coastal path, scenic Kealia Beach is the Eastside's best beach, bar none. Isolated from residential development, the beach begins at mile marker 10 as you head north on the Kuhio Hwy and continues for over a mile.

The sandy bottom slopes offshore very gradually, making it possible to walk out far to catch long rides back. But the pounding barrels can be treacherous and are definitely not recommended for novices; it's a crushing shore break. A breakwater protects the north end, so swimming and snorkeling are occasionally possible there.

Outdoor showers, restrooms, lifeguards, picnic tables and ample parking are available; natural shade is not, so sunscreen is a must.

Anahola

Blink and you'll miss sleepy Anahola, a Hawaiian fishing and farming village with rootsy charm and a stunning coastline. Pineapple and sugar plantations once thrived here, but today the area is mainly residential, with subdivisions of Hawaiian Homestead lots. The few who lodge here will find themselves in rural seclusion among true locals.

Grouped together at the side of Kuhio Hwy, just south of mile marker 14, Anahola's modest commercial center includes a post office, a burger stand and a convenience store.

🏝 Beaches

Anahola Beach Park   Beach
(Map p68; 🚻) Despite having no sign from the highway, this locals' beach is an easy getaway. Backed by pines and palms, it's blessed with excellent swimming thanks to a wide, sandy bay with a sheltered cove on the south end. At the beach's choppy northern end is the surf break **Unreals** (Map p68).

Because this county park sits on Hawaiian Home Lands, you'll probably share the beach with Hawaiian families, especially on weekends. Remember, it's their beach: respect the locals. There are two ways to get here: for the south end, turn off Kuhio Hwy onto Kukuihale Rd at mile marker 13, drive a mile down and then turn onto the dirt beach road. For the north end, take 'Aliomanu Rd at mile marker 14 and park in the sandy lot.

'Aliomanu Beach   Beach
(Map p68) Secluded 'Aliomanu Beach is a spot frequented primarily by locals, who pole- and throw-net fish and

Anahola Beach Park
ANN CECIL/GETTY IMAGES ©

The Airspace Issue?

For many, getting a bird's eye view of the verdant majesty of the Garden Island is a once-in-a-lifetime opportunity. As well, the chance to take a breath from above and witness the island at its finest is worth the discomfort (or thrill) of a soaring chopper and the dough the journey requires. But for many on the ground it's an audible thorn in their side.

The Sierra Club and other island advocacy groups have long pushed for the limits on the freedom of commercial aircraft to fly over residential neighborhoods and FAA–designated noise-abatement areas. But for now it's a voluntary system. Thus the Sierra Club recommends that passengers ask pilots to avoid sensitive areas, such as the Kalalau Trail, Na Pali Coast valleys and popular beaches. Whether these recommendations are successful remains to be seen, as it's like asking somebody who ordered a banana split to forego the ice cream and chocolate sauce.

To stop what they call 'disrespectful air tourism,' a group called StopDAT (www.stopdat.org) is seeking to pinpoint the best and worst tour companies. As is often the case, one person's pleasure is another person's pain.

Amid all the joy and conflict these tours can bring out is the fact that though locals have their gripes about noise pollution and dangers, most of the tour companies are owned by *other* locals and landing rights (which turn a profit) are leased by some deeply rooted multigenerational Kaua'i families.

gather *limu* (seaweed). It's a mile-long stretch of beach, with grittier golden sand, a few rocks in the shallows and crystalline water.

You can get to the beach's pretty northern end by turning onto the second 'Aliomanu Rd, just past mile marker 15 on the Kuhio Hwy. Turn left onto Kalalea View Dr, then drive around 0.5 miles and hang a right at the beach-access sign.

◎ Sights & Activities

Hole in the Mountain   Landmark
(Map p68) Ever since a landslide altered this once-obvious landmark, the *puka* (hole) in Pu'u Konanae has been a mere sliver. From slightly north of mile marker 15 on Hwy 56, look back at the mountain, down to the right of the tallest pinnacle: on sunny days, light shines through a slit in the rock face.

Legend says that the original hole was created when a warrior threw his spear through the mountain, causing the water stored within to gush forth as waterfalls.

TriHealth Ayurveda Spa   Spa
(Map p68; ☏808-828-2104; www.trihealthayur-vedaspa.com; Kuhio Hwy; treatments $140-325; ☙by appointment only) In a simple bungalow just off the highway, you can sample traditional ayurvedic therapies, practiced by therapists trained both locally and in India. Kudos if you can withstand a full-body (head and all) session in that horizontal steamer.

🛏 Sleeping & Eating

Oceanfront camping is allowed (except on Thursday nights) at Anahola Beach Park with an advance county camping permit.

'Ili Noho Kai O Anahola   B&B $
(Map p68; ☏808-821-0179; anahola@kauai.net; 'Aliomanu Rd; r with shared bath incl breakfast $100; 🛜) This simple guesthouse fronting Anahola Beach has four compact but tidy rooms (sharing two bathrooms) surrounding a central lanai, where guests talk story and fill up on home-cooked breakfasts (vegetarians welcome) made

Budget Wailua Activities

- Kaua'i's Hindu Monastery (p67)
- Kuilau Ridge & Moalepe Trails (p73)
- Nounou Mountain Trails (p75)
- Wailua Municipal Golf Course (p71)
- Smith's Tropical Paradise (p70)
- Self-guided Wailua River kayaking (p72)

by the musical hosts – both Native Hawaiian activists. Weekly and monthly rates available.

Hale Kiko'o Inn $$
(Map p68; www.halekikoo.com; 4-4382b Kuhio Hwy; s/d incl tax from $85/110; ☎) Along an unnamed, unpaved lane are these two charming, modern studios, each with a kitchenette. The bigger downstairs unit features slate floors, a garden patio and an outdoor shower. The upstairs unit is brighter, with windows aplenty and a sunny deck. There's beach gear to borrow and surfboards to rent. Three-night minimum stay; cleaning fee $100 to $125.

Kaleialoha Rental House $$
(Map p68; ☎888-311-5252; www.kauaialoha.com; 4934 'Aliomanu Rd; d $100-225; ☎) Set on the north end of the Anahola Beach area, these romantic, wooden houses are sprinkled in a lovely quiet neighborhood fronting the beach. Some have a kitchenette or full kitchen, but there's no telephone. Ask about weekly discounts.

Anahola Farmers Market Local $
(Map p68; Kuhio Hwy; meals around $10; ☺9am-dusk Fri-Sun) More of a permanent weekend market than a traditional farmers market. Stop by for wild boar plate lunches, *huli-huli* (rotisserie-grilled) chicken and fresh-baked mango bread.

Duane's Ono Char-Burger Fast Food $
(Map p68; ☎808-822-9181; 4-4350 Kuhio Hwy; items $3-9; ☺10am-6pm Mon-Sat, 11am-6pm Sun; 🚻) If you're a fan of In-N-Out and Dairy Queen, you'll go nuts over this drive-in. Try the 'old fashioned' (cheddar, onions and sprouts) or the 'local girl' (Swiss cheese, pineapple and teriyaki sauce). Burgers come slathered in mayo, just FYI. Add a side order of crispy onion rings and a milkshake.

ℹ Information

Anahola Post Office (Map p68; ☎808-822-4710; www.usps.com; 4-4350 Kuhio Hwy; ☺10am-1:30pm & 2-3:30pm Mon-Fri, 9:30-11:30am Sat)

ℹ Getting There & Away

Kaua'i Bus (p58) stops hourly on weekdays (limited weekend service) on the Kuhio Hwy across from the Whalers General Store at the bottom of the hill.

Ko'olau Road

Ko'olau Rd is a peaceful, scenic loop drive through rich green pastures, dotted with white cattle egrets and bright wildflowers. It makes a nice diversion and is the way to reach untouristed Moloa'a Beach or Larsen's Beach (no facilities in either). Ko'olau Rd connects with Kuhio Hwy 0.5 miles north of mile marker 16 and again just south of mile marker 20.

🏖 Beaches

Larsen's Beach Beach
(Map p68) This long, loamy, golden-sand beach, named after L David Larsen (former manager of C Brewer's Kilauea Sugar Company), is stunning, raw and all-natural, with a scrubby backdrop offering afternoon shade. Although it's shallow, snorkeling can be good when the waters are calm – usually only in the summer. Beware of a vicious current that runs westward along the beach and out through a channel in the reef.

To get here, turn onto Koʻolau Rd from whichever end (ie where it intersects either Kuhio Hwy or Moloaʻa Rd); go just over a mile then turn toward the ocean on a dirt road (it should be signposted) and take the immediate left. It's about a mile to the parking area and then a five-minute walk downhill to the beach.

Moloaʻa Beach   Beach

(Map p68; 🚻) Off the tourist radar, this classically curved bay appeared in the pilot for *Gilligan's Island*. There's a shallow protected swimming area good for families at the north end; to the south, the waters are rougher, but there's more sand. When the surf's up, stay dry and safe – go beach walking instead.

To get here, follow Koʻolau Rd and turn onto Moloaʻa Rd, which ends about 0.75 miles down at a few beach houses and a little parking area.

🍴 Eating & Drinking

Moloaʻa Sunrise Juice Bar   Cafe $

(Map p68; 📞808-822-1441; www.moloaasunrisejuicebar.com; 6011 Koʻolau Rd; items $3-11; ⏰7:30am-5pm Mon-Sat, 8am-4pm Sun; 🚻) A roadside shack sells fresh tropical fruit and unforgettably tasty smoothies, healthful multigrain-bread sandwiches, fish tacos, garden salads and addictive chocolate-chip and macadamia-nut cookies.

Hanalei & the North Shore

The North Shore's allure is inescapable. From the cliffside views of Kilauea and the fecund fields of Hanalei to the Na Pali Coast's rugged landscapes, a visit to the North Shore may very well be an exercise in believability.

Surfers, agricultural enthusiasts and Bohemian boppers are a selection of the mainland transplants whose three-week vacation – one or two decades ago – has turned into a sweet life in paradise. With the nearest traffic light almost 20 miles away, the North Shore carries a pace of its own – mellow. However, as demand for all the North Shore's glory is on the rise, local sentiments like 'Keep it Kauai-it' have grown out of these increasingly trodden peaks and valleys.

But fear not, change is the last item on Kaua'i's to-do list and the North Shore's staunchness always has and always will be that which prevails.

Hanalei Bay (p126)
M SWIET PRODUCTIONS/GETTY IMAGES ©

Hanalei & the North Shore Highlights

Hanalei Bay

With four beaches to choose from, two miles of golden sand, white frothy surf rolling onto the shore and a cloudless blue sky, you'll get the feeling that you've finally arrived. Spread your towel on the sand, pick up a board and paddle, or stroll along the water's edge, watching sailboats bob in the waves. Is this heaven? No, it's just Hanalei (p126).

Makua (Tunnels) Beach

Nicknamed for its caverns teeming with fish and other marine life that pocket the near-shore reef, this beach (p143) is a fierce beauty. In winter, the waves pound, but come summer, waters are usually calm enough for spectacular snorkeling and the North Shore's best diving. Always check with lifeguards before going in. If in doubt, stay out and just gaze rapturously from shore.

MATTHEW MICAH WRIGHT/GETTY IMAGES ©

Kalalau Trail

3

It's the most popular overnight trek (p149) in the state, and for good reason. You'll snake for 11 miles along the cliffs that gave the Na Pali Coast its name, past ancient Hawaiian settlements, beaches and waterfalls, with gobsmacking ocean views around nearly every corner. If you're day hiking, it's a challenging 4 miles to Hanikapi'ai Falls, and 4 miles back, with epic scenery and photo ops.

4

Kilauea Point

Drink in panoramic views of the North Shore before you jump in and take advantage of all it has to offer. Pop into the early 20th-century lighthouse then walk along the paths of this national wildlife refuge (p108) and sharpen your binocular skills. You'll spot a huge variety of birds, as well as humpback whales spouting offshore during winter.

5

Ho'opulapula Haraguchi Rice Mill & Taro Farm Tours

Hanalei's agricultural bounty is obvious to anyone who drives over the one-lane bridge into town and notices the valley's almost psychedelically green fields. But to really grasp the history and Hawaiian heart of this agricultural community, take a guided tour of this family-owned farm (p130) and its *lo'i kalo* (wet taro fields) set beside the peaceful Hanalei River.

Hanalei & the North Shore Itineraries

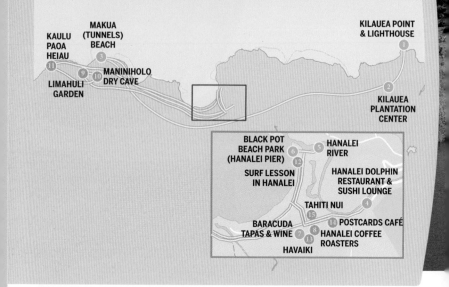

KAULU PAOA HEIAU · MAKUA (TUNNELS) BEACH · KILAUEA POINT & LIGHTHOUSE · MANINIHOLO DRY CAVE · LIMAHULI GARDEN · KILAUEA PLANTATION CENTER · BLACK POT BEACH PARK (HANALEI PIER) · HANALEI RIVER · SURF LESSON IN HANALEI · HANALEI DOLPHIN RESTAURANT & SUSHI LOUNGE · TAHITI NUI · BARACUDA TAPAS & WINE · POSTCARDS CAFÉ · HANALEI COFFEE ROASTERS · HAVAIKI

2 DAYS

21 MILES

DAYS ONE & TWO

Get your bearings with sweeping views from the northernmost point of the island at ❶ **Kilauea Point & Lighthouse**; it doubles as a National Wildlife Refuge and sanctuary for migratory and native birds. Next, head to ❷ **Kilauea Plantation Center** to browse the shops, buy souvenirs and enjoy a fresh fish wrap at Kilauea Fish Market.

You've seen the coast from afar, now drive it. Head north through Hanalei Valley past several one-way bridges. In Ha'ena, hit ❸ **Makua (Tunnels) Beach**, where reef-snorkeling and swimming opportunities abound. In the evening, grab a table at one of Hanalei's old-school restaurants, ❹ **Hanalei**

Dolphin Restaurant & Sushi Lounge, which serves roasted seafood and killer sushi rolls, or just grab a *poke* bowl to go.

Next day, take a kayak tour or stand-up paddle lesson at ❺ **Hanalei River** for almost-guaranteed athletic success in an idyllic setting. ❻ **Black Pot Beach Park (Hanalei Pier)** has turquoise, alluring water, pristine sailboats and waterfall-laden mountain views, making it a scenic, don't-miss spot. With lifeguards present, it's a great family spot. Later, if high-end is the name of the game for you, sip on a glass of vino or enjoy sliced honeycomb, apples and artisan cheese at candlelit ❼ **BarAcuda Tapas & Wine**.

14 MILES
DAYS THREE & FOUR

Rise and shine on day three with a cold, black-tea-and-milk Chai Anu or a spicy Point Break smoothie with ginger papaya and coconut milk at morning hot spot, ⑧ **Hanalei Coffee Roasters**. Continue the morning at ⑨ **Limahuli Garden** – honoring the Hawaiians who built agricultural terraces out of lava rock and planted taro. Then get a peek at the inside of ⑩ **Maniniholo Dry Cave**, across the street from Ha'ena Beach Park, which lost half its width to sand from a 1957 tsunami. Head from here to Ke'e Beach and while there take a moment to visit ⑪ **Kaulu Paoa Heiau**, one of the island's most cherished heiau (Hawaiian temples).

Give yourself a chance to get bitten by the surf bug on day four with a ⑫ **surf lesson in Hanalei** at one of several surf schools based by the pier. Afterwards, peruse artwork from all around the South Seas, and take home a handcrafted Polynesian souvenir from ⑬ **Havaiki**. Enjoy a healthy, well-prepared dinner at pescatarian ⑭ **Postcards Café**, a short stroll across the street. Finally, head to ⑮ **Tahiti Nui**. With lively music and a kinetic crowd (especially on the weekends), indulge in some well-earned late-night fun.

Hanalei River (p131)
ANN CECIL/GETTY IMAGES ©

Discover Hanalei & the North Shore

Kilauea

Kilauea is the quieter, more modest relative in the North Shore family. For numerous passersby it can be more of an entryway or a turnstile of sorts to the natural attractions that await further north and west. With nothing more than a gas station and a small sign marking their arrival, many who have been zipping north for half an hour from the Eastside are unaware of the charms that lie just beyond its unobtrusive entrance.

However, ye who venture shall be rewarded. The northernmost point on the island offers lush vistas, counterintuitive beach names ('Secrets Beach' is not so much a secret), a wildlife refuge, souvenir browsing, fish markets, remote accommodations (read: quiet), and arguably the top miniature golf facility within 2000 miles.

The town's logical layout and organized infrastructure are directly attributed to the practical needs of the working-machine-of-a-town that it used to be. Kilauea today very much reflects its rich history as a sugar-plantation town – only without the plantation.

🏖 Beaches

As all of Kilauea is perched several hundred feet above the ocean, reaching the beaches takes a bit of effort. But rest assured that effort will be rewarded, because where there are cliffs, there's privacy.

Kauapea (Secrets) Beach   Beach
Obviously a 'secret' no longer, these powdery white sands extend along massive cliffs for more than a mile, wrapping around two rock reefs, all the way to Kilauea Point. There's a sandy ocean floor and sea shells galore, with crystal-clear seas that are the domain of bait balls and occasionally dolphins. Alas, the swimming isn't always safe, thanks to a massive shore break, with frequent close-outs and tremendously strong currents that flow along the entirety of the beach.

Kilauea Lighthouse (p108)
MIKE SHAW/GETTY IMAGES ©

Detour:
Kalihiwai Valley

Sandwiched between Kilauea and 'Anini, Kalihiwai ('water's edge' in Hawaiian) is a hidden treasure that's easy to pass by. Most venture here to **Kalihiwai Beach**, an ideal spot for sunbathing and sandcastle building that is remote, small and surrounded by lush grounds. Swells permitting, you can also swim or go bodyboarding. Kalihiwai Rd was at one point a road that passed Kalihiwai Beach, connecting with the highway at two points. A tidal wave in 1957 washed out the Kalihiwai Bridge. The bridge was never rebuilt, and now there are two Kalihiwai Rds, one on each side of the river.

Kalihiwai Stream offers an ideal spot for a short kayak jaunt if you've rented one and don't feel like trying the more-crowded rivers of Wailua or Hanalei. Launch at the beach and into Kalihiwai Valley, where you should keep eyes peeled for **Kalihiwai Falls**. The closest outfit that will allow you an unsupervised rental on Kalihiwai Stream is Kayak Kaua'i (p73) in Wailua. The falls are on land leased by Princeville Ranch Stables and though all navigable waterways in Hawaii are public property, exiting the kayak and stepping foot on land (even land covered by water) is trespassing. So you can look, but not touch.

To go for a swim in one of the valley's waterfalls, take a jaunt on horseback at animal-friendly **Silver Falls Ranch** (Map p108; 📞808-828-6718; www.silverfallsranch.com; Kamo'okoa Rd; rides $99-139; 🕐by appointment only; 👫), where **Esprit de Corps Riding Academy** (📞808-822-4688; www.kauaihorses.com; tours per person from $99) also gives guided tours.

To get here, take the first Kalihiwai Rd if you're heading north on Kuhio Hwy, roughly 0.5 miles past Kilauea's gas station.

Swimming is especially hazardous during big swells (common in winter), which is why it's popular for surfing. This is a local spot, so mind your manners. Nudists also dig it, although technically they're breaking the law.

If you can handle such, ahem, sights, don't mind dirt roads or steep trails, adore virginal beaches and savor sunsets, you'll think Secrets is absolutely magical. However, if the swells are even a little bit big or rough, do not go out into even knee-high water and don't clamber on the rocky outcrops, as people have drowned here.

Turn *makai* (seaward) at Kalihiwai Rd (about 0.5 miles north of the gas station) and take a right on the first dirt road just after the initial bend. Drive toward the end of the road, park and find the steep trail down to the beach starting in plum trees.

Kahili (Rock Quarry) Beach   Beach
This scenically rugged stretch of beach is tucked away between two densely vegetated cliffs where Kilauea Stream meets the ocean. There's no protective barrier reef, so when the surf's up, waves can pound. Calm summer days are best for swimming, but beware the rip current from the stream's outflow. Public access is via Wailapa Rd, which begins at the Kuhio Hwy midway between mile markers 21 and 22. Follow Wailapa Rd north for less than 0.5 miles, then turn left onto the unmarked dirt road (4WD recommended) beginning at a bright-yellow water valve.

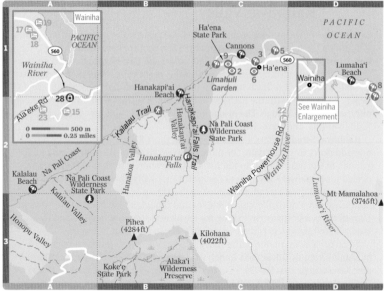

⊙ Sights

Kilauea Point National Wildlife Refuge
Wildlife Reserve

(☎808-828-1413; www.fws.gov/kilaueapoint; Kilauea Rd; adult/child under 16yr $5/free; ⊙10am-4pm Tue-Sun, closed federal holidays) 🌿 Home to some of Hawaii's endangered wildlife, this refuge claims sweeping views from atop the sea cliffs, where you'll also find a 1913 **lighthouse**. You can occasionally glimpse breaching whales in winter and spinner dolphins year-round offshore. Red-footed boobies, Pacific golden plovers, red-tailed and white-tailed tropic birds and Laysan albatrosses are among the birds spotted here, along with nene, the endangered Hawaiian goose. You'll also spy **Moku'ae'ae Island**, which is teeming with more protected wildlife.

To get here, turn seaward onto Kolo Rd, then take a left onto Kilauea (Lighthouse) Rd and follow it for about 2 miles through town to the end.

Na 'Aina Kai Botanical Gardens & Sculpture Park
Gardens

(☎808-828-0525; www.naainakai.org; 4101 Wailapa Rd; tours $35-85; ⊙tours 9am, 9:30am & 1pm Tue-Thu, 9am Fri; 🚻) In a somewhat over-the-top approach, this husband-and-wife operation pays tribute to Hawaiian culture on 240 acres of botanical gardens. Also on the grounds are a beach, a bird-watching marsh and a forest of exotic hardwood trees. Tour reservations are highly recommended.

To get here, turn right onto Wailapa Rd, between mile markers 21 and 22 on the Kuhio Hwy, and look for signs.

Kauai Fresh Farms
Ecotour

(☎808-651-1191; www.kauaifreshfarms.com; 5545 Kahiliholo Rd; 2hr tours incl lunch $45; ⊙tours 10am Tue, Wed & Fri, by reservation only) 🌿 The farm-curious might enjoy a this sustainable farm tour on Wai Koa Plantation. Learn about hydroponically grown fruits, veggies and herbs, and experience the beauty of the world's largest mahogany plantation before a farm-to-fork lunch. Reservations required.

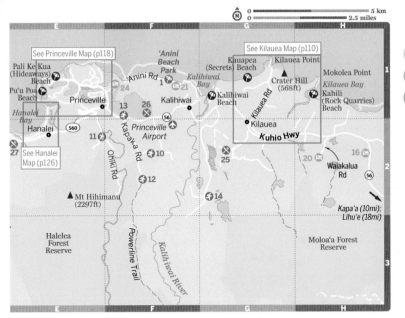

North Shore

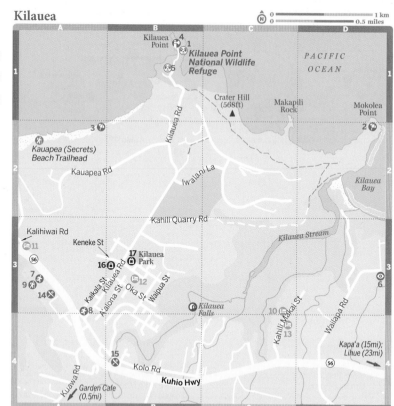

🏃 Activities

Though there are options for the activity-oriented traveler in Kilauea, the nexus of North Shore action takes place at Hanalei Bay, only 8 miles away.

Kauai Mini Golf & Botanical Gardens *Golf*

(📞808-828-2118; www.kauaiminigolf.com; 5-2723 Kuhio Hwy; adult/child under 5yr/child 5-10yr $18/free/10; ⏱11am-8pm, last entry 7:30pm; 🚼) Part mini-golf, part botanical gardens, this is one environmentally educational round of putt-putt. Winding past Native Hawaiian, Polynesian, plantation-era and East Asian plants, each hole offers a first-hand experience of exquisite flora. It gets busy on weekends, when there may be a wait.

Wai Koa Loop Trail *Hiking, Cycling*

(📞808-828-2118; www.anainahou.org; 5-2723 Kuhio Hwy; ⏱11am-9pm, closed Mon Sep-May) This 5-mile loop trail leads through the greater Namahana Plantation property, starting from Anaina Hou Community Park (also home to Kauai Mini Golf). Along the way you'll traverse a stream and walk through fruit orchards past signs explaining the plantation's history. Hike for free or rent a mountain bike ($25 for up to six hours).

Hikers must sign a waiver, available at the on-site Namahana Cafe, before hitting the trail.

Kilauea

Metamorphose Yoga Studio   Yoga
(☎808-828-6292; www.metamorphoseyoga.
com; Kilauea Plantation Center, 4720 Kilauea
Rd; drop-in classes $15) This studio nestled
in the heart of Kilauea town is sure to
redefine the phrase 'going on a bender'
with its Vinyasa flow and restorative yoga
classes. Go online for current schedules.

Pineapple Yoga   Yoga
(☎808-652-9009; www.pineappleyoga.com;
2518 Kolo Rd; drop-in classes/weekly pass
$20/90; ◷usually 7:30-9:30am Mon-Sat)
Mysore-style Ashtanga yoga links the
breath with 'moving meditation' to create
heat throughout the body and sweat (lots
of sweat) that detoxifies muscles and
organs. The studio is in the parish house
of Christ Memorial Church.

🛏 Sleeping

Sleepy Kilauea has some unique B&Bs.
What these lack in ocean views, they
make up for with lush, tropical farm
settings. Search **Vacation Rentals by
Owner** (www.vrbo.com) and **Airbnb** (www.
airbnb.com) for more hidden gems.

Anahata Spa & Sanctuary   Guesthouse $
(☎808-652-3698; www.anahatasanctuary.
net; 4356 Kahili Makai St; r with shared/private
bath from $80/145; P🤝) Stay over in this
uplifting home owned by a hospitable
couple. The great room features wood
floors, an open kitchen and gorgeous
leafy views. The outdoor shower is a
stunner, too. All rooms open onto a
common lanai with a Balinese daybed for
catching a sunrise.

Green Acres Cottages   Inn $
(Map p108; ☎808-828-0478, 866-484-6347;
www.greenacrescottages.com; 5-0421c Kuhio
Hwy; d $75-90; P🤝) The 'cottages'
are really just kitchenette rooms with
grandmotherly decor in the back wing of
someone's house. But mornings spent
picking fresh bananas and avocados, a
communal hot tub, and an old-school
nutcracker (macadamia nuts provided) perk things up at these roadside
lodgings.

North Country Farms   Cottage $$
(☎808-828-1513; www.northcountryfarms.
com; 4387 Kahili Makai Rd; d $160) 🌿 Run by

organic farmers, these cabin-like cottages come with a basket of breakfast goodies, and you're free to harvest fruit and veggies. The Orchard Cottage, a 500-sq-ft studio on stilts, has a full kitchen and a hammock on the lanai. The compact Garden Studio with a kitchenette sleeps four. Cleaning fee $95.

Kauai Vacation Cottages
Cottage $$

(Map p108; ☑808-828-1100; www.kauaisunrise. com; Waiakalua St; cottages $185; 🛜) 🍃 You might not want to ever go home after sleeping on this private estate. Spick-and-span twin cottages are contemporary, each with a full kitchen and outdoor BBQ grill, and there's beach gear to borrow. The Aloha Sunrise cottage's stacked layout features an airy skylit bedroom, while the Aloha Sunset cottage has expansive mountain views from the lanai. Cleaning fee $95.

🍴 Eating

Healthy Hut Market & Cafe
Health Food $

(☑808-828-6626; www.healthyhutkauai. com; 4480 Ho'okui Rd; ⏱7:30am-9pm; 🖉) 🍃 All of the gluten-free, dairy-free and all-natural groceries, snacks and supplies you'll need, and some you'll just want for your high-end, healthy lifestyle. Much of what this place carries is grown or made on Kaua'i. Thumbs up for the juice and smoothie bar, and organic coffee and espresso drinks.

For omnivores on a budget, tasty local **food trucks** (⏱hours vary) are permanently parked outside by the picnic tables.

Kilauea Sunshine Market
Market $

(Kilauea Neighborhood Center, 2460 Keneke St; ⏱4:30-6:30pm Thu; 🖉) 🍃 It's a modest market with a friendly hippie vibe.

Left: Kauapea (Secrets) Beach (p106); **Below:** Fish salad from Kilauea Fish Market

(LEFT) HAROLD G HERRADURA/GETTY IMAGES ©; (BELOW) LINDA CHING/GETTY IMAGES ©

A dozen or so local, often organic farmers show up to sell mangoes, papaya, cucumbers, tomatoes, salad greens, fresh coconuts and more.

Banana Joe's Fruitstand
Market $

(☏808-828-1092; www.bananajoekauai.com; 5-2719 Kuhio Hwy; items $4-8; ⊙9am-5:30pm Mon-Sat; ⚒🚼) Inside this tin-roofed shack they're making pineapple-banana frosties (dairy-free) that are worth pulling over for. Have you heard of *atemoya* or *mamey sapote*? Here's your chance to try these exotic fruits.

Namahana Farmers Markets
Market $

(☏808-828-2118; www.anainahou.org; Anaina Hou Community Park, 5-2723 Kuhio Hwy; ⊙4pm-dusk Mon, 9am-1pm Sat; ⚒) ✈ Two of Kilauea's three weekly farmers markets happen by the mini-golf course. Stop by and shop for Kaua'i-grown fruits and veggies, and handmade arts and crafts for souvenirs.

Kilauea Fish Market
Seafood $$

(☏808-828-6244; Kilauea Plantation Center, 4270 Kilauea Rd; mains $10-18; ⊙11am-8pm Mon-Sat) Serving healthy versions of over-the-counter plate lunches such as fresh *ono* (white-fleshed wahoo) or Korean BBQ chicken, mahi mahi (white-fleshed fish also called 'dolphin') tacos, and incredibly huge ahi wraps. Consider this island-style deli a necessity and build it into your itinerary. It's around back of the Kilauea Plantation Center, and has outdoor picnic tables.

Bring your own beer or wine, and be prepared to wait.

113

Kilauea Bakery & Pau Hana Pizza
Bakery, Pizza **$$**

(808-828-2020; www.kilaueabakery.word-press.com; Kong Lung Center, 2484 Keneke St; snacks & drinks from $3, pizzas $15-33; 6am-9pm, pizza from 10:30am;) Kilauea's go-to comfort food and social hub, this bakery has an impressive array of hearty soups, baked goods and pizzas (try the 'Billie Holliday,' with smoked *ono* and gorgonzo-la), although not everything is satisfying. That said, the espresso and chai tea are brewed fresh and the people-watching is superb. Don't expect smiles from the harried staff.

Bistro
Hawaii Regional Cuisine **$$**

(808-828-0480; www.lighthousebistro.com; Kong Lung Center, 2484 Keneke St; mains lunch $10-17, dinner $17-26; noon-2:30pm & 5:30-9pm) The tasteful, shabby-chic ambience works; the wine list is terrific; and it does burgers, fish sandwiches, salads, seafood and other carnivorous mains, but not equally well. The best dish in the house? Fish rockets (seared ahi wrapped in *lumpia* dough, fried with *furikake* – Japanese rice seasoning – and served with wasabi aioli). Live music happens some nights.

Garden Cafe
Cafe **$$**

(Map p108; 808-828-2192; www.common-groundlife.com; 4900 Kuawa Rd; mains $12-18; 9am-3pm Tue-Sun) Situated inland from the highway is the sustainability-motivated Common Ground complex. Its nature-chic cafe menu rotates, but always includes salads, wraps and grilled items made from seasonal crops grown on-site or by local farmers. Too bad the flavors tend to be dull, prices sky-high and service lacking.

🔒 Shopping

All of the shopping takes place within Kilauea's two outdoor malls – the **Kilauea Plantation Center** and the **Kong Lung Center** – located on opposite corners from each other at the intersection of Kilauea (Lighthouse) Rd and Keneke St.

Candles for sale

Island Soap & Candle Works   Souvenirs

(📞808-828-1955; www.islandsoap.com; Kong Lung Center, 2474 Keneke St; 🕙9am-8pm) 🌿 Though there are several similar shops on Kaua'i, at Island Soap & Candle Works the soap is all made in-house. Botanical lotions, body butters, bath oils and creamy shampoos and conditioners will make your friends back home envious. This local business uses solar power, forest-friendly packaging and sustainably harvested palm oil.

Kong Lung Trading   Arts, Clothing

(📞808-828-1822; www.konglung.com; Kong Lung Center, 2484 Keneke St; 🕙10am-6pm Mon-Sat, from 11am Sun) An Asian-inspired art and clothing boutique selling a wide array of artful tchotchkes (trinkets), silken clothing, and all-natural children's clothes, books and toys.

Oskar's Boutique   Clothing

(📞808-828-6858; www.oskarsboutique.com; Kilauea Plantation Center, 4270b Kilauea Rd; 🕙10:30am-6pm Mon-Fri, from noon Sat; ♿) 🌿 On the racks are some unique, island-inspired casual and beach wear for men, women and children, including pieces created by island fashion designers and jewelry makers.

Banana Patch Studio   Souvenirs

(📞808-828-6522; www.bananapatchstudio. com; Kong Lung Center, 2474 Keneke St; 🕙9am-5pm Mon-Sat, 10am-4pm Sun) This is a fun place to pick up touristy 'Hawaiian-style' souvenirs bearing local phraseology. Popular items include custom-designed ceramic tiles and Hawaiiana art.

Cake Nouveau   Clothing

(📞808-828-6412; Kong Lung Center, 2484 Keneke St; 🕙10am-6pm) The closest you'll come in town to an LA-meets-Polynesia-inspired selection of women's boutique-style clothes and accessories – perfect for those with a hot date coming up.

Local Knowledge

NAME: MIKE RODGER

OCCUPATION: OWNER, KAUAI ISLAND EXPERIENCE

What are some of the must-see spots on the North Shore? The Kilauea Point National Wildlife Refuge, Waipa Farmers Market, Limahuli Gardens and, for sure, the Na Pali Coast.

What about activities or adventures visitors might be hesitant to try, but should? I'd recommend going out on a traditional Polynesian sailing canoe, stand-up paddle boarding on a river or trying a private surf lesson.

About surfing, what is proper surfing etiquette? You definitely want to give children and locals plenty of space. If you can't read ocean conditions, talk with the lifeguards, surf instructors or locals before paddling out. There's so much unspoken communication that takes place out there. Take it slow, have patience, be observant of what others are doing and proceed with respect.

Favorite rainy-day activities? Well, you can still surf in the rain on Kaua'i. It's warm and there is a spiritual beauty to Kaua'i rain when it splashes in the ocean. Snuggling with a loved one is also fun! Or drinking some kava (Polynesian drink) and strumming ukulele.

What tips do you have for travelers wanting to feel a part of things up here? Try spending time at local Hawaiian music venues. Please remember to leave the beach and ocean cleaner than you found them, and have plenty of respect for locals.

'Anini

A popular destination for locals spending the day or weekend camping, fishing, diving or just 'beaching' it, 'Anini is unsullied, revered and golden. To get here, cross Kalihiwai Bridge – the swooping one with a distractingly incredible view – go up the hill and turn right onto (the second) Kalihiwai Rd, bearing left onto 'Anini Rd soon thereafter. The beach park will be the first visible land you pass after several bends along the ocean. For a quieter beach experience, drive past the beach park and find a space to call your own for a few hours.

◉ Sights & Activities

'Anini Beach Park   Beach

(Map p108; 'Anini Rd; 🚻) It may not be the island's best-looking beach, but 'Anini is Kaua'i's best spot for windsurfing and kiteboarding. It's just as popular for snorkeling and swimming, too, making it a good fit for families. In addition, it's protected by one of the longest and widest fringing reefs in Hawaii.

Lying less than 3 miles from the Kuhio Hwy, the park is unofficially divided into day-use, camping and windsurfing areas. Facilities include restrooms, outdoor showers, drinking water, picnic pavilions and BBQ grills.

At its widest point, the reef extends more than 1600ft offshore. Note that the shallows do bottom out at low tide, so timing your snorkel is key, or you may have to step awkwardly around exposed coral and sea urchins on your way in.

Weekends draw crowds; weekdays are low-key.

Windsurf
Kaua'i   Windsurfing

(Map p108; 📞808-828-6838; www.windsurf-kauai.com; 'Anini Beach Park; 2hr lessons $100, board & sail rental per hour $25; ⏱by appointment only) Learn what it's like to glide on water with Celeste Harvel. With 30 years of windsurfing experience, she guarantees you'll be sailing in your first lesson. Lessons are by appointment only, usually at 10am and 1pm on weekdays. Advanced lessons can be arranged (call for pricing).

'Anini Beach Park

STEVE KROEGER/GETTY IMAGES ©

Queen's Bath

This deadly spot – formed by a sharp lava-rock shelf – has pools that provide a natural swimming hole. Often hit by powerful waves, it's notorious for pulling visitors out to sea, as happens annually. Though the surf at times splashes in softly, what many people don't realize is that waves come in sets, meaning that a 15-minute flat period could be followed by a 10ft to 15ft wave, seemingly out of nowhere. People die here every year, most commonly by walking along the ledge used to access the pool. We recommend staying away.

Na Pali Sea Breeze
Snorkeling, Cruise

(✆808-828-1285; www.napaliseabreezetours.com; charter per person $135-195) The only tour leaving out of 'Anini, this aims for a personable experience. The pretrip rendezvous location is usually at the captain's house (except during winter, when departures are from Lihu'e's Nawiliwili Harbor). Ocean conditions permitting, sea cave exploration is a highlight, along with an hour of snorkeling and lunch.

Inquire about whale-watching and fishing charters.

🛏 Sleeping

High-end vacation rentals abound in 'Anini. Start by searching **Vacation Rentals By Owner** (www.vrbo.com) and **Airbnb.com** (www.airbnb.com) online.

Camping at the justifiably popular 'Anini Beach Park is another option. The campground hosts a mix of frugal travelers and long-term 'residents.' It's generally very safe. Note all campers must vacate the park on Tuesday nights.

Bamboo
Apartment $$

(Map p110; ✆808-828-0811; www.surfsideprop.com; 3281 Kalihiwai Rd; 1-bedroom apt per night/week $200/1300; 🛜) Overlooking the Kalihiwai Valley and a 10-minute walk to the beach, this airy getaway is attached to the owners' larger house. The private entrance stairs are steep, leading to a cozy but well-appointed apartment with a full kitchen, living-room lanai and spa tub in the bathroom. Cleaning fee $150.

Plumeria
Rental House $$$

(Map p108; ✆808-828-0811; www.surfsideprop.com; 3585 'Anini Rd; 3-bedroom house per night/week $375/2500; 🛜) A unique abode that's both comfortable and chic, Plumeria has an enviable location – it's such a short walk to the beach. Expect modest luxury, Hawaii-style, with a finely polished wood interior, sweeping views, and indoor and outdoor showers. Add to this amicable caretakers, and complimentary beach and snorkel gear, kayaks and bicycles to borrow. Cleaning fee $175.

Princeville

Kilauea's rich cousin, Princeville (dubbed 'Haolewood') is a methodically landscaped resort community that is about as carefully controlled – and protected – as a film set, especially when it actually is a film set. Its body is made up of high-end resorts, finely manicured golf courses, and a mixture of cookie-cutter residences, vacation rentals, and condominium complexes. What it may lack in personality it makes up for in convenience, as it's the most centrally located area on the North Shore. The St Regis Princeville – an incarnation of luxury – is Princeville's Oz at the end of the road. The only major commercial area is the Princeville Center (p125) with a grocery store, several restaurants and a mix of kiosks and retail stores.

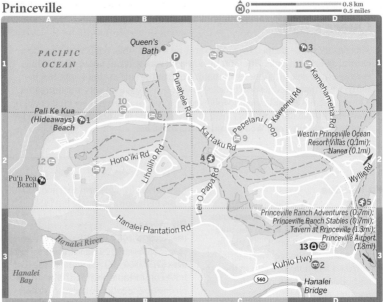

Princeville traces its roots to Robert Wyllie, a Scottish doctor who became foreign minister to King Kamehameha IV. In 1853, Wyllie established a sugar plantation in Hanalei. When Queen Emma and Kamehameha came to visit in 1860, Wyllie named his plantation and the surrounding lands Princeville to honor their two-year-old son, Prince Albert, who died only two years later. The plantation later became a cattle ranch.

Beaches

Pali Ke Kua (Hideaways) Beach   Beach

A cove notched in the cliffs, Hideaways has a short strand of golden sand and turquoise shallows. It's an ideal snorkel and swim spot (when it's calm), with a teeming reef just off the beach. Be wise and don't get caught out when the tide comes in.

Park at the tiny, always-crowded lot past the St Regis gatehouse, where a path between two fences followed by a steep railing- and rope-assisted scramble leads down to the beach.

A path to the left of the gatehouse takes you to Pu'u Poa Beach. Although public, it sits below and adjacent to the St Regis resort and serves as its on-campus beach.

Honu Cove   Beach

Beloved by locals but best visited only on calm days, this secret cove awaits at the end of Kamehameha Rd. Simply take the first right past the Westin, follow it all the way to the end and keep left. From the parking area, you'll see a trail that hugs the cliffs. At the bottom of the trail, stay left along the cliffs and you'll find a beach with good snorkeling and green sea turtles. Come at high tide.

Sights

Hanalei Valley Lookout   Viewpoint

Take in views of farmland that's been cultivated for more than 1000 years, including broad brushstrokes of valley, river and taro. Park opposite Princeville Center and take care to watch for other pedestrians when pulling out onto the busy highway.

Princeville

✪ Activities

Halele'a Spa   Spa
(☏808-826-9644; www.stregisprinceville.
com; St Regis Princeville, 5520 Ka Haku Rd;
treatments from $165; ⊙9am-7pm, by appoint-
ment only) Translated as 'house of joy,' this
11,000-sq-ft palatial escape offers massages, and has couples and VIP treatment
rooms. The interior incorporates native
Hawaiian woods and natural fibers, and
treatments are based upon a foundation
of traditional Hawaiian medicine, using

botanical and ocean resources such as
taro clay and seaweed-leaf body wraps.
Spa treatments include complimentary
fitness-center access.

Princeville Ranch
Stables   Horseback Riding
(Map p108; ☏808-826-7669; www.princeville
ranch.com; Kuhio Hwy at Kapaka St; tours $99-
135; ⊙Mon-Sat, by appointment only; ⊞) Offering a beautiful ride, even for beginners,
the pleasant 3½-hour trip to Kalihiwai
Falls includes picnicking and a swim. Find
the stables between mile markers 26 and
27 on the Kuhio Hwy, across from the
Prince Golf Course. Wear jeans and bring
sunblock and insect repellent. Minimum
ages for riders is eight to 10 years old;
maximum weight varies.

Makai Golf Club   Golf
(☏808-826-1912; www.makaigolf.com; 4080
Lei O Papa Rd; green fees incl car rental $159-
239, 9-hole round from $55) The St Regis
Princeville resort's golf club is divided into
three 9-hole courses designed by Robert
Trent Jones Jr. Each has its own distinctive personality and scenic flavor. The
Ocean Course runs out to the magnificent coastline and offers a signature par
3 overlooking Hanalei Bay. The Ocean
and Lakes Courses link up for traditional
18-hole play.

The **Lakes Course** winds around
serene lakes, while the **Woods Course** –
the cheapest and gentlest – meanders
through native woodlands.

Club and shoe rentals available.

Prince Golf Course   Golf
(☏808-826-5001; www.princeville.com;
5-3900 Kuhio Hwy; green fees $165-250) Most
call it difficult. Tiger Woods is rumored
to have called it 'unfair.' Regularly ranked
among the USA's best, this Robert
Trent Jones Jr–designed links-style golf
course offers breathtaking vistas. It's as
humbling as it can be rewarding – you
best bring your A-game, and possibly
extra sleeves of balls. Club and shoe
rentals available.

Princeville Ranch Adventures
Adventure Tour

(Map p108; ☎808-826-7669; www.princeville ranch.com; Kuhio Hwy at Kapaka St; tours $99-145; ⊗by reservation only; ⊛) This family-oriented enterprise can bring out your adventurous side, whether it's for a waterfall hike, a zipline ride, an off-road buggy drive, or a kayak tour to a secluded swimming hole. Age and weight requirements vary. Reservations required.

Powerline Trail
Mountain Biking

(Map p108) Measuring more than 11 miles each way, this bike ride presents challenging steep climbs, deep ruts and even deeper puddles (bike-tire deep) before finishing near Wailua's Keahua Arboretum (p71). The scenery doesn't measure up to the sheer audacious wild beauty of other island trails, however.

The trail starts about 2 miles down Kepaka St, the road to Princeville Stables. Look for the Na Ala Hele trailhead sign just past an obvious water tank, where the road turns to red dirt.

Tennis at the Makai Club
Tennis

(☎808-826-1912; www.makaigolf.com; 4080 Lei O Papa Rd; hourly court rental per person $25; ⊛) Newly remodeled, rust-tinted outdoor hard courts host lessons offered daily by the local pro, and also pickup games. Call up to a week in advance for reservations. Racket rental available.

Princeville Yoga
Yoga

(☎808-826-6688; www.princevilleyogakauai. com; Princeville Center, 5-4280 Kuhio Hwy; drop-in classes $15, 3-class pass $40) In Bikram style, a skilled team of yogis lead classes for any and all willing to practice in a room heated to between 95°F and 100°F. Mat and towel rentals available. Go online for current class schedules.

Mana Yoga
Yoga

(Map p108; ☎808-652-3823; www.manayoga. com; 3812 Ahonui Pl; classes $20, 4-class pass $60; ⊗usually 8:30-10am Mon & Wed) Michaelle Edwards has created her own version of yoga that may straighten even the most unruly of spines. Combining massage and yoga, it heals with natural poses rather than contortionistic ones.

🕹 Tours

Island Sails Kaua'i
Sailing

(☎808-212-6053; www.islandsailskauai. com; Pu'u Poa Beach; 90min cruises adult/child from $99/60; ⊗by reservation only) Whether snorkeling in the morning, cruising in the afternoon or catching a sunset, this is your chance to ride in a traditional Polynesian sailing canoe. The red-painted *Ku'upa'aloa* pulls right on the beach in front of the St Regis Princeville resort.

Makai Golf Club (p119)
MATTHEW MICAH WRIGHT/GETTY IMAGES ©

Sunshine Helicopters
Scenic Flights

(☎ 808-270-3999, 866-501-7738; www. sunshinehelicopters.com; 45min tours $245-295) Leaving out of Princeville airport, Sunshine Helicopters offers convenience if you're on the North Shore. Flights buzz along the Na Pali Coast and over Waimea Canyon. First-class seating with extra leg room next to the pilot costs extra.

🛏 Sleeping

Princeville, with an abundance of vacation rentals, is devoid of the quaint, personable accommodations found in neighboring Kilauea and Hanalei. It lacks much other than midrange to high-end options. Renting a condo or staying in a resort here may be pricey, but it will be worth it. Visitors who find themselves within Princeville's central positioning on the North Shore and among its elevated tropical milieu – whether for a day, a week, or a month – are among the lucky ones.

Sealodge
Condo $

(www.hestara.com; 3700 Kamehameha Rd; 1-/2-bedroom condo from $95/125; ❄ 🛜 ♨) These condos are wooden shingled affairs with gorgeous cliffside perches. Some units are in better shape than others and not all interiors are wonderful, so insist upon pictures prior to online booking through local rental agencies. Nonetheless, the setting will not disappoint. Cleaning fee $95 to $115.

Mana Yoga Vacation Rental
Apartment $$

(Map p108; ☎ 808-826-9230; www.kauai northshorevacationrentals.com; 3812 Ahonui Pl; studio/2-bedroom apt from $85/135; 🛜) Situated next to the serene Mana Yoga Center, the larger apartment features all natural wood details, teak cabinets and a tile floor. The lanai has vast 180-degree mountain views for contemplation. Though more compact, the studio nevertheless has a king-sized bed and private lanai. Farm-fresh eggs, coconuts and an orchard seal the deal. Cleaning fee $40.

Princeville Rental Agencies

The following companies also handle bookings for condos and vacation rentals in and around Princeville:

Kauai Vacation Rentals (☎ 866-922-5642; www.kauai-vacations-ahh.com)

Parrish Collection Kaua'i (☎ 800-325-5701; www.parrishkauai.com)

Princeville Vacations (☎ 808-828-6530, 800-800-3637; www.princeville-vacations.com)

Three-night minimum stay; ask about weekly discounts.

Holly's Kauai Condo
Condo $$

(☎ 480-831-0061; www.hollyskauaicondo.com; Ali'i Kai Resort, 3830 Edward Rd; 2-bedroom condo $195; ❄ 🛜) Perched cliffside with nothing but water between you and Alaska, this 1200-sq-ft, two-bedroom, two-bath unit is a real deal. Wintertime offers guaranteed whale sightings – basically from your bed – and the remodeled interior comes with HDTV, bamboo furnishings and a top-of-the-line kitchen. Three-night minimum stay; cleaning fee $135. Book far in advance.

Pali Ke Kua
Condo $$

(☎ 808-826-6585, 800-222-5541; www.ocean-frontrealty.com; 5300 Ka Haku Rd; 1-/2-bedroom condo from $175/225; ❄ 🛜 ♨) Situated cliffside, some condos here get both ocean and mountain views. Easy alternative access to Pali Ke Kua (Hideaways) Beach is on the property. Oceanfront Realty charges fees for reservations ($50) and cleaning ($130). Many other agencies also handle bookings here, so search online for the best quotes.

Nihilani
Condo $$

(☎ 808-987-3502, 877-877-5758; www.alohacondos.com; 4919 Pepelani Loop; 3-bedroom townhouse $139-209; 🅿 ❄ 🛜 ♨)

121

This manicured Princeville condo complex is not cliffside nor does it have sea views, but it's built with a certain Cape Cod panache. Townhouses show off louvered awnings and shutters, while an up-to-date pool area and outdoor BBQ grills make it ideal for family vacations. Cleaning fee $200.

Hanalei Bay Resort Resort $$

(808-826-6522, 877-344-0688; www.hanalei bayresort.com; 5380 Hono'iki Rd; r from $149;) Location is the name of the game. The suites are steeply priced, but you might see deals pop up at this timeshare property. Units vary drastically in quality and not all have the same amenities, so ask for details and photos before booking.

Emmalani Court Condo $$

(808-742-2000, 800-325-5701; www.parrish kauai.com; 5250 Ka Haku Rd; 1-/2-bedroom condo from $125/175;) Adjacent to the Makai Golf Club, these remodeled units are in a quieter part of town. They're roomy and well kept, and some afford ocean views. There's a small, tiled outdoor swimming pool. Five-night mimimum stay; there is a cleaning fee of $175 to $225.

St Regis Princeville Resort $$$

(808-826-9644, 866-716-8140; www. stregisprinceville.com; 5520 Ka Haku Rd; d from $500;) The Oz at the end of the road overlooks Hanalei Bay. More than 250 rooms range from merely opulent to 'what do I do with myself' extravagant. Decorated in upscale tropical fashion, all have custom-designed furniture, electronically controlled windows, and marble bathrooms. A 5000-sq-ft infinity pool with multiple hot tubs sits oceanside, with Pu'u Poa Beach just steps away.

Westin Princeville Ocean Resort Villas Condo $$$

(Map p108; 808-827-8700, 866-837-4254; www.westinprinceville.com; 3838 Wyllie Rd; studio/1-bedroom condo from $275/400;) Take advantage of this comparatively inexpensive Starwood property. Situated cliffside, the views are expansive, and from November to March whale sightings may only require you to gaze out at the ocean. Condo-like 'villas'

View of Makena (aka 'Bali Hai'), Ha'ena State Park (p147)

RANDY WELLS/GETTY IMAGES ©

boast full kitchens, flat-screen TVs and a washer-dryer, while studio units have kitchenettes. The resort's mutilevel pool complex is kid-friendly.

✖ Eating

Just a few miles down the road, Hanalei has many more eateries to match all budgets.

Foodland   Supermarket $
(☎808-826-9880; www.foodland.com; Princeville Center, 5-4280 Kuhio Hwy; ⏱6am-11pm) The North Shore's biggest supermarket has an abundance of fruits and vegetables, freshly prepared sushi and *poke,* wine, beer and a better selection overall than the Big Save in Hanalei.

Lappert's Hawaii   Ice Cream $
(www.lappertshawaii.com; Princeville Center, 5-4280 Kuhio Hwy; ⏱10am-9pm; ♿) The sweet smell of waffle cones beckons, as do scoops of island flavors such as Kauai Pie (Kona coffee ice cream with coconut flakes and macadamia nuts).

North Shore General Store & Café   American $
(☎808-826-1122; Princeville Center, 5-4280 Kuhio Hwy; items $2-10; ⏱6am-8pm Mon-Fri, 7am-8pm Sat, to 6pm Sun) A greasy-spoon minimarket that's also a coffee bar serving up bagel sandwiches, breakfast burritos, grass-fed Princeville beef burgers, plate lunches and more. It's inside the gas station.

Federico's FreshMex Cuisine   Mexican $
(☎808-826-7177; Princeville Center, 5-4280 Kuhio Hwy; mains $5-12; ⏱10:30am-8pm Mon-Sat; ♿) Just your standard strip-mall Mexican joint, but with relatively reasonable prices for fueling up on, say, shrimp seviche tostadas and chipotle fish tacos.

Lei Petite Bakery & Coffee Shop   Cafe $
(☎808-826-7277; Princeville Center, 5-4280 Kuhio Hwy; items $2-8; ⏱6am-4pm; 📶) Princeville's prime people-watching can

North Shore Sunsets

- Ke'e Beach (p148)
- Hanalei Pavilion Beach Park (p129)
- 'Anini Beach Park (p116)
- St Regis Bar (p124) terrace
- Kilauea Lighthouse (p108)

be found at this caffeine station dishing up acai bowls and fruit scones. Expect long lines in the morning.

Tiki Iniki Bar & Restaurant   American $$
(☎808-431-4242; www.tikiiniki.com; Princeville Center, 5-4280 Kuhio Hwy; mains lunch $10-14, dinner $14-32; ⏱11:30am-midnight; ♿) With a faux thatched roof and memorabila from the long-gone Coco Palms Resort, this place nails the retro Hawaiiana vibe. It's more suited to sipping tropical cocktails such as mai tais or the 'Hanalei Sling' than eating, although there are some satisfying plates of burgers, wraps, seafood, pasta and salads on the menu. They also serve later than anywhere else in Princeville.

Dinner reservations advised.

Kaua'i Grill   Hawaii Regional Cuisine $$$
(☎808-826-2250; www.kauaigrill.com; St Regis Princeville, 5520 Ka Haku Rd; mains $35-72; ⏱5:30-9:30pm Tue-Sat) An offshoot of the internationally venerated executive chef Jean-Georges Vongerichten, Kaua'i Grill is where the cuisine is sophisticated and the views extend for miles. Rice-cracker-crusted ahi in citrus-chili sauce and sautéed Kona lobster are some of the star cast, while black-truffle cheese fritters and mushroom spring rolls play well-crafted supporting roles. Wine pairings encouraged. Vegetarian and gluten-free menus available. Advance reservations essential.

Driving with Aloha

Lauded as one of the most scenic and breathtaking drives on the island, the drive to the 'end of the road' is impossibly beautiful. However, though you might want to pull over for that must-have photograph, please do so safely as accidents occur when drivers stop suddenly or in a bad place to snap a photo. (You'll likely see at least one other visitor doing this.) If you're heading to the road's end (Ke'e Beach), take it slowly and enjoy the crossing of each of the seven one-lane bridges, the first of which is in Hanalei.

When crossing these bridges, do as the locals do:

o When the bridge is empty and you reach it first, you can go.

o If there's a steady stream of cars already crossing as you approach, then simply follow them.

o When you see cars approaching from the opposite direction, yield to the entire queue of approaching cars for at least five cars, if not all.

o Give the *shaka* sign ('hang loose' hand gesture, with index, middle and ring fingers downturned) as thanks to any opposite-direction drivers who have yielded.

Nanea Hawaii Regional Cuisine **$$$**
(Map p108; ☎800-827-8808; www.westinprince-ville.com; Westin Princeville Ocean Resort Villas, 3838 Wylie Rd; mains lunch $12-18, dinner $20-45; ☺7-10:30am, 11am-2:30pm & 5:30-9:30pm Mon-Sat, 8:30am-12:30pm & 5:30-9:30pm Sun; ⊞) ✐ Nanea's Hawaii fusion dishes are elegant, but are not always quite worth the price tag. Alaska-born executive sous chef Eric Purugganan – whose family has roots on O'ahu – cut his culinary teeth at award-winning restaurants in the Pacific Northwest. His menu integrates locally caught seafood and island-grown greens, goat's cheese and honey. Lunch is definitely the better value. Reservations recommended.

Tavern at
Princeville American **$$$**
(Map p108; ☎808-826-8700; www.tavernbyroy. com; 5-3900 Kuhio Ave; mains lunch $13-24, dinner $18-46; ☺11am-4pm & 5-9:30pm) Don't let the golf-clubhouse location fool you: this eatery is the offspring of star chef Roy Yamaguchi. The atmosphere can feel hollow, but service is enthusiastic. Com-

plimentary popcorn and a creative drinks menu set the stage for an ambitious array of dishes that are at the very least original, such as baby back ribs with guava-*liliko'i* (passion fruit) barbecue sauce.

🍷 Drinking & Entertainment

While most restaurants in Princeville have barstools and bottles, the real social scene (relative to Kaua'i) can be found down the hill in Hanalei.

St Regis Bar Lounge
(☎808-826-9644; www.stregisprinceville. com; St Regis Princeville, 5520 Ka Haku Rd; ☺3:30-11pm) Don't let the elegance or the enormous crystal raindrop chandelier intimidate you. The lobby bar is for any and all wanting to take a load off. The vibe is a step more welcoming than the chichi surroundings, so relax and enjoy the ultimate location for a sunset cocktail and unforgettable views of Hanalei Bay.

Some nights musicians serenade imbibers with live jazz music.

🛍️ Shopping

Princeville Center · Mall
(📞8080-826-9497; www.princevillecenter.
com; 5-4280 Kuhio Hwy) If you're staying
in Princeville, you'll inevitably wind up
at this assortment of island and luxury
lifestyle shops. There's live local entertainment in the food court from 6pm to
8pm nightly.

Magic Dragon Toy & Art Supply Co · Toys
(📞808-826-9144; Princeville Center, 5-4280
Kuhio Hwy; 🕘9am-6pm; 🚻) A wonderland
of whirling, colorful and inspired toys,
from kites and beach gear to watercolors
and puppets, all packed into a tiny imaginative storefront. Prices aren't cheap,
though.

ℹ️ Information

Bank of Hawaii (📞808-826-6551; Princeville
Center, 5-4280 Kuhio Hwy; 🕘8:30am-4pm Mon-
Thu, to 6pm Fri) Has a 24-hour ATM.

Chevron Gas Station (Princeville Center,
5-4280 Kuhio Hwy; 🕘usually 6am-10pm Mon-
Sat, to 9pm Sun) The last fuel option before the
end of the road.

First Hawaiian Bank (📞808-826-1560; www.
fhb.com; Princeville Center, 5-4280 Kuhio
Highway; 🕘8:30am-4pm Mon-Thu, to 6pm Fri)
Has a 24-hour ATM.

Princeville Mail Service Center (📞808-826-
7331; Princeville Center, 5-4280 Kuhio Hwy;
per 15min $3; 🕘9am-5pm Mon-Fri) Internet
computer workstations available.

Princeville Post Office (📞808-828-1721;
www.usps.com; Princeville Center, 5-4280
Kuhio Hwy; 🕘10:30am-2:30pm Mon-Fri, to
noon Sat)

ℹ️ Getting There & Around

Princeville is great for walking or cruising on
bicycle, with one main arterial road (Ka Haku Rd)
running through the middle – the majority of
which has an adjacent bike path.

The Kaua'i Bus (p58) between Lihu'e and
Hanalei stops near Princeveille Center on the
Kuhio Hwy approximately hourly on weekdays
(limited weekend service).

St Regis Princeville (p122)

HOLGER LEUE/LOOK-FOTO/GETTY IMAGES ©

Hanalei

The drive down the hill from Princeville toward Hanalei will unveil even more inspired landscapes, soaring birds and drool-worthy views. Misted fields, the silhouettes of palm trees against the sky and afternoon rainbows collaborate to lure you in and pull you along.

The Hanalei Bridge is the first of seven bridges along the drive from the Hanalei River to the end of the road. The county has left the bridge as a historical landmark and, because of this, big trucks will never tear down any road in Hanalei or beyond (monster pick-up trucks excluded), and development has been kept at bay. During times of heavy rains (more common in winter), the Hanalei Bridge can close due to flooding, and all those on either side are stuck until it reopens.

The surfer-chic town of Hanalei has more than its fair share of adults with Peter Pan syndrome and kids with seemingly Olympian athletic prowess. Take a stroll down beachfront Weke Rd and you'll see men in their 60s waxing

Hanalei

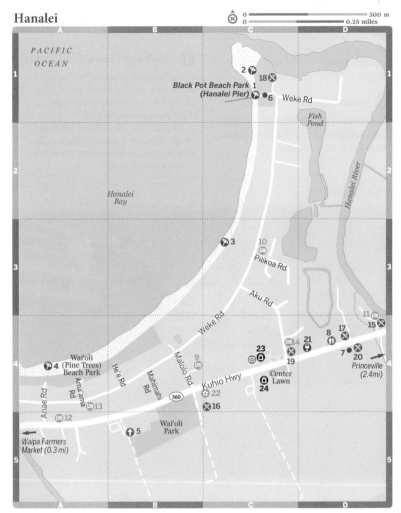

their surfboards and young 'uns carrying their 'guns' (big-wave surfboards) to the beach. Without a doubt, beach life is *the* life here, and how sweet it is. A water enthusiast's playground, Hanalei's rivers, beaches, and ocean access offer a plethora of frolicking fun in the sun.

History

With its remote location and epic landscapes, Hanalei Valley has always moved in a natural tempo. Realizing they were blessed with such fecund land, its earliest residents grew large amounts of *mai'a* (bananas), *'ulu* (breadfruit), *'uala* (sweet potatoes), *niu* (coconuts) and *kalo* (taro). Ancient Polynesians considered taro to be their direct ancestor and their 'staff of life.' As time passed, numerous other agricultural ventures took shape, including the growing of tobacco, coffee, rice, sugarcane, cotton and a variety of fruits such as pineapples, tamarinds, and even oranges and peaches. As with the rest of the Islands, the plantation era on Kaua'i brought groups of Japanese, Chinese, Filipino and Portuguese immigrants to help work the fields, resulting in the multiethnic population that remains today.

When ancient Hawaiian kings came to visit the valley, the residents practiced the custom of *ho'okupu* (gift giving) by bringing offerings such as fruits, vegetables, fish and pigs for their royalty. Though Hanalei has always carried a reputation of strong aloha, as recently as the 1970s the social temperature and lawlessness of these parts was something akin to the 'Wild West.' With the influx of mainland hippies seeking a tropical utopia, international surfers

Below: Paddling in Hanalei River (p131); **Right:** Black Pot Beach Park (Hanalei Pier)

(BELOW) KICKA WITTE/GETTY IMAGES ©; (RIGHT) MONICA & MICHAEL SWEET/GETTY IMAGES ©

pining for an endless summer and the lot of them on the lookout for anything but responsibility, growing pains were unavoidable for this haven.

Since the mid-20th century – many thanks to Hollywood's cameras – Hanalei and the surrounding North Shore's peaks, valleys and coastline have gained celebrity status, which might explain the recent influx of celebrity residents as well.

🏖 Beaches

A crescent-shaped bay and a near surfeit of surfers mean Hanalei Bay typifies what many envision when thinking of Kaua'i. Made up of four beaches (really one beach divided into four sections with four names), there's something for almost everyone here: sunbathing, bodyboarding and, of course, surfing. The winter

months can make this stretch of water an experts-only spot, though in summer months the water is sometimes so calm it's hard to distinguish between sky and sea, except for the smattering of yachts bobbing on the horizon.

The beaches are listed here going from the northeastern tip (at the Hanalei River) down the coast to the southwest.

Black Pot Beach Park (Hanalei Pier)   Beach

This small section of Hanalei Bay near the Hanalei River mouth usually offers the calmest surf among the wild North Shore swells. Also known as Hanalei Pier for its unmistakable landmark, this stretch of sand shaded by ironwood trees is popular mainly with surfers. In summer, swimming and snorkeling are decent, as is kayaking. Use extreme caution during periods of high surf because dangerous shore breaks and rip currents are common.

The sandy-bottomed beach slopes down gently, making it safe for beginning surfers. Lessons are typically taught just west of the pier, where you'll find surf schools galore. At the park's eastern end, where the Hanalei River empties onto the beach, is a small boat ramp where kayakers launch for trips upriver.

Facilities include restrooms and outdoor showers, and there are lifeguards.

Hanalei Beach Park   Beach

With its sweeping views, this makes a great place for a picnic, sunset or lazy day at the beach. Ideally located, its downside is the parking, which can be a challenge. Park along Weke Rd if you have to, as the public lot gets crowded. Facilities include restrooms and outdoor showers. Camping is allowed only with an advance county permit.

Hanalei Pavilion
Beach Park   Beach

Toward the middle of Hanalei Bay, you'll find this scenic beach park that possesses a white-sand crescent made for strolling. Waters are typically not as calm as further east by the pier, but swimming and stand up paddle surfing are possible during the calmest summer months. Facilities include restrooms and outdoor showers.

Wai'oli (Pine Trees)
Beach Park   Beach

Offering respite from the sun, this park is equipped with restrooms, outdoor showers and picnic tables. Winter months are when the North Shore is at its highest surf-wise and locals dominate the surf spot here known as **Pine Trees**. The shore break is harder here than any other spot on Hanalei Bay, and swimming is dangerous, except during the calmest summer surf.

129

Hanalei National Wildlife Refuge

Anywhere west of Kilauea will set you on a path ever more pristine the further you go. Following Kalihiwai Rd, you'll catch your first glimpses of even more vast Eden-like landscapes. Rolling hills abound as you pass through Princeville, where you'll spot the Hanalei National Wildlife Refuge. The Hanalei Valley Lookout (p118), across from the Princeville Center, is a great vantage point for the refuge.

One of the largest rivers in the state, the Hanalei River has nurtured its crops since the first *kanaka maoli* (Native Hawaiians) began cultivating taro in its fertile valley fields. Other crops have come and gone, including rice and oranges. In the mid-1800s, rice paddies were planted here to feed the Chinese sugar-plantation laborers. By the 1930s four rice mills were operating in the Hanalei area. Today, taro again dominates, but with only 5% of its original acreage.

The wildlife refuge, established in 1972, is closed to the public. However, from the lookout you might be able to spot a few of the 49 bird species using the habitat, including four endangered endemic waterbirds: *ae'o* (Hawaiian stilt; slender with a black back, white chest and long pink legs), *alae kea* (Hawaiian coot; slate-gray with white bill and frontal shield), *'alae 'ula* (Hawaiian moorhen; dark-gray with black head and distinctive red-and-yellow bill) and *koloa maoli* (Hawaiian duck; mottled brown with orange legs and feet).

To get here, turn left onto Ohiki Rd immediately after the Hanalei Bridge. You can enter the refuge only on the Ho'opulapula Haraguchi Rice Mill & Taro Farm Tours.

Middles Beach   Beach

(Map p108) At mile marker 4 on the *makai* (ocean) side of the road is a small, scrubby parking area. Walk along the beach or look out to the ocean to see three surf breaks; from left to right, they are **Waikokos**, **Middles** and **Chicken Wings**.

This beach is informally known as Middles because of the break. The highway bridge just past the parking area crosses over Waikoko Stream, so the shoreline from the bridge onward is known as Waikoko Beach.

Waikoko Beach   Beach

(Map p108) Protected by a reef on the western bend of Hanalei Bay, this sandy-bottomed beach with no facilities offers shallower and calmer waters than the middle of the bay. Local surfers call this break **Waikokos** (literally, 'blood water'); look for them in the water and you'll see where the break is.

◉ Sights

Ho'opulapula Haraguchi Rice Mill & Taro Farm Tours   Guided Tour

(☎808-651-3399; www.haraguchiricemill. org; tours incl lunch adult/child 5-12yr $87/52; ⊙tours usually 9:45am Wed, by reservation only) Learn all about cultivating taro on Kaua'i at this sixth-generation family-run, nonprofit farm and rice mill (the last remaining one in the Hawaiian Islands). On farmer-guided tours, which take you out into the *lo'i kalo* (wet taro fields), you'll also get a glimpse of the otherwise inaccessible Hanalei National Wildlife Refuge and learn about Hawaii's immigrant history.

Tours meet by Hanalei Taro & Juice Co (p136) food truck on Kuhio Hwy. A Hawaiian plate lunch is included in the price.

Wai'oli Hui'ia Church & Wai'oli Mission House   Church

(☎ 808-826-6253; www.hanaleichurch.org; 5-5363a Kuhio Hwy) A popular site for quaint church weddings, the original Wai'oli Hui'ia Church was built by Hanalei's first missionaries, William and Mary Alexander, who arrived in 1834 in a double-hulled canoe. Today the church, hall and mission house remain in the middle of town, set on a huge manicured lawn with a beautiful mountain backdrop.

The green American Gothic–style wooden church that passersby can see today was donated in 1912 by three sons of Abner Wilcox, another island missionary. The doors remain open during the day, and visitors are welcome. A 19th-century bible printed in Hawaiian is displayed on top of the old organ. The church choir sings hymns in Hawaiian at the 10am Sunday service.

Guided tours of the historic mission house are currently available for walk-in visitors (no reservations) between 9am and 3pm on Tuesdays, Thursdays and Saturdays. Check the Grove Farm website (www.grovefarm.org) for details.

Activities

Though its glory is of a more tame variety than that of the sacred Wailua River, the Hanalei River offers roughly 6 miles of tranquil scenery and is ideal for kayaking or stand-up paddle boarding.

Titus Kinimaka's Hawaiian School of Surfing   Surfing

(☎ 808-652-1116; www.hawaiianschoolofsurfing.com; 5-5088 Kuhio Hwy; 90min lessons from $65, board rental per hour/day/week $10/30/75; ⊙ by appointment only) Call in advance for a lesson with legendary pro

big-wave surfer Titus Kinimaka or, more likely, with one of his minions, who line up the boards daily on the beach or at the pier. No more than three students per instructor. Bonus: they'll let you use the boards for a couple of hours of practice after the lesson.

Kayak Hanalei   Water Sports

(☎ 808-826-1881; www.kayakhanalei.com; Ching Young Village, 5-5070a Kuhio Hwy; kayak/SUP set rental per day from $35/40, 2hr surfing or SUP lessons $90, kayak tours adult/child 5-12yr $105/95; ⊙ 8am-4:30pm) This long-standing, family-run outfitter rents SUP sets and surfboards at the in-town store, and kayaks at the river dock. Beginners surfing and SUP lessons are available daily except Sunday (reservations advised).

Hawaiian Surfing Adventures   Water Sports

(☎ 808-482-0749; www.hawaiiansurfingadventures.com; 5-5134 Kuhio Hwy; 90min group surfing or SUP lessons $65, surfboard/SUP rental per day $20/50; ⊙ store 8am-3:30pm, last lesson starts 2pm) Surfing lessons for novices

Wai'oli Hui'ia Church

LINDA CHING/GETTY IMAGES ©

include 30 minutes on land, and one hour in the water. SUP lessons could even get you doing yoga poses atop your board. The company is owned by local Hawaiian surfer Mitch Alepa and his family.

Pedal 'n Paddle Adventure Sports
(808-826-9069; www.pedalnpaddle.com; Ching Young Village, 5-5190 Kuhio Hwy; ⏰9am-6pm) This full-service rental shop is conveniently located and offers some of the best rates in town for renting snorkel sets, boogie boards, SUP sets, kayaks, bicycles and almost all the camping gear you could need for trekking the Na Pali Coast. Daily and weekly rental rates available.

Fathom Five Divers Diving
(808-742-6991, 800-972-3078; www.fathom-five.com; dives $90-155; ⏰by reservation only Mar-Oct) The PADI-certified Fathom Five outfit in Koloa also gears up for a North Shore dive at the reef off Makua (Tunnels) Beach. In summer, dare a night dive.

Kauai Island Experience Water Sports
(808-346-3094; www.kauaiexperience.com; 1½hr group/private surfing lessons $80/160, surfboard rental per day $20; 🚹) Waterman Mike Rodger's team will teach you to surf, stand up paddle, snorkel, fish, paddle a traditional Hawaiian canoe and more.

Hanalei Surf Company Surfing
(808-826-9000; www.hanaleisurf.com; Hanalei Center, 5-5161 Kuhio Hwy; 2hr group/private lessons $65/160, snorkel set/surfboard rental per day $5/20; ⏰8am-9pm) Pro surf instructors are especially suited for advanced surfers. If you're really serious, Russell Lewis has coached many of the pro surfers coming out of Kaua'i.

Kauai Outrigger Adventures Surfing, SUP
(808-212-5692; www.kauaioutriggeradventures.com; Hanalei Pier; surfboard/SUP rental from $20/40, SUP, outrigger canoe & surfing lessons from $75; ⏰usually 8am-5pm) The North Shore's only company for outrigger canoe surfing lessons and tours also offers surf and SUP lessons near the pier, near a Hanalei River put-in.

Yoga Hanalei Yoga
(808-826-9642; www.yogahanalei.com; Hanalei Center, 5-5161e Kuhio Hwy; drop-in classes $10-15) Instructors were all once

Makua (Tunnels) Beach (p143)

Island Insights

According to Hawaiian cosmology, Papa (earth mother) and Wakea (sky father), gave birth to Haloa, a stillborn brother to man. Haloa was planted in the earth, and from his body came taro, or *kalo,* a plant that has long sustained the Hawaiian people and been a staple for oceanic cultures around the world.

Kalo is still considered a sacred food, full of tradition and spirituality for Native Hawaiians. Hanalei is home to the largest taro-producing farm in the state, where the purple, starchy potato-like plant is grown in *lo'i kalo* (wet taro fields).

Kalo regained the spotlight in the 1970s thanks to the Hawaiian renaissance, a time during which Hawaiian culture enjoyed a long-overdue resurgence and reclaimed practice. *Kalo* is often boiled and pounded into poi, an earthy, starchy and somewhat sweet and sticky pudding-like food.

Families enjoy poi, defined by some Hawaiians as the 'staff of life,' a number of ways. Some prefer it fresh, while others prefer sour poi, or *'awa 'awa* (bitter) poi, possibly from the method in which poi used to be served – often it sat in a bowl on the table for quite some time.

All traditional Hawaiian households show respect for taro: when the bowl of poi sits on the table, one is expected to refrain from arguing or speaking in anger. That's because any bad energy is *'ino* (evil) – and can spoil the poi.

students of Bhavani Maki, who leads this Ashtanga-based studio. Classes tend to flow vinyasa or hatha style, except the ropes-wall class, which is for dangling. For something mellower, come later in the day.

Okolehao Trail
Hiking

(Map p108; Ohiki Rd) This 4.6-mile round-trip trail affords panoramic views of Hanalei's taro fields, the start of the Na Pali Coast and, on a clear day, Kilauea Lighthouse. It's rumored to be named for 'moonshine,' referring to distilled liquor made from the roots of *ti* plants. The visual spoils are worth the pain of the steep, sweaty uphill climb through the forest.

The first half-mile is a quad burner, which means few other hikers on what is a fairly quiet hike (except for your heavy breathing). After the initial vista at the power-line tower, the trail continues gradually upward, offering photo opportunities before ending 1250ft above the slow shuffle of Hanalei. Bring plenty of water.

Coming from Hanalei, veer right immediately before the Hanalei Bridge, between the river and the taro fields. Go down the road about 0.5 miles to a parking area on the left. The trail starts across the road.

North Shore Divers
Diving

(☎808-828-1223, 877-688-3483; www.northshoredivers.com; dives $79-149; ⊙by reservation only Mar-Oct) If you're already a certified diver, a night dive (during summer only) is an unforgettable experience. All dives take place at the reef off Makua (Tunnels) Beach.

Snorkel Depot
Water Sports

(☎808-826-9983; 5-5075 Kuhio Hwy; snorkel gear rental per day/week $5/20; ⊙8am-5pm) This little stand in the Hanalei Trading Co building rents budget-priced, well-used snorkel gear, SUP sets and boogie boards.

Tours

Na Pali Catamaran
Boat Tour

(☎808-826-6853, 866-255-6853; www.napali-catamaran.com; Ching Young Village, 5-5190 Kuhio Hwy; 4hr tours $180) This exceptional outfit has been running tours for 35 years, offering comfy catamaran cruises along the Na Pali Coast from Hanalei Bay. Depending on ocean conditions and the time of year, you might venture into some sea caves. Remember, though, the surf can pound and there's no reprieve from the elements. Minimum age five years.

Na Pali Explorer
Boat Tour

(☎808-338-9999; www.napaliexplorer.com; 4½hr tours adult/child $139/89; 🚼) Take a coastal snorkeling trip on a rigid-hull inflatable raft, which is hard-bottomed and gives a smoother ride than all-inflatable Zodiacs. The longer 49ft raft, which carries up to 36 passengers, has a restroom and a canopy for shade. Tours run out of Hanalei Bay. Minimum age for participants is five to eight years, depending on the boat.

Captain Sundown
Boat Tour

(☎808-826-5585; www.captainsundown.com; 6hr tours $185) This outfit is based out of Lihu'e most of the year, so take the advantage and board this sailing catamaran (17 passengers max) for a coastal snorkeling tour when it's here during the summer. A true character, Captain Bob has four decades of experience. No kids under seven years old.

Bali Hai Tours
Boat Tour

(☎808-634-2317; www.balihaitours.com; 3½hr cruises adult/child $165/95; 🚼) Explore the Na Pali Coast in a 20ft Zodiac (maximum six passengers) and splash your way to pure nature bliss. Cruise for up to four hours among humpbacks, dolphins and flying fish, and explore sea caves (weather permitting). Departs from Hanalei Pier.

Festivals & Events

Music & Mango Festival
Music, Food

(www.waipafoundation.org; ⏰mid-Aug; 🚼) 🏷 A late summer celebration of locally harvested food and live music happens at the nonprofit Waipa Foundation's farmlands on the outskirts of Hanalei.

Hawaii Sand Festival
Art, Music

(http://hawaiisandcastle.com; ⏰mid-Aug; 🚼) Magnificent sand castles and art sculptures are built on the sands of Hanalei Bay, with free lessons and live music.

Kalo Festival
Food, Cultural

(www.waipafoundation.org; ⏰Dec; 🚼) 🏷 In early December Halulu Fish Pond is host to demonstrations on growing taro and pounding poi, traditional Hawaiian games for kids, local food vendors and live music.

Sleeping

Though it requires a permit, camping at Black Pot Beach Park (Hanalei Pier) (p128) is fun, safe, and one of the only methods of keeping your stay on this pricey North Shore stop affordable, if that's a priority. Camping is allowed on Friday, Saturday and holidays only, with an advance county permit required.

Garden Surf Cottage
Cottage $$

(☎808-346-4371; 5278 Malolo Pl; 1-bedroom cottage $169; 🛜) Slumber inside this rustic wooden surf shack that has terracotta floors, a tiny kitchen with a two-burner stovetop, flat-screen TV and a BBQ grill out on the patio by the hammock. The location is quiet, yet right in the center of the action: you can stroll to downtown in one direction and the beach in the other. Cleaning fee $80.

Hanalei Vacation House
Apartment $$

(☎808-826-0006; www.hanaleivacationhouse.com; 4483 Aku Rd; studio/1-/2-bedroom apt $115/125/149; 🛜) Not far from the beach, and just a quick stroll from the river, this relaxed vacation rental is a no-fuss alternative to Hanalei's pricier lodging options. Tiled floors, knotty wood walls and old-fashioned kitschy furnishings give it a cabin-like atmosphere. Noise-sensitive types might want to look elsewhere, due to the next-door parking lot. Cleaning fee $75 to $85.

Hanalei Inn
Inn $$

(🖉 808-826-9333, 877-769-5484; www.hanalei inn.com; 5-5468 Kuhio Hwy; r $149-159; ❄ 🛜) Despite being a bit on the shabby side, these four studios – each with a kitchenette or full kitchen, HDTV, private lanai and classic retro Hawaiiana furniture – are in an ideal locale. On-site manager Bill works side by side with the resident cats and chickens to maintain a simple country atmosphere. Daily maid services cost extra.

Hale Reed
Rental House $$

(🖉 415-662-1086; www.hanalei-vacation.com; 4441 Pilikoa Rd; 5-bedroom house $245; 🛜) Approximately 89 paces from the white sand of Hanalei Bay, Hale Reed's location is key. The ground-floor, two-bedroom apartment has a full kitchen and a patio for barbecuing on. The airier upstairs unit has three bedrooms and a loft, along with a wraparound lanai. Boards and beach gear come with the territory. Three-night minimum stay; cleaning fee $150 to $250.

The apartment and upstairs can be rented separately, but only by the week.

Hanalei Dolphin Cottages
Cottage $$$

(🖉 808-826-1675; www.hanaleicottages.com; 5-5016 Kuhio Hwy; 2-bedroom cottage $260; 🛜) Launch a canoe, kayak or stand up paddle board right from your backyard on the Hanalei River. A lazy walk from the heart of Hanalei town, each cottage is styled similarly, with bamboo furniture, a full kitchen, BBQ grill, private outdoor (and indoor) showers, front-of-house bedrooms and airy quasi-lounge areas facing the river. There is a cleaning fee of $130.

Na Pali Coast (p148)

MAKENA STOCK MEDIA/GETTY IMAGES ©

Hanalei Surfboard House

Inn $$$

(☏ 808-651-1039; www.hanaleisurfboardhouse.com; 5459 Weke Rd; ste $325; ❄ 🛜) A work of art built with recycled and salvaged materials, this stylish surfer's haven is a one-minute walk to the beach. The two suites each feature unique vintage Hawaiiana decor, have a kitchenette, and share a backyard lanai with a BBQ grill. The ever-mellow owner, a former globe-trotting music executive, sets the mood at this adults-only property. Cleaning fee $95.

🍴 Eating

With a captive audience of day-trippers, Hanalei's eateries tend to be overpriced and underwhelming, but there are a few good-value exceptions to this rule.

Hanalei Taro & Juice Co

Hawaiian $

(☏ 808-826-1059; www.hanaleitaro.com; 5-5070a Kuhio Hwy; items $1.50-6, meals $9-11; ⏲ 11am-3pm Mon-Sat; ✍ 👪) 🚭 Find this roadside trailer for a taste of poi, the traditional Hawaiian staple food, made right on the family farm in Hanalei Valley. It does tropical taro smoothies, taro hummus, taro burgers, taro *mochi* cakes and Hawaiian plate lunches, too. If you miss the truck in Hanalei, look for the booth at farmers markets in Kapa'a (p91) and Lihu'e (p49).

Hanalei Farmers Market

Market $

(☏ 808-826-1011; www.halehalawai.org; Kuhio Hwy; ⏲ 9:30am-noon Sat; ✍ 👪) 🚭 One of the island's most popular farmers markets happens on the sports fields in front of the community center, Hale Halawai 'Ohana 'O Hanalei. Locals line up before the market opens, then literally run to their favorite farmers' booths. Don't miss a coconut-and-chocolate-covered banana from Kunana Dairy. North Shore artisans sell crafts, jewelry and tropical soaps, perfect for gifts or souvenirs.

Waipa Farmers Market

Market $

(Map p108; ☏ 808-826-9969; www.waipafoundation.org; Kuhio Hwy; ⏲ 2-4pm Tue; ✍ 👪) 🚭 Set on the Waipa Foundation's old Hawaiian *ahupua'a* (land division), just over the one-lane bridge from Hanalei proper on the way to Ha'ena, this market is small but still ample, with tropical fruit, leafy greens, flowers and handicrafts. To learn how to make poi as a hands-on volunteer on Thursday mornings, visit the website for details.

Pink's Creamery

Ice Cream, Sandwiches $

(☏ 808-824-9134; 4489d Aku Rd; items $4-9; ⏲ 11am-9pm; 🅿 ✍ 👪) A side-street ice-cream shop scoops tropical flavors such as banana-macnut brittle, mango and an unreal *haupia*

Hanalei Farmers Market

Island Insights

The Tahiti Nui has changed hands and menus, and seen its fair share of dated hairdos, barflies and beer bellies. But there's a part of 'the Nui' that always seems to remain the same. It's the liveliest spot in little Hanalei and, though certainly a dive, it remains *the* North Shore joint par excellence for regulars and visitors alike.

In 1964 a Tahitian woman named Louise Hauata and her husband Bruce Marston, founded the now iconic South Seas–style restaurant and bar. Its popularity grew and so did its draw – luring such names as Jacqueline Kennedy, who legendarily arrived unexpectedly, preceded by secret service agents. Yet despite the fact that it's seen its share of A-listers, you'd never guess it at first glance.

Bruce died in 1975, but Louise continued the spot's luau tradition, augmenting it with renditions of Tahitian songs in English, French or their original language. She was also well known for giving much aloha to her community in times of need.

Louise died in 2003, and Tahiti Nui is now run by her son, Christian Marston, and his daughter, Nanea Marston Correa. The Nui remains a lively, loud hangout long after the sun sets and police regularly set up shop outside its doors around 2am to ensure no one's drinking and driving.

(coconut pudding). It also whips up *liliko'i* and lychee sorbet, tropical fruit popsicles, date shakes, and absurdly tasty grilled cheese sandwiches on island-style sweet bread with munster cheese, *kalua* pork (cooked in the traditional method in an underground pit) and pineapple.

Harvest Market   Market $
(☎808-826-0089; www.harvestmarkethanalei. com; Hanalei Center, 5-5161 Kuhio Hwy; ⊙9am-7pm Mon-Sat, to 6pm Sun; 🖉) 🍴 If you like to treat your body well, pick up organic and all-natural snacks, groceries and produce with a locavore touch. Put together a beach picnic from the salad bar, smoothie station and weighable bulk-foods section (dried fruit, nuts and such), but beware that prices can sneak up on you.

Pat's Taqueria   Mexican, American $
(parking lot near Hanalei Pier; items $2-9; ⊙noon-3pm; 🖼) If you're by the pier and heading to the beach, a couple of *kalua* pork tacos or a mahimahi burrito with beans and rice on the side won't set you

back too much. Kids menu (mini burritos, quesadillas etc) available. Cash only.

Village Snack
Shop & Bakery   Bakery, Deli $
(☎808-826-6841; www.facebook.com/Village SnackShopBaker; Ching Young Village, 5-5190 Kuhio Hwy; mains $6-9; ⊙6:30am-4pm Mon-Sat, to 3pm Sun; 🖼) Just your basic mom-and-pop storefront, perfect for stuffing yourself with macnut pancakes before hiking the Na Pali Coast. Show up later in the day for heaping plate lunches and chocolate *haupia* pie.

Big Save   Supermarket $
(☎808-826-6652; www.timessupermarkets. com; Ching Young Village, 5-5172 Kuhio Hwy; ⊙7am-10pm; 🖼) For any basic grocery items and beach, hiking or road-tripping snacks and drinks you need.

Hanalei Dolphin
Restaurant &
Sushi Lounge   Seafood, Market $$
(☎808-826-6113; www.hanaleidolphin.com; 5-5016 Kuhio Hwy; mains lunch $12-16, dinner

137

$25-40; ⏱restaurant 11:30am-9pm, market 10am-7pm) At one of Hanalei's oldest restaurants (more than 30 years), the slow-roasted menu is abundant and the incisive sushi chefs will play culinary jazz with their daily fresh fish if decision-making is not your forte. Lunch is served riverside and the sushi bar seating fills up quickly. Wander around back to the fish market for takeout and DIY meals for grilling.

The fish market not only sells fish by the pound, but also assorted sushi rolls, *poke* bowls, a daily fresh-catch sandwich and a chunky seafood chowder.

Hanalei Gourmet   Cafe, Deli $$

(📞808-826-2524; www.hanaleigourmet.com; Hanalei Center, 5-5161 Kuhio Hwy; dinner mains $10-29; ⏱8am-10:30pm; 👪) At this lively sit-down spot, the best bets are huge sandwiches on house-baked bread. Meals – creatively skipping from a sampler of lox-style smoked Hawaiian fish to crunchy macadamia-nut fried chicken – are tasty and unpretentious, even if more mainstream American than local. Twice-weekly musical acts and happy hour (3:30pm to 5:30pm daily) are more good reasons to swing by.

Chicken in a Barrel   Barbecue $$

(📞808-826-1999; www.chickeninabarrel.com; Ching Young Village, 5-5190 Kuhio Hwy; meals $10-15; ⏱11am-8pm Mon-Sat, to 3pm Sun; 👪) Using a custom-made 50-gallon barrel drum smoker, this island BBQ joint is all about the bird. Grab a heaping plate of chicken or a hoagie sandwich with chili cheese fries. You won't have to eat again all day. Second location in Kapa'a.

BarAcuda
Tapas & Wine   Mediterranean $$$

(📞808-826-7081; www.restaurantbaracuda. com; Hanalei Center, 5-5161 Kuhio Hwy; shared plates $7-26; ⏱5:30-10pm, kitchen closes at 9:30pm) 🌱 A trendy wine and tapas bar presents ornately plated food that's noteworthy, but pricey. Pluses include inventive sustainability-driven uses of local products, such as North Shore honeycomb, goat's cheese and mizuna greens. A seductive 'see and be seen' at-

mosphere, service that's impeccable from start to finish and a groovy soundtrack all perpetuate the illusion that you're in a movie. Reservations essential.

Postcards
Café   Fusion $$$

(📞826-1191; www.postcardscafe.com; 5-5075 Kuhio Hwy; mains $19-38; ⏱6-9pm; 🌱) 🌿 With innocent charm, this riverside cottage could just as easily be found in the New England countryside. Vegan-friendly and seafood dishes, although hit and miss, often have an appealing world-fusion twist such as the wasabi-crusted ahi or *ono* in curried coconut broth. A genteel atmosphere will induce nostalgia like a Robert Redford film. Reservations recommended for groups of four or more.

🍸 Drinking & Entertainment

Tahiti Nui   Bar

(📞808-826-6277; www.thenui.com; 5-5134 Kuhio Hwy; ⏱11:30am-midnight Mon-Sat, from 2pm Sun) Usually crowded from mid-afternoon onward, the legendary Nui (which made a cameo appearance in *The Descendants*) can get rollicking with live Hawaiian music, and quite rowdy on weekends, when it's really the only place open past 10pm. It's a tiki dive bar with heart and history. On Wednesday nights, the **luau** (per adult/child $75/45) is a modest all-you-can-eat dinner show.

For luau reservations, call 📞808-482-4829.

Hanalei Coffee Roasters   Cafe

(📞808-826-6717; www.hanaleicoffeeandtea-company.com; Hanalei Center, 5-5183 Kuhio Hwy; ⏱6:30am-6pm; 📶) The caffeine isn't the only thing buzzing here. Coffee infusions are strong and waffles are sweetly topped with coconut syrup. The mellow vibes and lazy front porch will soothe strung-out psyches.

Hawaiian Slack Key
Guitar Concerts   Live Music

(📞808-826-1469; www.hawaiianslackkeyguitar. com; Hanalei Community Center, Malolo Rd; adult/child 6-17yr $20/15; ⏱4pm Fri & 3pm Sun)

Slack key guitar and ukulele concerts are performed by longtime musicians Doug and Sandy McMaster year-round in a refreshingly informal atmosphere.

🔒 Shopping

A testament to its popularity, Hanalei is full of charming shops selling everything from black pearls and Hawaiiana art to everyday surfwear and handcrafted souvenirs.

Kauai Nut Roasters   Food

(📞808-826-7415; www.kauainutroasters.com; Ching Young Village, 5-5190 Kuhio Hwy; ⏰10am-6:30pm Mon-Sat, to 5pm Sun) Some of the most delicious treats you can find on the island are found here in these unassuming little packages, bursting with unusual flavors. Coconut, wasabi, lavender, sesame, butterscotch and praline rank tops. Also in Kilauea and Koloa.

Hanalei Surf
Company   Clothing, Equipment

(www.hanaleisurf.com; Hanalei Center, 5-5161 Kuhio Hwy; ⏰8am-9pm) Surf, surf, surf

is this outfit's MO. Surfer-girl earrings, bikinis and rashies, as well as guys' boardshorts, flip-flops and all the gear you might need for hitting the surf: wax, shades and even the board itself. The **Backdoor** (www.hanaleisurf.com; Ching Young Village, 5-5190 Kuhio Hwy; ⏰8am-9pm) store is across the street.

Havaiki   Arts

(📞808-826-7606; www.havaikiart.com; Hanalei Center, 5-5161 Kuhio Hwy; ⏰10am-5pm) This hidden shop sells traditional, hand-crafted Polynesian art hand-picked by the owners, from inexpensive tchotchkes to museum-quality artworks. Keep an eye out for more exotic pieces such as penis gourds.

On the Road
to Hanalei   Clothing, Gifts

(📞808-826-7360; Ching Young Village, 5-5190 Kuhio Hwy; ⏰10am-6pm) Vibrant batik-print dresses and pareus, handcrafted silver jewelry and Japanese teapots are just a few of the treasures inside this rustic wooden-floored shop.

Postcards Café

Bikini Room
Clothing

(☎808-826-9711; www.thebikiniroom.com; 4489 Aku Rd; ☺10am-6pm Mon-Sat, 11am-5pm Sun) They're itsy bitsy and teeny weenie, but they show off a variety of wild, vibrant prints from Brazil instead of the said polka dots.

I Heart Hanalei
Clothing

(☎808-826-5560; www.shopihearthanalei. com; 5-5106 Kuhio Hwy; ☺11am-9pm) At one of Hanalei's cutest beachy boutiques, you can peruse racks of stylish bikinis, beach cover-ups, sun hats, shorts and yoga wear.

aFeinberg Gallery
Arts

(☎808-634-7890; www.afeinbergphotography. com; Ching Young Village, 5-5190 Kuhio Hwy; ☺noon-7pm) Photographer Aaron Feinberg captures international award–winning landscapes on Kaua'i and beyond.

ℹ Information

Hanalei has no bank, but there are ATMs at the Hanalei Liquor Store and Big Save supermarket.

Hanalei Post Office (☎808-826-1034; www. usps.com; 5-5226 Kuhio Hwy; ☺10am-4pm Mon-Fri, to noon Sat) is located on the *makai* (seaward) side of the road, just west of Big Save supermarket.

ℹ Getting There & Around

There's one road in and one road out. Parking can be a headache, and absent-minded pedestrians even more so. Everything in Hanalei is walkable, or do as the locals do and hop on a bicycle.

Pedal 'n Paddle (☎808-826-9069; www. pedalnpaddle.com; Ching Young Village, 5-5105 Kuhio Hwy; ☺9am-6pm) rents cruisers (per day/ week $15/60) and hybrid road bikes ($20/80), all including helmets and locks.

Beyond Hanalei

On turning out of Hanalei Bay one is immediately at the will of a dramatic coastal contour. The road winds its way around cliffside points that offer quick glimpses of what's ahead, then swoops through pasture-filled valleys and leads all who follow toward the grand finale – the start of the Na Pali Coast. Here is where the great amalgamation of mountain and ocean takes place, with a sliver of beach

Tahiti Nui (p138)

Island Insights

No doubt being attacked by a *mano* (shark) could be deadly: precautions, such as avoiding swimming in murky, post-rain waters, should be taken to avoid them. But statistically speaking, you're more likely to die from a bee sting than a shark attack, and you should be more concerned about contracting leptospirosis or giardiasis in those infamous muddy waters than becoming a midday snack.

Rather than letting any hardwired phobia of large predators get you down, try considering the creature from another perspective while in Hawaii: the *mano* as sacred. For many local families, the *mano* is their *'aumakua* (guardian spirit). *'Aumakua* are family ancestors whose *'uhane,* or spirit form, lives on in the body of an animal, watching over members of their living *'ohana*. Revered for their ocean skill, *mano* were also considered the *'aumakua* of navigators. Even today, *mano 'aumakua* have been said to guide lost fishers home, or toward areas of plentiful fish, to make for a bountiful sojourn.

and just enough road space in between for a passing stranger to travel by and contemplate all that is big (not us), and all that is small (us).

LUMAHA'I BEACH

Though it's a tidbit of useless knowledge, it's obligatory to mention that this beach is where the famous scene in which Mitzi Gaynor declared her intent to 'wash that man' out of her hair was shot for the 1958 movie *South Pacific*.

The beach, though beautiful, is known on-island as one of the most dangerous. Way too many visitors have drowned trying to swim at this beguiling spot, dubbed 'Luma-die,' as it's infamous for its rough rip currents and powerful waves. The inlet lacks barrier reefs and breaks, so swimming here is very risky.

Less morbid is the beach's other nickname, 'Nurse's Beach,' which pays tribute again to Gaynor as a US Navy nurse in the aforementioned movie. Plan for a nice stroll, however; it is scenic.

There are two ways onto Lumaha'i Beach. The first and more scenic is a three-minute walk that begins at the parking area 0.75 miles past mile marker 4 on the Kuhio Hwy. The trail slopes to the left at the end of the retaining wall. On the beach, the lava-rock ledges are popular for sunbathing and photo ops, but beware: bystanders have been washed away by high surf and rogue waves. The other way to access Lumaha'i is along the road at sea level at the western end of the beach, about 1 mile after the first entrance, just before crossing the Lumaha'i River Bridge. The beach at this end is lined with ironwood trees.

WAINIHA

Between Ha'ena and Hanalei rests this little spot marked by the 'Last Chance' Wainiha General Store. Steeped in ancient history, the narrow, green recesses of Wainiha Valley were the last hideout of the *menehune,* the legendary little people of the Hawaiian Islands. As late as the 1850s, 65 people in the valley were officially listed as *menehune* on the government census.

Today Wainiha Valley remains as it did in the old days: a holdout for Native Hawaiians, though some vacation rentals have encroached onto the area. Not as tourist-ready as neighboring areas east or west, Kaua'i's characteristic staunchness thrives here and an unwelcoming vibe is not uncommon. When the locals stare you down, don't take it personally.

But beyond that rough exterior is the true value of Wainiha – its offer of utter quietude and the chance to be nestled among lush greenery and flowing water where you can find a nook of your own; perhaps one that could lend itself to finally finishing (or starting?) that novel. A small but often empty beach also offers visitors some sandy solitude if they wish.

🛏 Sleeping & Eating

Coco Cabana Cottage Cottage **$$**
(Map p108; 📞 808-821-9836; www.vrbo.com/153703; 4766 Ananalu Rd; d $175-190; 📶) The hot tub, chirping birds, airy ambience and swimmable Wainiha River nearby make for a lovely secluded stay. This cute little cottage is perfectly suited to a couple wanting privacy and coziness, and so is the two-person outdoor jungle shower. Four-night minimum stay; cleaning fee $125.

Riverhouse at River Estate Rental House **$$$**
(Map p108; 📞 808-826-5118, 800-390-8444; www.riverestate.com; 5-6691 Kuhio Hwy; d from $295; ❄ 📶) Resting on stilts 30ft above the Wainiha River, this enchanting abode is fit for honeymooners or a family. Brazilian hardwood floors and marble countertops are deluxe, while a screened-in lanai allows for no-mosquito barbecues and soaks in the mini hot tub. Weekly rates available. Cleaning fee from $275.

Guesthouse at River Estate Rental House **$$$**
(Map p108; 📞 808-826-5118, 800-390-8444; www.riverestate.com; 5-6691 Kuhio Hwy; d from $275; ❄ 📶) This place is pricey, but one look and you'll see why. Airy, huge and open, set on jungly grounds, this vacation home features a master bedroom with a king bed, a second room with a queen bed, a decked-out kitchen, a wraparound lanai, beach gear to borrow, and almost anything else you could possibly need. Weekly rates available. Cleaning fee from $250.

Sushigirl Kauai Sushi **$$**
(Map p108; www.sushigirlkauai.fish; 5-6607b Kuhio Hwy; mains $12-15; ⏱ 11am-7pm Mon-Sat, to 4pm Sun) A roadside kitchen delivers generous *maki* (rolled) sushi, *poke* bowls drizzled with *ponzu* (Japanese citrus sauce), and sushi burritos made with 'yum yum' sauce, organic local veggies and heaps of TLC.

🛍 Shopping

7 Artists Arts
(Map p108; 5-6607 Kuhio Hwy; ⏱ 11am-5pm) Local painters, photographers, ceramic artists, jewelers, puka-shell-lei and beach-glass-mosaic makers staff this co-op gallery.

Kalalau Trail (p149)
JOHN ELK/GETTY IMAGES ©

Backyard Graveyards

Ancient burial sites lie underneath countless homes and hotels throughout Hawaii. Construction workers often dig up *iwi* (bones) and *moepu* (burial objects), while locals swear by eerie stories of equipment malfunctioning until bones are properly reinterred and prayers given.

In 1990 Congress enacted the Native American Graves Protection and Repatriation Act. In Hawaii, burial councils were established on each island to oversee the treatment of remains and the preservation of burial sites. Desecration of *iwi* is illegal, and a major affront to Native Hawaiians.

One recent case involved Ha'ena's Naue Point, the site of some 30 confirmed graves. Starting in 2002, and lasting close to nine years, the case went through numerous phases of court hearings, public demonstrations, burial treatment proposals, and ended with the state allowing the landowner to build after placing concrete caps over the burial grounds (an outcome that some Hawaiians found woefully inadequate).

As well, many hotels and condos were built on land with *iwi* now sitting in storage or still underground. And what happens to those restless spirits? Believe it or not, Po'ipu's Grand Hyatt Kauai Resort & Spa has a director of Hawaiian culture and community affairs who does blessings somewhere on resort grounds at least once a month to quell any 'spiritual disturbance.'

Wainiha
General Store   Market
(Map p108; 5-6607 Kuhio Hwy; ☺10am-dusk) If you've left Hanalei and need a few items, don't panic. The 'Last Chance' store sells last-minute beach essentials, including snorkel gear, drinks and snacks. Service can be eccentric.

Ha'ena

While the North Shore is Kaua'i's island within the island, Ha'ena is the island within the North Shore. Rural, remote, resplendent and idyllic, it's also a site of controversy, as many of the luxury homes on the point were built on top of *'iwi kupuna* (ancient Hawaiian burials).

Two tsunamis struck Ha'ena in the 20th century: the first in 1946 and the second in 1957. Both devastated homes along the beach. These events, combined with Hurricane 'Iniki's destruction in 1992, prompted laws regarding structures built a certain distance from the ocean. Therefore, any coastal houses built since 1992 must sit way above the ground (up to 16ft) as Federal Emergency Management Agency (FEMA) flood precautions dictate. Though they appear to lack stability, the idea is that in the event of a flood, most of the force will pass under the house. Sounds plausible, right?

Ha'ena is the aesthetic apex of (drivable) Kaua'i, with the road gradually squeezing between towering pinnacles of aggressive green growth and picture-perfect coastal curvatures. Though many humbly try, it is truly beyond verbal description.

🏖 Beaches

Makua (Tunnels) Beach   Beach
(Map p108) One of the North Shore's almost-too-beautiful beaches, named for the underwater caverns in and among the near-shore reef, this is

143

among the best snorkel spots on the island. It's also the North Shore's most popular dive site. Although the area is more suitable for the summer months, as the reef is adjacent to the beach, winter snorkeling may be possible. Always use caution and check with locals or lifeguards before heading into the water. Beware of a regular current flowing west toward the open ocean.

If you can't score a parking spot at one of the two unmarked lots down short dirt roads, park at Ha'ena State Park and walk.

Ha'ena Beach Park   Beach

(Map p108) Not ideal for swimming in winter, because of the regular pounding shore break that creates a strong undertow, this beach is nevertheless good for taking in some sun. During the summer months, the sea is almost always smooth and safe. Ask lifeguards about conditions before going in, especially between October and May. To the left is **Cannons**, an expert local surf break.

Facilities at the beach park include restrooms, outdoor showers, picnic tables and a pavilion.

◉ Sights & Activities

Limahuli Garden   Gardens

(Map p108; ☎808-826-1053; http://ntbg.org/gardens/limahuli.php; 5-8291 Kuhio Hwy; self-guided/guided tours $20/40; ☺9:30am-4pm Tue-Sat, guided tours 10am; ⬥) ♪ About as beautiful as it gets for living education, this garden offers a pleasant overview of endemic botany and ancient Hawai'i's *ahupua'a* (land division) system of management. Self-guided tours take about 1½ hours, allowing you to meditate on the scenery along a 0.75-mile loop trail; in-depth guided tours (minimum age 10 years, reservations required) last 2½ hours.

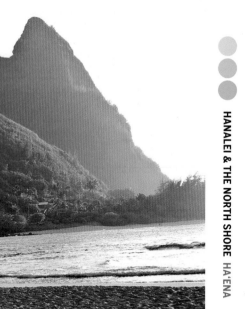

HANALEI & THE NORTH SHORE HA'ENA

Volunteer service projects in native ecosystem restoration give ecotourists a glimpse into the entire 985-acre preserve.

To get here, turn inland just before the stream that marks the boundary of Ha'ena State Park.

Maniniholo Dry Cave
Cave

(Map p108) Directly across from Ha'ena Beach Park, Maniniholo Dry Cave is deep, broad and high enough to explore. A constant seep of water from the cave walls keeps the dark interior dank. Drippy and creepy, the cave is named after the head fisherman of the *menehune* who, according to legend, built ponds and other structures overnight.

Hanalei Day Spa
Spa

(Map p108; ☎808-826-6621; www.hanaleiday-spa.com; Hanalei Colony Resort, Kuhio Hwy; ⊙9am-6pm Mon-Sat) If you're tired or need to revitalize, this friendly, though modest, spa offers some of the island's more competitively priced massages (including Hawaiian *lomilomi*) and body treatments.

🛏 Sleeping

Ha'ena Beach Park has campsites, restrooms and outdoor showers. If you plan to hike the entire Kalalau Trail, you might want to park and set up a base camp here, because your unattended car will probably be safer than parking at Ke'e Beach. Advance county camping permits are required.

There's an abundance of vacation rentals to be found in Ha'ena, although some have fallen through legal cracks. As always, **Vacation Rentals By Owner** (www.vrbo.com) and **Airbnb** (www.airbnb.com) are good resources for rental options.

Hale Ho'o Maha
B&B $$
(Map p108; ☏808-826-7083, 800-851-0291; www.halemaha.com; 7083 Alamihi Rd; r incl breakfast $220; @ 🛜) Though the word 'communal' is applicable, don't let it turn you off this quirky, four-room home. You'll share everything with your hosts, including an ozonated hot tub, high-end kitchen, an enormous flat-screen HDTV, a guest-use computer and even an elevator. Each suite has its own lanai.

River House
Rental House $$$
(Map p108; ☏808-826-7272, 800-715-7273; www.napaliprop.com; 5121 Powerhouse Rd; house & cottage per night $325-350) It's got a jungle paradise feel, just a mile from Tunnels Beach and close to the Kalalau Trail. Avocados, lychees, bananas, papayas and mountain apples abound. The sandalwood-floored main house comes with a queen bed, soaking tub and full kitchen. A separate cottage and a screened-in sleeping gazebo called the Bird's Nest are part of the rental. Cleaning fee $290.

Hale Oli
Rental House $$$
(Map p108; ☏808-826-6585; www.oceanfront realty.com; 7097 Alimihi Rd; 2-bedroom house per night/week from $300/1800; 🛜) Perched on stilts, this place boasts nothing but greenery between its front lanai and Ha'ena's jutting mountains. Inside it's Hawaiiana-meets-Zen decor. The bedrooms each have a queen-sized bed, and the kitchen is full-sized. On the back lanai, a spacious hot tub provides starry and foamy nights and a sliver of an ocean view. One-time rental ($50) and cleaning ($185) fees apply.

Hanalei Colony Resort
Hotel $$$
(Map p108; ☏808-826-6235, 800-628-3004; www.hcr.com; 5-7130 Kuhio Hwy; 2-bedroom ste from $255; @ 🛜 🏊) It'd be difficult to find a more knock-out location for a resort than this spot, the only resort west of Princeville. While the decor often looks dated, the property is waterfront and about as reclusive as it gets. Condos are scattered in several exceedingly charmless stucco out-buildings that arc

Maniniholo Dry Cave (p145)

Honopu Beaches

Though hailed as a thrilling side adventure, camping at or even stopping at Honopu Beach is considered by some Hawaiians as disrespectful, as it is full of *iwi* (bones) of Hawaiian ancestors. Only very skilled swimmers should venture to Honopu Beaches, just beyond the Kalalau campsite. You're not allowed to land a boat or surfboard or use any other craft on the beach, so if you opt to go, you have to swim in. The northern part of this beach has an immense waterfall that is beautifully scenic, but can push the life force out of you. Currents and rips abound and, of course, an infinite number of other risks are involved when you're frolicking in water below 1200ft cliffs.

If you're not deterred from the idea yet, aim to arrive on the southern side, but again, be respectful of the fact that it is the burial ground for many. Not a place for yelling, partying or anything you wouldn't do at a cemetery. Once there, you'll see the well-known **Honopu Arch**, featured in such films as *Honeymoon in Vegas*, *Six Days Seven Nights* and the 1976 remake of *King Kong* featuring Jessica Lange. You can also see the beaches from the water for a more respectful approach to seeing this historic site, either by kayaking past or on a raft or catamaran tour. To stay loose and limber for the hike back, or just to get some inland time, venture up the **Kalalau Valley Trail** to witness perpetuated time inlaid in the landscape, and maybe a hippie or two ambling nude in the woods or basking in the freshwater stream.

alongside an exquisite beach and bay. There's no TVs and no phones.

Eating

Mediterranean Gourmet
Mediterranean $$

(Map p108; 808-826-9875; www.kauaimed gourmet.com; Hanalei Colony Resort, 5-7130 Kuhio Hwy; mains lunch $12-17, dinner $26-37; noon-3:45pm & 4-8pm Mon & Wed-Sun, noon-3pm Tue) A taste of the Mediterranean literally on the Pacific (if the windows weren't there, you'd get salty ocean mist on your face), this fish out of water offers an eclectic range of Euro-inspired dishes such as rosemary rack of lamb and pistachio-crusted ahi. Food quality and service both tend toward mediocre, but there's live music on Saturday and Sunday evenings.

Shopping

Na Pali Art Gallery
Arts, Crafts

(Map p108; 808-826-1844; www.napaligallery. com; Hanalei Colony Resort, 5-7130 Kuhio Hwy; 7am-5pm Mon-Sat, to 3pm Sun;) Peruse a quality array of local artists' paintings, woodwork, sculptures, ceramics, art glass and jewelry such as coveted Ni'ihau shell necklaces. Skip the coffeehouse's weak brews.

Ha'ena State Park

Wind beaten and lava carved, Ha'ena State Park burns with the allure, mystique and beauty usually associated with some divine tale. Pele, the Hawaiian goddess of fire and volcanoes, is said to have overlooked the area as a home because of the water housed in its wet and dry caves. The 230-acre park is home to the 1280ft cliff commonly known in the tourism industry as 'Bali Hai,' its name in the film *South Pacific*. Its real name is Makana ('gift').

🏖 Beaches

Ke'e Beach   Beach
(Map p108) Memorable North Shore sunsets happen at this spiritual spot, where ancient Hawaiians came to practice hula. In summer, the beach offers a refreshing dip after hiking the nearby Kalalau Trail. But beware that Ke'e Beach may appear calm when it is, in fact, otherwise. Vicious currents have sucked some through a keyhole in the reef out into the open sea.

Facilities include outdoor showers and restrooms. Car break-ins are common in the parking lot, so don't leave any valuables behind.

👁 Sights

Wet Caves   Cave
(Map p108) Two wet caves lie within the boundaries of Ha'ena State Park. Formed by the constant pounding of waves many years ago, the massive cavern of **Waikapala'e Wet Cave** is as enchanting as it is spooky. It's on the opposite side of the street, a short walk from the visitor-overflow parking area. **Waikanaloa Wet Cave** is a little further down on the south side of the highway.

Though some enter the water to experience the sunlight's blue reflection in Waikapala'e's deeper chamber, note the water may be contaminated with leptospira bacteria, the rocks are slippery, and there's nothing to hold onto once you're in the water.

Kaulu Paoa Heiau   Temple
(Map p108) 🗡 The roaring surf was a teacher to those who first practiced the spiritual art of hula, chanting and testing their skills against nature's decibel levels. Ke'e Beach is the oceanfront site of a cherished heiau (ancient stone temple) dedicated to Laka, the goddess of hula. It's also where the volcano goddess Pele fell in love with Lohiau.

Lei and other sacred offerings found on the ground should be left as is. Enter the heiau through its entryway; don't be disrespectful by crosing over the temple walls.

....

Na Pali Coast Wilderness State Park

Kalalau, Honopu, 'Awa'awa-puhi, Nu'alolo and Miloli'i are the five major valleys on the Na Pali Coast, easily the most distinguished example of natural beauty on the island, if not within the entire archipelago. Whether by chopper, watercraft or foot – even if you have to go extra slowly, or busk ukulele for a week to cover the cost – *do what it takes* to see this 22-mile stretch of coast.

Ke'e Beach

Paddling the Na Pali Coast

While epic, kayaking the Na Pali Coast is strenuous and dangerous, and therefore not for everyone. Going with a guide helps manage the dangers; going without means you need to be an expert in ocean (not river) kayaking. It also means you shouldn't go alone. Always check several days of weather forecasting and ocean conditions before going out.

Hanakapi'ai Beach is about a mile in. About 6 miles more and you can set up camp at **Kalalau** (with a state-park permit). If you started very early, you can aim for setting up camp at **Miloli'i** (also requiring a permit), which is at the 11-mile point, 2 miles past Nu'alolo Kai. From there you have the often surf-less (May to September), hot, flat stretch to **Polihale**, for what feels like much longer than 3 miles.

Always start on the North Shore, end on the Westside (due to currents) and never go in winter (potentially deadly swells). Between April and October, the following outfitters offer a long day-trip that spans the entire Na Pali Coast:

Na Pali Kayak (☎ 808-826-6900; www.napalikayak.com; 5-5075 Kuhio Hwy, Hanalei) The Na Pali Coast trip is the only tour these folks lead, and their guides have over a decade of experience. Guided overnight camping trips start at $400 per person; a one-day trip costs from $225.

Kayak Kaua'i (p73) The original Na Pali kayaking outfitter's 'Odyssey' (from $240) paddles the entire stretch from Ke'e to Polihale in one long day.

History

Since the first waves of Polynesian settlers, these deep river valleys contained sizable settlements (read: tens of thousands of people). When winter seas prevented canoes from landing on the northern shore, trails down precipitous ridges and rope ladders provided access. Archaeologists maintain that the extreme, remote Nu'alolo Valley housed a civilization dating back more than a thousand years, based on ancient weapons and hunting tools recovered from the area. Irrigation ditches and agricultural terraces suggest the Kalalau Valley community was once one of the most advanced within the island chain.

In the mid-19th century, missionaries established a school in Kalalau, the largest valley, and registered the valley population at about 200. Influenced by Western ways, people gradually began moving to towns, and by century's end the valleys were largely abandoned.

◉ Sights & Activities

For views of the Na Pali Coast, hiking the 11-mile coastal Kalalau Trail into the Hanakapi'ai, Hanakoa and Kalalau Valleys is an adventure that's sure not to disappoint. Unfit for roads, the Na Pali Coast leads to the opposite side of drivable Kaua'i, at Koke'e State Park. You won't want to miss hiking the Westside of the island for those views, so close in distance but so far by car. If you're one of those 'ultimate' fitness fanatics, perhaps experiencing the Na Pali Coast by sea on a 17-mile kayak adventure is up your alley.

KALALAU TRAIL

Notorious for its difficulty and its dangerously eroded areas, the Kalalau Trail is also revered for the sublime beauty of its dynamic aqua-blue ocean setting and the crystal-clear mountain springs that constantly re-carve the 1000ft-plus cliffs. You came to Kaua'i seeking a real-life Eden (or Neverland?), and hiking this coast is the most intimate way to experience it. Hiking safety needs to be taken seriously here, though.

There are three hike options: **Ke'e Beach to Hanakapi'ai Beach**, **Hanakapi'ai Beach to Hanakapi'ai Falls** and **Hanakapi'ai Beach to Kalalau Valley**. There are hunters who can do the entire trail in and out in one day, but most people will either want to opt for the Hanakapi'ai Beach or Hanakapi'ai Falls hike. The full hike to Kalalau Valley is a true trek and will most likely necessitate

camping gear. In winter the trails can become rivers, streams can become impassable and the beaches will just plain disappear beneath the high surf. Give this trail a second thought before heading out on a rainy day. Always use extreme caution when swimming at the beaches along the Na Pali Coast, as dozens of people have drowned here over the years.

Note that although 11 miles may not sound like much, this is not an 11-mile *walk*. Also remember that its 11 miles *in*, after which point you have to come back out, unless you've got the proper camping equipment to stay. It is treacherous, steep and challenging to be sure – but it offers one of the sweetest series of views of ocean, cliffs and waterfalls you'll ever see.

Kalalau Trail

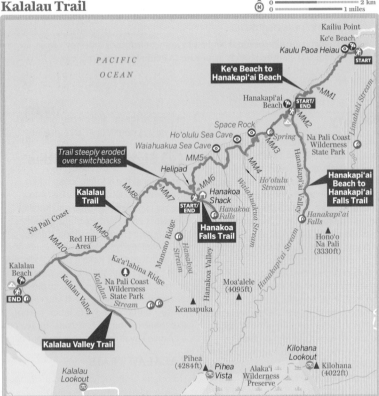

Safe Hiking on the Kalalau Trail

The Kalalau Trail is Rugged (yes, with a capital R) and therefore it's not for everyone. Being prepared is a tough call, too, as you won't want to pack too much, but you will need to stay hydrated, prepped for rain, and you *must* pack your trash out with you. You may see hikers with machetes, walkie-talkies, climbing ropes and reef shoes, but even the trekkers with the most impressive gear should know not to expect a rescue by emergency responders. These precipices are to be taken seriously. Anyone with a police scanner can tell you 'plenty story' about the braggart from the mainland who was warned by friends, family or an onlooker, but said something along the lines of these famous last words: 'Nah, I'm from the Rockies. This is nothing.' Finally, mosquitoes here are bloodthirsty and the sun can really ravage, so always wear insect repellent and sunblock.

The last section into Kalalau Valley should be done only by the extremely fit. Those who are of average mobility wanting an experience-and-a-half should opt for the hike to Hanakapi'ai, while those of modest physical prowess should feel justly accomplished with the 4-mile (one-way) hike to Hanakapi'ai Falls. While the falls hike offers a large and chilly waterfall pool to frolic in, the county's official stance on Hanakapi'ai Beach is that swimming is not allowed due to the many fatalities in its rough waters.

The **Division of State Parks** (Map p44; ☎808-274-3444; www.hawaiistateparks.org; Room 306, 3060 Eiwa St, Lihu'e; ☺8am-3:30pm Mon-Fri) office in Lihu'e can provide a Kalalau Trail brochure with a map. Even if you're not planning to camp, a camping permit is legally required to day-hike beyond Hanakoa. Camping permits ($20 per person per night for non-residents) are available from **Hawaii State Parks** (www.hawaiistateparks.org/camping) online or in person at the Lihu'e office. There's a five-night maximum per trip, with only one night allowed at Hanakoa (otherwise, you may camp only at Kalalau). Book permits as far in advance as possible, up to a year ahead.

Ke'e Beach to Hanakapi'ai Beach

It shouldn't take more than two to three hours to complete this 4-mile (round-trip) trek, the coast's most crowded hike. It's easy to see why it's so popular: it's a perfect mini–Na Pali experience, passing through the small hanging valleys and trickling streams, offering panoramic views down the entire coast. You'll end this hike at a white sand beach at the base of Hanakapi'ai Valley: Hanakapi'ai Beach. Swimming at this beach is not only dangerous but prohibited.

Hanakapi'ai Beach to Hanakapi'ai Falls

For a longer day hike, cross Hanakapi'ai Stream and follow the trail 2 miles up valley. Hanakapi'ai Falls is spectacular, falling 300ft into a wide pool that is gentle enough for swimming. Directly under the falls, the cascading water forces you back from the rock face – a warning from nature, as falling rocks are common. The setting is idyllic, though not very sunny near the falls because of the incredible steepness. You'll pass bamboo forests and see some of the most rugged, jagged and inspiring views the island has to offer.

The 4-mile round-trip side trail is relatively flat and pleasant going through the densely forested valley and crossing the stream at several swimming holes. Save the temptation to jump in for the falls, as there's not much that compares with floating in its brisk waters and looking up at the waterfall. Before you get there, listen for the water. It's sweet, sweet justice as you arrive and jump into this refreshingly clear pool as tropicbirds soar above.

The trail itself is periodically washed out by floodwaters, and sections occasionally get redrawn, but the path basically gradually ascends the side of Hanakapi'ai Stream. The first of three major stream crossings is about 1 mile or 25 minutes' walk up, at a sign that warns: 'Hazardous. Keep away from stream during heavy rainfall. Stream floods suddenly.' Be particularly careful of your footing on the rocky upper part of the trail. Some of the rocks are covered with a barely visible film of slick algae – worse than walking on ice.

During heavy rain, flash floods are likely in the narrow valley, so do this hike only in fair weather.

Hanakapi'ai Beach to Kalalau Valley

Going past Hanakapi'ai means you've got 9 miles left, and that you've committed to the whole 22-mile round-trip hike. The trail takes its longest climb out of Hanikapi'ai and proceeds in and out of the valleys along the Na Pali Coast. Hanakoa Valley usually marks the halfway point and a rest stop or campground for hikers – depending how you break up the trail – along with the turnoff for the 0.6-mile round-trip Hanakoa Falls Trail.

Past Hanakoa, the Kalalau Trail gets noticeably drier and more exposed, and the blue Pacific waters at the base of the cliff taunt you that much more. Hiking poles (which look like ski poles, but are for hiking) are helpful along the entire trail, but especially along these rocky ledges. The last hill to top is the saddle before dropping into Kalalau Valley. It's difficult to say from which vantage point

Kalalau Valley

M SWEET/GETTY IMAGES ©

the cliffs look more majestic, from the top at the lookout in Koke'e or here at the bottom (hint: it's the bottom). Either way, consider yourself lucky to get to ponder the question.

Near the end, the trail takes you across the front of Kalalau Valley, where you can feel dwarfed by 1000ft lava-rock cliffs before proceeding to the campgrounds on the beach, just west of the valley. You will need a state-park permit to camp here or even just to day-hike beyond Hanakoa Valley.

🖝 Tours

Kaua'i Nature Tours   Guided Tour
(📞808-742-8305, 888-233-8365; www. kauainaturetours.com; 10hr tours adult/ child 7-12yr $150/115; ⏰by reservation only) Geologist Chuck Blay's company guides an excellent 8-mile (round-trip) hike to Hanakapi'ai Falls. All-day tours depart by shuttle van from Po'ipu Beach Park on the South Shore.

ℹ️ Getting There & Away

The parking lot nearest the trailhead at Ke'e Beach is quite large, but fills quickly. By mid-morning and during the jam-packed summer

When in Doubt, Don't Go Out

Made evident by the knife-etched tally before the descent, has ended many a vacation – and life – too soon. Heed this warning. The waters in Hawaii are as powerful as anywhere on the planet and can catch many a toe-dipper off guard in the blink of an eye. Strong undertows can sweep even the most experienced swimmers off their feet and out to sea in a matter of seconds.

months, you may well be out of luck. Break-ins are rampant; some people advise leaving your car empty and unlocked to prevent damage such as window smashing.

Overnight hikers should consider parking at Ha'ena Beach Park (free, but not patrolled) or possibly at private YMCA Camp Naue (📞808-246-9090; www.ymcaofkauai.org/YMCA/ CampNaue.html; Kuhio Hwy) instead ($5 per night).

Poʻipu & the South Shore

Sun, surf, sand: the quintessential elements of a beach vacation are guaranteed in Poʻipu.

Here the weather and waves are welcoming almost year-round. To this we add a more intangible factor: good taste. While the long shoreline here is lined with hotels and vacation homes, you will find neither mini-golf nor plastic sharks, but people embracing natural treasures, from the raw beauty of the Mahaʻulepu Coast and family-centric Poʻipu Beach Park, to the world-renowned Allerton and McBryde Gardens.

Nearby Koloa also wears tourism well, its historic plantation cottages emptied of sugarcane workers and refilled with quirky shops and low-key restaurants, while in residential Kalaheo there is hardly any tourism at all.

All things considered, the South Shore welcomes you with a casual gentility, making it very easy – no, essential – to relax.

Bicolor anthias

Po'ipu & the South Shore Highlights

Ha'ula Beach

Indulge your inner Robinson Crusoe at this wild and secluded cove (p172). But you'll have to earn the right first by hiking here on the windswept Maha'ulepu Heritage Trail along a largely undeveloped stretch of South Shore coast, starting from Shipwreck Beach. Keep an eye open for rare, endangered Hawaiian monk seals hauled out on the beach, taking a snooze in the sun.

Seaview Terrace

The Grand Hyatt Kauai Resort really does evoke grandeur among all the cookie-cutter condos of Po'ipu. Step into the hotel's graceful lobby, then swish through the open-air atrium until suddenly a panorama of tropical greenery and blue sea opens at your feet (p186). Order a mai tai and grab a terrace table to watch the sunset. Then exhale: your vacation starts *now*.

IRENE CHAN/ALAMY ©

Old Koloa Town

3

Hawaii's first sugar plantation was established here in the 1830s, forever changing the way of life in the Hawaiian Islands. Take a peek back in time along the main street of this small town (p160), whose historic buildings still stand, today housing restaurants and shops. The scenic way to get here is to drive through the Tree Tunnel on Maluhia Rd (Hwy 520). Tree Tunnel (p159)

4

Allerton & McBryde Gardens

Forget Shangri-La, you'll find paradise here at the National Tropical Botanical Garden (p179). If you're a botany geek or just anyone who appreciates carefully cultivated beauty of the floral kind, reserve ahead for a guided tour of Allerton Garden (p172), the fantastical estate deep in the Lawa'i Valley, or wander around the smaller but still impressive McBryde Garden (p173) next door.

5

Snorkeling the Coast

The South Shore offers some of the island's finest snorkeling, bar none. Best of all, you can reach several of the hot spots right from shore (p176). So don a mask and fins, and get ready to meet and greet schools of colorful tropical fish, eels, turtles, waving corals and more. To get even further offshore, paddle a kayak or hop on a boat cruise.

Po'ipu & the South Shore Itineraries

KOLOA FISH MARKET ④ ⑤ OLD KOLOA TOWN

ALLERTON GARDEN ③

JOSSELIN'S TAPAS BAR & GRILL ⑬ ⑨

MAHA'ULEPU HERITAGE TRAIL ⑦ ⑧ MAKAUWAHI SINKHOLE

KEOKI'S PARADISE

BEACH HOUSE RESTAURANT ⑥ ⑪ ②

SHOPS AT KUKUI'ULA SNORKEL THE COAST ① ⑩ ⑫ SEAVIEW TERRACE & ANARA SPA

PO'IPU BEACH PARK

---

2 DAYS

10 MILES
DAYS ONE & TWO

Start by getting in the local swing of things by relaxing at ❶ **Po'ipu Beach Park**. If you're looking for lunch, Brennecke's Beach Deli is across the street, as is Nukumoi Surf Company for rental boards. The local choice for in-the-know dining, partying and general fun-having, ❷ **Keoki's Paradise** jungle lodge (a spin-off from the Duke's franchise) will also put you in the proper mood, beginning with its popular happy hour.

On day two, head west to ❸ **Allerton Garden**. Far more than a garden tour, this trip through one man's tropical Shangri-La turns an entire paradise valley into a work of landscape art.

You still haven't got your local bearings until you've ordered a takeout lunch at ❹ **Koloa Fish Market**. Have your picnic at the Sugar Monument, the remains of an old mill across the street.

Spend the afternoon leisurely nosing around ❺ **Old Koloa Town**, a strip of historic buildings, where plantation cottages from the days of Big Sugar have been converted into an eclectic range of shops and restaurants. Finally, it just isn't a complete trip to Po'ipu until you've enjoyed a sunset table at waterfront icon ❻ **Beach House Restaurant**. Take our advice and book far, far ahead.

15 MILES

DAYS THREE & FOUR

On day three, the awesome yet easy 4-mile ❼ **Mahaʻulepu Heritage Trail** coastal hike takes you past bays, streams, monk seals, wild waves and more. Bring a picnic lunch, snorkel gear and the whole family. Make sure to check out the unique ❽ **Makauwahi Sinkhole**. This geological oddity off the trail is both beautiful and fascinating.

Take a late-afternoon stroll down the central pedestrian zone of ❾ **Shops at Kukuiʻula**. This attractive mall, which appears in the form of a village of plantation-style buildings, is worth a look. Visit the Grand Hyatt's panoramic ❿ **Seaview Terrace** for a drink at sunset when there's free entertainment, or on day four, when it becomes a morning cafe.

Head out to ⓫ **snorkel the coast** on day four at one of the South Shore's five great snorkeling sites. Take a kayak tour with Outfitters Kauai for more snorkeling adventures.

Next, indulge in a massage at the Grand Hyatt's mega-spa, ⓬ **Anara Spa**, where you'll have a tropical gazebo to yourself. In the evening, head to ⓭ **Josselin's Tapas Bar & Grill** for the famous chef's Hawaii Regional Cuisine, and imaginative cocktails.

Beachside resort, Poʻipu (p168)
MATTHEW MICAH WRIGHT/GETTY IMAGES ©

Discover Poʻipu & the South Shore

Koloa

The district of Koloa contains a charming historic town of quaint painted cottages, now filled with tourist shops, restaurants, and galleries. Known as **Old Koloa Town**, it lines one side of Koloa Rd, making it a breeze to navigate: just start at one end and work your way toward the other.

Coming from Lihuʻe, be sure to take Maluhia Rd (Hwy 520), which will lead you through the romantic **Tree Tunnel**, a mile-long canopy of towering eucalyptus trees. Pineapple baron Walter McBryde planted them as a community project in 1911, with leftover trees from his estate at Kukuiolono.

History

When William Hooper, an enterprising 24-year-old Bostonian, arrived on Kauaʻi in 1835, he took advantage of two historical circumstances: Polynesians' introduction of sugarcane to the islands and Chinese immigrants' knowledge of refinery. With financial backing from Honolulu businesspeople, he leased land in Koloa from the king and paid a stipend to release commoners from their traditional work obligations.

He then hired the Hawaiians as wage laborers and Koloa became Hawaii's first plantation town. Visitation led to the establishment of the first hotel in Kauaʻi, the Koloa Hotel, which you can still see today. The town withered following the decline of Big Sugar, but like the rest of Kauaʻi has made a successful transition to tourism, while retaining its historic facade.

◎ Sights

Koloa Jodo Mission
Temple

(☎ 808-742-6735; www.koloajodo.com; 3480 Waikomo Rd; ⓒservices usually 10:30am Sun) Serving the local Japanese community for more than a century, this sect of Buddhism practices a form of chanting meditation. The temple on the left is the original, which dates back to 1910, while the larger temple on the right

Spouting Horn Park (p173)
LINDA CHING/GETTY IMAGES ©

Lawa'i International Center

Magical. Enchanting. Stirring. Such words are often used to describe this quiet spiritual site (☏ tour reservations 808-639-4300; www.lawaicenter.org; 3381 Wawae Rd, Lawa'i; admission by donation; ⊘ 2nd & last Sun of the month, tours depart 10am, noon & 2pm) in the Lawa'i Valley, just east of Kalaheo. Originally the site of a Hawaiian heiau, whatever mana (spiritual essence) this site has also attracted local Japanese plantation families seeking to develop a religious community. In 1904, they placed 88 miniature Shingon Buddhist shrines (each about 2ft tall) along a steep hillside path to symbolize the famous 88 pilgrimage shrines in Shikoku, Japan. For years, island pilgrims would journey here to meditate upon these shrines, but the site was abandoned by the 1960s, and half of the shrines were scattered in shards.

In the late 1980s, a group of volunteers led by Lynn Muramoto formed a nonprofit group, acquired the 32-acre property and embarked on a backbreaking project to repair or rebuild the shrines. Today all 88 shrines are beautifully restored, and there's a newly built wooden temple, the Hall of Compassion. Leisurely tours include a detailed history and hillside trail walk that amounts to a mini-pilgrimage. While the shrines are of Buddhist origin, the center is a nondenominational sanctuary.

is used for a weekly service followed by a Dharma talk – everyone is welcome. For a guided tour, call ahead.

Check the website for the dates of summer Obon festivities, which feature Japanese drumming, folk dancing and more.

Koloa History Center   Museum
(www.oldkoloa.com; Koloa Rd; ⊘9am-9pm) **FREE** This tiny open-air museum traces the town's history through old photos and historic artifacts such as old barber chairs and kerosene dispensers, plows, yolks, saws and sewing machines. In effect, the entire town is part of this museum, as many buildings have placards describing their history.

Sugar Monument (Old Mill)   Historic Site
(Koloa Rd) The sugar industry, once Hawaii's largest, began here in 1835. This memorial stands on the site of the first mill. There's little left besides a foundation, an old stone chimney and a bronze sculpture depicting the ethnically diverse laborers of Hawaii's plantation era.

🏃 Activities

Fathom Five Ocean Quest Divers   Diving
(☏808-742-6991, 800-972-3078; www.fathom five.com; 3450 Po'ipu Rd; dives $75-350) Considered Kaua'i's best dive outfit, Fathom Five offers a full range of options, from Ni'ihau boat dives to certification courses and enticing night dives. Newbies can expect reassuring hand-holding during introductory shore dives. Groups max out at six people, and mixing skill levels is avoided. Scuba and snorkel gear are rented at the full-service shop. Book well in advance.

Koloa Zipline   Ziplining
(☏808-742-2894, 877-707-7088; www.koloazip line.com; 3477a Weliweli Rd; tours $145-185; ⊘tours daily, by reservation only) Take the plunge and zip upside down as you enjoy superlative views from the longest (measured in feet, not minutes) zipline tour on the island, and the only one to allow tandem zipping. Try to book at least two weeks ahead, or call the day before to ask about last-minute openings. Minimum age is seven years; maximum weight is 270lbs.

161

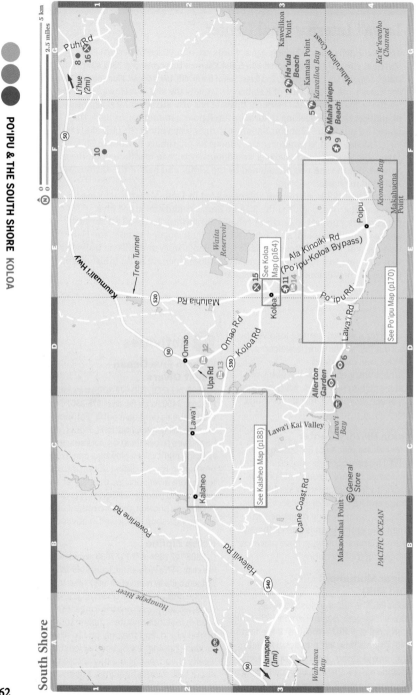

0   2.5 miles
0   5 km

Kaumuali'i Hwy
Tree Tunnel
Waita Reservoir

Li'hue (2mi)
Puhi Rd
8 16

10

50

Omao
12
Upa Rd
13
Omao Rd
Koloa Rd

520
Maluhia Rd
15
Koloa
11
14
Ala Kinoiki Rd
(Po'ipu-Koloa Bypass)

See Koloa Map (p164)

See Po'ipu Map (p170)

Poipu
Po'ipu Rd
Lawa'i Rd
Makahuena Point
Koomeloa Bay

6
1
7
Allerton Garden
Lawa'i Bay

Lawa'i Kai Valley
See Kalaheo Map (p188)

Lawa'i
Kalaheo

Powerline Rd

Halewili Rd
Cane Coast Rd

Hanapepe River
Hanapepe (1mi)

540

50

4

Wahiawa Bay
Makaokahai Point
PACIFIC OCEAN
General Store

2 Ha'ula Beach
Kawelikoa Point
Kamala Point
5 Kawailoa Bay
3 Maha'ulepu Beach
9
Mahā'ulepu Coast
Ka'ie'iewaho Channel

Ha'ula Beach
Maha'ulepu Beach

50
530

South Shore

Snorkel Bob's   Water Sports

(Map p162; 📞808-742-2206, 800-262-7725; www.snorkelbob.com; 3236 Po'ipu Rd; ◷8am-5pm) The king of snorkel gear rents and sells enough styles and sizes to assure a good fit. Wetsuits, flotation devices and boogie boards are all rented here. You can return snorkel gear to any location on Kaua'i, O'ahu, Maui or the Big Island.

Boss Frog's Dive,
Surf & Bike   Water Sports

(📞808-742-2025, 888-700-3764; www.bossfrog.com; 3414 Po'ipu Rd; ◷8am-5pm) This outfit rents well-used snorkel gear pretty darn cheaply. You can even return snorkel gear to their Maui or Big Island shops. Rental boogie boards, surfboards, underwater cameras, beach chairs and umbrellas are also available (but no bikes).

Kauai Z Tourz   Boat Tour

(📞808-742-7422; www.kauaiztours.com; 3417e Po'ipu Rd; tours adult/child 5-12yr from $99/84)

The 'Z' is for Zodiac boat, which whisks you off on a snorkeling tour of the South Shore. Options include reefs off Spouting Horn, Prince Kuhio Park and Allerton Gardens. You may wish to avoid sites you can reach from shore yourself. Winter boat trips go out dolphin- and whale-watching (no snorkeling).

🎉 Festivals & Events

Koloa Plantation
Days Celebration   Cultural, Music

(📞808-652-3217; www.koloaplantationdays.com; 👪) In mid- to late July, the South Shore's biggest annual celebration spans nine days of family-friendly fun with a gamut of attractions (many free), including a parade, *paniolo* (Hawaiian cowboy) rodeo, traditional Hawaiian games, Polynesian dancing, a craft fair, film nights, live music, guided walks and hikes, a beach party and plenty of 'talk story' about the old days.

🛏 Sleeping

Listed here are accommodations in the Koloa and Omao Rd residential neighborhoods.

Yvonne's B&B   B&B $

(📞808-742-2418; yvonne.e.johnson@gmail.com; 3857 Omao Rd; s/d with shared bath $89/99, incl breakfast $99/119; 📶) World traveler, collector of oddities and teller of hilarious stories, Yvonne makes this homey B&B sing. Guests will enjoy a good chat on the charming verandah and showers of kindness. Her two rooms are decorated with Hawaiiana artifacts, retro furnishings and original art. While the bathroom is shared, only one room is typically rented at a time. Three-night minimum stay.

Boulay Inn   Apartment $

(Map p162; 📞808-742-1120; www.boulayinn.com; 4175 Omao Rd; 1-bedroom apt $85; 📶) This airy apartment in quiet residential Omao sits atop a garage, but has its own wrap-around lanai, full kitchen, high ceilings, washer-dryer and complimentary use of beach gear. There's a sofa bed in the living

Koloa

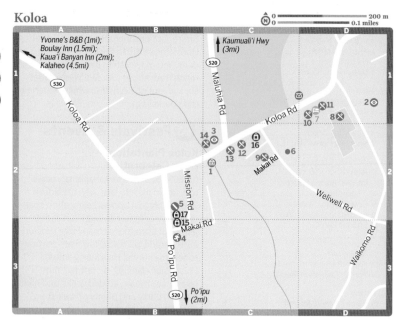

Koloa

room, so you can bring the kids or another adult. Fresh flowers and a breakfast basket welcome your arrival. Three-night minimum stay; cleaning fee $50.

Kaua'i Banyan Inn   Inn $$
(Map p162; ☏888-786-3855; www.kauaibanyan.com; 3528b Mana Hema Pl, Lawa'i; ste incl breakfast $155-230; ⊕) Perched on a lush hillside in Lawa'i, this inn is chic enough for even the most discerning guests. Each impeccable suite features polished hardwood floors, a kitchenette (or full kitchen),

vaulted ceilings, private lanai and quality wood furnishings. The top suite (Ali'i) has mountain and (distant) ocean views. Guests make their own breakfast from food provided. Cleaning fee $45.

Hale Kipa O Koloa   Cottage $$
(☏808-651-4493; www.vrbo.com/68868; 1-bedroom cottage per night/week $135/810; ⊕) This plantation-style house is a walkable half-mile to Old Koloa Town and affords much privacy. With one queen and three

twin beds, a full kitchen and a washer-dryer, a family can settle in and have plenty of room. The inland location can be hot, but the cottage has high ceilings and cool tile floors. Free beach gear to borrow.

🍴 Eating

Koloa Fish Market   Seafood $

(☎808-742-6199; 5482 Koloa Rd; meals $7-11; ⊙10am-6pm Mon-Fri, to 5pm Sat) Line up with those in the know at this hole-in-the-wall. It serves outstanding *poke* in all kinds of flavors (spicy kimchi is the hands-down winner), Japanese-style *bentō* (boxed meals), sushi rolls, seaweed salads and both Hawaiian and local plate lunches grilled to order. Thick-sliced, perfectly seared ahi and rich slabs of homemade *haupia* (coconut) or sweet-potato pie are quite addictive.

Fresh Shave   Dessert $

(www.thefreshshave.com; 3540 Koloa Rd, Lawa'i; shave ice from $5.50; ⊙11am-3pm Wed-Fri, to 5pm Sat; 🖉 👶) 🍴 Out of a shiny vintage Aristocrat trailer comes the best shave ice on the island, made using fresh, organic and often local ingredients such as apple bananas and coffee. Opening hours vary, but be forewarned that this roadside pit stop is always mobbed with neighborhood moms and kids after school in the afternoon.

Koloa Farmers Market   Market $

(Map p162; www.kauai.gov; Knudsen Park, Maluhia Rd; ⊙noon-2pm Mon; 🖉) 🍴 Vendors sell mostly flowers and produce, including exotic fruit; try drinking the milk from a whole coconut. Bring small bills and change, and show up on time, as competition is fierce once the whistle blows.

Koloa Mill Ice Cream & Coffee   Cafe $

(☎808-742-6544; http://koloamill.ahez.com; 5424 Koloa Rd; items from $3; ⊙7am-9pm) Homemade cotton candy, Kaua'i coffee and nothing but the best Maui-made Roselani Tropics ice cream are always served with a smile. If you're indecisive, start with the Kona coffee, macadamia

nut or 'Pauwela Sunrise' containing pineapple chunks.

Sueoka Snack Shop   American $

(☎808-742-1112; www.sueokastore.com; 5392 Koloa Rd; items $2-5, meals around $7; ⊙9am-5pm or 6pm Tue-Sun) Next door to Sueoka's grocery store, this little yellow takeout window is the smart place to order that picnic lunch, be it teriyaki burgers, fish and chips, or mixed plates. For better or worse, all the food tastes home-cooked. It's as inexpensive a meal as you'll find anywhere on Kaua'i. Cash only.

Chalupa's   Mexican $

(☎808-634-4016; www.chalupaskauai.com; 3477 Weliweli Rd; items $3-10, meals $10-13; ⊙10am-7pm Mon-Fri, 11am-4pm Sat & Sun) Hailing from Veracruz, this Mexican chef and his food truck is worth seeking out behind the shops. Fish tacos and shrimp (garlic, Cajun or spicy *diabla*) plates are what everyone's chowing down on at the picnic tables. BYOB.

Big Save   Supermarket $

(☎808-742-1614; www.timessupermarkets.com; 5516 Koloa Rd; ⊙6am-11pm) Fill up the kitchen of your vacation rental at this local chain supermarket; this is one of its best branches, and it stocks some locally

---

Island Insights

The Koloa Heritage Trail (www.koloaheritagetrail.info) is a 10-mile walk, bike ride or drive with 14 stops highlighting the archaeology, culture and history of the South Shore. Some stops are little more than bronze plaques, while others, like Spouting Horn and Po'ipu Beach Park, are popular sights. If you want to combine fresh air and exercise with an overview of the region, this will do it. Download a free trail guide online or stop by the Poipu Beach Resort Association (p187) office for a free brochure.

grown produce. Pick up the value-priced ahi *poke*.

Sueoka Store
Supermarket $
(☎808-742-1611; www.sueokastore.com; 5392 Koloa Rd; ⏰6:30am-8:30pm Mon-Sat, 7:30am-8.30pm Sun) On the town's main drag, this small local grocery store holds its own by stocking the basics, plus pre-packaged Japanese snacks and Kaua'i-made Taro Ko chips.

La Spezia
Italian, American $$
(☎808-742-8824; www.laspeziakauai.com; 5492 Koloa Rd; mains breakfast $8-14, dinner $14-22; ⏰7:30-11am Mon, Tue & Thu-Sat, 8:30-11am Wed, 8am-1pm Sun, 5:30-10pm daily) A step up in sophistication from everywhere else in town, this Italian *ristorante* with polished wooden floors and a wine bar crafts flatbreads, crunchy crostini and house-made sausage and pasta. Surprisingly, it doubles as a creative breakfast spot – turn up for stuffed French toast and Bloody Marys at Sunday brunch.

Yanagi Sushi
Fusion $$
(5371 Koloa Rd; mains $12-15; ⏰11am-3pm Mon-Thu) Look for the 'Dragon Wagon' parked at the old mill site, across the street from the main shopping strip. The enthusiastic, superfriendly Kaua'i-born sushi guru is creative and generous in his plating of fusion rolls. Show up too late and you might find everyone has gone surfing, brah.

Pizzetta
Italian, American $$
(☎808-742-8881; www.pizzettakauai.com; 5408 Koloa Rd; mains $12-20, pizzas $17-25; ⏰11am-9:30pm) More than the pasta bowls, it's the baked pizzas, with toppings such as *kalua* pig, Hawaiian BBQ chicken or spinach with goat's cheese, that are the draw at this casual spot. Nab a patio table out back.

🛍 Shopping

Island Soap & Candle Works
Beauty, Gifts
(☎808-742-1945, 888-528-7627; www.kauai-soap.com; 5428 Koloa Rd; ⏰9am-9pm) 🌿 The

PO'IPU & THE SOUTH SHORE KOLOA

aromas wafting out of this shop are enough to turn your head. Wander in and sample the all-natural Hawaii botanical bath and body products, including lip balms, soaps, lotions and tropically scented candles. Some of the products are made on-site at the back of the store, which was established in 1984.

Pohaku T's   Clothing
(📞 808-742-7500; www.pohaku.com; 3430 Po'ipu Rd; 🕐10am-6pm Mon-Sat, to 5pm Sun) Spot the Kaua'i-made clothing hanging out on the lanai (when it's not raining), including unique aloha shirts, and a grab bag of souvenirs indoors. Stonewashed (*pohaku* means stone in Hawaiian) T-shirt designs are printed with Hawaiian themes such as petroglyphs, Polynesian carvings and navigational maps.

Art House   Arts & Crafts
(📞 808-742-1400; www.arthousehawaii.com; 3440 Po'ipu Rd; 🕐11am-6pm) Local artists show their plein-air paintings, mixed media and groovy handicrafts, such as sweet silver jewelry and art boxes, at this brightly lit gallery. Owner Julie Berg's acrylic images shine with an unusual additive: surfboard resin.

ℹ Information
First Hawaiian Bank (📞808-742-1642; www.fhb.com; 3506 Waikomo Rd; 🕐8:30am-4pm Mon-Thu, to 6pm Fri) Has a 24-hour ATM.

Koloa Post Office (📞808-742-1319; www.usps.com; 5485 Koloa Rd; 🕐9am-4pm Mon-Fri, to 11am Sat) Serves both Koloa and Po'ipu.

ℹ Getting Around
The Kaua'i Bus (p58) stops in Koloa on its route between Po'ipu and Kalaheo; the latter has onward connections to Lihu'e and the Westside.

167

Po'ipu

Po'ipu is the most popular vacation spot on the South Shore for good reason: it's a great deal of fun. There is a lot of sun here (far more than the North Shore), a wide range of easy-access beaches, an excellent hiking trail, two shopping centers, a wide variety of restaurants, and a truly Grand Hyatt. You won't be alone in enjoying all of this: the coast is blanketed with hotels, condos and vacation homes, making this section of Kaua'i feel like a vast resort. But it is all done in good taste, with no building taller than a palm tree, and this won't be changing anytime soon.

Alas, there is no town center. The Shops at Kuku'ula dining and shopping complex is, however, an attempt to create one from scratch. Inevitably, the result feels somewhat artificial, but at the same time, the design is as good as one could reasonably expect, with a pedestrian zone lined by bright and attractive plantation-style houses, each one unique. Shops here are upmarket and the dining options are a welcome addition to the area.

Po'ipu Beach Park

Beaches

Po'ipu has two different beach areas: the in-town beaches, which front resorts and condos, and the wild beaches to the east, along the Maha'ulepu Coast. The former are popular and crowded, the latter unspoiled and surprisingly private. With a total of nine beaches to choose from, you'll find a favorite soon enough.

IN-TOWN BEACHES

Po'ipu Beach Park   Beach
(🏖) At the South Shore's most popular beach, there are no monster waves and no idyllic solitude, but it's a go-to spot with something for everyone. Patrolled by resident *honu* (green sea turtles) in the shallows, the beach is protected by a rocky reef that attracts fish of all kinds.

The beach spills into two separate bays connected by the reef outside and bisected by a sandbar. Add in lifeguards, picnic tables, toilets and outdoor showers, and you have one safe, family-friendly beach.

At the end of Ho'owili Rd, there's parking located right across from the beach. There are also three nearby surf

ANN CECIL/GETTY IMAGES ©

breaks and a grassy lawn connecting to Brennecke's Beach just east.

Brennecke's Beach · Beach

With a sandbar bottom and a notch of sand and sea wedged between two lava rock outcrops, this little beach attracts a cadre of bodyboarders, bobbing in the water, waiting for the next set at any time of day or year. No surfboards are allowed near shore, so bodyboarders rule. Tourists sit on the roadside stone wall, gawking at the action.

The beach flanks the eastern edge of Po'ipu Beach Park. Check with lifeguards there before venturing out.

Po'ipu Beach · Beach

Although it's nicknamed Sheraton Beach or Kiahuna Beach, this long swath of sand is not private. It merely fronts the hotel and the condo complexes, both of which scored big-time with their location here, lying west of Po'ipu Beach Park.

The waters are often too rough for kids, although an offshore reef tames the waves enough for strong ocean swimmers and snorkelers. To get to the beach, drive to the end of Ho'onani Rd.

Experienced surfers and bodyboarders can attempt the breaks near the Sheraton, but those waters are famous for sneaker sets (rogue waves that appear out of nowhere) and the rocky coast makes it difficult to get offshore and back.

Shipwreck Beach · Beach

Unless you're an expert surfer, body-boarder or bodysurfer, keep your feet dry at 'Shipwrecks.' Instead, come for an invigorating walk along the half-mile crescent of light-gold sand. You'll have some company, as the Grand Hyatt over-looks much of the beach along Keoneloa Bay. Row after row of waves crash close to shore, giving this beach a rugged, untamed feel.

To the east of the bay looms **Makawehi Point**, a gigantic lithified sand dune. Beware that cliff-jumpers (or those who accidentally fall due to erosion) have been seriously injured and have even died. To the west is **Makahuena Point**, the southernmost tip of Kaua'i, a rocky

cliff overlooking crashing waves that is covered with condos.

Baby Beach · Beach

(👶) Introduce tots to the ocean at this beach, where the water is barely thigh

169

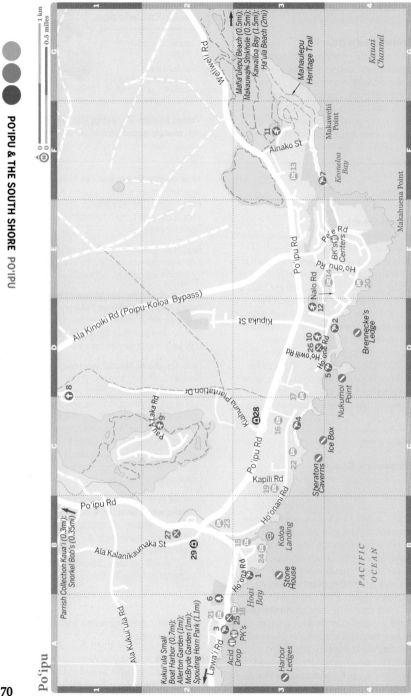

Po'ipu

high. The sandy shore runs behind a row of beach homes on Ho'ona Rd west of Koloa Landing. Access is easy, but parking is limited (don't block any driveways). Look for the beach-access sign that marks the path down to the beach.

Don't confuse this Baby Beach with the one in Kapa'a on the island's Eastside.

Lawa'i (Beach House) Beach
Beach

For such a tiny beach, this snorkeling and surfing spot gets lots of attention. Almost adjacent to Lawa'i Rd, just west of the landmark Beach House Restaurant, it's not especially scenic or sandy. But during calm surf, the waters are rich snorkel turf, especially for novices. Expect a crowd of vacationers from nearby timeshares and condos.

Restrooms, outdoor showers and a smidgen of public parking are found across the street from the beach.

MAHA'ULEPU COAST BEACHES

The windswept Maha'ulepu Coast resembles no other on Kaua'i: lithified sand-dune cliffs, pounding surf, secluded coves, and three outstanding beaches with very few people on them. A popular way to see them all is by walking the

Po'ipu on a Budget

McBryde Garden (p173) The self-guided tour (half the price of the Allerton tour) lets you stroll at your own pace amid palms, orchids and rare native species.

Maha'ulepu Heritage Trail (p174) Walk the island's last accessible undeveloped coastline and bear witness to striking limestone cliffs unlike anything else across the Hawaiian Islands.

Shoreline snorkeling If you don't have a boat, you don't need a snorkel cruise. Rent or buy your own snorkel gear and explore Po'ipu's eye-catching marine life from just beyond the shore.

Beach House Restaurant lawn (p185) If you can't afford dinner at this fine-dining icon, park yourself on the adjacent grassy knoll and enjoy the free show: lithe local surfers, an unobstructed horizon and blazing sunsets.

Kukuiolono Golf Course (p189) In Kalaheo, this neighborhood nine-hole course is welcoming, unpretentious – and only $9.

Maha'ulepu Heritage Trail (p174). Swimming can be dicey in spots, even in summer, so use your best judgment.

Maha'ulepu Beach   Beach
(Gillin's Beach; Map p162; http://malama-mahaulepu.org) You feel like you're sitting on the reef in this secluded spot, so it's no surprise that there's excellent snorkeling. To get here, hike the Maha'ulepu Heritage Trail from Shipwreck Beach or drive 1.5 miles on the dirt road that begins after the Grand Hyatt, turning right where it dead-ends at a gate (open 7:30am to 6pm daily, to 7pm in summer, and strictly enforced). Continue to the parking area, where a trail leads to the beach.

Look out for the sole house on the entire coast, the **Gillin Beach House**, originally built in 1946 by a civil engineer with the Koloa Sugar Plantation.

Kawailoa Bay   Beach
(Map p162) The beach at Kawailoa Bay has sand dunes at one end and cliffs at the other. The reliable breeze here makes it a popular spot for windsurfing and kitesurfing, while the ironwood trees bordering the beach create an impromptu picnic area. It's also a local fishing spot. Coming from Maha'ulepu Beach, continue down the coastal Maha'ulepu Heritage hiking trail on foot or follow the inland dirt road by car until you run into Kawailoa Bay.

Ha'ula Beach   Beach
(Map p162) Ha'ula is an isolated bay and pocket beach nestled into the shoreline. You'll feel like Robinson Crusoe here, particularly when swinging in a hammock made from a washed-up fishing net. If you're lucky, you might see a monk seal hauling out on the beach. Please stay back at least 50yd to avoid disturbing these critically endangered marine mammals. The beach is a 15-minute walk beyond Kawailoa Bay along the coast, past a rusty fence.

◎ Sights

Allerton Garden   Gardens
(Map p162; ☏808-742-2623; www.ntbg.org; 4425 Lawa'i Rd; 2½hr tours adult/child 6-12yr $40/15; ⏲visitor center 8:30am-5pm, tours by reservation only) An extraordinary tour of this garden, part of the multi-site National Tropical Botanical Garden, wanders deep into Lawa'i Valley. Robert Allerton, a wealthy Chicago transplant, spent three

decades modifying this beautiful tropical valley, which has its own jungle river and ocean beach, by adding stone walkways, pools, sculptures, waterfalls, gazebos and a tremendous variety of plants. Book ahead for all tours.

Tour guides are knowledgeable and enthusiastic as they leisurely lead groups through the meticulously landscaped grounds. Highlights include otherworldly Moreton Bay fig trees (as seen in *Jurassic Park*), golden bamboo groves, a pristine lagoon, and valley walls blanketed with purple bougainvillea during summer. More expensive three-hour sunset tours peek inside Allerton's historic home, where drinks and appetizers are civilly served on the lanai.

McBryde Garden   Gardens

(Map p162; ☎808-742-2623; www.ntbg.org; 4425 Lawa'i Rd; self-guided tours adult/child 6-12yr $20/10; ⏱visitor center 8:30am-5pm, tours by reservation only; ♿) ∅ This garden showcases palms, flowering and spice trees, orchids, and rare endemic species, plus a pretty stream and a waterfall. For budget travelers, the self-guided tour allows you to wander in the vast grounds without watching the clock. Advance reservations are required, however.

Spouting Horn Park   Viewpoint

(Map p162) A concrete walkway and a grassy picnic area sit just above two blowholes in the lava-rock reef where the surf juts through like a mini geyser. The waves can be unpredictable, so you might need to wait for some action. Eruptions are typically less than 30ft and last only seconds, but they can reach twice that height during big surf.

To get here, turn right off Po'ipu Rd onto Lawa'i Rd and continue along the coast for less than 2 miles.

Moir Pa'u a Laka   Gardens

(☎808-742-6411; www.outrigger.com; Kiahuna Plantation, 2253 Po'ipu Rd; ⏱sunrise-sunset) **FREE** On the grounds of Outrigger's Kiahuna Plantation condo complex, this historical cactus and exotic flower garden is a diverting, if modest, collection interspersed with winding paths, a koi pond and colorful shocks of orchids. Established in the 1930s by Hector Moir, manager of Koloa Sugar Plantation, and his wife Alexandra, the gardens were once far better known than they are today.

McBryde Garden

St Raphael's Catholic Church   Church

(☎808-742-1955; www.st-raphael-kauai.org; 3011 Hapa Rd) Kaua'i's oldest Catholic church is the burial site of some of Hawaii's first Portuguese immigrants. The original 1854 church was made of lava rock and coral mortar with walls 3ft thick – a type of construction visible in the ruins of the adjacent rectory. When the church was enlarged in 1936 it was plastered over, giving it a more typical, whitewashed appearance. Church service hours vary, but you can poke around the old cemetery during daylight.

🏃 Activities

HIKING

Maha'ulepu Heritage Trail   Hiking

(www.hikemahaulepu.org) This outstanding coastal hike runs for 2 miles each way between Shipwreck Beach and Ha'ula Beach. Leaving from Shipwreck Beach, park in the Grand Hyatt lot at the end of Ainako St; from the beach, head east through the ironwood trees. Windblown and mostly deserted, the trail offers tremendous variety: stark cliffs, pounding seas, secluded bays and beaches, heiau ruins, tidepools and more.

If you want to shorten the hike, start from Maha'ulepu Beach, or simply turn back at any time. For an interpretive trail guide and map, visit the website or the Poipu Beach Resort Association (p187) office.

DIVING

The Po'ipu coast offers the majority of the island's best dive sites, including **Sheraton Caverns (Map p170)**, a series of partially collapsed lava tubes, with shafts of glowing sunlight illuminating their dim, atmospheric interior; **General Store (Map p162)**, with sharks, octopuses, eels and the remains of an 1892 shipwreck; and **Nukumoi Point (Map p282)**, also known as Tortugas, a shallow site as well as a habitat for green sea turtles.

Dive boats and catamaran cruises typically depart from **Kukui'ula Small Boat Harbor (Map p162; Lawa'i Rd).**

Seasport Divers   Diving

(☎808-742-9303, 800-685-5889; www.seasportdivers.com; Po'ipu Plaza, 2827 Po'ipu Rd; shore/boat dives from $90/135; ⊙by reservation only) This leading outfit schedules a variety of dives from shore or by boat, including twice-daily South Shore boat trips, and a rare and wonderful three-tank dive to Ni'ihau, available twice-weekly from late spring through early fall. All dives are guided by instructor-level dive masters; any group with noncertified divers includes an additional instructor. Rental equipment available. Book in advance.

Scorpionfish, Sheraton Caverns
CASEY MAHANEY/GETTY IMAGES ©

Detour:
Makauwahi Sinkhole

So you've never been to the Land of the Lost? You may well think this enormous sinkhole is it. The only way in is by squeezing through a tiny opening in a rock wall. Suddenly you find yourself in a beautiful, open-air atrium, with palm trees dwarfed by high cliffs, and an enormous cave system beneath – a dramatic sight.

To paleontologists, this sinkhole, which was once full of water, represents a large pickling jar. Since 1996 it has been excavated by David and Lida Burney with the aid of numerous volunteers, yielding fascinating results. Now a 17-acre reserve, the site has provided evidence for widespread extinction of species in Hawaii following human settlement 1000 years ago, a phenomenon also found in Australia, North America and New Zealand. David Burney's well-written book, *Back to the Future in the Caves of Kaua'i*, tells this cautionary tale with verve.

While this is arguably the richest fossil site in the Hawaiian Islands, very few people seem to know about it. The sinkhole is located at the western end of Maha'ulepu Beach, but is best approached from above by following the short Makauwahi Cave trail to marker 15. First take the unpaved road after the Hyatt past CJM ranch, park where the road splits into spurs, and follow the leftmost one. Trail guides are usually available in a self-serve box, or downloadable online. The sinkhole is currently open to visitors for free guided tours (no reservations) from 9am to 2pm on Wednesday, Friday, Saturday and Sunday. Check the website (www.cavereserve.org) for up-to-date tour times and directions.

Kauai Down Under   Diving

(☏808-742-9534; www.kauaidownunderscuba. com; Sheraton Kauai Resort, 2440 Ho'onani Rd; boat dives incl equipment rental from $159; ☺by reservation only) With one instructor per four guests, personal attention is guaranteed. This outfit offers introductory noncertified one-tank dives, two-tank scooter dives, and night dives for the truly adventurous. It also has a multitude of classes including the recommended pre-arrival online academic portion of the certification for those wanting to maximize playtime while on the island. Make reservations in advance.

SNORKELING

For shore access, three popular snorkeling areas are at Po'ipu Beach Park (p168; ideal for kids and newbies), Lawa'i (Beach House) Beach (p171; if you don't mind crowds), and best of all, secluded Maha'ulepu Beach (p172; if you're a strong swimmer and conditions are calm). To reach further out or down the coast, you'll need a boat.

KAYAKING
Outfitters
Kauai   Kayaking, Snorkeling

(☏808-742-9667, 888-742-9887; www.outfitters kauai.com; Po'ipu Plaza, 2827a Po'ipu Rd; full-day tours adult/child 12-14yr $156/126; ☺guided tours usually 7am-3pm Tue & Thu mid-Sep–mid-May, by reservation only) Take a unique kayaking tour of the Po'ipu coastline, and go snorkeling and surfing at beaches only accessible by boat. Tandem, open-cockpit kayaks or sit-on-top, self-bailing kayaks with pedal rudders make it easy for novices, but if you get seasick, think twice. Make tour reservations in advance. No nonswimmers or children under 12 years old.

175

Snorkeling Hot Spots

These are the top-rated snorkeling areas with beach access on the South Shore.

Koloa Landing (Map p170) Once Kaua'i's largest port, this site is known for the best shore diving on the South Shore, with a quick drop-off to 45ft. The edge is also great for advanced snorkeling. Expect to see large schools of fish, eels and the usual turtles. Avoid the sandy middle ground.

Lawa'i (Beach House) Beach (p171) If you don't mind the crowds, you'll find good coral here, lots of reef fish and sea turtles, all within a depth of 3ft to 12ft. There are bathrooms and outdoor showers on shore.

Maha'ulepu Beach (p172) Though often overlooked because of its seclusion, this near-shore reef is perhaps the best of the lot, though you'll need calm wind and water. Monk seals are often seen here.

Po'ipu Beach Park (p168) Ranging from 3ft to 12ft, this shallow protected bay is great for families, although experts will enjoy it as well. It's best on the left side as you enter. Lifeguard, outdoor showers and restrooms.

Prince Kuhio Park (Map p170) Directly across the street from this park, this site ranges from 3ft to 21ft, appealing to both beginners and advanced snorkelers. There's a rocky shoreline, but the bay is well-protected.

SURFING & STAND UP PADDLE BOARDING

Po'ipu's killer breaks and year-round sun make it a popular spot for surfing lessons and rentals. Avoid large classes with more than four students per instructor.

Kaua'i Surf School   Surfing, SUP
(☎808-651-6032; www.kauaisurfschool.com; Ho'onani Rd; 2hr group/private surfing lessons $75/175; ⏰by reservation only; 🚻) With 90 minutes of teaching, 30 minutes of free practice, and only four students per instructor, you get your money's worth. Ages four and up are welcome in group lessons as long as they can swim; alternatively, book a special one-hour private lesson for kids. Ask about surf clinics, surf camps, private surf coaches and SUP lessons.

Kauai Stand-up Paddle & Surf   SUP, Surfing
(☎808-652-9979; www.kauaisurfandsup.com; 2hr group/private surfing lessons $75/120, 2hr SUP lessons $85, surfing & SUP tours $120-150; 🚻) This locally owned, small-group outfitter runs kids' surf camps in summer, offers family discounts and has 30 years

of experience to bring to the table. It also offers island-wide custom SUP tours.

Surf Lessons by Margo Oberg   Surfing
(☎808-332-6100; www.surfonkauai.com; 2hr group/semiprivate/private surfing lessons $68/90/125; ⏰by appointment only) Owned and operated by a seven-time world champ, one of the longest-running surf schools on Kaua'i has a fine rep. Group classes can include up to six people.

Garden Island Surf School   Surfing, SUP
(☎808-652-4841; www.gardenislandsurfschool.com; Po'ipu Beach; 2hr group/private surfing lessons $75/150, 80min SUP lessons $65, outrigger canoe tours $50; ⏰by reservation only) Group surfing lessons include just one hour with an instructor and an hour of free surfing. For a unique experience, surf the waves while paddling a Hawaiian outrigger canoe. Reservations required.

Po'ipu Surf   Surfing
(☎808-742-8797; www.facebook.com/poipu surf; Shops at Kukui'ula, 2829 Ala Kalanikaumaka

St; surfboard/SUP rental per day from $20/40; ⏱9am-9pm) Local surf and skate shop renting beginner and performance surfboards and SUP sets at competitive rates. Weekly discounts available.

Nukumoi Surf Shop Water Sports

(☎808-742-8019; www.nukumoi.com; 2100 Ho'one Rd; snorkel set & boogie board/surfboard/SUP rental per day from $6/25/60; ⏱8am-sunset) For surfboard, snorkel and SUP rentals, this shop is right across from Po'ipu Beach Park. Check your gear carefully before heading out.

HORSEBACK RIDING

CJM Country
Stables Horseback Riding

(Map p162; ☎808-742-6096; www.cjmstables.com; off Po'ipu Rd; 2hr group rides $110-140, private rides from $140; ⏱rides usually 9:30am & 2pm Mon-Sat, also 1pm Wed & Fri; 👫) The Maha'ulepu Coast is a perfect landscape to see by horse. CJM offers two gentle tours of the purely nose-to-tail walking variety suitable for the whole family. More experienced riders may opt for a private ride.

GOLF & TENNIS

Po'ipu Bay Golf Course Golf

(☎808-742-8711, 800-858-6300; www.poipubaygolf.com; 2250 Ainako St; green fees incl cart rental $130-255) Known for its magnificent views of mountains and sea, this 18-hole, par-72 course designed by Robert Trent Jones Jr hosted the PGA Grand Slam for 13 years. It sports 85 bunkers, multiple water hazards and unpredictable winds. Rates drop dramatically in the afternoons. Club and shoe rentals available.

Kiahuna Golf Club Golf

(☎808-742-9595; www.kiahunagolf.com; 2545 Kiahuna Plantation Dr; green fees incl cart rental $75-110) A relatively inexpensive and forgiving 18-hole, par-70 course designed by Robert Trent Jones Jr, interestingly incorporating some archaeological ruins. The scenery is excellent, with some ocean views, although the course is often windy. Rental clubs available.

Poipu Kai Tennis Club Tennis

(☎808-742-8706; www.poipukai.org/tennis; 1775 Po'ipu Rd; per person per day $20, racket rental $5; ⏱8am-noon & 2-6pm) Rent one of six hard courts or two artificial-grass

Surf lessons

177

courts with ocean views at this resort racquet club. It has tennis clinics and round-robin tourneys. You can either make a reservation or just show up.

SPAS

Anara Spa
Spa

(☏808-742-1234; www.anaraspa.com; Grand Hyatt Kaua'i Resort & Spa, 1571 Po'ipu Rd; ⊙by appointment only) The Grand Hyatt does everything grandly, and this 45,000-sq-ft spa, embellished with tropical gardens and waterfalls, is no exception. Spa treatments inspired by Hawaiian healing arts are given in private garden-view rooms. Don't miss the lava-rock showers. Access to the lap pool and a fitness center offering yoga and wellness classes is complimentary with a minimum 50-minute treatment. Reservations required.

Spa at Koa Kea
Spa

(☏808-828-8888; www.koakea.com; Koa Kea Hotel & Resort, 2251 Po'ipu Rd; ⊙by appointment only) A boutique spa with just five treatment rooms (including one for couples) that puts a variety of massage styles on the menu. Choose from Hawaiian *lomilomi* and *pohaku* (hot stone), as well as body scrubs and treatments utilizing island-sourced ingredients such as *kukui* (candlenut) and coconut oils, Kaua'i coffee and red clay. Book ahead.

👉 Tours

Captain Andy's Sailing Adventures
Boat Tour

(Map p162; ☏808-335-6883, 800-535-0830; www.napali.com; Kukui'ula Small Boat Harbor; 2hr tours adult/child 2-12yr $79/59; ⊙departs 4pm or 5pm Sat) If you're dreaming of a scenic sunset cruise down the Maha'ulepu Coast by catamaran, Captain Andy is a real pro. Cross your fingers to spot whales between December and April. Tours, which depart only once a week, include appetizers, cocktails and live music. Book at least three days ahead.

✹ Festivals & Events

Prince Kuhio Celebration of the Arts
Cultural, Art

(www.princekuhio.net) The South Shore hosts this two-week celebration in mid- to late March. Events include hula dancing and slack key guitar music, a rodeo,

Snorkeling with butterfly fish

The National Tropical Botanical Garden

The National Tropical Botanical Garden (www.ntbg.org) is not a single place, but a nonprofit organization. It is chartered by the US Congress and runs five gardens and three preserves, four of which three are on Kaua'i: the Allerton Garden and the McBryde Garden in Po'ipu, and the Limahuli Garden and Preserve near Ha'ena, on the North Shore. Of the rest, the Kahanu Garden is near Hana on Maui, the Awini and Ka'upulehu Preserves are on the Big Island, and the Kampong is on Biscayne Bay in Coconut Grove, Florida. Headquartered in Kalaheo, the organization is focused on research, conservation and education aimed at the preservation and survival of tropical plants. The name can be confusing sometimes, as it is often used to refer to the Allerton and McBryde Gardens, where the organization began.

canoe racing, 'talk story' time, an artisan fair and Hawaiian cultural presentations on *kapa* (bark cloth), lei and poi making, stone and wood carving, and much more.

🛏 Sleeping

Po'ipu offers two major resorts, the Grand Hyatt and the Sheraton; one boutique hotel, Koa Kea; numerous vacation homes; and a horde of condos. The Po'ipu Beach Resort Association website (www.poipubeach.org/places-to-stay) provides a good overview and helpful photos. Private rentals tend to have better prices, while a good agency can help connect you with the right property and assist with any problems during your stay. In any case, condo rates depend on the owner of the unit, not the complex; typical rates are listed here.

Prince Kuhio Resort   Condo $
(☎888-747-2988; www.prince-kuhio.com; 5061 Lawa'i Rd; studio/1-/2-bedroom condo from $75/125/275; 🛜🏊) This 72-unit complex has an enviable location across from Lawa'i Beach. Although varying in quality and amenities, most condos here have views across the road to the ocean. All have full kitchens and lanai. The pool is no slouch, and the grounds are well kept. A last-minute rental here can be great value. Cleaning fee $85 to $150.

Kuhio Shores   Condo $$
(www.kuhioshores.net; 5050 Lawa'i Rd; 1-/2-bedroom condos from $175/275) Set on a grassy outcrop jutting into the sea opposite Prince Kuhio Park, this three-story oceanfront complex claims the most stunning vistas in Po'ipu. Privately owned condos each spill out onto a patio or lanai. That makes them perennially popular, even though some units are showing their age and amenities vary. Book well ahead. Cleaning fee $95 to $150.

Hideaway Cove
Poipu Beach   Condo $$
(☎808-635-8785, 866-849-2426; www.hideawaycove.com; 2307 Nalo Rd; studio/1-/2-/3-bedroom condos from $185/215/275/425; ❄🛜) Near Po'ipu Beach Park, these impeccable, modern and professionally managed units that come with concierge services are a cut above their peers. All condos feature private lanai, hardwood flooring, genuine art and antiques, name-brand appliances, whirlpool tubs and 50in flat-screen HDTVs, making them feel like private homes. Air-con is only in the bedrooms. Cleaning fee $140 to $325.

Complimentary concierge services and loaner beach gear.

Kaua'i Cove   Cottage, Inn $$
(☎808-742-2562, 800-624-9945; www.kauaicove.com; 2672 Pu'uholo Rd & 2367 Ho'ohu Rd; r/ste from $129/159, cottage $149-229; @🛜)

In a low-key neighborhood near Koloa Landing, this trio of lodgings deftly blends modern amenities with a tropical bungalow feel. In the private studio cottage, an efficient layout allows for a bamboo canopy bed, vaulted ceilings and a fully loaded kitchenette. Add tastefully exotic decor, lustrous hardwood floors and parking right outside your doorstep. Cleaning fee $50 to $75.

Beach gear is free to borrow, and guests have access to a nearby pool and hot tub.

Kiahuna Plantation
Condo $$

(☎808-742-6411, 800-542-4862; www.outrigger.com; 2253 Po'ipu Rd; 1-/2-bedroom condo from $115/235; ☒) This aging beauty is still a hot property because it's among the rare Po'ipu accommodations flanking a swimmable beach. Buildings are spread around a tidy oceanfront park. Comfy units have fully equipped kitchens and large lanai, but vary in quality. Guests can use the Poipu Beach Athletic Club fitness center and pool across the road. Cleaning fee $35 to $175.

On-site property management agencies include **Outrigger** (☎808-742-6411, 866-733-0587; www.outriggerkiahunaplantationcondo.com) and **Castle Resorts** (☎808-742-2200, 877-367-1912; www.castleresorts.com), but **Kiahuna Beachside** (☎808-742-2200, 800-937-6642; www.kiahuna.com) manages some of the best (and most expensive) oceanfront units.

Waikomo Stream Villas
Condos $$

(☎808-742-2000, 800-325-5701; www.parishkauai.com; 2721 Po'ipu Rd; 1-/2-bedroom condos from $135/165) Because it's neither beachfront nor oceanfront, this condo can be a steal. The 60 units vary in decor, but are huge, with full kitchens, washer-dryers and lanais (an unlucky few look onto the parking lot and Po'ipu Rd roundabout). The split-level, two-bedroom units soar with vaulted ceilings and an upstairs sleeping loft. Cleaning fee $135 to $165.

Sheraton Kaua'i Resort
Resort $$

(☎808-742-1661, 866-716-8109; www.sheraton-kauai.com; 2440 Ho'onani Rd; r from $209; ✳@☎☒) While it can't compete with top resorts such as the Hyatt, the Sheraton has one enviable advantage: a prime stretch of sandy, swimmable, sunset-perfect beach, ideal for families.

Rooms are unmemorable, however. The hotel's open-air design highlights its ocean setting, yet the cheapest garden-view and partial ocean-view rooms are flung across the street, where they feel like a different hotel. Mandatory per-night resort fee $30.

Complimentary activities, including yoga, hula and lei-making classes, guided tidepool tours and introductory surfing and snorkel lessons make it fun.

White egret
HOLGER LEUE/GETTY IMAGES ©

Grand Hyatt Kauai Resort & Spa
Resort $$$

(☎808-742-1234, 888-591-1234; www.grand-hyattkauai.com; 1571 Po'ipu Rd; r from $309; P✳@🛜🏊) Po'ipu's glamour girl is 600-rooms strong and loves to show off, with a soaring lobby, tropical gardens, a huge spa, a world-renowned golf course, oceanfront restaurants and meandering 'river pools.' Rooms are simple yet elegant with tropical wood crown mouldings, marble entryways and baths, and rain showerheads. Adjacent Shipwreck Beach is a natural wonder. Mandatory per-night resort fee $25.

There's plenty to do here, with saltwater lagoons you can kayak around or even scuba dive in, tennis courts, and Camp Hyatt for kids. Guests can learn Hawaiian crafts or watch cultural demonstrations in the hotel atrium or sign up for volunteering with local nonprofit organizations.

Whalers Cove
Condo $$$

(☎808-742-7571, 800-225-2683; www.whalers coveresort.com; 2640 Pu'uholo Rd; 1-/2-bedroom condos from $360/500; 🛜🏊) These luxury condos with private check-in and daily maid service will suit discriminating travellers. Although somewhat impersonal, the units are palatial (1300 sq ft on average), elegantly appointed and immaculate, with outstanding ocean views. Prized koa wood has been used on some doors and furnishings. Mandatory nightly resort fee $15, but no cleaning fee.

Koa Kea Hotel & Resort
Hotel $$$

(☎808-828-8888, 888-898-8958; www.koakea. com; 2251 Po'ipu Rd; r from $369; ✳🛜🏊) This romantic boutique hotel occupies a unique niche in Po'ipu. It's a bold exploration of design instead of the Hawaiiana leitmotif of so many other hotels. With 121 rooms, it's intimate and inwardly focused: the U-shaped building opens onto the beach, leaving many rooms looking across the central pool at each other. Mandatory nightly resort fee ($26) includes valet parking.

Po'ipu Rental Agencies

Ocean Kaua'i Vacation Rental Condos
(☎888-747-2988; www.kauai-vacation-rental-condos.com) Reasonable rates on privately owned condos at Prince Kuhio Resort.

Parrish Collection Kaua'i
(Map p162; ☎808-742-2000, 800-325-5701; www.parrishkauai.com; 3176 Po'ipu Rd, Koloa) Top-rated rental agency for condos and vacation homes not just in Po'ipu, but also on the North Shore and the Westside. Professional staff is friendly and accommodating.

Po'ipu Connection Realty
(☎808-742-2233, 800-742-2260; www.poipuconnection.com; 5488 Koloa Rd, Koloa) A variety of condo rentals at decent rates (mostly at Prince Kuhio Resort), plus personalized service.

Po'ipu Shores
Condo $$$

(☎808-742-7700, 877-367-1912; www.poipu shores.com; 1775 Pe'e Rd; 2-/3-bedroom condos from $450/525; @🛜🏊) Location, location, location. This seemingly ordinary 39-unit condo sidles up to the coast, overlooking lava rock and pounding surf. Although there's no sandy beach, guests can swim in a heated pool. Search online for much lower rates offered by local rental agencies and private owners.

Po'ipu Kapili
Condo $$$

(☎808-742-6449, 800-443-7714; www.poipukapili.com; 2221 Kapili Rd; 1-/2-bedroom condos from $255/385; 🛜🏊) This 60-unit complex features landscaped grounds and spacious condos with lots of hardwood, big plush beds, extra bathrooms, tech electronics and air-con in some bedrooms. With tennis and pickleball courts, BBQ grills and a saltwater pool, the property is walking distance to the beach. One-bedroom units can, however, have iffy views.

Below: Papaya fruit on the tree; **Right:** Papaya for breakfast

(BELOW) RICH REID/GETTY IMAGES ©; (RIGHT) MARC MORITSCH/GETTY IMAGES ©

chefs and *pau hana* (happy hour) drinks in an outdoor beer and wine garden.

Eating

'The better the view, the worse the meal.' Unfortunately this restaurant truism often applies in Po'ipu, where some of the top names rely on ambience to get you through an average dinner – and still makes you pay heavily for it. On the other hand, there is quite a line-up of restaurants here, so if you ignore the hype, you can find the standouts. For the budget-conscious, several restaurants have split-level menus targeting two different price ranges.

Kaua'i Culinary Market   Market $

(☎855-742-9545; www.kukuiula.com; Shops at Kukui'ula, 2829 Ala Kalanikaumaka St; ⏰3:30-6pm Wed; ✈👫) 🖉 An upscale take on the traditional island farmers market features not only a couple dozen local farmers and food vendors, but also free live music, cooking demonstrations by South Shore

Papalani Gelato   Ice Cream $

(☎808-742-2663; www.papalanigelato.com; Po'ipu Shopping Village, 2360 Kiahuna Plantation Dr; scoop $4; ⏰11am-9:30pm; 👫) Deliciously sweet treats are all made on-site. You can't go wrong with classic pistachio, but for local flavor, get a scoop of macnut butter or coconut gelato, or guava, *liliko'i* or lychee sorbet. Second location at the **Anchor Cove Shopping Center** (Map p40; 3416 Rice St) in Lihu'e.

Da Crack   Mexican, American $

(☎808-742-9505; www.dacrack.com; Po'ipu Plaza, 2827 Po'ipu Rd; mains $5-10; ⏰11am-8pm Mon-Sat, to 4pm Sun; 👫) A guilty pleasure, this taco shop (literally, it's a hole in the wall) cooks up tacos, burritos and rice-and-beans bowls overstuffed with batter-fried fish, *carnitas* (braised pork), shredded chicken or chipotle shrimp. Expect to wait.

Kukui'ula Market Supermarket $

(📞808-742-1601; Po'ipu Plaza, 2827 Po'ipu Rd; 🕐8am-8:30pm Mon-Fri, to 6:30pm Sat & Sun) Locally owned grocery store stocking almost everything a vegan, vegetarian or gluten-free DIY eater needs, and it has a sushi bar, too. A juice bar at the back makes smoothies and acai bowls until 4pm on weekdays, 3pm on weekends.

Puka Dog Fast Food $

(📞808-742-6044; www.pukadog.com; Po'ipu Shopping Village, 2360 Kiahuna Plantation Dr; hot dogs $7-8; 🕐10am-8pm; 🖊) Popular with tourists more than with locals, these specialty hot dogs come with a toasty Hawaiian sweet bread bun, a choice of Polish sausage or a veggie dog, a 'secret' sauce and tropical fruit relish (mango and pineapple, yum).

Keoki's Paradise Hawaii Regional Cuisine $$

(📞808-742-7534; www.keokisparadise.com; Po'ipu Shopping Village, 2360 Kiahuna Planta-tion Dr; mains bar $11-20, restaurant $22-35; 🕐restaurant 4:45-9:30pm, bar 11am-10:30pm) Natural woods, tiki torches and water features combine to form a warm jungle-lodge atmosphere. The higher-priced dining room offers grilled meats and seafood, while the Bamboo Bar is all about tropical *pupu* (snacks) and pub grub. Throw in a great selection of draft beers and nightly live music, and Keoki's is a winner.

Brennecke's Beachfront Restaurant & Beach Deli American $$

(📞808-742-7588; www.brenneckes.com; 2100 Ho'one Rd; deli sandwiches $6-10, restaurant mains lunch $11-20, dinner $14-30; 🕐deli 7am-9pm, restaurant 11am-10pm, bar 10am-close; 🖐) Part sports bar, part restaurant, this institution across from Po'ipu Beach Park has served up endless plates of ribs, steak, fresh fish, pasta, burgers and tacos for three decades, along with tropical cocktails and cold brewskis.

The downstairs deli is the only breakfast burrito or club sandwich within range of your beach towel.

Tortilla Republic
Mexican $$

(📞808-742-8884; www.tortillarepublic.com/ hawaii; Shops at Kukui'ula, 2829 Ala Kalanikaumaka St; mains bar $11-21, restaurant $14-32; ⏰restaurant 5:30-9pm Sun-Thu, to 10pm Fri & Sat, bar 8am-1pm Mon-Fri, from 9am Sat & Sun) In a plantation-style building with two levels, you'll find a buzzing margarita bar and taqueria downstairs, and a dining room upstairs that's intriguingly decorated with an onyx bar top, metalwork sculpture and carved wooden doors from Guadalajara. While the food is just as artfully designed, with some new takes on old favorites, portions are awfully small for these prices.

Living Foods Gourmet Market & Café
Market, Cafe $$

(📞808-742-2323; www.shoplivingfoods.com; Shops at Kukui'ula, 2829 Ala Kalanikaumaka St; mains $10-18; ⏰7am-9pm; 🅿🚻) 🍃 High-priced even by island standards, the often organic, gluten-free and/or all-natural groceries sold here include cheeses, meats and imported wines, along with a selection of local produce and artisanal foodstuffs such as Kaua'i-made juices, nuts, honey, salts, coffee and cookies.

Island Insights

Here's a little Po'ipu secret: if you want a front-row sunset table at the iconic Beach House Restaurant, but failed to reserve well in advance, don't worry, there's more than one way to fillet that fish. The bar and lounge has the same great view, serves the dinner menu – and you can just walk in at 5pm!

Josselin's Tapas Bar & Grill
Hawaii Regional Cuisine $$$

(📞808-742-7117; Shops at Kukui'ula, 2829 Ala Kalanikaumaka St; shared plates $11-32; ⏰5-9pm or 10pm) Heading up the restaurants at the Shops at Kukui'ula is this creative take on tapas by revered chef Jean-Marie Josselin. His Asian-influenced food is culinary high art, yet somehow still understated and approachable, with explosions of unexpected flavor combinations that leave you contemplating a second go at duck confit tacos or a deconstructed ahi roll. Reservations strongly recommended. There's always a lively, multigenerational crowd here, yet the low lighting and decor are stylish enough for dates. Table service begins with the sangria cart rolling up – try the lychee flavor – but the creative cocktails are even better.

Roy's Po'ipu Bar & Grill
Hawaii Regional Cuisine $$$

(📞808-742-5000; www.royshawaii.com/ roys-poipu.html; Po'ipu Shopping Village, 2360 Kiahuna Plantation Dr; mains $28-42; ⏰5:30-9:30pm; 🚻) Popular with everyone from tourists to longtime locals, bustling Roy's continues to deliver above-average dishes such as miso-marinated *misoyaki* (butterfish), blackened ahi and pesto-steamed monchong. The prix-fixe menu ($50) comes with an appetizer sample and Roy's signature dark chocolate soufflé for dessert. Set in a shopping mall, it manages not to suffer much for it. Make reservations.

Red Salt
Fusion $$$

(📞808-828-8888; www.koakea.com; Koa Kea Hotel & Resort, 2251 Po'ipu Rd; mains $29-39; ⏰restaurant 6-10pm, lounge 5:30pm-midnight) At this romantic hideaway, fusion dishes such as pan-seared *opah* (moonfish) with king crab and a sake-spiked coconut broth or vanilla bean-seared mahimahi elevate the culinary game. Seafood appetizers, sushi and strong cocktails are served in the svelte lounge, and there's always that root beer float with warm macnut cookies or *liliko'i*-ginger crème brûlée for dessert. Valet parking is complimentary.

Beach House Restaurant

Seafood **$$$**

(📞 808-742-1424; www.the-beach-house.com; 5022 Lawa'i Rd; mains lunch $10-19, dinner $20-48; ⏰ 11am-10pm; 🚻) There are many oceanfront restaurants in Po'ipu, but only one iconic spot for sunset dining and special occasions such as weddings, birthdays and anniversaries. The focus of the Pacific Rim cuisine is fresh fish – island fishers are identified by name on the menu – but sauces are heavy. For sunset dining, reserve a 'first seating' weeks in advance. Vegan and gluten-free menus available.

Merriman's Fish House

Hawaii Regional Cuisine **$$$**

(📞 808-742-8385; www.merrimanshawaii.com; Shops at Kukui'ula, 2829 Ala Kalanikaumaka St; mains bar $11-17, restaurant $24-40; ⏰ bar 11:30am-10pm, restaurant 5-9pm) 🌿 Upstairs is a breezy surf-and-turf dining room, where 90% of all menu ingredients are locally caught or grown, and the fusion cuisine is designed by a famous chef. The sunset views are excellent from the plantation house's upper lanai, so book ahead to secure a spot. Downstairs is a family-friendly spot for burgers and pizza (happy hour 3:30pm to 5:30pm daily).

Plantation Gardens Restaurant & Bar

Hawaii Regional Cuisine **$$$**

(📞 808-742-2121; www.pgrestaurant.com; Kiahuna Plantation, 2253 Po'ipu

Luxe Po'ipu

- Koa Kea Hotel & Resort (p181)
- Anara Spa (p178)
- Allerton Garden (p172) sunset tour
- Beach House Restaurant (p185) sunset dinner
- Po'ipu Bay Golf Course (p177)

Rd; mains $24-37; ⏰ restaurant 5:30-9pm, bar from 5pm) Set in a historic plantation house, this longstanding favorite is known more for its ambience than its food. The open-air setting in tropical gardens is lovely, particularly when illuminated by tiki torches. The mostly seafood menu is mercifully concise and features local ingredients. However, the taste just isn't there with many dishes. Book ahead.

Living Foods Gourmet Market & Café

KICKA WITTE/GETTY IMAGES ©

Drinking & Entertainment

Seaview Terrace   Bar
(📞808-240-6456; www.kauai.hyatt.com; Grand Hyatt Kauai Resort & Spa, 1571 Po'ipu Rd; 🕐5:30-11am & 4:30-10pm) Don't miss Po'ipu's grandest and most memorable ocean view. In the morning, this stepped terrace is an espresso and pastry cafe. Later in the day, a torch-lighting ceremony announces sunset, with live music and occasionally hula dancing before 9pm. Show up early for a prime viewing table (no reservations). Head directly through the hotel lobby and atrium toward the sea.

'Auli'i Luau   Luau
(📞808-634-1499; www.auliiluau.com; Sheraton Kaua'i Resort, 2440 Ho'onani Rd; adult/child 3-12yr/youth 13-17yr from $101/49/74; 🕐6pm Mon & Thu Mar-Sep, 5:30pm Mon & Thu Oct-Feb) The Sheraton's luau banks on its oceanfront setting. The Polynesian revue and dinner buffet are both pretty standard. Beware: the jokester emcee demands audience participation. When it rains, the luau happens in a hotel ballroom – not fun.

Havaiki Nui Luau   Luau
(📞808-240-6456; www.grandhyattkauailuau. com; Grand Hyatt Kaua'i Resort & Spa, 1571 Po'ipu Rd; adult/child/teen $109/70/97; 🕐5:15-8pm Thu & Sun) The Havaiki Nui Luau is a well-oiled pan-Polynesian production befitting the Grand Hyatt's beachfront setting. But the price is too steep, especially when the show takes place indoors instead of outside in the resort's gardens.

🔒 Shopping

Shops at Kukui'ula   Mall
(📞808-742-9545; www.kukuiula.com; 2829 Ala Kalanikaumaka St; 🕐10am-9pm) This upscale outdoor shopping mall conveniently located at the Po'ipu roundabout offers more than 30 restaurants and designer shops, including fine-art galleries such as cutting-edge Galerie 103 and aFeinberg Gallery from Hanalei, a few high-end jewelry stores and some only-in-Hawaii fashion boutiques such as Mahina and Blue Ginger.

Po'ipu Shopping Village   Mall
(📞808-742-2831; www.poipushoppingvillage. com; 2360 Kiahuna Plantation Dr; 🕐most shops

Grand Hyatt Kauai Resort & Spa (p181)

DENNIS FRATES/ALAMY ©

9am-9pm Mon-Sat, 10am-7pm Sun) A small-scale outdoor mall sports affordable, vacation-centric shops (think aloha wear, T-shirts, swimwear and souvenirs) such as the beachy boutique Sand People, Honolua Surf Co and Honolua Wahine for surf-style fashions, and By the Sea for a huge variety of rubbah slippah (flip-flops).

Malie Organics Boutique
Beauty, Gifts

(📞808-332-6220, 866-767-5727; www.malie.com; Shops at Kukui'ula, 2829 Ala Kalanikaumaka St; ⏰10am-9pm) 🍃 Kukui nuts, mangoes, coconuts and vanilla are just a few of the island plant 'essences' utilized by this homegrown bath and body products company. It stocks Kaua'i's high-end resorts with its sprays, soaps, body creams and candles, but this is its only retail outlet.

Allerton Garden Gift Shop
Books, Gifts

(Map p162; 📞808-742-2623; www.ntbg.org; 4425 Lawa'i Rd; ⏰8:30am-5pm) Stocks an excellent array of books (especially nature and Hawaiiana titles), as well as quality nature-themed gifts and souvenirs.

🛈 Information

Poipu Beach Resort Association (📞808-742-7444, 888-744-0888; www.poipubeach.org; Shops at Kukui'ula, 2829 Ala Kalanikaumaka St; ⏰9:30am-2pm Mon-Fri) Go online for general visitor information about Po'ipu and the entire South Shore, including beaches, activities, accommodations, dining, shopping and events.

🛈 Getting There & Around

You'll need a car (or scooter) to go anywhere here besides the beach. You can walk along the main roads and beaches, but the vibe is more suburbia than surf town. Navigating is easy, with just two main roads: Po'ipu Rd (along eastern Po'ipu) and Lawa'i Rd (along western Po'ipu). Parking is free.

The Kaua'i Bus (p58) runs through Koloa and into Po'ipu, stopping along Po'ipu Rd at Ho'owili Rd (the turnoff to Po'ipu Beach Park) and also by the Hyatt. It's an option to get here from other towns, but a limited in-town mode of transportation.

Outfitters Kauai (📞808-742-9667, 888-742-9887; www.outfitterskauai.com; Po'ipu Plaza, 2827a Po'ipu Rd; bicycle rental per day $25-45; ⏰9am-4:30pm) Perhaps because of the lack of bike lanes, cyclists are scarce in Po'ipu. However, you can rent bikes here, including road, mountain and hybrid models. Rates include a helmet and lock. Phone reservations recommended.

Kalaheo

Kalaheo is a one-stoplight cluster of eateries and little else. But along the back roads, this neighborly town offers peaceful accommodations away from the tourist crowd. If you plan to hike at Waimea Canyon and Koke'e State Parks, but also want easy access to Po'ipu beaches, Kalaheo's central location is ideal.

The town's post office and handful of restaurants are centered on the intersection of Kaumuali'i Hwy and Papalina Rd.

🔘 Sights

Kaua'i Coffee Company
Farm

(📞808-335-0813, 800-545-8605; www.kauaicoffee.com; 870 Halewili Rd; ⏰9am-5:30pm Jun-Aug, to 5pm Sep-May; guided tours usually 10am, noon, 2pm & 4pm daily) 🍃 A short drive east of town on Hwy 540, the island's biggest coffee estate is planted with more than 4 million trees, producing about 60% of the state's entire crop. Around the back of the plantation store and visitor center, you can glimpse the roasting process, peruse historical photographs and sample estate-grown coffees including a robust peaberry and flavored chocolate macadamia nut. Afterward, take a quick self-guided walking tour of the farm, or join a free guided tour (check current schedules online).

The rolling seaside plantation, where coffee berries are cooled by tradewinds, is 100% powered by renewable energy.

Hanapepe Valley Lookout
Viewpoint

(Map p162) Popping up shortly after mile marker 14, this lookout offers a view

Kalaheo

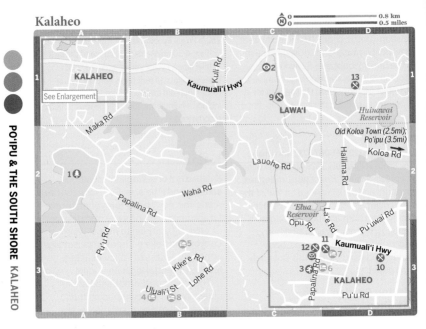

Kalaheo

◎ Sights
1 Kukuiolono Park A2
2 Lawa'i International Center C1

✪ Activities, Courses & Tours
3 Kalaheo Yoga C3
  Kukuiolono Golf Course .... (see 1)

🛏 Sleeping
4 Hale Ikena Nui B3
5 Hale O Nanakai B3
6 Kalaheo Inn D3

7 Kalaheo Neighborhood Center D3
8 Sea Kauai B3

✖ Eating
9 Fresh Shave C1
10 Kalaheo Café & Coffee Co D3
11 Kalaheo Farmers Market D3
12 Kauai Kookie Bakery & Kitchen C3
13 Lanakila Kitchen D1

🛍 Shopping
  Collection at the Cafe .... (see 10)

deep into Hanapepe Valley, where the red-clay cliffs are topped by wild green sugarcane. This sight is but a teaser for the dramatic vistas awaiting at Waimea Canyon.

While the sugar business has faded, Hanapepe Valley remains an agriculture stronghold with grazing cattle and local farmers growing taro. Look *makai* (seaward) across the highway and you'll see the region's cash crop: coffee.

Kukuiolono Park   Park

(854 Pu'u Rd; ⏲6:30am-6:30pm) Unless you're staying in Kalaheo, you'll miss this little park with a nine-hole **golf course**, modest **Japanese garden**, sweeping views and grassy grounds for strolling or running. Kukuiolono means 'light of Lono,' referring to the torches that Hawaiians once placed on this hill to help guide canoes safely to the shore.

To get here, turn left onto Papalina Rd from Kaumuali'i Hwy (heading west).

🏃 Activities

Kukuiolono Golf Course   Golf
(☎808-332-9151; Kukuiolono Park, 854 Pu'u
Rd; green fees $9; ⏰6:30am-6:30pm, last tee
time 4:30pm) There are only nine holes,
but they come with spectacular ocean
and valley views and zero attitude.

The course was built in 1927 by Walter
McBryde (think McBryde Garden) and
later donated to the public. McBryde
clearly loved golf: he's buried by the
eighth hole. The driving range and cart
and club rentals are about as cheap as
the green fees.

Kalaheo Yoga   Yoga
(☎808-652-3216; www.kalaheoyoga.com;
4427 Papalina Rd; per class $18, 3-/4-class pass
$48/62) A bright, harmonious yoga space
one block from the highway teaches a few
classes daily, including gentle, restorative
and vinyasa flow. Pre-register for classes
online.

🛏 Sleeping

Hale Ikena Nui   Inn $
(☎808-332-9005, 800-550-0778; www.kauai-
vacationhome.com; 3957 Uluali'i St; d $75-95;
📶) Located at the end of a cul-de-sac,
this spacious in-law apartment (1000 sq
ft) includes a living area with a queen-
sized sofa bed, a full kitchen and washer-
dryer. There's a three-night minimum
stay. The B&B room is less private, but
has its own bathroom and rates include
breakfast.

Sea Kauai   Apartment $
(☎808-332-9744; www.seakauai.com; 3913
Uluali'i St; d $75-95; 📶) Choose between two
comfortable ground-floor units with Japanese *shōji* (rice-paper sliding doors) and
sunset ocean views. The one-bedroom
suite has a full kitchen, separate living and
dining areas and beds for four (one king
and two twins). The compact studio, with
a kitchenette, is a steal. Free beach gear to
borrow. Three-night minimum stay.

Kukuiolono Park

ROSANNE TACKABERRY/ALAMY ©

Kalaheo Inn
Inn **$**

(☎808-332-6023; www.kalaheoinn.com; 4444 Papalina Rd; r & ste $88-119; 🛜) Like most plain Janes, this one is dependable, low-key and quiet (except it has thin walls). Resembling a typical motel, Kalaheo Inn best suits budget travelers looking for kitchenette studios. For couples and families, the one- and two-bedroom suites are decent, but you could do better. All have basic furnishings, TV/DVD combos and access to BBQ grills and beach gear.

Hale O Nanakai
B&B **$$**

(☎808-652-8071; www.nanakai.com; 3726 Nanakai Pl; s $75-85, d $115-175, most incl breakfast; 🛜) A sky-blue family house turned five-room B&B has plush wall-to-wall carpeting, beamed ceilings and spectacular sea views. Rooms range in size, yet all but the cheapest digs have similar amenities including HDTVs and queen- or full-sized beds with high-end mattresses. The tiny Maile Room has but a single bed for the wandering nomad. Cleaning fee $40 to $45.

🍴 Eating

Kalaheo Farmers Market
Market **$**

(www.kauai.gov; Kalaheo Neighborhood Center, 4480 Papalina Rd; ⏲3-5pm Tue; 👪) 🗲 Just a straightforward, small-town produce market. It's one of the county-wide Sunshine Markets, so no shopping allowed before the whistle blows.

Lanakila Kitchen
Cafe **$**

(☎808-332-5500; www.lanakilapacific.org/services/lanakila-kitchen; 2-3687 Kaumuali'i Hwy; meals $8-10; ⏲6:30am-2:30pm Mon-Fri) A local's haunt, this tiny cafe with a cause serves a steam table of meat and fish dishes, which you can pick and mix for plate lunches, such as chicken *laulau*, teriyaki fish, tofu stir-fry and more. It also does *ono* fish burgers, ahi *poke* bowls, soups, salads and pies. Proceeds benefit an employment program for people with disabilities.

Kauai Kookie Bakery & Kitchen
Cafe, Bakery **$**

(☎808-332-0821; 2-2436 Kaumuali'i Hwy; mains $5-13; ⏲5:30am-4pm) Stop at this roadside diner for simple but filling breakfasts, *bentō*, and Asian and island-style fusion dishes served as plate lunches to an almost exclusively local customer base. It does an authentic oxtail soup, too. For a bigger selection of the famous cookies, visit the Hanapepe factory store (p212).

Kalaheo Café & Coffee Co
Cafe, Breakfast **$$**

(☎808-332-5858; www.kalaheo.com; 2-2560 Kaumuali'i Hwy; mains breakfast & lunch $5-15, dinner $16-28; ⏲6:30am-2:30pm Mon-Sat, to 2pm Sun, 5-8:30pm Tue-Thu, to 9pm Fri & Sat) Adored by

Ni'ihau shell lei
ALVIS UPITIS/ALAMY ©

locals and visitors alike, this always-busy cafe has a spacious dining room and brews strong coffee. Order egg scrambles with grilled cornbread for breakfast, or a deli sandwich (*kalua* pork with guava BBQ sauce) and a salad of local greens for lunch. Weightier dinner plates include hoisin-glazed fresh catch and salt-rubbed ribs.

🔒 Shopping

Collection at the Cafe
Arts, Gifts

(📞808-332-5858; 2-2560 Kaumuali'i Hwy; 🕐9am-3pm) An airy walk-though gallery displaying ever-changing works by local artists, including oil paintings, watercolors and prints, hand-crafted shell jewelry and more.

Waimea Canyon & the Westside

The Westside could well be called the Old West–side. It is a surprising marriage of the Old West and a tropical island, like some new genre of film. With false-front buildings lining its main street, Hanapepe looks like it's ready for a shoot-out. Waimea is a frontier town, the doorway to the Grand Canyon (of the Pacific). A dash of *paniolo* (Hawaiian cowboy) peppers the culture, in which hunting is popular. There's even a saloon.

This is a land of deep valleys, big sky and relatively few overnight tourists. At the same time, those valleys, full of postcard waterfalls, lead to a glittering Pacific, where you can hop aboard a catamaran or raft.

And there are some spectacular beaches, from Polihale to the lost paradise of Nu'alolo Kai. For the hiker-poet, this impossible mélange provides a bottomless source of inspiration, as well as some perplexity. After all, what do you call a surfer-cowboy?

Waimea Canyon State Park (p224)

Waimea Canyon & the Westside Highlights

Polihale State Park

The vast grandeur here will even stop the kids talking. Reached via a bumpy 5-mile-long road, which might not even be passable after recent rains (or if your car-rental contract prohibits it), this feels like the edge of the planet. For ancient Hawaiians, Polihale (p223) represented the jumping-off point for souls leaving for the underworld. Sit. Stay. Ponder eternity.

Waimea Canyon

It's so striking, you may well wonder if this painterly vision is real or not. Here, layer upon layer of colorful volcanic rock strata is laid bare for your inspection, gashed open by the Waimea River. Whether you simply stand on the canyon rim and look down, or hike into its wild depths, the 'Grand Canyon of the Pacific' (p224) is an unmissable place.

SAMI SARKIS/GETTY IMAGES ©

Na Pali Coast Boat Tour

3

Zipping into sea caves, bouncing over waves and snorkeling remote reefs – aah! Leaving from Port Allen Harbor (p198) or Waimea (p212), cruises along the Na Pali Coast (p286) are more thrilling when you opt for a raft instead of a catamaran ride. In summer sign up for a landing at remote Nuʻalolo Kai, where you can almost hear Mother Nature and ancient Hawaiians talking at once.

4

Art Night in Hanapepe

Sleepy Hanapepe awakens every Friday for Art Night (p207), when the town's pint-sized main street fills with local artists, food vendors and crowds of visitors and locals who come to shop, eat and mingle. Get a custom-made aloha shirt, peruse watercolor paintings and photographs of the Westside's natural beauty, and take a stroll over the swinging bridge.

5

Kokeʻe State Park

It's entirely another world up here (p229), thousands of feet high atop the Na Pali cliffs and in the rain shadow of Mt Waiʻaleʻale. Stop at roadside lookouts to peek over into remote valleys, and then lace up your hiking boots and hit the trails. For nature lovers who don't mind a bit of a slog, the Alakaʻi Swamp Trail (p232), with its rare birds and dwarfed trees, awaits.

Waimea Canyon & the Westside Itineraries

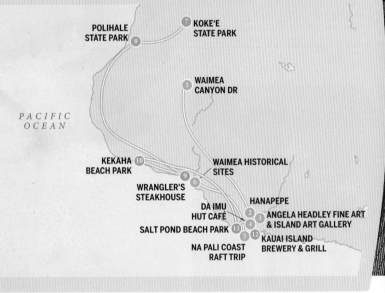

KOKE'E STATE PARK

POLIHALE STATE PARK

WAIMEA CANYON DR

PACIFIC OCEAN

KEKAHA BEACH PARK

WAIMEA HISTORICAL SITES

WRANGLER'S STEAKHOUSE

HANAPEPE

DA IMU HUT CAFÉ

ANGELA HEADLEY FINE ART & ISLAND ART GALLERY

SALT POND BEACH PARK

KAUAI ISLAND BREWERY & GRILL

NA PALI COAST RAFT TRIP

2 DAYS

57 MILES

DAYS ONE & TWO

The ❶ **Waimea Canyon Dr** will be the drive of your trip. Follow Hwy 550 all the way to Pu'u o Kila in Koke'e State Park, stopping at the many stunning lookouts along the way. Pause at the Koke'e Museum (where you can also plan a hike for day three).

Next, head to ❷ **Hanapepe**. Stroll the main street here for souvenirs, objets d'art, and a few shots of the 'Old West,' ideally during Friday's Art Night. Hanapepe's ❸ **Angela Headley Fine Art & Island Art Gallery** has pulled together some of the brightest artists at work on Kaua'i today. Later, rub elbows with the locals at strip-mall joint ❹ **Da Imu Hut Café**.

The morning of day two brings the chance to head out on a ❺ **Na Pali Coast raft trip** to see the great Na Pali from the sea – a very different experience than by land. If you're interested in visiting Nu'alolo Kai, arrange a trip with Kaua'i Sea Tours. If you want to rock and roll with your waves, then join the Na Pali Riders.

End the day with a visit to ❻ **Waimea's historical sites**. Where else can you visit a Russian fort, Captain Cook's statue and an ancient Hawaiian aqueduct, all in an hour? Be sure to stop by the West Kaua'i Technology & Visitor Center first to check out its historical and cultural exhibits.

60 MILES

DAYS THREE, FOUR & FIVE

On day three, choose a few trails, or maybe just one, and spend the day enjoying one of nature's great works of art on a ➐ **Koke'e hiking adventure**. If you're in good shape, opt for the descent into the otherworldly Alaka'i Swamp, ending at Kilohana Lookout. Day four provides some well-deserved reflection time on a ➑ **Polihale Picnic**. Contemplate eternity beneath the cliffs at Polihale Beach. No answers? Have a few more deli eats from Waimea's Ishihara Market. After a few days of Westside adventures, you deserve a thick steak, not to mention a saloon, so pop into ➒ **Wrangler's Steakhouse**.

A ➓ **sunset at Kekaha Beach Park** is as good as the ol' yellow orb gets on the Westside, with great views to Ni'ihau, its satellite isle, and Lehua, so don't miss it.

If the kids need a break from the action, spend day five at ⓫ **Salt Pond Beach Park**, a mellow, family-style beach replete with lifeguard and facilities. Make sure you pack a snorkel, and if you're really ambitious, a BBQ picnic. Later, head to ⓬ **Kauai Island Brewery & Grill**, the Westside's own brewery – a laid-back spot, with plenty of pub grub.

Swinging Bridge (p205), Hanapepe
ANN CECIL/GETTY IMAGES ©

Discover Waimea Canyon & the Westside

Port Allen & Around

The Hanapepe River, which empties into its namesake bay, separates two communities: 'Ele'ele (to the south and east) and Hanapepe (to the north and west). 'Ele'ele contains Port Allen Harbor, the island's second-largest port. Once known as 'Ele'ele Landing, it's used primarily for importing fuel, as the dock for the Pacific Missile Range Facility and, most importantly for visitors, as the departure point for most Na Pali Coast tours. The nearby **Port Allen Marina Center** (Map p204) is where you'll find tour company offices. The small Port Allen Airport faces the harbor from across the bay, but is adjacent to Hanapepe, not 'Ele'ele.

The main reason to visit 'Ele'ele is to access the harbor. If you have some time to kill before or after your tour, there are a few ways to spend it.

🏖 Beaches

Glass Beach   Beach
(Map p200) Trash as art – many a visitor has pored through the colorful well-worn remnants of glass spread along the shoreline here. Glass 'pebbles,' along with abandoned metals (some with newfound patina, some not so much), are washed up from an old dumpsite nearby.

To get to the little cove, take Aka'ula St (the last left before entering the Port Allen wharf) past the fuel storage tanks, then curve to the right down a bumpy dirt road about 100yd to the beach.

🕐 Tours

If you're considering a Westside boat-trip departure, look at Waimea tour operators as well. Also be sure to check online for deals.

The following companies offer very similar Na Pali snorkeling, sunset and dinner tours. Differentiators are landings at Nu'alolo Kai and snorkeling trips to Ni'ihau. Be aware that motion sickness is common, especially on Zodiac rafts, which

Glass Beach
DENNIS FRATES/GETTY IMAGES ©

Detour:
Nu'alolo Kai: the Last Paradise?

Kaua'i is often associated with paradise, and there is no better place to contemplate this connection than the remains of a Hawaiian settlement in a remote Na Pali valley, accessed only by sea. Nu'alolo Kai is perhaps the ultimate end-of-the-Earth location, its beach trapped between two soaring cliffs, framing an empty ocean that goes on for thousands of miles. The site is blessed by a fringing reef that is teeming with fish and shellfish. It was once linked by a precarious cliffside path to Nu'alolo 'Aina, a terraced valley whose fertile soil was planted with taro, and whose walls held burial caves.

This isolated paradise was inhabited by about 100 people for 600 years, until 1919. They lived in thatched pole houses, commuting between reef and fields, completely self-sufficient. Men did most of the fishing, while women and children harvested seaweed and shellfish. They weren't entirely cut off from the rest of the island, however. There was once a trail here from Koke'e (now washed away), and their beach was the safest stop for Native Hawaiians canoeing between Hanalei and Waimea. Today all that is left is the stone foundations of various structures, but it is enough to get you thinking.

To help preserve Nu'alolo Kai, only three companies currently have landing rights: Kaua'i Sea Tours and Captain Andy's Sailing Adventures provide guided tours of the archaeological site, while Waimea-based Na Pali Explorer (p215) only lands on the beach. Weather usually restricts boat landings to between mid-April and late October only.

offer little protection from the waves and sun.

Captain Andy's
Sailing Adventures   Boat Tour
(Map p204; ☎808-335-6833, 800-535-0830; www.napali.com; Port Allen Marina Center, 4353 Waialo Rd; tours adult/child from 2-12yr $119/89) This outfit offers a high-end sailing experience aboard the *Southern Star* – its 65ft flagship luxury catamaran – and a more rugged, adrenaline-addled Zodiac raft tour of the sea caves and secluded beaches of the Na Pali Coast. Six-hour raft trips include a beach landing at Nu'alolo Kai (weather permitting, April to October only), along with snorkeling and easy hiking.

Sunset dinner cruises add an awesome sky to the coast's bewitching cliffs, as well as a chef-prepared meal washed down with a 'sneaky tiki.'

Kaua'i Sea Tours   Boat Tour
(Map p204; ☎808-826-7254, 800-733-7997; www.kauaiseatours.com; Port Allen Marina Center, 4353 Waialo Rd; tours adult/child under 13yr/youth 13-17yr from $115/75/105) Take a seat on the 60ft catamaran *Lucky Lady* for a snorkel or sunset dinner cruise, or clamber aboard a rigid-hull inflatable raft for a more adventurous Na Pali trip. Six-hour raft tours add a beach landing and a guided walking tour of Nu'alolo Kai (weather permitting, between April and October only), along with sea cave and waterfall explorations.

Holo Holo Charters   Boat Tour
(Map p204; ☎808-335-0815, 800-848-6130; www.holoholocharters.com; Port Allen Marina Center, 4353 Waialo Rd; tours adult/child 5-12yr from $115/99) Holo Holo's 50ft sailing catamaran and rigid-hull inflatable rafts happily do Na Pali snorkeling tours and sunset sails that include food and

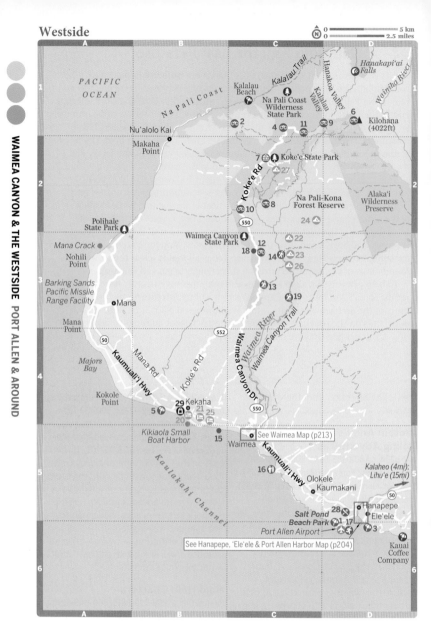

WAIMEA CANYON & THE WESTSIDE PORT ALLEN & AROUND

drinks. The power cat takes you on a longer, 3½-hour sunset tour serving substantial appetizers and cocktails, or the marathon seven-hour Ni'ihau and

Na Pali Coast snorkeling combo that includes continental breakfast and a buffet lunch.

Westside

Blue Dolphin Charters Boat Tour
(Map p204; ☎808-335-5553; www.bluedol-phinkauai.com; Port Allen Marina Center, 4353 Waialo Rd; tours adult/child 5-11yr/youth 12-17yr from $117/90/106) Sailing 65ft catamarans, this outfit offers a standard array of tours, including a seven-hour Na Pali and Ni'ihau snorkel trip and a four-hour sunset dinner cruise. Uniquely, Blue Dolphin Charters will take you on a one-tank dive – even if it's your first time scuba diving – and the Zodiac rafts are equipped with hydrophones for listening underwater to whales in winter.

Inquire about the sportfishing charters available.

Catamaran Kahanu Boat Tour
(Map p204; ☎808-645-6176, 888-213-7711; www.catamarankahanu.com; Port Allen Marina Center, 4353 Waialo Rd; tours adult/child from $79/60) This small-group catamaran affords a more personal experience, whether you take a Na Pali snorkel trip or a sunset dinner or winter whale-watching cruise. The superfriendly captain and his crew talk story about Hawaiian culture and marine traditions

on your way out to sea. You'll find big discounts for online bookings.

✗ Eating & Drinking

Da Imu Hut Café Cafe $
(Map p204; ☎808-335-0200; 'Ele'ele Shopping Center, 4469 Waialo Rd; meals $7-11; ⊙10am-1:30pm & 5-8pm Mon-Fri) Try specials such as the teriyaki fried chicken, traditional-style *kalua* pig or any of the Hawaiian plates (especially the fried saimin), which change daily. If you don't want to intrude on the mostly local vibe, meals are also great to order in advance and take out for a picnic.

Kauai Ramen Asian $
(Map p204; ☎808-335-9888; 'Ele'ele Shopping Center, 4469 Waialo Rd; mains $7-11; ⊙11am-10pm; 👪) A hot bowl of spicy seafood ramen with grilled *gyoza* (pork dumplings) and fried rice on the side might just be what your tummy needs after being rollicked by the waves on a Na Pali Coast boat tour. The bargain-priced menu is nominally Japanese, but with Chinese and local island-style dishes rolled in.

A Soiled Shirt

The well-known dirt shirt originated on Kaua'i back in the 1990s, after Hurricane Iniki covered the island with its trademark red soil. As the legend goes, a stack of white Ts was stained in the process...and the dirt shirt was born. The rich red color is essentially rusted volcanic rock, with the redness coming from iron oxide. Among the Hawaiian Islands, only Kaua'i features such plentiful red dirt, thanks to five million years of erosion.

Now minds differ on who actually discovered the dirt shirt, but more importantly (for the shopper) there is only now one factory outlet on the island. The Original Red Dirt Shirt has an unmissable red store in 'Ele'ele. It has also expanded to other islands and to the US mainland, cleverly using the red dirt of Arizona and Utah.

When it's new, be sure to wash your dirt shirt separately, at least the first few times. Manufacturers now claim that the dye holds fast, but in the past one dirt shirt thrown in the laundry had the surprising ability to replicate.

Grinds Café   Diner $$

(Map p204; ☏808-335-6027; www.grindscafe. net; 'Ele'ele Shopping Center, 4469 Waialo Rd; mains $8-20; ⏱5:30am-9pm Fri-Mon, 6am-3pm Tue-Thu) This family restaurant in a barn-like building is good for a hearty meal with the locals. It's strong on sandwiches, salads and specialty pizzas, and big breakfasts are served all day. Dinners aren't particularly cheap, however.

Kauai Island Brewery & Grill   Brewery

(Map p204; ☏808-335-0006; www.kauaiisland brewing.com; 4350 Waialo Rd; ⏱11am-9:30pm) The founder of the once beloved, now defunct brewery in Waimea is still brewing in Port Allen. Sample the hoppy, high-alcohol IPAs, the lauded Pakala Porter, South Pacific Brown or light liliko'i-infused ale. Drinks and decent pub grub are discounted during happy hour (3:30pm to 5:30pm daily).

Port Allen Sunset Grill & Bar   Bar

(Map p204; ☏808-335-3188; www.portallen sunsetgrillandbar.com; Port Allen Marina Center, 4353 Waialo Rd; ⏱11am-10pm) This is the place to hang out while you are waiting for your tour to start or if you want to grab a bite afterwards. Located at the water end of the Port Allen Marina Center, it has a small bar and covered outdoor seating area. Popular bar-food picks include the macnut-crusted calamari steak.

🔒 Shopping

Kauai Chocolate Company   Food

(Map p204; ☏808-335-0448; www.kauaichoco-late.us; Port Allen Marina Center, 4341 Waialo Rd; ⏱10am-6pm Mon-Fri, 11am-5pm Sat, noon-3pm Sun) Sample the fudge and truffles with creamy ganaches, mousses and delicate creams of papaya, liliko'i, coconut, guava, Kaua'i coffee or sugarcane. The chocolate 'opihi (limpet) is the biggest seller, followed by handmade chocolate bars chock full of macnuts.

Original Red Dirt Shirt   Clothing

(Map p204; ☏800-717-3478; www.dirtshirt.com; 4350 Waialo Rd; ⏱8am-6pm) With punny slogans such as 'Older than Dirt' and 'Life's Short, Play Dirty,' these shamefully touristy T-shirts can be useful if you're planning on hiking, since most of Kaua'i's dirt wants to destroy your clothing and dye your shoes permanently red.

Information

Hanapepe

Hanapepe calls itself 'Kaua'i's Biggest Little Town,' and that's not just advertising. This is the funkiest, artiest town on the island, its Old West architecture lending it a unique vibe. Lining a single bend of the highway, the main street is chock-full of galleries, crafts shops and restaurants, yet for all its tourist appeal Hanapepe manages to be local to the core and brims with liberal personality. Of the town's 69 buildings, 43 are listed on state and national registers, many with placards describing their history. A walking tour map ($2), available at most stores in town, ties it all together. Don't miss a bouncy trip over the Swinging Bridge, which crosses the Hanapepe River. Be aware that some establishments close by 2pm or 3pm on most weekdays, and may not be open at all on weekends. The notable exception is Friday's Art Night (p207), the very best time to visit.

History

Hanapepe was not a plantation town, but was built by entrepreneurial immigrants, largely from Asia. The architectural style of false fronts and porches came from them, as it did in the Old West. Many who retired from the sugar plantations or disliked their working conditions came here to begin small farms or businesses. This included labor union organizers in the early 1900s who were not allowed to reside at plantation camps. In 1924 a pitched battle between Filipino strikers and police, known as the Hanapepe Massacre, left 20 dead.

Hanapepe was the island's commercial center until overtaken by Lihu'e in the 1930s. It then morphed into a military R&R town. After a period of decline, artists began settling in, and the town reinvented itself once again, propelled by an activist spirit that seems to be rooted in the local soil.

Banana Patch Studio (p211)

/GETTY IMAGES ©

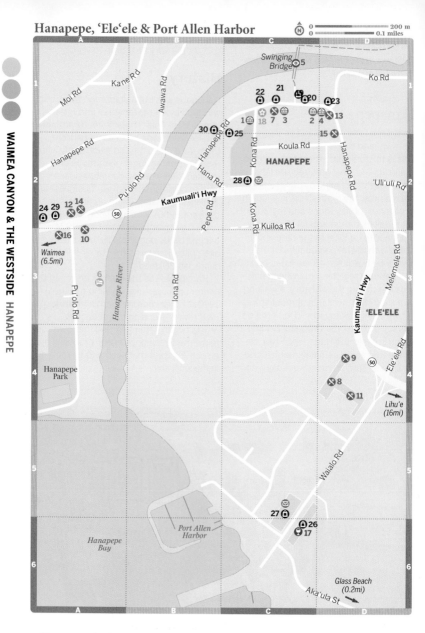

Hanapepe also has its own cinematic history: it doubled as the Australian outback in the TV miniseries *The Thorn Birds* (1983), the Filipino Olongapo City in the movie *Flight of the Intruder* (1991) and as a model for the Hawaiian town in Disney's animated movie *Lilo and Stitch* (2002).

Hanapepe, 'Ele'ele & Port Allen Harbor

🏊 Beaches

Salt Pond Beach Park   Beach
(Map p200; 👪) Named for its saltwater flats, where seawater is still drained and harvested for reddish-pink sodium crystals, this crescent-shaped beach is great for lounging. With a shallow (but not too shallow) swimming area accessible from the sand and sheltered by a rock reef, it's popular with local families. Full facilities include BBQ grills, outdoor showers, restrooms, lifeguards and camping.

Turn *makai* (seaward) onto Lele Rd, off the Kuhio Hwy just west of Hanapepe, then hang a right on Lokokai Rd.

Stronger swimmers and snorkelers may venture through the narrow keyhole in the reef and swim further west where the water clarifies and fish gather along a rugged coast defined by lava jagged cliffs. But beware of ocean conditions, because currents and tides can shift in a blink. Check with the lifeguards before venturing out.

◎ Sights

The best sights in Hanapepe are the galleries, although their owners would undoubtedly prefer that you think of them as stores. For Kaua'i, this is a unique concentration of artists, so if you're looking to purchase some art, this is the place to do it.

Swinging Bridge   Landmark
(Map p204) Built in 1911 and rebuilt after the 1992 hurricane, this narrow wood and cable suspension bridge spans the Hanapepe River just before it snakes inland between stark red-earth cliffs. It does swing and moan a bit in the wind. It's tucked behind the Aloha Spice Company. No diving!

Angela Headley Fine Art & Island Art Gallery   Gallery
(Map p204; 📞808-335-0591; www.islandart kauai.com; 3876 Hanapepe Rd; ◷11am-5pm Mon-Thu & Sat, 11am-5pm & 6-9pm Fri) Make this your first stop in Hanapepe for

The Hanapepe Massacre?

On September 9, 1924, a surprisingly little-known chapter in Hawaii's (and the USA's) history unfolded in Hanapepe.

That year a sugar workers' strike spread to Kaua'i. Strikers were demanding a decent minimum wage, an eight-hour workday and equal pay between men and women. Filipino workers had their own particular grievances. They were the last group of laborers to arrive in Hawaii, and were generally given the worst housing and lowest-paying jobs. More than half weren't even considered residents.

On Kaua'i 575 Filipino workers joined the strike and set up a headquarters in Hanapepe. After six weeks of little progress, the frustrated strikers seized two Filipinos who had not joined the strike, and held them in a schoolhouse. Kaua'i deputy sheriff William Crowell arrived with 40 troops, including many trained sharpshooters, whom he positioned on a nearby hill. Crowell went in with three deputies and demanded that the strikers turn over their captives, which they did. But a crowd also followed Crowell from the schoolhouse, waving their cane knives in the air. It is not clear what happened next – whether Crowell and his men were attacked, or whether the sharpshooters opened fire prematurely – but in the ensuing melee, 16 strikers were gunned down and four deputies were stabbed to death. Crowell was injured, but survived. There was little public outcry and the Hanapepe Massacre disappeared into the history books. Today no one knows where the strikers are buried.

contemporary Hawaiian art: reverse acrylic paintings and giclée prints on wood and metal that are luminous blends of color. It's a somewhat more adventurous gallery than the rest, but it also sells a few baubles, bracelets and foodstuffs.

Amy-Lauren's Gallery
Gallery

(Map p204; ☎808-335-2827; www.amylaurens gallery.com; 4545 Kona Rd; ☺11am-5pm Mon-Thu, to 9pm Fri, noon-5pm Sat) Here's a chance to buy (or at least gaze upon) an original instead of a giclée print. This boutique gallery invites passersby inside with vibrantly colored oil paintings, photography and mixed media.

Art of Marbling & Robert Bader Wood Sculpture
Gallery

(Map p204; ☎808-335-3553; 3890 Hanapepe Rd; ☺10am-5pm Sat-Thu, to 9pm Fri) Becky J Wold's original marbled silk scarves and

sarongs hang from bamboo poles alongside her husband's wooden bowls and sculpture, making this a unique gallery experience.

Arius Hopman Gallery
Gallery

(Map p204; ☎808-335-0227; www.hopmanart. com; 3840c Hanapepe Rd; ☺10am-2pm Mon-Thu, 10am-2pm & 6-9pm Fri) Art photography and plein-air watercolors spotlight Kaua'i's tropical landscapes, flora and fauna, from mango and banana trees to sunrise breaking over the Na Pali Coast.

Dawn Traina Gallery
Gallery

(Map p204; ☎808-335-3993; 3840b Hanapepe Rd; ☺6-9pm Fri or by appointment) Traditional Hawaiian themes come to life in many different media, including oil paintings, limited-edition giclées and scratchboards (hard-panel carving reminiscent of scrimshaw).

Activities

These companies both operate out of Port Allen Airport (take the road for Salt Pond Beach Park).

Skydive Kauai Adventure Sports
(Map p200; ☎808-335-5859; www.skydivekauai.com; Lele Rd, Port Allen Airport; per person from $239; ⊙by reservation only) For a real adrenaline rush, jump out of an airplane (in tandem with an instructor) and freefall back down to earth witth this adventure tour company. The experience may seem expensive, but considering it includes a free 25-minute flightseeing tour on the way up, it's not such a bad deal.

Birds in Paradise Scenic Flights
(Map p200; ☎808-822-5309; www.birdsinparadise.com; 3666 Kuiloko Rd, Port Allen Airport) Take a flying lesson in an ultralight plane: a 25-minute flight allows you to see the Westside from above, while 50-minute flights glide into Waimea Canyon and along the Na Pali Coast; 80-minute flights may get you around the entire island. At the time of writing, flights were on temporary hiatus; call ahead for reservations, updated schedules and pricing.

Festivals & Events

Art Night Art, Food
(www.hanapepe.org; ⊙6-9pm Fri) On any given Friday night, Hanapepe comes to life and gives everyone an extended peek into its art world. Galleries stay open later and the town's main drag is transformed by musicians and street vendors. Visitors and locals come to stroll, browse and snack

streetside on everything from barbecue to hot, sugary *malasadas* (Portuguese fried dough, served warm and sugar-coated).

During this weekly event, galleries hold open houses, and artists often make themselves available. On egalitarian display are island-inspired originals, Hawaiiana vintage, pure kitsch and the works of Sunday dabblers through to fine-art photography, watercolors and a sampling of Asian art.

Sleeping

Salt Pond Beach Park (p205) offers convenient camping; an advance county permit is required. Otherwise, there are hardly any accommodations in Hanapepe.

Hanapepe Riverside Apartment $
(Map p204; ☎808-635-7860; 4466 Puolo Rd; 1-bedroom apt $85; 🛜) This one-bedroom cottage on stilts faces the Hanapepe River on a residential street. It has a

Salt Pond Beach Park (p205)
KEVIN LEVESQUE/GETTY IMAGES ©

full kitchen, a shared washer-dryer, a king-sized bed, a living room and an amiable upper deck for morning coffee. The decor needs sprucing up, but the cottage is near town, and the price is right. Three-night minimum stay; cleaning fee $85.

Eating

Taro Ko Chips Factory   Fast Food $
(Map p204; 808-335-5586; 3940 Hanapepe Rd; per small bag $4-5; 8am-5pm) Thinly sliced *kalo* (taro) that's been seasoned with garlic salt, slathered with oil and tortured in a deep wok makes for some crispy, slightly sweet, but mostly salty crunching. The farmer who grows the taro is also the chef, so show aloha.

Lappert's Hawaii   Ice Cream $
(Map p204; 808-335-6121; www.lapperts hawaii.com; 1-3555 Kaumuali'i Hwy; scoops from $4; 10am-6pm) The famed ice-cream chain started operations right here along the highway in 1983 at this quaint little roadside shop and factory. The business is way too big for Hanapepe-based

production now, but this humble shop still scoops the goodness of tropical flavors such as 'Kauai Pie' (Kona coffee ice cream, chocolate fudge, macadamia nuts, coconut flakes and vanilla cake crunch). Deadly.

Kaua'i Pupu Factory   Hawaiian $
(Map p204; 808-335-0084; 1-3566 Kaumuali'i Hwy; mains $7-10; 9am-5:30pm Mon-Fri, to 3pm Sat) A down-home-style deli is your source for fresh *poke* – try a scoop of *tako* (octopus) or ahi with *limu* (seaweed) – and Hawaiian plate lunches with bundles of *laulau* and *lomilomi* salmon. If you've got a big group, get enough for everyone, pack a cooler and head to the beach.

Bobbie's   Island Contemporary $
(Map p204; 808-334-5152; 3824 Hanapepe Rd; meals $9-12; 10am-3pm & 5-8pm Mon-Wed & Fri, 10am-2:30pm Thu & Sat) In a small storefront, this humble lunch counter makes huge plate lunches of local faves such as *loco moco* and chicken katsu (deep-fried fillets), as well as BBQ

Tour through taro fields

CARINI JOE/GETTY IMAGES ©

Island Insights

With minimal light pollution, the Westside of Kaua'i is an ideal locale to take in the night sky. The **Kaua'i Education Association for Science & Astronomy** (KEASA; ☎808-332-7827, 808-652-2373; www.keasa.org) holds free monthly 'Starwatches' on Saturdays closest to the new moon (the dark one). KEASA educators share both their gear and insights with the public, beginning at sunset.

First, arm yourself with a light jacket, a lawn chair, insect repellent and a small flashlight, preferably covered with red cellophane. Then follow Hwy 50 west past Hanapepe. After mile marker 18, turn right at the fork to Kaumakani School. Follow the signs to the ball field, and remember to turn your headlights off when approaching or you will not make any new friends. Now prepare to have your mind blown.

Space: it goes on forever.

---

chicken and ribs on Friday nights. It's not good-for-you food, but it certainly tastes darn good.

Little Fish Coffee
Cafe $

(Map p204; ☎808-335-5000; www.facebook. com/LittleFishCoffee; 3900 Hanapepe Rd; items $3-11; ⏱6:30am-5pm Mon-Thu & Sat, to 9pm Fri; 🛜) The colorful chalkboard menu at this cute coffee shop lures you with espresso drinks, fruit smoothies, granola bowls, homemade soups, garden salads and bagel and panini sandwiches. Sit inside amid the retro artwork and music, or on the back patio splashed with both sun and shade.

Hanapepe Farmers Market
Market $

(Map p200; Hanapepe Town Park; ⏱3-5pm Thu) 🌿 One of the county-wide Sunshine Markets. Small-scale farmers truck in the goods themselves and locals line up before the whistle blows just to score the best produce.

Wong's Restaurant & Omoide Bakery
Chinese $

(Map p204; ☎808-335-5066; www.wongs omoide.com; 1-3543 Kaumuali'i Hwy; mains $8-12; ⏱8am-9pm Tue-Sun) A popular diner

that serves up local plantation-style fare such as saimin noodle soup with pork or a whole roasted duck. But the real reason to stop by is the *liliko'i* chiffon pie.

Paco's Tacos
Mexican $

(Map p204; ☎808-335-0454; 4505 Puolo Rd; mains $4-16; ⏱10am-8pm Mon-Sat) Grab takeout or sit at picnic tables outside this Baja-style roadside shack offering all the usual suspects, including *carne asada* (grilled meat) tacos, shrimp burritos and enchilada platters.

⭐ Entertainment

Storybook Theatre of Hawaii
Theater

(Map p204; ☎808-335-0712; www.storybook. org; 3814 Hanapepe Rd; 90min walking tour per individual/couple/family $18/25/30; ⏱tours depart 9:30am Tue & Thu; 👶) The Storybook Theatre, which tours Hawaii with puppets who 'talk story' (chat), has been around for 35 years. Schedules vary, but it's worth a peek on Art Night (p207), when it sometimes hosts kids' activities. Book ahead to join one of its historical walking tours of Hanapepe (no puppets, sorry!), which finishes with a relaxing Chinese herbal tea served in the garden.

Captain Cook's Landing

The great British explorer Captain James Cook traversed the Pacific in three voyages of discovery over the course of a decade. On the third voyage, in 1778, he spotted Kaua'i. Though anxious to get on with his mission, he decided to quickly investigate and reprovision his ships. Native Hawaiians paddling canoes came alongside, and the crew offered nails in exchange for food. When the islanders were invited aboard, they could not believe what they saw, and some historians say they mistook Cook for a deity. When Cook went ashore on the morning of January 20, they prostrated themselves in his honor. All was not completely peaceful, however, as one of his lieutenants shot and killed a Hawaiian. Despite this, Cook stayed on Kaua'i and nearby Ni'ihau for two weeks before heading off in search of the Northwest Passage.

This short visit ended nearly half a millennium of isolation, and irrevocably altered the course of Hawaiian history. While Cook was already familiar with Polynesians, Hawaiians knew nothing of Europeans, nor of the metal, guns and diseases their ships carried, not to mention the world view they presented. Hawaiians lived in a natural world inseparable from the spiritual realm, while Cook embodied a culture in which God ruled heaven and men walked the earth. In some ways those two world views continue to collide today.

Interestingly, Captain Cook was not the only famous sailor to pull into Waimea in 1778. His sailing master was William Bligh, the very Captain Bligh later set adrift by the mutinous crew of the *Bounty*.

🔒 Shopping

Talk Story Bookstore Books, Music
(Map p204; ☎808-335-6469; www.talkstory-bookstore.com; 3785 Hanapepe Rd; ⏰10am-5pm Mon-Thu, to 9:30pm Fri, noon-5pm Sat) The USA's westernmost bookstore is a funky indie bookseller's paradise, the kind that may even fill e-reader enthusiasts with musty page-turning nostalgia. New books by local authors are stocked up front, but it's mostly used fare here, with more than 40,000 books (organized by both genre and, curiously, author gender), vintage Hawaiian sheet music and vinyl records.

Machinemachine Clothing
(Map p204; www.machinemachineapparel.com; 3800 Hanapepe Rd; ⏰5:30-9pm Fri) Shannon Hiramoto, a fifth-generation Kaua'i-born designer, scours flea markets and thrift stores for aloha wear and other tossed-out fashions, which she upcycles into funky, elegant dresses, skirts and cloth-covered journals. She has a devoted cult following, and does most of the sewing out of her Hanapepe workshop.

Puahina Clothing
(Map p204; ☎808-335-9771; 4141 Kona Rd; ⏰11am-4pm Mon-Thu, 11am-4pm & 6-8:30pm Fri, Sat & Sun by appointment) Bold designs set this small boutique apart. You'll find wearable keepsakes that fuse traditional motifs with contemporary styles here. Look for original-design shirts, skirts and tops adorned by native ferns, as well as unusual shell jewelry. The shop also carries Maui-made Hana Lima Soap Co bath and body products with alluring tropical scents.

Jacqueline on Kaua'i Clothing
(Map p204; ☎808-335-5797; 3837 Hanapepe Rd; ⏰9am-6pm Mon-Thu, Sat & Sun, to 9pm Fri) Friendly Jacqueline makes her mark with aloha shirts custom-made while you wait ($60 to $200; usually one to two hours), including children's sizes, and

with coconut buttons no less. You choose the fabric, and she does the rest. Place an order at the beginning of Art Night (p207) and you're good to go by the end.

Banana Patch Studio
Arts & Crafts

(Map p204; ☎808-335-5944, 800-914-5944; www.bananapatchstudio.com; 3865 Hanapepe Rd; ⊙10am-4:30pm Mon-Thu, to 9pm Fri, to 4pm Sat) This studio puts out functional crafts rather than fine art – koi watercolors, wooden tiki bar signs, pottery with tropical flowers, souvenir ceramic tiles and coasters – but there's plenty to behold in this crowded little space, which is usually packed with shoppers. Also in Kilauea on the North Shore.

Salty Wahine
Food

(Map p204; ☎808-378-4089; www.saltywahine.com; 1-3529 Kaumuali'i Hwy; ⊙9am-5pm) Beside the highway on the outskirts of town, this factory shop is a smorgasbord of salt and spice-blends with island flavors, from herbs to fruit. 'Black Lava' and kiawe (Hawaiian mesquite) sea salt, coconut-infused cane sugar and *li hing mui* maragarita salt are bestsellers.

JJ Ohana
Gifts, Souvenirs

(Map p204; ☎808-335-0366; www.jjohana.com; 3805b Hanapepe Rd; ⊙8am-6pm Mon-Thu, to 9pm Fri, to 5pm Sat & Sun) There aren't many places that you can find both $2.50 comfort food and a $7000 necklace. This family-run spot offers affordable daily food specials (such as chili and rice) and high-quality, Hawaii-made crafts and souvenirs, such as koa wood bowls, coral and abalone-shell jewelry, and Ni'ihau shell lei.

Aloha Spice Company
Food

(Map p204; ☎808-335-5960, 800-915-5944; www.alohaspice.com; 3857 Hanapepe Rd; ⊙10am-4:30pm Mon-Thu, to 9pm Fri, to 4pm Sat) You can smell the savory, smoky goodness as soon as the bells on the swinging front door announce your presence. In addition to local spices, this place also sell sauces and jams, lotions and oils, nuts and chocolate, teas and Kaua'i-made tropical-fruit popsicles.

Kauai Fine Arts
Arts

(Map p204; ☎808-335-3778; 3751 Hanapepe Rd; ⊙9:30am-4:30pm Mon-Thu & Sat, to 9pm Fri) If you want to get your hands on a unique piece of memorabilia, step inside

Talk Story Bookstore

LINDA CHING/GETTY IMAGES ©

to peruse fossilized shark teeth, antique and newer tiki carvings, prints of old Pan Am ads, old-world maps and vintage botanical prints.

Kauai Kookie Company   Food
(Map p204; ☎808-335-5003; www.kauaikookie. com; 1-3529 Kaumuali'i Hwy; ⏲8am-5pm Mon-Fri, 10am-5pm Sat & Sun) Though some say it's more novelty than delicious, Kauai Kookie has a local following rivaling that of Girl Scout cookies. Classic tastes sold at the factory warehouse shop include Kona coffee and chocolate chip–macnut.

ℹ Information

American Savings Bank (☎808-335-3118; www.asbhawaii.com; 4548 Kona Rd; ⏲8am-5pm Mon-Thu, to 6pm Fri) Has a 24-hour ATM.

Bank of Hawaii (☎808-335-5021; www.boh. com; 3764 Hanapepe Rd; ⏲8:30am-4pm Mon-Thu, to 6pm Fri) Has a 24-hour ATM.

Hanapepe Post Office (Map p204; ☎808-335-5433; www.usps.com; 3817 Kona Rd; ⏲9am-1:30pm & 2-4pm Mon-Fri)

ℹ Getting There & Away

Coming from Waimea, veer *mauka* (inland) onto Hanapepe Rd at the 'Kaua'i's Biggest Little Town' sign.

Waimea

Waimea ('reddish water') is a popular name in Hawaii, belonging to both an O'ahu valley and a historic ranch town on the Big Island. But on Kaua'i, it's the name of what is arguably the island's landmark town – historically speaking. It was here that Captain Cook first landed in 1778, where King Kaumuali'i welcomed the first New England missionaries in 1820, and where the first Chinese contract laborers arrived in 1852 to work in a new sugar business. In 1884, the Waimea Sugar Company moved in and the settlement evolved into a plantation town.

Today, Waimea thrives as the heart of the Westside, though it still feels like a frontier town, with the great expanse of Waimea Canyon, Koke'e State Park, and the Na Pali Coast lying beyond. That, of course, is the main reason to pass through or to stay the night. Otherwise, there is an eclectic collection of historic sites to see. For a nice elevated view of the town, follow Waimea Canyon Rd about a mile *mauka* (toward the mountains).

🏄 Beaches

Waimea State Recreational Pier   Beach
(www.hawaiistateparks.org; La'au Rd) This wide black beach, flecked with microscopic green crystals called olivine, stretches between two scenic rock outcroppings and is bisected by the namesake fishing pier. It's especially beautiful at sunset.

Facilities include restrooms, picnic areas and drinking water.

◎ Sights

West Kaua'i Technology & Visitor Center   Museum
(☎808-338-1332; www.westkauaivisitorcenter. org; 9565 Kaumuali'i Hwy; ⏲12:30-4pm Mon, 9:30am-4pm Tue & Wed, to 12:30pm Fri; 👪) 🔗 FREE Orient yourself historically to the Westside with modest exhibits on Hawaiian culture, Captain Cook, sugar plantations and the US military. The gift shop sells locally made artisan crafts, including rare Ni'ihau shell lei.

This complex doubles as a visitor center and offers a free, three-hour historic Waimea walking tour at 9:30am Monday (call to register by noon on the previous Friday).

Waimea Town Center   Architecture
Surprisingly, Waimea offers some interesting architecture, including the neoclassical First Hawaiian Bank (1929), the art-deco Waimea Theater (1938), and a historic church, the crushed coral-covered **Waimea United Church of Christ (Makeke Rd)**, first built during the early missionary era and faithfully reconstructed after Hurricane 'Iniki.

Waimea

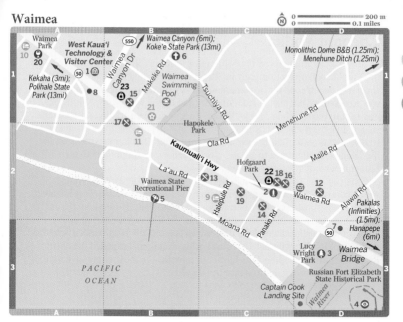

Waimea

Russian Fort Elizabeth State Historical Park
Historic Site

(www.hawaiistateparks.org; off Kaumuali'i Hwy; ⊙dawn-dusk) FREE A Russian fort in Hawaii? Yes, it's true. Constructed in 1817 and named after the Empress of Russia, Fort Elizabeth commanded the entrance to Waimea River. The octagonal design ranges from 350ft to 450ft across. In addition to a cannon, it once harbored

Coconut Vodka

So how did the Russians end up with a fort in Kaua'i? In the early 19th century the Russian American Company in Sitka, Alaska, wished to open trade with Hawaii to access food for its settlements. They sent several ships, one of which was wrecked off Waimea in 1815. Another, led by the wily Georg Anton Schäffer, was sent to recover the cargo and to set up a permanent trading post. Schäffer signed an agreement with King Kaumuali'i of Kaua'i giving the Russians certain trading rights. After failing to win assistance from King Kamehameha on the Big Island, Schäffer tried to get the already rebellious Kaumuali'i to turn against Kamehameha in favor of Russian protection.

Construction of three forts followed, two in Hanalei and one in Waimea, which commanded the river. Named after the Russian Empress, Fort Elizabeth was the largest, with cannon, barracks, a trading house, gardens, homes for 30 families and a Russian Orthodox chapel. The fort was not yet complete, however, when allegiances shifted decisively against the high-handed Schäffer. Acting on King Kamehameha's request, King Kaumuali'i expelled the entire Russian contingent. Today Fort Elizabeth remains the most impressive reminder of Russian efforts to gain influence in Hawaii.

a Russian Orthodox chapel. Apart from impressive walls, some 20ft high, there is little else to see nowadays.

Captain Cook Monument
Monument

(Hofgaard Park, cnr Waimea Rd & Kaumuali'i Hwy) Captain James Cook changed the course of Hawaii history when he sailed into Waimea Harbor with his ships *Resolution* and *Discovery* in January 1778. Partly obscured by trees, Cook's likeness is a replica of the original statue by Sir John Tweed in Whitby, England.

Menehune Ditch
Archaeological Site

(Kikiaola; Menehune Rd) Not much remains to be seen of this unique and still functional aqueduct, yet its archaeological significance is immeasurable. It's the only example of precontact cut and dressed stonework in Hawaii, said to be the work of the *menehune* (the little people), who allegedly completed it within one night for *ali'i* (royalty).

To get here, follow Menehune Rd inland from Kaumuali'i Hwy nearly 1.5 miles to the bridge along the Waimea River. Look for the interpretive signboard opposite.

Lucy Wright Park
Park

At this small municipal park next to the Waimea River, you'll find picnic tables, restrooms and outdoor showers. Camping is permitted on the flat grassy area, but the site doesn't hold much appeal. A plaque commemorating the landing sites of Captain Cook has gone missing.

Activities

Na Pali Sportfishing
Fishing

(808-635-9424; www.napalisportfishing.com; Kikiaola Small Boat Harbor, Kekaha; 4/6/8hr trips per person $145/180/245) If there is anything to upend a deep-sea fishing trip, it's hanging green over the side. This outfit has lessened that risk with a 34ft catamaran, which makes for a much steadier platform. Standard catch includes yellowfin, skipjack, marlin, mahimahi and wahoo. All gear supplied.

Pakalas
Surfing

(Infinities; Kaumuali'i Hwy) Between mile markers 21 and 22 on Kaumuali'i Hwy, you'll notice cars parked on the side of the highway in an area known as Makaweli. It's the access point to Pakalas

(Infinities), an experts-only surf break said to offer the 'longest lefts' anywhere on the island. Conflicts between locals and nonlocals are common here, so leave this break alone.

🖐 Tours

These outfits offer Na Pali Coast tours from Kekaha's Kikiaola Small Boat Harbor, instead of from Port Allen in Hanapepe. This can be important, as the journey there and back is not as rough.

Na Pali Explorer   Boat Tour
(Map p200; ☎808-338-9999; www.napali -explorer.com; Kikiaola Small Boat Harbor; 4½hr tour adult/child $119/99) Snorkeling excursions zoom around on rigid-hull inflatable rafts, which are hard-bottomed and give a smoother ride than all-inflatable Zodiacs. The 49ft-long *Explorer 2* includes a restroom and canopy for shade, and the 26ft-long *Explorer 1* makes seasonal beach landings at Nu'alolo Kai. Expect between 14 and 36 passengers. Tours depart every morning and afternoon, with whale-watching during winter. Minimum age varies across tours; for some it is five years of age, for other it is eight.

Na Pali Riders   Boat Tour
(☎808-742-6331; www.napaliriders.com; 9600 Kaumuali'i Hwy; 4hr tour adult/child 5-12yr $150/120) Get a first-hand peek at sea caves (weather permitting) with Captain Chris Turner, who likes to think of his Zodiac raft tour as being 'National Geographic' in style (read: he likes to travel fast, blare Led Zeppelin and talk story). Warning: the no-shade, bumpy ride isn't for the faint of heart. Morning and afternoon departures available. Cash discounts.

Liko Ho'okano   Boat Tour
(☎808-338-0333, 888-732-5456; www.liko -kauai.com; 4516 Alawai Rd; 4hr cruise adult/child 4-12yr $140/95) Run by a Kaua'i-born-and-raised Hawaiian, whose ancestors hailed from Ni'ihau, this outfit sails to the Na Pali Coast in its 49ft power catamaran with a shade canopy and forward-facing padded seats. Tours go as far as Ke'e Beach during summer. Snorkel gear provided.

Na Pali Coast (p148)

Ni'ihau

Only 72 sq miles, Ni'ihau is the smallest and flattest of the inhabited Hawaiian Islands. Nicknamed the 'Forbidden Island,' it remains an intriguing mystery due to its private ownership and unique isolation. Accessible only to its owners, Native Hawaiian residents, government officials, occasional US Navy personnel and invited guests, Ni'ihau is the last bastion of traditional Hawaiian culture.

HISTORY

Captain Cook anchored off Ni'ihau on January 29, 1778, less than two weeks after 'discovering' Hawaii. Cook noted in his log that the island was lightly populated and largely barren – a description still true today. His visit was short, but it had a lasting impact. Cook gave two things to Ni'ihau that would quickly change the face of Hawaii: he left goats, the first of the grazing animals that would devastate the island's native flora and fauna; and his men introduced syphilis, the first of several Western diseases that would strike down Hawaiians.

In 1864 Elizabeth Sinclair, a Scottish widow who was moving from New Zealand to Vancouver when she got sidetracked in Hawaii, bought Ni'ihau from King Kamehameha V for $10,000 in gold. Kamehameha originally tried to sell her the 'swampland' of Waikiki, but she passed it up for the 'desert island.' Interestingly no two places in Hawaii could today be further apart, either culturally or in land value. Mrs Sinclair brought the first sheep to Ni'ihau from New Zealand and started the island's longstanding, but now defunct, ranching operation.

Today the island is owned by Mrs Sinclair's great-great-grandsons Keith and Bruce Robinson, brothers who also own a vast expanse of land on Kaua'i, where they live. The Robinsons are outdoorsmen and are fluent in Hawaiian. Keith, who worked for years in ranching and fishing, is often found in red-dirt-covered jeans, driving a beat-up pickup or doing heavy labor to save endangered plants. Bruce, whose wife Leiana is Ni'ihauan, holds top management positions in the family businesses – while also leading efforts to safeguard Ni'ihau's monk seals.

POPULATION & LIFESTYLE

Ni'ihau's residents are predominantly Native Hawaiian. Over the years the island's population has dropped from over 250 in 1960, to 160 in the 2000 census. Today Ni'ihau's population is a mere 130, and it is the only island where the primary language is still Hawaiian. Business is conducted in Hawaiian, as are Sunday church services. Inside a solar-powered schoolhouse, teachers hold classes from kindergarten through 12th grade; courses are taught solely in Hawaiian up to the fourth grade, and students learn English as a second language.

Residents are known for being humble, generous and mellow, and most live in Pu'uwai ('heart'), a village on the dry leeward coast. Their lifestyle is extremely rustic, with no sense of hurry. The island has no paved roads, no airport, no phones and no plumbing or running water. Rainwater is collected in catchments, and toilets are in outhouses. While there is no island-wide electricity, homes have generators and solar power. Alcohol and guns are banned, and a code of ethics advocates honesty and monogamy. It all sounds utopian.

Despite their isolation, residents are not unacquainted with the outside world. Ni'ihau residents are permitted to go to Kaua'i or even Las Vegas to shop, drink a few beers or just hang out. However, there are restrictions on Ni'ihauans bringing friends from other islands back home with them. If Niʻihauans marry people from other islands, or if the Robinsons view particular residents as undesirable, they are rarely allowed to return.

While the Robinsons consider themselves protectors of Niʻihau's isolation and its people, and most Niʻihauans point out that their traditional Hawaiian lifestyle isn't possible on any other island, some outsiders have been critical. Some Hawaiians on other islands see the Robinsons as colonialists and believe that Niʻihau's inhabitants should be granted their own land and the right to self-determination.

ECONOMY & POLITICS

The island economy long depended on Niʻihau Ranch, the sheep and cattle business owned by the Robinsons. But it was always a marginal operation on windy Niʻihau, with droughts devastating the ranch's herds. In 1999 the ranch ceased operations, putting most of the island's residents on federal welfare. A few artisans make a living by hand-crafting highly valued Niʻihau shell lei, which can sell for thousands of dollars each.

Historically the Robinsons diverted funds from their (now defunct) sugar company on Kauaʻi to provide Niʻihauans with subsidized housing, food staples, medical care and education.

Since 1999 the US Navy has leased sites on the uninhabited southern end of the island for remotely operated radar surveillance and periodic, small-scale training maneuvers. The Robinsons have also pushed for Niʻihau's participation in major Navy missile testing, which they consider less invasive and damaging (both to the physical land and to the preservation of Niʻihau's culture and privacy) than tourism.

Apart from the income derived from military operations, the only other realistic option is tourism, which is why the Robinsons started offering helicopter and hunting safari tours. Neither is a booming moneymaker, probably due to the steep tour prices as well as the Robinsons' ambivalence about opening the island to tourists.

Politically, Niʻihau falls under the jurisdiction of Kauaʻi County.

VISITING NIʻIHAU

Although outsiders are not allowed to visit Niʻihau independently, the Robinsons offer helicopter flights and hunting excursions, and several dive outfits on Kauaʻi offer scuba diving tours to the waters around Niʻihau and Lehua Islands (a typical three-tank dive costs around $350). Book all tours well in advance.

Niʻihau Helicopters (☎877-441-3500; www.niihau.us; per person $385) The pilot flies over much of Niʻihau (but avoids the population center of Puʻuwai) and lands beachside for snorkeling. Lunch, snacks and drinks are included; five-person minimum required.

Niʻihau Safaris (☎877-441-3500; www.niihau.us; per hunter from $1750) Provides everything you'll need (air transportation, guide, preparation and shipping of trophies) to hunt Polynesian boar and feral sheep, mostly, but also wild eland, Barbary sheep and wild oryx. Organizers promote this as 'useful harvesting of game' (due to overpopulation and overgrazing) and obey the norms of free-chase hunting.

⚛ Festivals & Events

Waimea Town Celebration
Cultural

(www.waimeatowncelebration.com) ✦ Free fun in mid-February includes a *paniolo* (Hawaiian cowboy) rodeo, storytelling, canoe, SUP and surf-skiing races, local food vendors, carnival games, an arts-and-crafts fair, and lei-making and ukulele-playing contests.

🛏 Sleeping

Monolithic Dome B&B
B&B $

(📞808-651-7009; Menehune Rd; r $95; 🛜) Constructed by the hard-working owner herself, this unique concrete creation – looking like a spaceship getting ready to blast off – rises above the neighbors on a residential street. The private studio apartment can be hot and a tad buggy, but it has modern conveniences: a bathroom with painted walls, a queen bed with memory-foam mattress, a kitchenette and a lanai. Note that there's a three-night minimum stay and a cleaning fee of $75.

Coco's Kaua'i B&B
B&B $$

(📞808-338-0722, 808-639-1109; www.cocos kauai.com; ste $120-140; ❄🛜) ✦ This off-the-grid retreat on sprawling ranch lands is run by one of the descendants of the Robinson family, who own the island of Ni'ihau. With its own private entrance, the suite offers a king bed, kitchenette, outdoor BBQ grill, and cowboys riding by on horses. There's free beach gear to borrow and seasonal tropical fruit for snacking. Two-night minimum stay. Address given upon booking.

Inn Waimea
Inn $$

(📞808-338-0031; www.innwaimea.com; 4469 Halepule Rd; r & ste $110-120, cottages $150; 🛜) This inn feels like a family summer house that has seen the passing of many generations. Situated in the heart of town, the suites feature clawfoot tubs and other vintage-style furnishings, while the king-bedded Taro Room is ADA–compliant with a roll-in shower. The inn's two-bedroom cottages are even more quaint (the Ishihara Cottage is the better pick).

There's a three-night minimum stay in the cottages. A $25 surcharge applies for one-night stays in the room or suites.

Waimea Plantation Cottages

More Hawaiian Islands?

If you're staring out to sea thinking that Kaua'i and its neighbor, Ni'ihau, mark the end of the Hawaiian Islands, think again – there's more! The Northwestern Hawaiian Islands begin more than 150 miles northwest of Kaua'i, and stretch for 1200 miles. They represent an enormous area of some 140,000 sq miles of ocean known as **Papahānaumokuākea Marine National Monument** (www.papahanaumokuakea.gov), the largest protected marine area in the world.

This 'other Hawaii' is grouped into 10 clusters, containing both atolls and single-rock islands. From east to west, the clusters are Nihoa Island, Mokumanamana (Necker Island), French Frigate Shoals, Gardner Pinnacles, Maro Reef, Laysan Island, Lisianski Island, Pearl and Hermes Atoll, Midway Atoll and Kure Atoll. The total land mass is just less than 6 sq miles, however, which is why they remain incognito. Managed by the **US Fish & Wildlife Service** (FWS; www.fws.gov), Midway Atoll is normally the only island open to visitors.

Interestingly, Nihoa and Necker islands, the two closest to Kaua'i, were inhabited by Native Hawaiians from around AD 1000 to 1700. More than 135 archaeological sites have been identified there. As many as 175 people lived on Nihoa, while Necker was used for religious ceremonies. The fact that anyone at all could live on these rocks is remarkable. Nihoa juts from the sea like a broken tooth, with 900ft sea cliffs, and is only 1 sq km in size. Necker is one-sixth that. What some people will do for a bit of sun.

West Inn Inn $$
(808-338-1107; www.thewestinn.com; 9690 Kaumauli'i Hwy; r from $200; ※ 🛜) Across from Waimea Theater, this feels like a budget chain hotel, but isn't one. Some buildings have been recently renovated with spacious rooms that have king or double beds, high ceilings, granite countertops, flat-screen TVs, microwaves and minifridges. More expensive suites are equipped with full kitchens. The decor won't win any awards, though, and rates are comparatively overpriced.

Waimea Plantation Cottages Inn $$
(808-338-1625, 800-992-4632; www.waimea-plantation.com; 9400 Kaumuali'i Hwy; d from $199; 🛜 🛝) These rebuilt plantation cottages from the 1930s and 1940s once housed sugarcane laborers. The 57 tin-roofed, clapboard, pastel-painted sweethearts with wide porches and rattan seating are scattered over a wide lawn, studded with golden bamboo, swaying palm groves and a cathedral banyan tree. The only downsides are poor upkeep of some of the arguably too-rustic cottages and spotty wi-fi.

Oceanside yoga classes, massages and spa services are priced à la carte.

🍴 Eating

Ishihara Market Supermarket, Deli $
(808-338-1751; 9894 Kaumuali'i Hwy; 🕑6am-7:30pm Mon-Thu, to 8pm Fri & Sat, to 7pm Sun) It's an ad-hoc lesson in local cuisine shopping at this historic market (c 1934) with deli. Trusty takeout meals (get here before the lunch rush) include sushi, spicy ahi *poke* and smoked marlin. Daily specials and marinated ready-to-go meats are available for those wanting to barbecue. The parking lot is often full – it's that popular.

Yumi's
Diner $

(📞808-338-1731; 9691 Kaumuali'i Hwy; mains $5-10; 🕐7:30am-2:30pm Tue-Thu, 7am-1pm & 6-8pm Fri, 8am-1pm Sat) Friendly, filling and reasonably priced sums up this local institution, where you can get a plate lunch with some chicken katsu or teriyaki beef, a burger, a mini *loco moco* or a special bowl of saimin. Be sure to order a slice of coconut pie or the pumpkin crunch for dessert.

G's Juicebar
Health Food $

(📞808-634-4112; 4492 Moana Rd; snacks from $7; 🕐7am-6pm Mon-Fri, 9am-5pm Sat) Your quest for Kaua'i's top acai bowl might reach the finish line inside this Rastafarian corner shack. A Marley bowl comes with kale and bee pollen, and the Kauai Bowl with mango juice and shaved coconut. Fresh tropical juice smoothies and yerba maté tea will quench your thirst.

Super Duper Two
Ice Cream $

(📞808-338-1590; 9889 Waimea Rd; snacks from $3; 🕐noon-9pm Mon-Thu, to 10pm Fri & Sat) Across the street from Captain Cook's statue, this place lives up to its moniker. Stop in for tropically flavored shakes, sundaes, floats or old-fashioned scoops of Roselani ice cream (made on Maui) in crispy handmade waffle cones.

Island Taco
Mexican $

(📞808-338-9895; www.islandfishtaco.com; 9643 Kaumuali'i Hwy; mains $6-13; 🕐11am-5pm) At this island fusion taqueria, tortillas are stuffed with wasabi-coated or Cajun-dusted seared ahi, fresh cabbage and rice. Have the same trick done with mahimahi, tofu, shrimp with papaya seeds or *kalua* pork with spinach instead. Wet burritos and taco salads round out the menu.

Jo-Jo's Anuenue Shave Ice & Treats
Desserts $

(9899 Waimea Rd; snacks from $3; 🕐10am-5:30pm; 🚻) Now in a new location, this shack delivers icy flavor: all syrups are homemade without additives and won't knock you out with sweetness. The superstar item is the *halo halo* (Filipino-style mixed fruit) with coconut.

Shrimp Station
Seafood $

(📞808-338-1242; 9652 Kaumuali'i Hwy; mains $8-12; 🕐11am-5pm; 🚻) Want shrimp? Whether sautéed scampi-style, coconut- or beer-battered, in taco form or ground up into a 'shrimp burger,' crustaceans is what this roadside chow hut is all about. Look for the flamingo-pink sign out front.

Da Booze Shop
Fast Food $

(📞808-338-9953; 9883 Waimea Rd; mains $5-10; 🕐10:30am-9pm Mon-Sat, to 5pm Sun) For down-home burgers, box lunches, BBQ ribs and plates full of artery-clogging local faves

Shave ice
BILL ADAMS/GETTY IMAGES ©

such as katsu *loco moco* covered in gravy, step inside this family-owned storefront deli and grill. Ironically, no alcohol is served.

Wrangler's Steakhouse   Steak $$
(☎808-338-1218; www.wranglersrestaurant. com; 9852 Kaumuali'i Hwy; lunch meals around $10, dinner mains $18-30; ⏰11am-8:30pm Mon-Thu, 4-9pm Fri & Sat, to 8:30pm Sun; ☷) Yes, it's touristy, but this Western-style saloon dishes up plantation lunches in authentic *kaukau* (food) tins full of shrimp and vegetable tempura, teriyaki steak, rice and kimchi. Sizzling dinner steaks are decent, but the seafood and soup-and-salad bar less so. Save room for peach cobbler. There's atmospheric seating on the front lanai or back porch.

🍸 Drinking & Entertainment

Kalapaki Joe's   Sports Bar
(☎808-338-1666; www.kalapakijoes.com; Waimea Plantation Cottages, 9400 Kaumuali'i Hwy; ⏰11am-10pm) Calling itself the USA's westernmost sports bar, this outpost of the Lihu'e original inhabits a charming plantation building with a full bar, ceiling fans, ocean-view verandahs and local music some nights. Take your pick of two dozen beers on tap, including made-in-Hawaii brews. Skip the pub grub, except for happy-hour specials (from 3pm to 6pm daily).

Waimea Theater   Cinema
(☎808-338-0282; www.waimeatheater.com; 9691 Kaumuali'i Hwy; adult/child 5-10yr $8/6) This art-deco movie theater is the place for a rainy day or for an early-evening reprieve from sun and sea. Kaua'i is a little behind with new releases and schedules are erratic, but since this is one of only two functioning cinemas on the island (the other is in Lihu'e), no one's complaining.

Fun for Kids

- Salt Pond Beach Park (p205)
- Hanapepe's Swinging Bridge (p205)
- Waimea Canyon Drive (p225)
- Ice cream at Lappert's Hawaii (p208) or Super Duper Two (p220)
- Jo-Jo's Anuenue Shave Ice & Treats (p220)

🛍 Shopping

Aunty Lilikoi Passion Fruit Products   Food, Gifts
(☎808-338-1296, 866-545-4564; www.aunty lilikoi.com; 9875 Waimea Rd; ⏰10am-6pm) Find something for almost any occasion: award-winning passion fruit–wasabi mustard, passion-fruit syrup (great for banana pancakes), massage oil (the choice for honeymooners), and a tasty lip balm (ideal for après surf), all made with at least a kiss of, you guessed it, *liliko'i*.

Kaua'i Granola   Food
(☎808-338-0121; www.kauaigranola.com; 9633 Kaumuali'i Hwy; ⏰10am-5pm Mon-Sat) Before you head up to Waimea Canyon and Koke'e State Parks, drop by this island bakery for snacks such as trail mix, macadamia-nut cookies, chocolate-dipped coconut macaroons and tropically flavored granola.

ℹ Information

First Hawaiian Bank (☎808-338-1611; www. fhb.com; 4525 Panako Rd; ⏰8:30am-4pm Mon-Thu, to 6pm Fri) Has a 24-hour ATM.

Waimea Post Office (☎808-338-9973; www. usps.com; 9911 Waimea Rd; ⏰9am-1pm & 1:30-4pm Mon-Fri, 9-11am Sat)

Waimea Public Library (☎808-338-6848; 9750 Kaumuali'i Hwy; ⏰noon-8pm Mon & Wed, 9am-5pm Tue, Thu & Fri; 📶) Free wi-fi; online computer terminals available with temporary nonresident library card ($10).

West Kauai Medical Center (☎808-338-9431; www.kvmh.hhsc.org; 4643 Waimea Canyon Dr) Basic 24-hour emergency services.

West Kaua'i Technology & Visitor Center (☎808-338-1332; www.westkauaivisitorcenter. org; 9565 Kaumuali'i Hwy; ⏰12:30-4pm Mon, 9:30am-4pm Tue & Wed, to 12:30pm Fri) Free internet computer access.

Kekaha

If you're looking for a scenic beach near the base of Waimea Canyon, Kekaha could be the ideal spot for your stay. In fact, Kekaha Beach Park offers one of the most beautiful sunsets on the island. However, the town is largely a bedroom community for the nearby military base, and a bit remote for some. On the flip side, Kekaha is near Kikiaola Small Boat Harbor, the start of many an exciting expedition to the Na Pali Coast.

🏖 Beaches

Kekaha Beach Park   Beach
(Map p200) Kaua'i's Westside is known for its unrelenting sun and vast beaches. Just west of Kekaha town, this long stretch of sand is best for beachcombing and catching sunsets. Before jumping in, find a lifeguard and make sure it's okay to swim, since the beach lacks reef protection. In high surf, the currents are extremely dangerous. Under the right conditions, however, it's good for surfing and bodyboarding.

Facilities include outdoor showers, restrooms and picnic tables.

🛏 Sleeping

For more vacation rental homes and beach cottages, contact **Kekaha Ocean-side** (☎800-351-4609; www.kekahaocean sidekauai.com).

Mindy's   Apartment $
(Map p200; ☎808-337-9275; 8842 Kekaha Rd; ste from $95; 📶) Featuring a private lanai, this second-story, fan-cooled apartment,

Kekaha Beach Park

ROYCE BAIR/GETTY IMAGES ©

with a full-sized bed and a kitchen, feels large and open. There's free beach gear to borrow, and complimentary fruit and coffee in the mornings.

Hale Makai Rental House **$$**
(Map p200; ☏760-492-7583; www.vrbo.com/135835; 4635 Palila Loop; 2-bedroom house $180-200; ❄🛜) Children are welcome at this two-bedroom house, a short walk inland from the beach. Polished wooden floors, a full kitchen, two en-suite bedrooms (one king, one queen), a screened-in lanai and a private hot tub are among many welcome amenities. Minimum four-night stay. Cleaning and reservation fees $150.

Hale La Rental House **$$$**
(Map p200; ☏808-652-6852; www.kekaha kauaisunset.com; 8240a Elepaio Rd; 3-bedroom house $395; ❄🛜) This modern, green-painted, oceanside house offers three suites with cherrywood and bamboo furnishings, and two with private lanai and ocean views. Watch whales breach off the beach in winter. One hiccup: traffic noise. Three-night minimum stay. Cleaning fee $250.

🍴 Eating

Kekaha Farmers Market Market
(Map p200; Kekaha Neighborhood Center, 8130 Elepaio Rd; ⏰9-11am Sat) A handful of local farmers and flower growers gather every Saturday morning just off the Kaumuali'i Hwy.

Barking Sands

Between Kekaha Beach Park and Polihale State Park, the Westside's biggest beach stretches for approximately 15 miles. However, much of this is taken up by the US Navy's Barking Sands Pacific Missile Range Facility, which is closed to the public. Established during WWII, it has the world's largest instrumented underwater listening range (more than 1100 sq

Island Insights

A massive expanse of beach – the end of one of the longest (15 miles) and widest (300ft) in the state – Polihale is as mystical as it is enchanting. Translated as 'home of the underworld,' traditional Hawaiian belief holds Polihale as the place where souls depart for the afterlife. The cliffs at the end of the beach are home to ancient Hawaiian ruins constructed over the ocean as the jumping-off place for spirits.

mi) and controls over 40,000 sq mi of airspace. If you see a flame streaking through the sky at night, don't worry, it is not a UFO.

Polihale State Park

Vast and inspiring, Polihale is where Kaua'i appears to end, and the Earth with it. An epic stretch of beach backed by dunes leads to the base of an impassable line of giant cliffs stretching as far as you can see: the beginning of the Na Pali Coast. The effect is quite different than one feels elsewhere on the island. There is a sense of eternity here that other dramatic vistas can't match. If you feel vacation frazzle, this is a great place to relax and reflect.

People may warn you about the 5-mile dirt road to get here, starting from Mana village off the Kaumuali'i Hwy, but it's usually passable in the absence of severe flooding. The park has restrooms, outdoor showers and a picnic area, but no lifeguards – you must be careful if you go swimming, and only enter the water during calm conditions. Camping is allowed with an advance state park permit (required).

Below: Waipo'o Falls; **Right:** Waimea Canyon
(BELOW) BOB POOL/GETTY IMAGES ©; (RIGHT) JERRY ALEXANDER/GETTY IMAGES ©

Waimea Canyon State Park

When someone named Waimea Canyon 'the Grand Canyon of the Pacific' (and contrary to popular belief, it was not Samuel Clemens), they weren't kidding. This vast chasm opens up into the same awesome network of colored valleys that defines its namesake, making you wonder how it ever came to be here on a remote Pacific island. The Waimea River that twists through it is no Colorado, but the waterfalls that plunge into it are certainly compensation. The fact that this natural wonder merges into another, radically different one, the Na Pali, is one of Kaua'i's quiet miracles.

The stats: this is the largest canyon in the Pacific, measuring 10 miles long, 1 mile wide, and 3500ft deep. It was formed by two causes, the long process of erosion, and the sudden, catastrophic collapse of Mt Wai'ale'ale, the volcano that created Kaua'i, forming a deep fault in the entire island. This exposed layer upon layer of ancient lava flows, like some enormous twisting cake. Mercifully, access is simpler than it sounds, at least along the rim. A single road takes you from one end of the canyon to the other, with plentiful lookouts along the way. For a closer look, there are 45 miles of hiking trails with various levels of difficulty.

⊚ Sights & Activities

Drives here on a clear day are phenomenal. But don't be disappointed by rain, as that's what makes the waterfalls gush. Sunny days following rain are ideal for prime views, though slick mud makes hiking a challenge then.

DRIVING

Waimea Canyon Drive
Driving Tour

(Map p200; Hwy 550) This spectacular drive, the best on the island, follows the entire length of Waimea Canyon into Koke'e State Park, ascending 19 miles from the coast to Pu'u o Kila Lookout. It begins as Waimea Canyon Dr by Waimea's West Kaua'i Technology & Visitor Center, then merges into and becomes Koke'e Rd. You can stop at scenic lookouts and take short hikes during the drive. There are no gas stations along the way, but major signposted lookouts have restrooms.

Waimea Canyon Lookout
Viewpoint

(Map p200) This breathtaking vista is about 0.3 miles north of mile marker 10, at an elevation of 3400ft. The canyon running in an easterly direction off Waimea Canyon is Koai'e Canyon, an area accessible to backcountry hikers.

Waipo'o Falls
Waterfall

This 800ft waterscape can be seen from a couple of small unmarked lookouts before mile marker 12 and then from a lookout opposite the picnic area shortly before mile marker 13. The picnic area has restrooms and drinking water.

Pu'u Hinahina Lookout
Viewpoint

(Map p200) A majestic canyon lookout (elevation 3640ft) showing the river glistening in the distance and giving panoramic views down to the ocean. There are two lookouts near the parking lot at a marked turnoff between mile markers 13 and 14.

HIKING

For serious hikers, there are trails that lead deep into Waimea Canyon. Trail maps are available at the Koke'e Museum (p230) in Koke'e State Park, further uphill. Hiking safety needs to be taken seriously here. During weekends and holidays, pig and deer hunters use these trails, so wear bright colors.

Hiking poles or a sturdy walking stick will ease the steep descent into the canyon. Note the time of sunset and plan to return well before dark, as daylight will fade inside the canyon long before sunset. Beware of rain, which creates hazardous conditions in the canyon: red-dirt trails quickly become slick and river fords rise to impassable levels.

While packing light is recommended, take enough water for your entire trip, especially the uphill return journey. Do not drink freshwater found along the trails without treating it. Cell phones will not work here. If possible, hike with a companion or, at the very least, tell someone your expected return time.

Kukui Trail

Iliau Nature Loop   Hiking
(https://hawaiitrails.ehawaii.gov; off Waimea Canyon Dr) This easy, mostly flat 0.3-mile nature loop is a good leg-stretcher for those itching to get out of the car, but who are ill-equipped for a big trek. *Iliau*, a plant endemic to Kaua'i's Westside, grows along the route and produces stalks up to 10ft high. The marked trailhead comes up shortly before mile marker 9 on Hwy 550.

For a top-notch panorama of Waimea Canyon and its waterfalls, you only have to walk for about three minutes past the bench on your left.

Kukui Trail   Hiking
(http://hawaiitrails.ehawaii.gov; off Waimea Canyon Dr) This narrow switchbacking trail drops 2000ft in elevation over 2.5 miles without offering much in the way of sweeping views, though there's a river at the bottom. The climb back out of the canyon is for seriously fit and agile hikers only. Another option is to only hike about a mile down, where there's a bench with an astonishing view.

JIM KRUGER/GETTY IMAGES ©

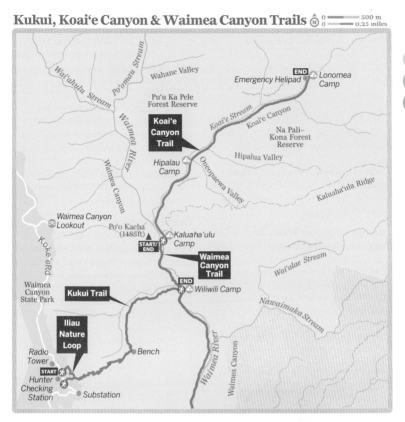

To get to the trail, first find the Iliau Nature Loop trailhead just before mile marker 9 on Hwy 550. Keep your eyes peeled for a small sign directing hikers to turn left and hike down the steep slope, with the hill at your back. When you hear the sound of water, you're near the picnic shelter and **Wiliwili Camp** (www.hawaiistateparks.org/camping; tent site $18) area, where overnight camping is allowed with an advance permit. Mostly it's hunters who camp here.

Depending on weather, the sun can be unrelenting, so be sure to bring a hat and sunblock.

Koaiʻe Canyon Trail · Hiking

(http://hawaiitrails.ehawaii.gov) After traversing roughly half a mile up the canyon along the Waimea Canyon Trail, you'll intersect the Koaiʻe Canyon Trail, a moderate 3-mile (one-way) trek that takes you down the south side of the canyon to some swimming holes (avoid them during rainy weather due to the possibility of hazardous flash floods).

This route offers three camps. After the first, **Kaluahaʻulu Camp** (www.hawaiistateparks.org/camping; tent site $18), stay on the eastern bank of the river – do not cross it. Later you'll come upon the trailhead for the Koaiʻe Canyon Trail (marked by a brown-and-yellow Na Ala

Hele sign). Watch for greenery and soil that conceal drop-offs alongside the path.

Next up is **Hipalau Camp** (www.hawaiistateparks.org/camping; tent site $18). Following this, the trail is hard to find. Keep heading north. Do not veer toward the river, but continue ascending at approximately the same point midway between the canyon walls and the river.

Growing steeper, the trail then enters Koai'e Canyon, recognizable by the red-rock walls rising to the left. The last camp is **Lonomea** (www.hawaiistateparks.org/camping; tent site $18). Soak up the best views at the emergency helipad before retracing your steps.

Waimea Canyon Trail   Hiking
(http://hawaiitrails.ehawaii.gov) The relatively flat, 11.5-mile (one-way) Waimea Canyon Trail fords the Waimea River several times. You can pick it up at the bottom of Waimea Canyon at the end of Kukui Trail, then follow it out to Waimea town, or hike upstream in reverse. An entry permit is required (available at self-service trail-head registration boxes). Bring mosquito repellent.

You might see locals carrying inner tubes on the upstream hike, so they can float home the easy way.

CYCLING

Waimea Canyon is a mountain biker's dream. Riders are allowed on all 4WD hunting-area roads off of Waimea Canyon Dr, even when the yellow gates are closed on nonhunting days. The exception to this is Papa'alai Rd, managed by the Department of Hawaiian Home Lands, which is only open for hunting.

Outfitters Kauai   Cycling
(Map p40; 808-742-9667, 888-742-9887; www.outfitterskauai.com; Po'ipu Plaza, 2827a Po'ipu Rd, Po'ipu; 4½hr tours adult/child 12-14yr $106/86; tour check-in usually 6am & 2:30pm daily, by reservation only) For lazy two-wheeled sightseeing, it's hard to beat this 13-mile downhill glide along Waimea Canyon Dr. The experience is much better than looking out a car window, as you

Kalalau Lookout (p230)

cruise along with a comfy, wide saddle and high-rise handlebars. Morning tours avoid the setting sun's glare. Tours include snacks and drinks. Reservations are required.

🛏 Sleeping

All four backcountry campsites (per night $18) on the canyon trails are on forest reserve land. They have open-air picnic shelters and pit toilets, but no other facilities; all fresh-water must be treated before drinking.

Advance state park camping permits are required.

ℹ Getting There & Away

The southern boundary of Waimea Canyon State Park is about 6 miles uphill from Waimea. You can reach the park by two roads: more scenic Waimea Canyon Dr (Hwy 550), which starts in Waimea just past mile marker 23, or Koke'e Rd (Hwy 552), starting off in Kekaha off Mana Rd. The two routes merge between mile markers 6 and 7.

Koke'e State Park

The expansive Koke'e (ko-*keh*-eh) State Park is a temple for nature lovers. Lush, unspoiled, primordial and highly three-dimensional, it's home to some famously inspirational views, like that of the Kalalau Valley, as well as some of the island's most precious ecosystems. Botanists will revel in the variety of endemic species here, from the rainforest to the vast Alaka'i Swamp, while birders will have their binoculars full, particularly at Kalalau and Pu'u o Kila Lookouts, and on the Pihea and Alaka'i Swamp Trails. Hikers will enjoy some reprieve from the sun while tackling a full range of options, from short walks to highly advanced, multiday treks.

The park experiences a rainy season from October to May, although you may need a raincoat at any time. The elevation (2000ft to 4000ft above sea level) necessitates a light jacket as well, and a heavier one if you are camping in wintertime, when temperatures can dip into the high 30s. Though one of the park's locally revered charms is its choppy 4WD roads, the state has thankfully paved the main one from beginning to end.

⊙ Sights

Koke'e Museum   Museum

(Map p200; ☏808-335-9975; www.kokee.org; donation $1; ⏱9am-4:30pm; ♿) ⬦ Inside this two-room museum you'll find detailed topographical maps, exhibits on flora and fauna, and local historical photographs. It also has botanical sketches of endemic plants and taxidermic representations of some of the wildlife that calls Koke'e home.

The gift shop sells a handy fold-out map of the park and its hiking trails, as well as a self-guiding brochure for the short nature trail out back.

Kalalau Lookout   Viewpoint

(Map p200) At mile marker 18, the Kalalau Lookout stands up to the ocean, sun and winds with brave, severe beauty. Hope for a clear day for views of Kalalau Valley, but know that even on a rainy day, the clouds could quickly blow away to reveal gushing waterfalls and, of course, rainbows.

Though it might be hard to imagine due to the extremity of the terrain, as late as the 1920s Kalalau Valley was home to many residents who farmed rice. The only way into the valley nowadays is via the North Shore's Kalalau Trail (p149) or by sea kayaking.

Pu'u o Kila Lookout   Viewpoint

(Map p200) The paved park road (subject to periodic closures) heads a mile beyond the Kalalau Lookout before it dead-ends at a parking lot. The views of Kalalau Valley are similarly spectacular to those at Kalalau Lookout, but usually less crowded. Pu'u o Kila is also the trailhead for the Pihea Trail.

Alaka'i Swamp Trail (p232)

BEN KLAUS/GETTY IMAGES ©

🏃 Activities

HIKING

Koke'e's sheer size can make it tough to nail down where to start. The 4WD roads that access many trailheads complicates things more. Be prepared for wet, cold weather anytime. For trail information, stop at the Koke'e Museum and consult the Na Ala Hele website (http://hawaiitrails.ehawaii.gov).

In total, this state park boasts 45 miles of trails that range from swampy bogs to wet forest to red-dirt canyon rim with clifftop views that can cause vertigo even in wannabe mountain goats. Hiking here offers the chance to spy endemic species of animals and plants, including Kaua'i's rare, endangered forest birds.

Halemanu Rd, just north of mile marker 14 on Koke'e Rd, is the starting point for several scenic hikes. Whether or not the road is passable in a non-4WD vehicle depends on recent rainfall. Note that many rental-car agreements forbid any off-road driving.

Cliff & Canyon Trails   Hiking

The 0.1-mile Cliff Trail is a relatively easy walk with rewarding canyon views. Keep going on the 1.7-mile Canyon Trail, a steep forested trail that descends before opening up to a vast red-dirt promontory with cliffs to one side and charming log-steps to guide you further. Shortly thereafter it'll take some huff-and-puff climbing to get to **Waipo'o Falls**.

If it's getting to be too much, you could turn around at the falls. Otherwise, follow the trail across the stream to the canyon rim. The trail ends at **Kumuwela Lookout**, where you can rest at a picnic table before backtracking to Halemanu Rd.

For an alternate return route, make a right at the signed intersection with the **Black Pipe Trail** at the top of the switchback where you leave the canyon rim. This 0.5-mile alternative trail stops at the 4WD road, where you turn left

Cliff, Canyon & Halemanu-Koke'e Trails

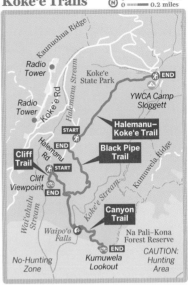

(downhill) and walk back to where you started.

To get to the trailhead for the Cliff and Canyon Trails, walk down Halemanu Rd over 0.5 miles. Keeping Halemanu Stream on your left, turn right onto a footpath leading to the Cliff and Canyon Trails. At the next junction, the Cliff Trail veers right and uphill to a viewpoint.

Awa'awapuhi & Nu'alolo Trails   Hiking

The Awa'awapuhi Trail (3.2 miles one-way) and more challenging Nu'alolo Trail (3.8 miles) are the best of Koke'e. Both ultimately afford unforgettable vistas of 2000ft cliffs rising above the Na Pali Coast. If you're undecided as to which trail to take, Awa'awapuhi is much less technical and Nu'alolo is steeper, though each require a good amount of endurance.

The Awa'awapuhi Trail sees more people, and there are some steep steps where you might find yourself hugging

Awa'awapuhi & Nu'alolo Trails

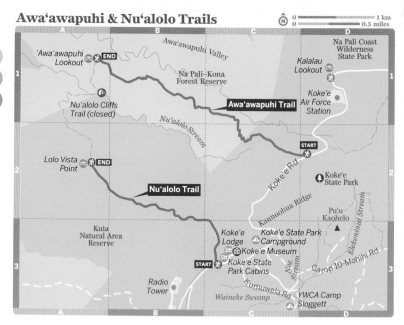

a tree. At the trail's end you'll arrive at a breathtaking view of the cliffs below **Awa'awapuhi Lookout**.

Perhaps nothing is more exhilarating than the connecting **Nu'alolo Cliffs Trail** (2.1 miles), where you'll sometimes feel like more of a rock climber or makeshift acrobat than a hiker. As of 2014, this trail was closed indefinitely, however, due to erosion and a washout.

The trailhead for the Nu'alolo Trail is just south of the Koke'e Museum. The Awa'awapuhi Trail begins off Koke'e Rd, about 1.5 miles uphill past the museum.

Pihea Trail to
Alaka'i Swamp Trail   Hiking
This rugged, strenuous 7.5-mile round-trip trek begins off Koke'e Rd at Pu'u o Kila Lookout (p230). A mere mile in, **Pihea Lookout** appears. After a short scramble downhill, the boardwalk begins. About 1.8 miles later, you'll come to a crossing with the Alaka'i Swamp Trail.

Taking a left at this crossing puts you on the trail toward **Kilohana Lookout**.

Continuing straight on the Pihea Trail will take you to Kawaikoi Campground instead. Most hikers begin this trip at Pu'u o Kila Lookout because it's accessible via the paved road.

Both of these trails may be muddy and not recently maintained. The stretch between Alaka'i Crossing and Kilohana Lookout includes hundreds of steps, which can be hell on your knees.

Halemanu–Koke'e Trail   Hiking
This trail starts off Halemanu Rd, along from the Cliff and Canyon Trails. A gentle recreational nature hike, the 1.2-mile trip passes through a native forest of koa and ohia trees, which provide habitat for endemic birds. The trail ends near YWCA Camp Sloggett, about 0.5 miles from Koke'e Lodge.

One common trailside plant is banana *poka*, a member of the passion-fruit family and a serious invasive pest. It has pretty pink flowers, but it drapes the forest with its vines and chokes out less-aggressive native plants

Kawaikoi Stream Trail   Hiking
This easy, 1.8-mile loop trail initially follows Kawaikoi Stream through a grove of Japanese cedar and California redwood trees, rises up on a bluff, then loops back down to the stream before returning to where you started. Find the trailhead upstream from Sugi Grove Campground on Camp 10–Mohihi Rd (4WD only).

🏵 Festivals & Events

Eo e Emalani I
Alaka'i   Dance, Music
(www.kokee.org) A one-day outdoor dance festival at the Koke'e Museum in early October, commemorating Queen Emma's 1871 journey to Alaka'i Swamp. The festival includes a royal procession, hula dancing, live music and more.

Banana Poka
Round-Up   Art, Music
(www.kokee.org) 🖉 This unique festival in late May strips Koke'e of an invasive pest from South America, the banana *poka* vine, then weaves baskets from it. Come for live music, a rooster-crowing contest and the 'Pedal to the Meadow' bicycle race.

🛏 Sleeping & Eating

Koke'e State Park
Campground   Campground $
(Map p200; www.hawaiistateparks.org/camping; tent site $18-30) The most accessible camping area is Koke'e State Park Campground, which is north of the meadow, just a few minutes' walk from Koke'e Lodge. The campsites sit in a grassy area beside the woods and have picnic tables, drinking water, restrooms and outdoor showers. There's a five-night maximum stay. Book online in advance.

Pihea, Alaka'i Swamp & Kawaikoi Stream Trails

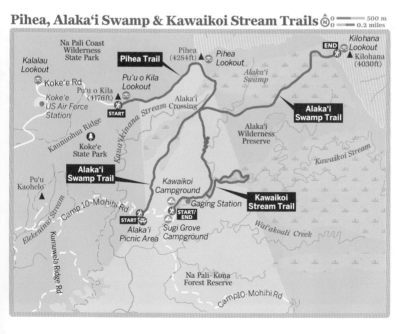

YWCA Camp Sloggett
Campground, Cabin $

(Map p200; ☎808-245-5959; www.camping kauai.com; tent site $15, cottage, lodge or bunkhouse $120-200) Choose basic cottage, lodge or bunkhouse accommodations, or camp on the grass; all have hot showers available. The cottage has a king-sized bed, kitchen and wood-burning fireplace, while the bunkhouse and lodge are outfitted for large groups, with a kitchen or kitchenette. Bring sleeping bags and towels. No reservations typically needed for camping, but call ahead to check. These facilities are extremely rustic, even run-down.

To get here, turn right off Koke'e Rd, just past the lodge, at the YWCA sign and follow that dirt road for around 0.5 miles.

Koke'e State Park Cabins
Cabin $$

(Map p200; ☎808-335-6061; www.thelodgeat kokee.net; Koke'e Rd; cabin incl taxes $115) Minimally maintained, these dozen cabins are for folks seeking a remote, bare-bones experience – pretend you're reliving college dorm life (without a phone or TV). All cabins have a double bed and twin beds with sagging mattresses, a kitchen, hot shower, wood-burning stove (your only heating source), linens and blankets. There's a small cleaning fee, depending on how long you stay.

Koke'e Lodge
American $

(Map p200; ☎808-335-6061; Koke'e Rd; mains $5-8; ⏰cafe 9am-2:30pm, takeout until 3pm; 👪) This summer camp-style restaurant's strong point is convenience. And that goes a long way in Koke'e, where you're a 30-minute drive from any other dining options. Pancakes, salads, sandwiches, burgers and booze are served. The gift shop, which stays open until 3:30pm or 4pm daily, sells sundries, souvenirs, snacks and drinks.

ⓘ Information

This park's southern boundary lies beyond the Pu'u Hinahina Lookout. After mile marker 15, you'll pass a brief stretch of park cabins,

Pihea Trail (p232)

The Otherworldly Alaka'i Swamp

Nothing really provides that out-of-the-ordinary hiking experience the way the Alaka'i Swamp does. Designated a wilderness preserve in 1964, this soggy paradise has a hiking trail that is almost completely lined with wood planks, mainly to discourage off-trail trekking. The state started laying these planks around 1989 – a time-consuming process that was delayed when Hurricane 'Iniki hit in 1992. Today there are still ambitious plans to cover some of the Pihea Trail, but in reality the Alaka'i Trail has already degraded some. Nevertheless, you'll traverse truly fantastic terrain on this hike, including misty bogs where plants dwarf you. On a clear day, look for outstanding views of the Wainiha Valley and during winter, whales breaching in the distant ocean. If it's raining, don't fret: search for rainbows, enjoy the mist and tone down the talk with your fellow hikers. This is a spiritual place: Queen Emma was said to have been so moved by tales from the Alaka'i that she ventured there, chanting in reverence during her sojourn.

The swamp has its own unique biological rhythms as well. There are far more endemic birds than introduced birds here – elsewhere in Hawaii the opposite is true. Many of these species are endangered, some with fewer than 100 birds remaining. The Kaua'i 'o'o, the last of four species of Hawaiian honeyeaters, was thought to be extinct until 1971, when a nest with two chicks was discovered. Unfortunately the call of the 'o'o – that of a single male – was last heard in 1987.

a restaurant, a museum and a campground. Remember, the nearest place for provisions and gas is Waimea, 15 miles away.

Koke'e Museum (☎808-335-9975; www.kokee.org; Koke'e Rd) Sells inexpensive trail maps and provides basic information on trail conditions. You can call for real-time mountain weather reports.

Kaua'i
In Focus

Stand up paddler, Hanalei Bay (p126)
MICHELE FALZONE/GETTY IMAGES ©

Kaua'i Today

Hanalei (p126)

> *Community is what almost all island residents care most about.*

ethnicity
(% of population)

33 White
31 Asian
25 Mixed
8 Native Hawaiian
3 Other

if Kaua'i were 100 people

31 would be 0-24 years old
25 would be 25-44 years old
30 would be 45-64 years old
14 would be 65+ years old

population per sq mile

≈ 40 people

Kaua'i
Hawai'i the Big Island
Maui

Economy & Community

For an island that is in many ways unique and prides itself on being so, Kaua'i is being shaped by issues today that are not unique at all. The first of these is economic recovery. During the recent US recession and the global economic downturn, a decline in tourism halted or curtailed many large construction projects on Kaua'i, particularly in Po'ipu. Of course, this also had a negative impact on the local construction industry and island-wide unemployment.

Another impact of the economic slowdown was an increase in what you might call 'social turnover.' As businesses downsized or closed, some people had to leave the island for good, while demand for temporary or contract employees has attracted others. Similarly, some property owners were forced to sell to shore up their declining finances, while others have been attracted by fire-sale opportunities. The end

ANN CECIL/GETTY IMAGES ©

Toward Sustainability

Another global trend that has found its way to Kaua'i's shores is the sustainability movement. Perhaps it would be more accurate to say that Kaua'i has rediscovered its sustainable roots, as ancient Hawaiians, who weren't even aware of the profit motive, were inherently green.

The first area of interest here is sustainable agriculture. There is a major movement on Kaua'i towards becoming self-sufficient in food production. And why not? We are talking about an island with hundreds of thousands of acres of fertile fields, and relatively few people. Consequently, imported food is increasingly viewed like fossil fuels – necessary at the present moment, but definitely to be avoided in the future. This passionately held local view fuels everything from the development of Hawaii Regional Cuisine to the proliferation of farmers markets. In addition, there is a growing struggle against the use of genetically modified organisms (GMOs), including two recent lawsuits against local GMO grower Pioneer Hi-Bred International, a DuPont company. In 2013, Kaua'i County passed a law requiring large-scale agribusinesses to disclose whether they use pesticides and grow GMO crops on the island, but that groundbreaking law was later overturned by a federal judge.

The other area of interest is renewable energy. In the past Kaua'i has had a surprising deficit in this area, as evidenced by the many gas-guzzling pick-ups prowling island highways. Spurred by the statewide Hawaii Clean Energy Initiative, Kaua'i has become a leader in solar power, and is making progress with hydropower, the latter targeting island rivers. Now if they could only find a way to tap into the power of the waves!

result is a quickening of the rate at which people come and go on Kaua'i, which has put a quiet strain on the social fabric of the community.

And community is what almost all island residents care most about. Under the leadership of Mayor Bernard Carvalho Jr, Kaua'i County is working toward achieving the ambitious goals set by the 'Holo Holo 2020' program, which aims to 'grow Kaua'i responsibly.' Tangibly, it involves more than three dozen separate community improvement projects, ranging from the mundane, but very necessary – repaving roads, expanding bus service, upgrading local parks etc – to the forward-thinking and inspiring, for example, working to increase Native Hawaiian stewardship of the island's important cultural sites and building the county's first 'green' affordable housing.

History

LONELY PLANET/GETTY IMAGES

Hawaii has two periods of history: before Western contact, and after. Prior to Captain Cook's arrival, Native Hawaiians had a traditional culture. Afterwards came Big Sugar, statehood and tourism. This profound transformation occurred peacefully, but still incites a mix of emotions, ranging from rage to pride. However you see this change, it raises important questions for a world still struggling to find peace between Western capitalism and the natural environment.

The First Settlers

Most archaeologists believe that the first humans migrated to the Hawaiian Islands from the Marquesas Islands between AD 300 and 600. This settlement was part of a 2000-year period of migration by ancient seafarers, originally from Southeast Asia, that populated Polynesia. They made their journeys in double-hulled canoes, without any modern navigational tools. Instead they relied on the 'star com-

AD 300–600
Polynesian colonists traveling thousands of miles across open seas in double-hulled canoes arrive in Hawaii.

pass,' a celestial map based on keen observation (and perfect memory) of star paths. They had no idea what, if anything, they would find thousands of miles across open ocean. Amazingly, experts estimate that Hawaii's discoverers sailed for four months straight without stops to restock food and water.

The Ancient Way of Life

Ancient Hawaiians had a hierarchical class system. At the top were the *ali'i nui* (high chiefs, descended from the gods), who each ruled one of the four major islands (including Kaua'i). One's rank as an *ali'i* was determined by one's mother's family lineage, making Hawaii a matrilineal society.

The second class comprised *ali'i 'ai moku* (district chiefs) who ruled island *moku* (districts) and *ali'i 'ai ahupua'a* (lower chiefs) who ruled *ahupua'a*, pie-shaped sub-districts extending from the mountains to the ocean. Also ranked second were kahuna (priest, sorceror, healer, or master), experts in important skills such as canoe building, religious practices, healing arts and navigation.

The third, and largest, class were the *maka'ainana* (commoners), who were not chattel of the *ali'i* and could live wherever they pleased but were obligated to support the *ali'i* through taxes paid in kind with food, goods and labor.

The final *kauwa* (outcast) class was shunned and did not mix with the other classes, except as slaves. In this 'natural order,' Ancient Hawaiians based their identity on the group rather than on individuality.

Although the hierarchy sounds feudal, Hawaiian society was quite different because *ali'i* did not 'own' land. It was inconceivable to the Hawaiian mind to own land or anything in nature. Rather the *ali'i* were stewards of the land – and they had a sacred duty to care for it on behalf of the gods. Further, the ancients had no monetary system or concept of trade for profit. They instead exchanged goods and services through customary, reciprocal gift giving (as well as through obligations to superiors).

Strict religious laws, known as the *kapu* (taboo) system, governed what people ate, whom they married, when they fished or harvested crops, and practically all human behavior. Women, for example, could not dine with men or eat bananas, coconuts, pork and certain types of fish.

1300
Na Pali Coast settled at Nu'alolo Kai. Settlement survives 600 years.

1778
Captain James Cook lands at Waimea; Hawaii will never be the same again.

1810
Kamehameha I unites the major Hawaiian Islands under one kingdom, called Hawai'i after his home island.

From Hawaiian Kingdom to US Territory

Captain Cook

When esteemed British naval captain James Cook inadvertently sighted the uncharted island of Oʻahu on January 18, 1778, the ancient Hawaiians' centuries of isolation were forever lost. This singular event transformed Hawaii in ways inconceivable at the time.

Strong winds on that fateful day pushed Cook away from Oʻahu and toward Kauaʻi, where he made landfall on January 20 at Waimea Bay. Cook promptly named the islands the Sandwich Islands, after his patron, the Earl of Sandwich.

Cook and his men were enthralled with Kauaʻi and its inhabitants, considering them to be robust and handsome in physical appearance, and friendly and generous in trade dealings. Meanwhile the Hawaiians, living in a closed society for hundreds of years, found the strange white men to be astounding. Some historians believe that they regarded Cook as the earthly manifestation of the great god Lono.

After two weeks, Cook continued to the Pacific Northwest for another crack at finding the elusive Northwest Passage across North America. Searching in vain for eight months, he returned south to winter in the Hawaiian Islands.

In November 1778, Cook sighted Maui for the first time, but did not land, choosing instead to head further south to explore the nearby island of Hawaiʻi with its towering volcanic mountains. After returning to picturesque Kealakekua Bay in February 1779, Cook's luck ran out. When one of his ship's boats was stolen, Cook attempted to kidnap the local chief as ransom, and was driven back to the beach. A battle ensued, killing Cook, five of his men, and 17 Hawaiians.

The Hawaiian Kingdom

Among the Hawaiian warriors that felled Captain Cook was a robust young man named Paiʻea. Between 1790 and 1810, this charismatic leader, who became known as Kamehameha the Great, managed to conquer the islands of Hawaiʻi, Maui, Molokaʻi and Oʻahu.

To make his domain complete, Kamehameha tried to conquer Kauaʻi, too, but was thwarted by the formidable chief Kaumualiʻi. Kamehameha did, however, negotiate a diplomatic agreement with the chief, which put both Kauaʻi and Niʻihau into Kamehameha's new kingdom, but gave Kaumualiʻi the right to rule the islands somewhat independently.

Kamehameha is credited with unifying all of the islands, establishing a peaceful and solidified kingdom. He was widely acknowledged as being a benevolent and just ruler, much loved by his people until his death in 1819.

Enter the Missionaries

When Kamehameha died, his 22-year-old son Liholiho (Kamehameha II) became *moʻi* (king) and one of Kamehameha's wives, Queen Kaʻahumanu, became *kuhina nui* (regent) and co-ruler. In a shocking blow to tradition, the two broke a strict taboo against men and women eating together, and later many heiau (temples) and *kiʻi* (carved

1815–17

Georg Scheffer fails to conquer Hawaiʻi for Russia, departing before finishing Fort Elizabeth on the southwest coast.

1819

King Kamehameha I dies and the Hawaiian religious system is cast aside.

1820

First Protestant mission established at Waimea. Without the *kapu* system, Hawaiians prove ready to convert.

Top History Books

Kauaʻi: The Separate Kingdom (Edward Joesting) Definitive history of Kauaʻi emphasizes its iconoclastic bent.

Kauaʻi: Ancient Place-Names and Their Stories (Frederick B Wichman) Traditional stories about island sites give context and meaning to sightseeing.

Ancient Hawaiʻi (Herb Kawainui Kane) Renowned artist-historian's gorgeously illustrated book stirs the imagination about old Hawaii.

Shoal of Time: A History of the Hawaiian Islands (Gavan Daws) Classic history book covering the period from Captain Cook's arrival to statehood.

Pau Hana: Plantation Life and Labor in Hawaii, 1835–1920 (Ronald Takaki) Well-researched account of Hawaii's sugar-plantation laborers and subsequent unique multiculturalism.

deity images) were destroyed. Hawaiian society fell into chaos. Thus when the first missionaries to Hawaii arrived in April 1820, it was a fortuitous moment for them. The Hawaiian people were in great social and political upheaval and some, particularly the *aliʻi* (chiefs), found the Christian faith an appealing replacement.

The Hawaiians had no written language, so the missionaries established a Hawaiian alphabet using Roman letters and taught them how to read and write. This fostered a high literacy rate and the publication of dozens of Hawaiian-language newspapers. Eventually, however, missionaries sought to separate the Hawaiians from their 'hedonistic' cultural roots. They prohibited hula dancing because of its 'lewd and suggestive movements,' denounced the traditional Hawaiian chants and songs that honored 'heathen' gods, taught women to sew Western-style clothing, abolished polygamy, and even banned from schools and governments the language they had taught Hawaiians to write.

Many missionaries became influential advisors to the monarchy and received large tracts of land in return, prompting them to leave the church altogether and turn their land into sugar plantations.

Big Sugar

Foreigners quickly saw that Hawaii was ideal for growing sugarcane and established small plantations using Hawaiian labor. But by then the native population had severely declined, thanks to introduced diseases. To fill the shortage, workers were imported

1835
First successful commercial milling of sugar in Hawaii begins in Koloa.

1848
Under the influence of Westerners, the first system of private land ownership is introduced.

1864
Sugar baron-to-be George Norton Wilcox takes over the lease for Grove Farm in Lihuʻe.

from overseas starting in the 1850s, first from China, and soon after from Japan and the Portuguese islands of Madeira and the Azores.

The influx of imported foreign labor and the rise of the sugar industry had a major impact on the islands' social structure. Caucasian plantation owners and sugar agents rose to become the elite upper economic and political class, while the Hawaiians and foreign laborers became the lower class, without much of a middle class in between. Labor relations became contentious, eventually resulting in the formation of unions and strike action.

Overthrow of the Monarchy

In 1887 the members of the Hawaiian League, a secret antimonarchy organization run by sugar interests, wrote a new constitution and by threat of violence forced King David Kalakaua to sign it. This constitution, which became known as the 'Bayonet Constitution,' limited voting rights and stripped the monarchy's powers, effectively making King Kalakaua a figurehead.

Human Arrival

Human arrival has always been problematic in Hawaii. Excavation at the Makauwahi Sinkhole (p175) near Po'ipu reveals mass extinction of flora and fauna, particularly large birds, following the first wave of Polynesian settlers over 1500 years ago, due to a combination of hunting and the introduction of invasive species. In the 18th century, this brutal process began repeating itself – but this time it affected Native Hawaiians.

When news of Captain Cook's discovery spread, a flood of largely European and American foreigners came to explore Hawaii, which became a prime Pacific waystation for shipping. In particular, by the 1840s the islands had become the whaling capital of the Pacific, with over 700 ships stopping at Hawaiian ports annually. This influx of foreigners brought not only new religious, social, political and dietary habits, but also a slew of lethal infectious diseases, including syphilis, tuberculosis, measles, influenza and smallpox. In 1778, Captain Cook had found a thriving native population of about 400,000 (estimates range from 100,000 to one million). A century later, the count had dropped to an estimated 40,000.

Today, about 140,000 Hawaiian residents (10% of the population) identify themselves as part Native Hawaiian.

1887

Members of the antimonarchy Hawaiian League force King David Kalakaua to sign the 'Bayonet Constitution'.

1890

Lihu'e's Fairview Hotel opens with emphasis on sunbathers; it's the first fully fledged tourist hotel in Kaua'i.

1893

The Hawaiian monarchy, under Queen Lili'uokalani, is overthrown, ending 83 years of rule.

When Kalakaua, Hawai'i's last king, died in 1891, his sister and heir, Princess Lili'uokalani, ascended the throne. She tried to restore the monarchy, but on January 17, 1893, the leaders of the Hawaiian League, supported by both John L Stevens (the US Department of State Minister to Hawaii) and a contingent of US marines and sailors, forcibly arrested Queen Lili'uokalani and took over 'Iolani Palace in Honolulu – a tense but bloodless coup d'état. The Kingdom of Hawai'i was now the Republic of Hawai'i.

Annexation, War & Statehood

American interests pushed hard for annexation, while Hawaiians fought to prevent this final acquisition. In 1897, more than 21,000 people (almost half the population of Hawai'i) signed an anti-annexation petition and sent it to Washington. In 1898, President William McKinley nevertheless approved the annexation, perhaps influenced by the concurrent Spanish-American War, which highlighted Pearl Harbor's strategic military location.

Statehood was a tough sell to the US Congress, but a series of significant historical events paved the way. In 1936, Pan American airlines launched the first commercial flights from the US mainland to Hawaii, thus launching the trans-Pacific air age and the beginning of mass tourism. A wireless telegraph (and later telephone) service between

Traditional Hawaiian tattoos
KAREN KASMAUSKI/GETTY IMAGES ©

1897
More than 21,000 people (almost half of Hawaii's population) sign an anti-annexation petition.

1898
Annexed by Congress, the Republic of Hawai'i becomes a US territory.

1924
Hanapepe Massacre leaves 20 dead as Filipino strikers confront police.

Hawaii and the mainland alleviated doubts about long-distance communication. Most importantly, WWII proved both the strategic military role of Pearl Harbor and the loyalty and heroism of Hawaii's residents of Japanese ancestry.

During WWII, Japanese immigrants and locals of Japanese ancestry were initially banned from joining the armed forces, due to great suspicion about their loyalty. In 1943, the US government yielded to political pressure and formed an all-Japanese combat unit, the 100th Infantry Battalion. While less than 3000 men were needed for this unit, more than 10,000 men volunteered.

By the war's end, another all-Japanese unit, the 442nd Regimental Combat Team, composed of 3800 men from Hawaii and the US mainland, had received more commendations and medals than any other unit. The 100th Infantry also received special recognition for rescuing the so-called 'Lost Battalion,' stranded behind enemy lines in France.

Despite being a controversial candidate, the Hawaiian Islands were finally admitted as the 50th US state on August 21, 1959.

Polynesian-style thatched huts
PHOTOBLUEICE VIEW PORTFOLIO/ISTOCK ©

1934
First movie, *White Heat*, shot on Kaua'i.

1941
Japanese attack Pearl Harbor on O'ahu, catapulting the US into WWII.

1946
Tsunami generated off Alaska strikes Hawaiian Islands – 45ft waves hit the North Shore, killing 14 and knocking out bridges.

The Hawaiian Renaissance

After WWII, Hawaii became America's tropical fantasyland. The tiki craze, surfer movies, aloha shirts and Waikiki were all Westernized, commercial images, but they made Hawaii iconic to the masses. Simultaneously, Native Hawaiians were increasingly marginalized by Western social, political and economic influences. The Hawaiian language had nearly died out, land was impossible for most Native Hawaiians to buy, and most of the traditional ways of life that had supported an independent people for over a millennium were lost. Without these, Native Hawaiians lost much of their own identity and indigenous pride.

The 1970s introduced a cultural awakening, due largely to two events: in 1974 a small group called the **Polynesian Voyaging Society** (www.hokulea.com) committed themselves to building and sailing a replica of an ancient Hawaiian voyaging canoe, to

Promised Land

Ancient Hawaiians had no concept of land ownership. The gods owned the land and people were stewards. In practical terms, the king controlled the land and foreigners had no means to own any.

In the 1840s, Americans sought to secure long-term property rights. In 1848, they convinced the Hawaiian government to enact the Great Mahele, a revolutionary land reform act that redistributed all kingdom lands into three parts: crown lands, chief lands and government lands (for the benefit of the general public).

Two years later the government went further and allowed foreign residents to buy land. Sugar growers and land speculators bought huge parcels for minimal sums from chiefs lured by quick money and from commoners ignorant of deeds, taxes and other legal requirements for fee-simple land ownership.

Native Hawaiians lost much of their land and struggled with ensuing economic problems. In 1921, Kaua'i's native son Prince Kuhio (congressional delegate for the Territory of Hawaii) convinced the US Congress to pass the Hawaiian Homes Commission Act, which set aside almost 200,000 acres of government land for Native Hawaiians to lease for $1 per year. It sounds terrific, but there are problems. Much of this land is remote and lacks basic infrastructure, such as roads and access to water and electricity. Lessees must build their own homes, which many applicants cannot afford. And applicants end up waiting for years, even decades. Today there are over 22,000 residential applicants waiting across the state. Only about 9200 leases have been granted since 1921.

1958

Mitzi Gaynor's *South Pacific* becomes an international hit. The movie was shot on Kaua'i's North Shore.

1959

Hawaii becomes the 50th US state.

1982

Hurricane 'Iwa strikes Kaua'i – 1900 homes damaged or destroyed, 44 boats sunk, resorts wrecked.

Eye of the Storm

Almost two decades after Hurricane 'Iniki blasted Kaua'i, residents can still give blow-by-blow accounts of their survival on September 11, 1992. 'Iniki blew in with sustained winds of 145mph and gusts of 165mph or more (a weather-station meter in mountainous Koke'e broke off at 227mph). It snapped trees by the thousands and totally demolished over 1400 homes (and swept over 60 out to sea). Another 5000 homes were severely damaged while over 7000 sustained minor damage. Most of the island lacked electricity for over a month, and some areas lacked power for up to three months. Thirty-foot waves washed away entire wings of beachfront hotels, particularly those in Po'ipu and Princeville.

During the immediate aftermath, residents were remarkably calm and law-abiding despite the lack of power, radio or TV. Communities held parties to share and consume perishable food. Looting was minor, and when grocers allowed affected residents to take what they needed, they insisted on paying.

Miraculously, only four people died, but the total value of the damage to the island was over $1 billion. While locals notice the changed landscape, newcomers would never realize the havoc wreaked 15 years ago.

prove that the first Polynesian settlers were capable of navigating the Pacific without the use of Western technology such as sextants and compasses. When the *Hokule'a* made its maiden 4800-mile roundtrip voyage to Tahiti in 1976, it instantly became a symbol of rebirth for Hawaiians, prompting a cultural revival.

The same year, a small grassroots group, the Protect Kaho'olawe 'Ohana (PKO), began protesting against the treatment of Kaho'olawe, an island the US military had used as a training and bombing site since WWII. The PKO's political actions, including the island's illegal occupation, spurred new interest in reclaiming not only Kaho'olawe (which the US Navy relinquished in 2003) and other military-held lands, but also Hawaiian cultural practices, from hula to *lomilomi* massage.

Public schools have started teaching Hawaiian language and culture classes, while Hawaiian immersion charter schools proliferate. Hawaiian music tops the charts, turning island-born musicians into superstars. Small but vocal contingents still push for Hawaiian sovereignty, from complete secession from the United States to a nation-within-a-nation model.

1992
Hawai'i's most powerful hurricane ever, 'Iniki, destroys 1400 houses; four people are killed. Kaua'i declared a disaster area.

2007
Protesters prevent Superferry from entering Nawiliwili Harbor on its inaugural voyage, ending service to Kaua'i.

2009
Age of sugar ends on Kaua'i with closure of Gay & Robinson mill in Kaumakani.

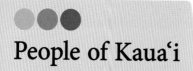

People of Kaua'i

Hula performance

PHOTO RESOURCE HAWAII/ALAMY ©

In many people's minds Kaua'i's visual splendor seems to act as a composer, orchestrating social harmony among its residents. Well, it does and it doesn't. As with any multicultural atmosphere, seamless fusion is rare and cultural disparities exist. However, whether the residents are Native Hawaiian, kama'aina (born here) or transplants, they undoubtedly share one thing in common: aloha 'aina (love of the land).

Kaua'i Identity

Local Versus Transplant

Born-and-raised Kauaians tend to be easygoing and low-key for the most part, preferring the unpretentious small-town life. Multigenerational locals take pride in their roots and enjoy knowing and being known within in their community – which is a good thing since anonymity is a state short-lived, thanks to the 'coconut wireless' (see p241). Stereotypes of an unwelcoming local contingent do exist, and there is some justification for that. Resistance has been one of Kaua'i's strong suits throughout its history and the way that this still manifests itself today is in an insider-outsider mentality that can linger beneath the surface of everyday interactions. However, we find that if you give aloha, you get aloha.

What's in a Name?

Haole White person (except local Portuguese). Translates as 'shallow breather.' Often further defined as 'mainland haole' or 'local haole.'

Hapa Person of mixed ancestry, most commonly referring to *hapa haole,* who are part white and part other. such as Hawaiian or Asian.

Hawaiian Person of Native Hawaiian ancestry. It's a faux pas to call any Hawaii resident 'Hawaiian' (as you would a Californian or Texan), thus ignoring the existence of an indigenous people.

Kama'aina Literally defined as 'child of the land', refers to a person who is native to a particular place. In the retail context, '*kama'aina* discounts' apply to any resident of Hawaii (ie anyone with a Hawaii drivers license).

Local Person who grew up in Hawaii. Locals who move away retain their local 'cred,' at least in part. But longtime transplants never become local. To call a transplant 'almost local' is a welcome compliment, despite its emphasis on the insider-outsider mentality.

Neighbor Islander Person who lives on any Hawaiian Island other than O'ahu.

Transplant Person who moves to the islands as an adult.

Island life is different, and its pace of life is a few gearshifts down from that of the modern get-it-done-yesterday world. For most island residents, tradition trumps change. Locals can grow resentments with the influx of mainland transplants and their progressive ideals diluting traditional communities, especially on the North Shore. Yet other transplants seem to quickly find their feet: befriending neighbors, immersing themselves in the culture and simply slowing down and respecting local ways. As the saying goes, 'Kaua'i will either suck you in or spit you out.'

Typical transplants include post-college wanderers, surfer dudes, wealthy retirees or middle-aged career switchers seeking idyllic seclusion.

Regional Differences

Despite the island's compact size, each geographical location has its own distinct vibe. Lihu'e, the county seat, is a functional town where people go to work, not to play. Wailua's upcountry remains a favorite residential area while coastal Kapa'a has taken on a burgeoning hippie front. Hanalei is a surf town, dominated by suntanned blonds and affordable only to multimillionaires. Po'ipu's sun-splashed beaches serve as a perennial summer camp for retirees and the Westside – more so than any other region – has retained an audible echo of its multiethnic plantation-history traditions.

Lifestyle

Most residents focus on the outdoors. With the ocean as the primary playground, surfing is the sport of choice, along with fishing, free diving, hunting and just hanging out as popular pastimes. The workday starts and ends early, and most find a comfortable work/home balance.

Locals and transplants tend to diverge in their careers and ambitions. Locals tend toward more conventional, 'American dream' lives, meaning marriage, kids, a modest home, stable work and free nights and weekends. Mainland transplants are here for other reasons: retirement, a dream B&B or organic farm, waves, art, or all around youthful shenanigans. Most feel free to be unconventional on Kaua'i.

Family

In Hawaii, locals define 'family' much more inclusively than mainstream mainlanders. Here, the *'ohana* (family) can extend beyond bloodlines to friends, teammates, coworkers and classmates. If people demonstrate the *''ohana* spirit,' it means that they are generous and welcoming, like family should be.

Hanai (adopted or foster) children are common in Hawaiian families. To be a *hanai* child or to *hanai* a child is not odd or pejorative in Hawaii. Instead, *hanai* children are fully accepted into the family.

Locals might refer to a 'calabash cousin,' meaning a close friend akin to a cousin but not a blood relation. More commonly, you'll hear locals refer to 'aunty' or 'uncle' even if the person is not related at all. These elders are beloved community members, and calling them aunty or uncle connotes respect and affection.

Multiculturalism

The overwhelming majority of Kaua'i's current immigrants are white, so the island's diversity is based on historic minorities: Native Hawaiians and plantation immigrants (predominantly Filipino, Japanese and Chinese).

During plantation days, whites were wealthy plantation owners, and their legendary surnames remain household words (eg Wilcox Memorial Hospital and Rice St). Their ingrained privilege is one reason why some resentment toward haole lingers. As time passes and the plantation era fades, the traditional stereotypes, hierarchies and alliances have softened.

Hawaiian Pidgin Phrases

brah – shortened form of *braddah* (brother)

chicken skin – goose bumps from cold, fear, thrill

coconut wireless – the 'grapevine'; local gossip channels

da kine – whatchamacallit; used whenever you can't think of the appropriate word

fo' real? – Really? Are you kidding me?

grind – to eat (grinds means local food)

high makamaka – stuck-up, snooty, pretentious, high-maintenance; literally high 'eyes,' meaning head in the air

howzit? – Hey, how's it going? As in 'Eh, howzit brah?'

lolo – crazy, stupid, moronic

rubbah slippah – literally 'rubber slippers'; flip-flops

stink eye – dirty look

talk story – chitchat or any casual conversation

to da max – used as an adjective or adverb to add emphasis, as in 'da waves was big to da max!'

That said, no ethnic group in Hawaii ever remained exclusive; instead, they freely adopted and shared cultural customs, from food to festivals to language. Folks of all backgrounds dance hula, craft hardwood bowls, play the ukulele and study the Hawaiian language.

Today there is no ethnic majority in the Hawaiian Islands. Due to this multiculturalism, you will find a blend of cultural influences and names. Many local Hawaiians have Caucasian or Asian surnames, for example.

Generally, locals feel bonded with other locals. While tourists and transplants are usually welcomed with open arms, they must earn the trust and respect of the locals by being *pono* (respectful and proper). It is unacceptable for an outsider to assume an air of superiority and try to 'fix' local ways.

Hawaiian Words

aloha – love, hello, welcome, goodbye

hale – house

kane – man

kapu – taboo, restricted

kokua – help, please

mahalo – thank you

makai – a direction, toward the sea

mauka – a direction, toward the mountains (inland)

pau – finished, completed

wahine – woman

Social Issues

Among social issues on Kaua'i, two stand out: education and substance abuse. With only three public high schools on the island, education remains a weak point. North Shore students, for example, can average three hours a day commuting to and from school. With an 'us versus them' mentality sometimes present between the student body and the faculty, public school can end up being more of a containment facility than

Preparing meat for a luau
BOYKOV/GETTY IMAGES ©

Island Etiquette

- Practice acquiescence, be courteous and 'no make waves' (don't make a scene).
- Treat ancient Hawaiian sites and artifacts with respect. Do not move any stones.
- Dress casually as the locals do.
- Remove your shoes before entering homes and B&Bs.
- Drive slowly. Don't honk your horn unless you're about to crash – it's a sure way to attract 'stink eye'.
- Give a thank-you *shaka* ('hang loose' hand gesture, with index, middle and ring fingers downturned) if a driver lets you merge or stops before a one-lane bridge.
- Don't assume being called a haole is an insult (but don't assume it's not either).
- Tread lightly with locals when surfing; it can quickly become unpleasant if you do otherwise.
- Ask permission before you pick fruit or flowers from private property.

an institution of learning. Parents, especially if they're mainland transplants, often try to get their kids into private schools.

Crystal methamphetamine, or 'ice' as it's referred to locally, is an issue growing at an alarming rate. With Hawaii's considerable reliance on importing goods, ice has been able to make its way onto the islands with ease. As there is no inpatient rehab facility on the island, progress is something residents can only hope for with fingers crossed. And with the extremely addictive nature of the drug, crimes like theft (including gas siphoning), and even fatalities are inevitably one or two paces behind. Yet even with all of these stern facts clearly visible, this issue seems to remain half-swept under the collective social carpet of denial – perhaps an example of the darker (and sadder) repercussions of a remote and rural community's exposure to the outside world.

Food & Drink

Sashimi *pupu* (appetizer) with soybeans, *ogo* (edible seaweed) and *onigiri* (Japanese rice balls)

ANN CECIL/GETTY IMAG

Island-caught fish. Island-grown produce. Island-casual setting. Kaua'i likes to keep it simple. Whether you're savoring four-star Hawaii Regional Cuisine or sampling that curious Spam musubi (rice ball), you'll find a fascinating fusion of flavors – from Polynesian staples such as taro, banana and coconut to Japanese teriyaki, Chinese noodles and Hawaiian kalua pork. The real spoils go to those willing to hunt down the best fish markets, local bakeries and farmers markets.

The Island Diet

The island diet is more than just a meal. It's a window on the islands themselves. But defining it is no simple matter. It's multiethnic, yet distinct from fusion cooking. It's got a full-fledged highbrow cuisine, yet its iconic dishes are lowbrow local grinds (casual food). The only way to understand the island diet is to partake of its pleasures, which have the following elements in common:

○ The primary starch in Hawaii is sticky, medium-grain white rice. Jasmine rice is tolerated with Thai food, but fluffy rice is considered *haole* (Caucasian) food (and Uncle Ben's is thought of as inedible).

○ The top condiment is soy sauce (ubiquitously called by its Japanese name, *shōyu*), which combines well with sharp Asian flavors, such as ginger, green onion and garlic.

○ Meat, chicken or fish is often integral to a

dish. For quick, cheap eating, locals devour anything tasty, from Portuguese sausage to hamburger steak to canned Spam. But the dinner-table highlight is always seafood, especially succulent, freshly caught ahi (tuna).

○ Non-local classics (such as pizza and bagels) are usually disappointing. Also bear in mind that 'barbecue' typically means teriyaki-marinated.

○ While Kaua'i's top restaurants can hold their own among statewide peers, you generally won't find the cutting-edge culinary creativity that you'd get on O'ahu, Maui or the Big Island.

Two excellent resources on Hawaii cuisine are **Edible Hawaiian Islands** (www.edible hawaiianislands.com), which covers the gamut, and **Hawaii Seafood** (www.hawaii -seafood.org) which is all about just that. For an explanation of our review system, see p288.

Hawaii Regional Cuisine

If pineapple-topped entrées epitomized Hawaii cuisine till the late 1980s, locals are partly to blame. Fine dining in Hawaii meant copycat 'continental' fare that hid the basic appeal of local ingredients. While there were many decent, mid-range Asian eateries, Hawaii lacked a recognizable local cuisine. Further, the local appetite for cheap, filling food (never mind that it's made with canned goods) did nothing to push the gourmet envelope.

In the early 1990s, 12 Hawaii chefs changed all that. Led by some now-famous names, they established Hawaii Regional Cuisine, a culinary movement that inventively blends Hawaii's diverse, ethnic flavors with the cuisine of the world. Some classic menus include Roy's (p184) and Merriman's Fish House (p185) at Po'ipu Beach and Princeville's Kaua'i Grill (p123) and Hanalei's Postcards Café (p138). You'll also hear this cuisine called 'Pacific Rim'. It has since led to more sophisticated fusion menus in general, such as the Mediterranean-inspired tapas restaurant BarAcuda (p138) in Hanalei and culinary superstar Josselin's Tapas Bar & Grill (p184), another tapas restaurant with a focus on Asian fusion, in Po'ipu.

Regional Treats

Don't miss these local Kaua'i specialties:

○ Homemade taro chips from Taro Ko Chips Factory (p208)

○ Steaming noodle soups at Hamura Saimin (p50)

○ Spam *musubi* and homemade *manju* (Japanese sweet bean-filled pastry) at Pono Market (p91)

○ *Bentō* (Japanese-style boxed meal) from Ishihara Market (p219)

○ Taro smoothies, taro burgers and Hawaiian plate lunches with poi at Hanalei Taro & Juice Co (p136)

○ Spicy kim-chi or traditional Hawaiian *poke* from Koloa Fish Market (p165)

○ Coconut almonds, Kona-coffee pecans and other addictive crunchies at Kauai Nut Roasters (p139)

○ Sorbetto made from exotic island-grown fruits at Papalani Gelato

Hawaii Regional Cuisine started as a four-star phenomenon, but is not just defined by complex culinary fusions. It is also rooted in local, seasonal, organic ingredients, handpicked if possible. This trend toward eating local, known as locavarianism, might help struggling island farms survive. In part by necessity, 90% of the state's basic food supply is imported. By frequenting farmers markets, you'll not only eat better, you'll help sustain Kaua'i's budding farming industry. For more on sustainable agriculture, see p263.

Local Food

Cheap, filling and tasty, local food is the stuff of cravings and comfort. Such food might be dubbed 'street food' but street vendors are uncommon, except at farmers markets.

No list is complete without the classic plate lunch, a fixed-plate meal containing 'two scoop rice,' macaroni salad and your choice of a hot protein dish, such as *tonkatsu* (breaded, fried pork cutlets), fried mahimahi or teriyaki chicken. Often eaten with disposable chopsticks on disposable plates, they are tasty and filling. Typically fried, salty, gravy-laden and meaty, more health-conscious contemporary plate lunches now include grilled fish, brown rice and green salad.

The local palate prefers hot rice or noodle entrées to cold cuts and sliced bread. Thus another favorite is *saimin,* a soup of chewy Chinese egg noodles and Japanese broth, garnished with colorful toppings such as green onion, dried nori, *kamaboko* (steamed fish cake), egg roll or *char siu* (Chinese barbecued pork). If you're in a hurry, pick up a *bentō* (prepackaged Japanese-style boxed meal) containing rice, meat or fish, and Japanese garnishes such as pickles, at deli counters and corner stores. And you can't go home without trying a Big Island invention called *loco moco,* a bowl of rice, two eggs (typically fried over-easy) and a hamburger patty, topped with gravy and a dash of *shōyu.*

Consider yourself lucky if you snag an invitation to a *pupu* (appetizer) party at a local home. Go casual and expect an endless spread of grazing foods (forget the cheese and crackers), such as fried shrimp, *edamame* (boiled soybeans in the pod) and *maki* (rolled) sushi. A must-try is *poke* (pronounced 'po-keh'), Hawaii's soul food, a savory dish of bite-sized raw fish (typically *'ahi*), seasoned typically with *shōyu,*

Seafood Decoder

The following species are most commonly eaten in Hawaii:

ahi – yellowfin or bigeye tuna; red flesh, excellent raw or rare

aku – skipjack tuna; red flesh, strong flavor; *katsuo* in Japanese

kajiki – Pacific blue marlin; firm white to pinkish flesh; *a'u* in Hawaiian

mahimahi – dolphin fish or dorado; firm pink flesh

nairagi – striped marlin; firm flesh, colored pink to deep red-orange; *a'u* in Hawaiian

onaga – long-tailed red snapper; soft and moist

ono – wahoo; white-fleshed and flaky

opah – moonfish; firm and rich flesh

'opakapaka – pink snapper; delicate flavor, firm flesh

'opelu – mackerel scad; pan-sized, delicious when fried

shutome – swordfish; succulent and meaty

tako – octopus, chewy texture

The Other Pink Meat

Simply put, locals love Spam. Yes, *that* Spam. It's a local comfort food, typically eaten sliced and sautéed to a light crispiness in sweetened *shōyu*. Expect to see Hormel's iconic canned ham product served with eggs for breakfast or as a *loco moco* option. It's especially enjoyed as Spam *musubi* (rice ball topped with fried Spam and wrapped with dried seaweed, or *nori*) – folks of all stripes savor this only-in-Hawaii creation that's culturally somewhat akin to an easy, satisfying PB&J sandwich.

The affinity for Spam arose during the plantation era, when canned meat was cheap and easy to prepare for *bentō* (box) lunches. In Hawaii, unlike on the mainland, there's no stigma to eating Spam. If you acquire a taste for it, plan a trip to Honolulu for the annual **Waikiki Spam Jam** (www.spamjamhawaii.com) and go wild in your own kitchen with *Hawai'i Cooks with SPAM: Local Recipes Featuring Our Favorite Canned Meat,* written by prolific cookbook author Muriel Miura.

sesame oil, green onion, sea salt, *ogo* (seaweed) and *inamona,* a flavoring made of roasted and ground *kukui* (candlenut).

Nowadays kids veer toward mainstream candy and gum, but the traditional local treat is preserved fruit (typically plum, cherry, mango or lemon) known as crack seed. It can be sweet, sour, salty or licorice-spicy. On a hot day, go for shave ice, the island version of a snow cone.

Traditional Hawaiian Dishes

Native Hawaiian food is like no other. Today, several dishes are staples in the local diet, but they're generally harder to find than other cuisines. The best venues for good, authentic Hawaiian food are plate-lunch shops, diners, fish markets and supermarket delis. Commercial luau buffets include all the notable dishes, but the quality can be mediocre.

Perhaps the most famous (or infamous) Hawaiian dish is poi, or steamed and mashed wetland taro, which was sacred to ancient Hawaiians. Locals savor the bland to mildly tart flavor as a starchy palate cleanser, but its slightly sticky and pasty consistency can be off-putting to others. Taro is highly nutritious, low in calories, easily digestible and versatile to prepare. Also try taro chips (made with dryland/upland 'Chinese' taro), available from local grocers.

Locals typically eat poi as a counterpoint to strongly flavored fish dishes such as *poke* and *lomilomi* salmon (minced salted salmon tossed with diced tomato and green onion). Salmon is actually an imported food, first introduced to Hawaiians by the crews of 19th-century whaling ships.

No Hawaiian feast is complete without *kalua* pig, which is traditionally roasted, whole, underground in an *imu,* a sealed pit of red-hot stones. Cooked this way, the pork comes out smoky, salty and quite succulent. Nowadays *kalua* pork is typically oven-roasted and seasoned with salt and liquid smoke. But if you attend the Luau Kalamaku (p53) you'll see it done the old way.

A popular restaurant dish is *laulau,* a bundle of pork or chicken and salted butterfish, wrapped in taro leaves, and steamed in ti leaves. When cooked, the melt-in-your-mouth taro leaves blend perfectly with the savory meats.

Another food rarely appearing on menus is raw *'opihi,* or limpet shells. You might see locals picking these off shoreline rocks.

Island Drinks

Although Kona coffee grown on the Big Island gets all the acclaim, 40% of the state's entire coffee crop is grown right here on Kaua'i. Sample local brews at island farmers markets and take a working farm tour at Kaua'i Coffee Company (p187).

While fresh fruit is plentiful at farmers markets, fresh fruit juice tends to be pricey and sold mainly at health-food markets and roadside fruit stands, such as the Coconut Cup Juice Bar & Cafe (p91), which makes tropical smoothies to order. An offshoot of the smoothie is the frosty, an icy dessert with the texture of ice cream, made by puréeing frozen fruit in a food processor. Try it at Banana Joe's Fruitstand (p113). Forgo the supermarket cartons and cans, which tend to be sugary drinks.

Unique to Hawaii are two fruit-juice 'tonics' nowadays marketed mainly to tourists: 'awa (kava), a mild sedative, and noni (Indian mulberry), which some consider to be a cure-all. Both fruits are pungent, if not repulsive, in smell and taste, so they are typically mixed with other juices.

Among alcoholic beverages, beer is the local drink of choice. Knock back locally brewed pints at Kauai Beer Company (p53) in Lihu'e and the Kauai Island Brewery & Grill (p202) at Port Allen. Wine is gaining in popularity, and all top-end restaurants offer a decent selection.

Food & Drink Festivals

Now that agri-tourism and gourmet cuisine are trendy, food festivals are garnering much attention. The annual Kalo Festival (p134) in Hanalei features poi-pounding and taro-cooking demonstrations. More extravagant is Taste of Hawaii (p76), a line-up-and-sample extravaganza dubbed the 'ultimate Sunday brunch.' Look for the Garden

Tropical fruit and smoothie at a fruit stand
LINDA CHING/GETTY IMAGES ©

Island Range & Food Festival (p48) at Kilohana Plantation.

Many public festivals and events offer family-friendly outdoor food booths, serving much more than standard concession grub. The Waimea Town Celebration (p218), Koloa Plantation Days celebration (p163), Kapa'a's Coconut Festival (p89) and Lihu'e's Kaua'i County Farm Bureau Fair (p47) showcase not only local culture but also local food, from shave ice to plate lunches.

Luau

In ancient Hawaii, a luau commemorated auspicious occasions, such as births, war victories or successful harvests. Today, only commercial luau offer the elaborate Hawaiian feast and hula dancing that tourists expect. A $75 to $100 ticket buys you a highly choreographed Polynesian dance show and an all-you-can-eat buffet of luau standards – usually toned down for the Western palate – such as poi, *kalua* pig, steamed mahimahi, teriyaki chicken and *haupia* (coconut-cream custard).

For the most impressive show, Kilohana Plantation's Luau Kalamaku (p53) offers a theatrical production with professional-caliber dancers. The long-running luau at Smith's Tropical Paradise (p70) is a family affair and, while touristy, the multicultural performances with dancers of all ages has its appeal.

Private luau celebrations, typically for weddings or first birthdays, are often large banquet-hall gatherings. The menu might be more daring – perhaps including raw *'a'ama* (black crab) and *'opihi* (limpet) – but the entertainment is more low-key. No fire eaters.

Habits & Customs

In most households, home cooking is integral to daily life, perhaps owing to the slower pace of living, backyard gardens and a common obsession with food. Meals start early and on the dot: typically 6am breakfast, noon lunch and 6pm dinner. At home, locals rarely (perhaps never) serve formal sit-down meals with individual courses. Even when entertaining, meals are typically served in a potluck style, often with a spread of unrelated dishes.

If you're invited to a local home, show up on time and bring dessert. Remove your shoes at the door. And don't be surprised if you're forced to take home a plate or two of leftovers. Except at top resort restaurants, the island dress code means that T-shirts and flip-flops are ubiquitous. But the local, older generation tends toward neat and modest attire.

Kaua'i restaurants typically open and close early; late-night dining is virtually nonexistent. Smoking is not allowed at any restaurants in Hawaii. Tipping (normally 18% to 20%) is expected.

The Best...
Desserts

1 Right Slice (p50)

2 Pink's Creamery (p136)

3 Papalani Gelato (p182)

4 Omoide Bakery (p209)

5 Jo-Jo's Anuenue Shave Ice & Treats (p220)

6 Lappert's Hawaii (p123)

IN FOCUS FOOD & DRINK

Vegetarians & Vegans

Although locals love their sashimi and Spam, vegetarians and vegans won't go hungry on Kaua'i, especially at lively local farmers markets held weekly island-wide. A handful of restaurants cater to vegetarian, vegan, gluten-free or health-conscious diets. Notable venues include Postcards Café (p138), Kaua'i Pasta (p85), Kalaheo Café & Coffee Co (p190) and Rainbow Living Foods (p92), which focus on vegetarian dishes. High-end Hawaii Regional Cuisine menus always have vegetarian options. Asian eateries offer varied tofu and veggie options, but beware of meat- or fish-based broths.

Food Glossary

Hawaii cuisine is multiethnic and so is the lingo.

adobo – Filipino chicken or pork cooked in vinegar, *shōyu*, garlic and spices

arare – *shōyu*-flavored rice crackers; also called *kaki mochi*

'awa – kava, a Polynesian plant used to make a mildly intoxicating drink

bentō – Japanese-style boxed meal

broke da mout – delicious; literally 'broke the mouth'

char siu – Chinese barbecued pork

crack seed – Chinese-style preserved fruit; a salty, sweet and/or sour snack

furikake – a catch-all Japanese seasoning or condiment, usually dry and sprinkled atop rice; in Hawaii, often used for *poke*

grind – to eat

grinds – local food; *'ono kine grinds* is good food

guava – fruit with green or yellow rind, moist pink flesh and lots of edible seeds

haupia – coconut-cream custard

hulihuli chicken – rotisserie-cooked chicken

imu – underground earthen oven used to cook *kalua* pig and other luau food

inamona – roasted and ground *kukui* used to flavor *poke*

izakaya – a Japanese pub serving tapas-style dishes

kaki mochi – see *arare*

kalo – Hawaiian word for taro

kalua – Hawaiian method of cooking pork and other luau food in an *imu*

kamaboko – cake of puréed, steamed fish

katsu – Japanese deep-fried cutlets, usually pork or chicken; see *tonkatsu*

kaukau – food

The Best...
Fish Markets

1 Kilauea Fish Market, Kilauea (p113)

2 Koloa Fish Market, Koloa (p165)

3 Ishihara Market, Waimea (p219)

4 Fish Express, Lihu'e (p51)

5 Hanalei Dolphin Restaurant & Sushi Lounge (p137)

kukui – candlenut

laulau – bundle of pork or chicken and salted butterfish, wrapped in taro and *ti* leaves and steamed

li hing mui – sweet-salty preserved plum; type of crack seed; also refers to the flavor powder

liliko'i – passion fruit

limu – Hawaiian term for *ogo*

loco moco – dish of rice, fried egg and hamburger patty topped with gravy and other condiments

lomilomi salmon – minced, salted salmon, diced tomato and green onion

luau – Hawaiian feast

mai tai – 'tiki bar' drink typically containing rum, grenadine, rum and tropical fruit juices

malasada – Portuguese fried doughnut, sugar-coated, no hole, often filled with flavored custard

manapua – Chinese steamed or baked bun filled with *char siu*

manjū – Japanese steamed or baked cake, often filled with sweet bean paste

mochi – Japanese pounded-rice cake, sticky and sweet

noni – type of mulberry with smelly yellow fruit, used medicinally

nori – Japanese seaweed, usually dried

ogo – crunchy seaweed, often added to *poke; limu* in Hawaiian

'ohelo – shrub with edible red berries similar in tartness and size to cranberries

'ono – delicious

'ono kine grinds – good food

pho – Vietnamese soup, typically beef broth, noodles and fresh herbs

poi – staple Hawaiian starch made of steamed, mashed wetland taro

poke – cubed, marinated raw fish

pupu – snacks or appetizers

saimin – local-style noodle soup

shave ice – cup of finely shaved ice doused with colorful sweet syrups

shōyu – soy sauce

soba – thin Japanese buckwheat-flour noodles

star fruit – translucent green-yellow fruit with five ribs like the points of a star and sweet, juicy pulp

taro – staple plant with edible roots and stems (used to make *poi*) and edible leaves (eaten in *laulau); kalo* in Hawaiian

teishoku – Japanese set meal

teppanyaki – Japanese style of cooking with an iron grill

tonkatsu – Japanese breaded and fried pork cutlets, also prepared as chicken *katsu*

tsukemono – Japanese pickled vegetables

ume – Japanese pickled plum

unagi – freshwater eel, usually grilled and served with sweet sauce over sushi rice

Hawaiian Arts & Crafts

Playing the ukulele

DANA EDMUNDS/GETTY IMAGES

It's no surprise that the island's arts and crafts are rooted in nature and are used to celebrate mana (spiritual essence). Underneath it all beats a Hawaiian heart, pounding with an ongoing revival of Hawaii's indigenous language, artisan crafts, music and the hula. E komo mai (welcome) to these unique Polynesian islands, where storytelling and slack key guitar are among the sounds of everyday life.

Hawaiian Music

Traditional Hawaiian music meant *mele oli* (solo chants), performed a cappella at rituals or ceremonies, and *mele hula* (hula chants), accompanied by dance and percussion instruments. While stirring, *mele* were repetitive and not exactly melodic. Once the missionaries arrived, Hawaiians sang hymns with gusto and soon were composing songs still sung today. Queen Lili'uokalani's 'Aloha 'Oe' is a prime example.

After the arrival of string instruments, Hawaiians displayed their musical gifts by making three instruments their own. The resonant Hawaiian steel guitar *(kika kila)* is fundamental to the signature Hawaiian sound. Most cite Joseph Kekuku as the inventor of the iconic lap guitar in the 1880s; by the 1900s, he and other Hawaiians burst onto the international scene, introducing both their guitar and *hapa haole* (Hawaiian music with English lyrics) songs to the world.

To hear a diverse selection of Hawaiian music, stream the Hawaiian Rainbow (www.hawaiianrainbow.com) radio station online. An excellent online Hawaiian music retailer, Mele.com (www.mele.com) links to more streaming radio stations.

Ukulele

Heard all across the islands is the ukulele, derived from the *braguinha*, a Portuguese stringed instrument. Ukulele means 'jumping flea' in Hawaiian, referring to the way players' deft fingers swiftly move around the strings. While it's often present in the background to accompany *hula 'auana* (modern-style hula), it's also a solo instrument for bestselling musicians such as Eddie Kamae and Jake Shimabukuro (who became a YouTube hit with his mesmerizing cover of 'While My Guitar Gently Weeps').

Slack Key Guitar

Slack key guitar (*ki ho'alu*, which means 'loosen the key') is not an instrument but a finger-style method in which the thumb plays the bass and rhythm chords, while the fingers play the melody and improvisations, in a picked style. Traditionally, slack key tunings were closely guarded secrets among *'ohana* (extended family and friends).

Since Gabby Pahinui first recorded his slack key tunes for the public in the 1940s, it has become the most famous and commercially successful Hawaiian genre. To find out more about slack key guitar, visit George Winston's Dancing Cat music label website (www.dancingcat.com) to listen to sound clips and browse bios of some of the living legends.

Vocals

Hawaiian vocalists are known for a distinctive falsetto of 'high voice' style called *leo ki'eki'e*, which stresses *ha'i*, a vocal break between lower and upper registers. Among females, the archetype is the late Genoa Keawe, whose impossibly long-held notes in the song 'Alika' set the standard (and set it high). Other notables include

Island Literature for All Ages

All I Asking for is My Body (Milton Murayama) First published in 1975, this 1980 American Book Award winner is a realistic account of the Japanese American experience in Hawaii around WWII.

Saturday Night at the Pahala Theatre (Lois-Ann Yamanaka) This prolific writer's breakthrough collection of poems, written in pidgin, won the 1993 Pushcart Prize.

Kaua'i Tales (Frederick B Wichman) This beautifully illustrated collection (the first in a series) gives imaginative context to real-life places on Kaua'i.

Where are My Slippers? A Book of Colors (Dr Carolan and Joanna Carolan) With lost slippers, zoo animals, rhymes, a musical CD and colorful illustrations, this is a guaranteed go-to fave. See the Carolans' entire collection of children's books at www.bananapatchpress.com.

jazz-turned-Hawaiian songbird Amy Hanaiali'i and the younger superstar Raiatea Helm, both widely considered to be Keawe's successors.

Since the early 1900s, Hawaii music has shifted between Westernized and Hawaiian sounds. Nowadays, the trend is toward Hawaiian lyrics, both modern pop compositions and traditional chanting with minimal accompaniment. The singer who best captured both worlds is the late Israel 'Iz' Kamakawiwo'ole, whose rendition of the classic 'Over the Rainbow' enchanted audiences worldwide.

Hula

Modern audiences assume that hula is entertainment or creative expression. But ancient Hawaiians regarded hula as much more. They had no written language, so hula and chanting served as essential communication, to record historical events, myths and legends. It was also a religious offering to the gods.

Hawaiian Quilting

With their vibrant colors and graphic patterns, the striking beauty of Hawaiian appliqué quilting is easy to see. But look more closely and you'll discover the story behind the beauty. Each part has meaning, and each design is thought to contain the very spirit of the crafter – early quilts were even buried with their makers so their souls couldn't go wandering.

Missionaries introduced quilting to the islands in the 19th century, but Hawaiian women already sewed *kapa* (pounded-bark cloth) to make bedding, imprinting the top with natural motifs. Most scholars believe appliqué quilting took hold because of its 19th-century popularity in the US and easy adaptation to *kapa*-like designs.

Even today, traditional quilts usually have one bright fabric – say, magenta – that is cut into a repeating pattern after being folded in fourths or eighths (remember making paper snowflakes in grade school?). The bright fabric is then appliquéd, usually by hand, onto a white or natural-color foundation cloth, and the design is quilted around in an echoing pattern.

At the center of the quilt is the *piko* (navel); an open center is seen as a gateway linking the spiritual world and the physical one, while a solid core symbolizes the strength of the family. Fruits and plants have meaning, too, but you won't see any human figures (it's believed they could come alive at night). Some typical symbols:

breadfruit – abundance

pineapple – hospitality

mango – wishes granted

taro – strength

Exquisite antique quilts are on display at the Kaua'i Museum (p39) in Lihu'e. If you want to buy one of these treasures, expect to pay thousands of dollars. (If prices are low, the quilts were likely machine-made in the Philippines.) Better still, sew your own! Ask the friendly staff at Kapaia Stitchery (p56) in Lihu'e or Vicky's Fabrics (p94) in Kapa'a for tips.

Kaua'i's Contemporary Art Scene

Most artwork by Kaua'i artists is highly commercial: colorful, representational works that appeal to the tourist eye. Unique pieces that go beyond the stereotypes do exist, but they're harder to find, displayed mainly in Honolulu's museums and galleries. On Kaua'i, start by browsing the cluster of art galleries in Hanapepe during 'Art Night' held every Friday, and drop by **Galerie 103** (www.galerie103.com) in Po'ipu's Shops at Kukui'ula (p186).

Notable fine artists (to name only a few) who live and work on Kaua'i include:

Carol Bennett (www.carolbennettart.com) Meditative paintings of underwater movement.

A Kimberlin Blackburn (www.akimberlinblackburn.com) Uninhibitedly colorful, stylized sculptures and paintings.

Liedeke Bulder (www.liedekebulderart.com) Unusual botanical paintings and skyscape watercolors.

Margaret Ezekiel Pastel drawings of cloudscapes or the human figure.

Mac James (www.macjamesonkauai.com) Nature paintings, drawings and sculptures with contemporary environmental themes.

Bruna Stude (www.brunastude.com) Elegant black-and-white underwater photography.

Today's commercial hula shows, which emphasize swaying hips and nonstop smiling, might be compelling but they're not 'real' hula. Serious students join a hula *halau* (school), where they undergo rigorous training and adopt hula as a life practice.

Contemporary hula *halau* have embraced the concept of competition. In major competitions held in Hawaii, on the US mainland and abroad, dancers vie in *kahiko* (ancient) and *'auana* (modern) categories. *Kahiko* performances are raw and primordial, accompanied only by chanting and *ipu* (gourd instruments), and dancers use a bent-knee stance to absorb the earth's energy. *Kahiko* dancers' costumes show primary colors and often lots of skin. Accompanied by harmonious singing (often in English) and stringed instruments, *'auana* brings Western-influenced clothing, sinuous arm movements and smiling faces.

Traditional Hawaiian Crafts

In the 1970s, the Hawaiian renaissance sparked interest in artisan crafts. The most beloved traditional craft is lei-making, stringing garlands of flowers, leaves, berries, nuts or shells. More lasting souvenirs include wood carvings and decorative works of handmade fabric art.

Traditional Hawaiian woodwork is sold island-wide, ranging from keepsake rocking chairs and masterful calabash bowls to affordable desk accessories and kitchen utensils. Stop by the Koa Store (p55) in Lihu'e to buy handmade koa souvenirs, from chopsticks to display canoe paddles.

The best advice for buying any Hawaiian crafts, whether you've got a budget of $10 or $10,000 is to beware of cheap, foreign, mass-produced imitations. Buy locally made goods, directly from the artists themselves whenever possible.

Literature

Hawaii's first examples of literature were ancient Hawaiian myths and legends, originally transmitted by oral tradition. But in modern times, novels by nonlocal writers, such as James Michener's *Hawaii,* long dominated the literature about Hawaii.

Beginning in the 1970s, novels and poems by local authors expanded the definition of Hawaii literature. A good intro to the pidgin vernacular and local personalities is *Growing up Local: An Anthology of Poetry and Prose from Hawai'i* (1998), published by Bamboo Ridge Press (www.bambooridge.com), a pioneer in the genre. Visit the publisher's website to get more familiar with notable island writers.

For traditional myths and legends of Kaua'i, you can't go wrong with master storyteller Frederick B Wichman's anthologies, including *Polihale & Other Kaua'i Legends, Touring the Legends of Koke'e* and *Touring the Legends of the North Shore,* all published by Bamboo Press or the Kaua'i Historical Society (www.kauaihistoricalsociety.org).

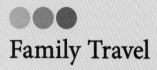
Black Pot Beach Park (Hanalei Pier; p128)

LINDA CHING/GETTY IMAGES ©

Kaua'i is an amusement park of sorts, just of the more natural variety. Instead of riding roller coasters, na keiki (children) can snorkel amid tropical fish, zipline through forest canopies and splash off sandy beaches – from body-boarding hot spots to shallow, toddler-sized lagoons. If you came to Kaua'i to recapture a child-like free-spiritedness, those tots you're toting may prove an inspiration for letting go and diving into fun in the sun.

Practicalities

Calling Kaua'i 'kid-friendly' would be an understatement, because *na keiki* are adored here. There's an explanation for this – cuteness aside. The entire island has a small-town vibe and, as the Hawaiian saying goes, 'we're all in the same canoe.' When it comes down to it, people look out for each other, and each others' kids, because almost everybody else has kids, too.

Not much can go wrong when you're visiting Kaua'i. Coastal temperatures rarely drop below 65°F, driving distances are relatively short and everyone speaks English. Still, proper planning can be a game-changer, especially when traveling with children. With just a few tidbits of insider information, you can minimize your vacation costs and maximize adventure.

Finding a convenient home base is the first step. Resorts and hotels typically allow children under 18 to stay for free with their parents; some can provide rollaway beds or cribs, usually for a nightly surcharge. A few top-end beach hotels and resorts offer professionally supervised 'day camps.' At vacation rentals, rates often apply for two adults, while kids above a certain age might count as extra guests and incur a nightly surcharge. B&Bs are generally not kid-friendly, although there are exceptions.

Baby supplies, such as disposable diapers and infant formula, are sold island-wide. Try going shopping in Lihu'e or on the Eastside for the best selection and prices.

Food & Drink

Kaua'i is a family-oriented and unfussy place, so almost all restaurants welcome children. Notable exceptions are some high-end resort dining rooms. Otherwise, children's menus and highchairs are usually available everywhere – but if a highchair is a necessity at every meal, bring your own collapsible chair.

If restaurant dining is not your family's strong suit, no problem! Eating outdoors is among the simplest and best island pleasures. Pack finger foods for a picnic, pick up fruit at farmers markets, stop for smoothies at roadside stands, and order plate lunches at takeout counters. Accommodations providing full kitchens are convenient for eat-in breakfasts.

Finding food should pose little trouble, as supermarkets and convenience stores stock mainstream national brands – just at around 150% or more of the cost you'd normally expect.

Need to Know

Babysitting Licensed child-care providers who come to your accommodations can be arranged by **Babysitters of Kaua'i** (☎808-632-2252; www.babysittersofkauai.com; up to 2 siblings per hour $18). Otherwise, ask your concierge.

Breastfeeding Generally done discreetly (cover up) or in private.

Changing facilities A few public toilets have a baby-changing table, but these can be sparse away from hotels and resorts. Elsewhere, plan on improvisation.

Cots Available at some hotels and resorts (a nightly surcharge may apply); try to reserve them in advance.

Diapers (nappies) Widely sold at supermarkets, pharmacies and convenience stores.

Highchairs Ubiquitous at sit-down restaurants, except for some upscale dining rooms.

Kids' menus Available at most sit-down restaurants, as well as at many drive-ins, food trucks and takeout kitchens.

Strollers You can rent them from **Kauai Baby Rentals** (☎866-994-8886, 808-651-9269; www.kauaibabyrentals.com), along with everything else families might need, including cribs, toys, booster seats and backpacks.

Transportation Car seats are rented by rental-car companies for around $10 to $15 per day, but supply is limited, so reserve them in advance.

Activities

Although you can't hike the steepest trails or go scuba diving when you're traveling with a toddler, parents will find equally enjoyable substitutes for outdoor family fun for all ages. Some activities (eg ziplining, surfing, horseback riding) and guided tours require that children be of a certain age, height or weight to participate; always ask about restrictions when making reservations to avoid disappointment – and tears.

For valuable tips and amusing tales, read Lonely Planet's *Travel with Children*. You can also ask questions and get advice from other travelers in the Thorn Tree's online 'Kids to Go' and 'USA' forums at www.lonelyplanet.com.

In the Water

With 90 miles of coastline, ocean activities are bound to be a part of the agenda. If your child cannot swim or fears the ocean, try one of Kaua'i's gentle 'baby beaches' in Po'ipu or Kapa'a. Lydgate Beach Park is an ideal starter beach for grade-schoolers or anyone who needs well-protected waters.

Snorkeling is generally family-friendly on Kaua'i, exciting for young kids and teens alike, especially in Po'ipu. Local snorkel-gear rental shops are a great starting point, as they can fit kids with custom-sized masks and have a wealth of knowledge to share. Book ahead if you want to take a thrilling snorkel cruise up the iconic Na Pali Coast. If your kid has never sailed before, a smoother catamaran ride will be much safer than a zippy raft adventure.

Surf lessons are another fun family activity and can be a big hit with teens. Kaua'i's waters are relatively uncrowded and beginner groups are generally small and personalized. If your child (or you) associate the word 'surf' with iPads more than set waves and 'hanging ten,' go bodyboarding before trying the real thing. Bodyboarding (also called 'boogie boarding') is much easier to learn and provides that all-important seed of confidence.

On Land

For when all fingers and toes are thoroughly wrinkled, many land-based activities on Kaua'i are especially geared towards children.

At Lydgate Beach Park, you'll find a massive wooden playground with swings, slides and bridges. Smith's Tropical Paradise is a family-friendly botanical garden where there are no time limits to strolling the island-themed 30-acre grounds. A kayaking adventure up the Wailua River and ziplining are usually a hit with teens, as is cruising around the shops of Hanalei or Kapa'a for souvenirs.

Hiking trails abound on Kaua'i, though some are geared more towards older kids who are experienced hikers. At Waimea Canyon and Koke'e State Parks, you'll find trails ranging from simple nature walks to strenuous treks amid the striking landscape of a gargantuan gorge and wet, rugged forest land. On the Na Pali Coast, hiking even a short way up the Kalalau Trail offers unforgettable views.

Other great landlubber adventures include horseback riding in Kilauea, Princeville or Po'ipu; cycling the Eastside's coastal path; and monthly stargazing parties in Hanapepe.

The Best...
Kid-Friendly Attractions

1 Kamokila Hawaiian Village (p69)

2 Kauai Plantation Railway (p45)

3 Kauai Mini Golf & Botanical Gardens (p110)

4 Kaua'i Museum (p39)

5 Limahuli Garden (p144)

Green Kaua'i

View over Ke'e Beach and Na Pali Coast (p148)

M SWIET PRODUCTIONS/GETTY IMAGES ©

The foundation of life for ancient Hawaiians was the philosophy of aloha 'aina – love, care and respect for the land. Eco-concepts such as 'green' and 'sustainable' weren't catchphrases introduced by foreigners. They were principles already built into the fabric of everyday life, based upon a spiritual relationship with the land. Today those principles and that love may be coming full circle on the Garden Island.

The Island Goes Green

Truth be known, being 'green' is not easy, especially on an island where staunchness is a positive attribute and change is met with resistance nearly every step of the way. Taking a broad overview of Kaua'i, one can see an isolated island threatened by over-development, traffic, a lack of affordable housing, waste creation, and an extreme reliance on imported fuel and food. However, look closer and what becomes visible are the efforts of a community working together to create and implement realistic future-based alternatives to the unsustainable practices that have taken over.

Idyllic Isolation

Arguably the best thing Hawaii has going for it is the same factor that led to its state of dependence on global currents: isolation. Yet this isolation can also now be transformed into the freedom to invent a new system.

But any progress must come from the ground up. In the next decade or two, with consistent and concerted efforts, Kaua'i could go from being almost completely regulated by the outside world to being significantly self-sustaining. And that change is already underway. From photovoltaic and hydroelectric power to waste utilization and GMO-free initiatives, the future has been set in motion. After all, with a nickname like the 'Garden Island,' it just makes sense, right?

Impact of Tourism

High up on the list of ecological concerns is tourism, an issue with which Kauaians have a love-hate relationship. It drives the economy, but also affects the environment and increases the cost of living.

In the mid-2000s resort and luxury developments went gangbusters, with over 5000 residential units and 6100 resort units set on the drawing board. The largest project, Po'ipu's massive Kukui'ula community, is on its way to being another enclave of wealthy second-home buyers. While Kukui'ula gets some credit for their Club Cottages, which were designed to meet LEED (Leadership in Energy and Environmental Design) certification standards, their asking price of almost $3 million is unaffordable for most. Exclusive communities like this can't help but shift island demographics away from people who are truly connected to the land.

Environmentally, the biggest impacts of tourism are from cruise ships and helicopters. Cruise ships burn diesel fuel, releasing exhaust fumes equivalent to thousands of cars into the island's atmosphere. Their discharge of ballast water and wastes can pollute the ocean, damage coral reefs and accidentally release invasive species. Helicopter tours are popular with visitors, but some residents and environmental groups point out that those pleasure flights contribute to both air and noise pollution. They also diminish the enjoyment of Kaua'i's natural areas for those who choose to visit them in low-impact ways, such as by hiking, biking or kayaking.

Helpful Resources

Island Breath (www.islandbreath.org) Dig deep into local issues with these links to newspaper and independent articles on Kaua'i's hot-button sustainability topics.

Kauai Explorer (www.kauaiexplorer. com) While known mainly for its beach guide and ocean-safety advice, this refreshingly concise site also contains preservation and conservation tips and a handy 'Where to Recycle' guide.

Malama Kaua'i (www.malamakauai. org) This Kilauea-based grassroots organization is the island's watchdog, dedicated to protecting ecosystems and local culture with a community farm, volunteering opportunities, educational efforts, political advocacy, public events and more.

On the Ground

When it comes to putting green theory into practice there are definite steps you can take as a visitor to reduce further harm to the 'aina (land) without forgoing any of its charms. Available as a free mobile app, the handy Green Kaua'i Map (www. malamakauai.org) provides a list of local businesses and organizations with environmentally, socially and culturally responsible practices. Though the list is based on self-identification as being 'green,' it's a good starting point.

Transportation

Given limited bus services and safe bicycle lanes, there's no getting around the fact that you'll probably need a car on Kaua'i. But choosing a small rental car and efficiently planning daily excursions can make a difference. Perhaps pick a couple of home-based accommodations around the island. Then, at each place, keep your sightseeing to within that region. Along with saving on unnecessary fuel costs this will allow you to really plug in to your immediate surroundings, and most likely will result in a richer, more local travel experience.

Food & Accommodations

When it comes to eating, where you buy is as important as what you buy. Buying locally grown produce, locally caught fish and locally made cheeses, preserves and baked goods are all easily managed. Wherever you're located on the island there is a weekly farmers market and a daily fish market within a 20-minute drive or so. To find unique, homegrown food and drinks made around the island, visit the Kaua'i Made website (www.kauaimade.net) or look for its purple-and-green stickers on products when you're out shopping.

In 2009, Kaua'i County passed a ban on plastic bags at retail shops. Grocery stores and big-box chains now charge a small fee for recyclable paper bags, but bringing a reusable tote bag can earn you lots of points with the environmental karma police. The garbage dumps on Kaua'i are nearly overflowing, so it's always important to minimize your waste production. Try to patronize restaurants and food retailers who use biodegradable utensils, avoid styrofoam and feature local produce, dairy, seafood and meats as ingredients on their menus.

Standout ecofriendly accommodations include hydroelectrically powered Coco's Kaua'i B&B near Waimea; solar-powered Aikane Kaua'i, a beach house in Po'ipu; and organic North Country Farms and eco-conscious Kauai Vacation Cottages in Kilauea. Camping is another way to make your vacation more green. Kaua'i offers state and county park campgrounds by the coast and in inland forests. All require getting advance permits, reservable online or available in person from government offices (most are in Lihu'e), so plan ahead.

Activities

For the price of an ATV or helicopter tour, you could instead get an up-close and personal experience with some of the same terrain on an expert-led hike with Kaua'i Nature Tours. Outrigger-canoe sailing with Kauai Outrigger Adventures or Island Sails Kaua'i in Hanalei, Garden Island Surf School or Kauai Island Experience in Po'ipu, or the Kamokila Hawaiian Village in Wailua makes for a great time on the water.

Possibly the most Kaua'i-friendly activities you can try are those that teach about Hawaiian history and local culture, such as Limahuli Garden on the North Shore, the Kaua'i Museum in Lihu'e and the Eastside's Kaua'i Cultural Center. Agrotourism is also big on Kaua'i, including with Ho'opulapula Haraguchi Rice Mill & Taro Farm Tours in Hanalei, sustainable Kauai Fresh Farms in Kilauea and the renewable energy–powered Kaua'i Coffee Company.

Renewable Energy

With a dismal dependence on petroleum for energy production, and higher energy costs than the other Hawaiian Islands (and anywhere else in the USA, for that matter), Kaua'i has sprung into action and gotten on board with the Hawaii Clean Energy Initiative – a statewide push to have 70% of Hawaii's energy for electricity and ground transportation come from renewable resources by 2030.

Voluntourism

While relishing all of the tropical delights Kaua'i has to offer, an hour or two spent volunteering can be satisfying. Listed here are a few volunteering opportunities. When possible, make arrangements in advance.

Hui O Laka (☎ 808-335-9975; www.kokee.org) Get dirty while working to restore forested areas impacted by overuse or invasive species, or participate in the annual bird count.

Kaua'i Habitat for Humanity (☎ 808-335-0296; www.kauaihabitat.org/volunteer) 🖉 Help build affordable housing in the island's low-income communities.

Koke'e Resource Conservation Program (☎ 808-335-0045; www.krcp.org) 🖉 Accepts short-term and long-term volunteers and interns to help with weed-control projects in and around Koke'e, Waimea Canyon and Na Pali Wilderness Coast State Parks. It involves strenuous hiking and use of herbicides. Bunk-bed housing is provided at the historic Koke'e Civilian Conservation Corps (CCC) Camp.

Malama Kaua'i (☎ 808-828-0685; www.malamakauai.org) Half-day volunteering projects take place at the community gardens and 'Food Forest' in Kilauea.

National Tropical Botanical Garden (NTBG; ☎ North Shore 808-826-1668, South Shore 808-332-7324; www.ntbg.org/donate/volunteer.php) Call or email in advance to find out about the 'Vacation and Volunteer' program.

Sierra Club (www.hi.sierraclub.org/kauai) A pioneer in the environmental movement, this nonprofit organization's Kaua'i chapter offers guided outings, such as full-moon hikes, and half-day volunteer projects cleaning up beaches and restoring native plants.

Surfrider Foundation (☎ 808-625-2593; http://kauai.surfrider.org) Public beach clean-ups happen regularly, and can always use more volunteers.

Waipa Foundation (☎ 808-826-9969; www.waipafoundation.org) Join the Hanalei community for a hands-on lesson in making poi, a traditional Hawaiian food staple. Call ahead to sign up and to ask about other volunteer opportunities with this nonprofit organization.

Solar Power

Major steps on Kaua'i towards this goal began with the 1.21-megawatt solar farm near Kapa'a that was completed in 2011. The farm, connected to the KIUC (Kauai Island Utility Cooperative) grid, provides electricity to 300 homes. A 6-megawatt solar plant in Po'ipu, which began operations in 2012, supplies even more. As well, the Port Allen facility has a battery storage system to stabilize short-term fluctuations in energy output during cloudy spells. Currently under construction, another 12-megawatt project in Anahola will eventually meet 20 percent of the island's daytime electricity needs; it will also become the state's largest solar power plant after completion in 2016.

It's projected that soon Kaua'i could have the highest percentage of solar energy on its system of any in the country. KIUC has committed to generating 50% of the island's power from renewable sources by 2023. Who knows, in the coming decades Kaua'i could do a complete 180-degree turnaround and one day be exporting energy.

Hydroelectricity

Plans have also been proposed for four possible hydroelectric plants to be constructed across the island on the Hanalei and Wailua Rivers, as well as the Koke'e and Kekaha Ditches. However, there are concerns from the community about how these facilities may impact the aesthetic beauty of these waterways. The Wailua River project is proposing a dam to be placed only 1000ft up from Wailua Falls, one of Kaua'i's trademark wonders. While the solar panels may be a minor eyesore in some places, hydroelectric plants have the potential to permanently affect the physical harmony of the island.

On the other hand, hydroelectric energy is considered by many to be the most stable form of renewable energy, lacking the fluctuations that come from wind and sunlight. Hydroelectric facilities in Kalaheo and Wainiha, owned by the McBryde Sugar Company, have been running for over a century (yes, over 100 years), and currently generate about 5 megawatts of electricity for the island. A new 6-megawatt plant, privately owned by the ex-sugar plantation company Gay & Robinson, is in the works for the Westside.

Powering the Future

As with any change, compromise is a must, and underlying all these nifty propositions for a greener future is the continued threat to the sanctity of Hawaiian culture. With new technologies come the companies that can afford to research and run these technologies, and those companies are not based on Kaua'i. This inevitably results in more of Kaua'i's land, while being used for 'good' ends, also being controlled by strangers, whose ultimate goal may very well be to turn a profit.

Fig tree
DANITA DELIMONT/GETTY IMAGES ©

Sustainable Agriculture

Another hot issue on Kaua'i is food security. About 90% of the island's food is imported, despite its natural biodiversity. At any given time there is only enough food on Kaua'i to feed the island for three to seven days.

A growing contingent of small-scale organic farmers argues that island agriculture is no longer viable by the old model of corporate-scale, industrialized mono-cropping (of pineapples and sugarcane, for example) enabled by chemical fertilizers, pesticides and herbicides. Instead, family farms growing diverse crops – for the table or for sale locally, not only globally – would always be sustainable.

Nobody goes into farming to make money, especially on Kaua'i, where limited resources mean that land, water and labor costs are comparatively high. Huge parcels of agricultural land are occupied by major multinational corporations growing genetically modified (GMO) crops, mainly corn. Minds differ on the risks of genetic modification, but many agree that island crops should benefit residents, not multinational corporations.

The Land

Kaua'i is the oldest and fourth largest of the major inhabited Hawaiian Islands, with volcanic rocks dating back over five million years and most of the island boasting the tropical trifecta of ocean, beach and mountain. Unlike the shiny black terrain seen on much of the lava-spewing Big Island (a baby at less than 500,000 years old), Kaua'i displays the effects of time and erosion, with weathered summits, mountaintop bogs and rainforests, deeply cut valleys and rivers, extensive sandy beaches, coral and algal reefs, and rust-colored soil indelible to both memory and your white sneakers.

Reduce, Reuse, Recycle

Here's a list of convenient island recycling centers:

Eastside (4900 Kahau Rd) In Kapa'a at the end of Kahau Rd, behind the ball field near the bypass road.

Lihu'e (4303 Nawiliwili Rd) At the back of the Kmart parking lot on the pavilion side of the store.

Nawiliwili Harbor (3343 Wilcox Rd) At Reynolds Recycling, just north of the harbor, at the corner of Kanoa Rd.

North Shore (5-3751 Kuhio Hwy) At the Hanalei Transfer Station, across from the Prince Golf Course in Princeville.

Port Allen (4469 Waialo Rd) North of the harbor at 'Ele'ele Shopping Center.

South Shore (2100 Ho'one Rd) In the Brennecke's parking lot opposite Po'ipu Beach Park.

Westside At Waimea Canyon Park (4643 Waimea Canyon Dr) and Kekaha Landfill (6900-D Kaumuali'i Hwy).

Volcanic Origins

Because its volcanic origins lie hidden under a carpet of forests, ferns and shrubland, Kaua'i's landscape, particularly along the North Shore, is overwhelmingly lush and strikes many as the ultimate tropical beauty – which partly explains the frequency of visitors showing up for a week or two and staying a lifetime. Many folks' lives have shifted as a result of just driving down the hill from Princeville to Hanalei.

Perhaps duped by its round shape, scientists for decades believed that a single volcano formed Kaua'i. But on the basis of evidence collected since the 1980s, scientists now think that Kaua'i's entire eastern side 'slumped' along an ancient fault line, leaving a steep *pali* (cliff) along Waimea Canyon's western edge. Then, lava from another shield volcano flowed westward to the *pali* and pounded against the cliffs. The black and red horizontal striations along the canyon walls represent successive volcanic eruptions; the red color shows where water seeped through the rocks, oxidizing the iron inside.

Highs & Lows

Now shrunken by age, Kaua'i is also slowly subsiding into the ocean floor. Don't worry, the rate is less than an inch per century. Still, over eons those inches have cost the island 3000ft in elevation, making today's high point the 5243ft Kawaikini. Among the most visually spectacular valleys is Kalalau, with its curtain-like folds and knife-edge ridges, topping out just above 4000ft at lookouts where the road ends in Koke'e State Park. Views of the Na Pali sea cliffs are spectacular, but can be seen only from the deck of a boat, the windows of a helicopter – or, for the fit and eco-conscious, from the Nu'alolo or Awa'awapuhi Trails in Koke'e State Park, or the grueling 11-mile Kalalau Trail in Na Pali Coast Wilderness State Park.

Hawaiian monk seal

Wildlife

The Hawaiian Islands are the most isolated land masses on earth. Born of barren lava flows, they were originally populated only by plants and animals that could traverse the Pacific – for example, seeds clinging to a bird's feather or fern spores that drifted thousands of miles through the air. Most flora and fauna that landed here didn't survive. Scientists estimate that new species became established maybe once every 70,000 years – and these included no amphibians, no browsing animals, no mosquitoes and only two mammals: a bat and a seal.

The wildlife that did make it here found a rich, ecologically diverse land to colonize. Developed in isolation, many of these species became endemic to the islands, meaning that they're found nowhere else in the world. Unfortunately, Hawaii has the highest rate of extinction in the nation, and nearly 25% of all federally listed threatened and endangered species in the US are endemic Hawaiian flora and fauna. Only time will tell how climate change will affect the islands' unique species.

Marine Wildlife 911

Federal and state laws protect all of Hawaii's wild marine mammals and turtles from harassment. Legally, this usually means you may not approach them closer than 50yd (100yd for whales, or 20ft for turtles) or do anything that disrupts their normal behavior. The most important actions for island visitors to avoid are disturbing endangered monk seals and sea turtles that have 'hauled out' and are resting on beaches. If you see a fellow beach-goer hassling one of these sand-lounging beasts, feel free to get righteous on them.

Animals

For wildlife enthusiasts, the island's main attractions are both resident and migratory birds, as well as myriad ocean creatures.

Ocean Life

Up to 10,000 migrating North Pacific humpback whales come to Hawaiian waters for calving each winter, and whale watching can be especially excellent off Kaua'i's South Shore. Pods of spinner dolphins, with their acrobatic spiraling leaps, regularly approach boats cruising in Kaua'i's waters, and can also be seen from the shoreline off Kilauea Point.

Threatened *honu* (green sea turtles) are traditionally revered by Hawaiians as an 'aumakua (protective deity). Snorkelers often see *honu* feeding on seaweed along rocky coastlines or in shallow lagoons. Endangered Hawaiian monk seals also occasionally haul up on shore, a thrill for beachgoers, who by law must observe turtles and seals from a distance.

Birds

Kaua'i is a birder's dream, with copious creatures soaring over its peaks and down its valleys. Lowland wetlands feature four endangered waterbirds that are cousins of mainland species: the Hawaiian duck, Hawaiian coot, Hawaiian moorhen and Hawaiian stilt. The best place to view all four species is the North Shore's Hanalei National Wildlife Refuge. Although public access to the refuge is

strictly limited, an overlook opposite Princeville Center provides a great view of the birds' habitat, with a serene river, shallow ponds and cultivated taro fields.

The endangered nene, Hawaii's state bird, is a long-lost cousin of the Canada goose. Nene once numbered as many as 25,000 on all the islands, but by the 1950s only 50 were left. Intensive breeding programs have raised their numbers to around 2500 on three main islands: Maui, Kaua'i and Hawai'i (Big Island). You might see them in Hanalei wetlands, around golf courses and open fields, and at Kilauea Point National Wildlife Refuge.

Native forest birds are more challenging to observe, but the keen-eyed may spy eight endemic species remaining at Koke'e State Park, especially in the Alaka'i Wilderness Preserve. The 'apapane, a type of honeycreeper, is the most abundant: a bright-red bird the same color as the lehua flowers from which it takes nectar.

Today, two-thirds of all endemic Hawaiian birds are extinct, the victims of aggressive, introduced birds and infectious diseases. In 1992, Hurricane 'Iniki also contributed to this catastrophic decline: it was the last time three species were seen on Kaua'i. To learn more about Kaua'i's birds, Birds of Kaua'i (www.kauaibirds.com) is a good starting point and SoundsHawaiian (www.soundshawaiian.com) is a real treat for the ears, offering crisp recordings of island birdsong.

Plants

Ancient Hawaiians would scarcely recognize Kaua'i, having never encountered the tropical flowers, fruit trees and lush landscape that today epitomize the island. Mangoes came from Asia, macadamia nuts from Australia and coffee from Africa. Today, many botanists and farmers advocate biodiversity, so alien species aren't necessarily bad. But, of Hawaii's 1300 endemic plant species, over 100 are already extinct and 273 are endangered.

Kalalau Valley, Koke'e State Park (p229)

Native Forest Trees

Over 90% of Hawaii's 1000-plus plant species are endemic to the islands. To see native forest trees, visit Koke'e State Park and the 10,000-acre Alaka'i Swamp Wilderness Preserve. Along the Pihea and Alaka'i Swamp Trails, you'll see the most abundant rainforest tree, *'ohi'a lehua*, a hardwood with bright-red or orange pompom-like flowers that provide nectar for forest birds. Another dominant forest tree (or shrub) is lapalapa, with long-stemmed leaves that flutter in the slightest breeze. Among the best-known tree species is koa, an endemic hardwood that is Hawaii's most commercially valuable tree for its fine woodworking qualities, rich color and swirling grain. You can identify koa trees by their distinctive crescent-shaped leaves.

Coastal Plants

Despite the rampant development along some parts of Kaua'i's coast, the shoreline is also a good place to find endemic plants. The harsh environment – windblown, salt-sprayed, often arid land with nutrient-poor, sandy soil – requires plants to adapt to survive, for example, by growing flat along the ground, becoming succulent or developing waxy leaf coatings to retain moisture. You can also see many endemic coastal plants at Kilauea Point National Wildlife Refuge on the North Shore.

National, State & County Parks

About 30% of Kaua'i is protected as state parks and nature reserves. For hiking, don't miss Waimea Canyon State Park and Koke'e State Park, with their spectacular elevated views and numerous trails and campsites. On the Eastside, Nounou Mountain, with three steep but scenic hiking trails, is well-maintained forest-reserve land.

Ha'ena State Park is another favorite, as it has Ke'e Beach, a fantastic snorkeling spot, and the nearby Kalalau Trail leading into Na Pali Coast Wilderness State Park. The miles of sandy beach at Polihale State Park offer an escape from crowds, but beware two potential threats: hazardous ocean conditions and the bone-rattlingly rough 5-mile unpaved road to get there.

Most of Kaua'i's best easy-access beaches are designated as county parks, such as sunny Po'ipu Beach Park (South Shore), serene 'Anini Beach Park (North Shore), calm Salt Pond Beach Park (Westside) and family-friendly Lydgate Beach Park (Eastside).

There are no national parks on the island, but there are three federal refuges, including the accessible Kilauea Point National Wildlife Refuge, which has spectacular wildlife watching, including migratory whales in winter and the only diverse seabird colony on the main Hawaiian Islands.

Outdoor Activities & Adventures

Scuba diving with a *honu* (green sea turtle)

ISLAND EFFECTS/GETTY IMAGES

Kaua'i is blessed with a bounty of outdoor adventures. Whether in the air, on the ground or at sea, there are uncountable ways to engage with this fascinating island and its unique, often idyllic environment. That means there is something for everyone to do, no matter what your age, fitness or skill level. Get ready, then dive right on in.

At Sea

Tucked into Kaua'i's 90 miles of coastline are more than 60 beaches. You need not drive far to find another (and yet another) gorgeous strand. Water conditions are changeable, however. Note the seasonal changes in surf conditions: North Shore and Westside beaches are most hazardous during winter (November through March), when South Shore and Eastside beaches are relatively calm. The pattern reverses in summer. Of course, conditions change daily and exceptions can become the rule.

Before plunging in, click to **Kaua'i Explorer** (www.kauaiexplorer.com), a Hanalei-based resource on beaches, ocean safety, marine life, eco-travel and much more. The best printed watersports guide, available at bookstores, outdoor outfitters and ocean-sports shops, is **Franko's Kaua'i Dive Map** (www.frankosmaps.com), a waterproof, rip-proof plastic fold-up map ($8) that identifies all the top diving, snorkeling, surfing and kayaking sites island-wide.

Bodyboarding & Bodysurfing

While bodyboarding (aka boogie boarding) is less glamorous than surfing, it's more popular, more affordable and more doable (from day one). Bodysurfing appeals to minimalists who prefer to catch waves without a board, using only specialized fins (if that). It feels like you're riding a conveyor belt to the shore.

Good South Shore breaks include Po'ipu Beach and, for the skilled, Brennecke's Beach or Shipwreck Beach. In Lihu'e, newbies should start at Kalapaki Beach. Further north up the Eastside, experts can test themselves at Kealia Beach. Hanalei Bay near the pavilion is a top North Shore spot. On the Westside, head to Kekaha Beach Park when conditions are right.

Boogie board rentals cost around $5 per day and $20 per week at local surf or snorkel shops.

Lifeguard-Protected Beaches

Lifeguard staffing is subject to change, so check with **Hawaii Beach Safety** (☎808-241-6506; www.hawaiibeachsafety.com/kauai) online to confirm that the following beaches still have lifeguards:

- Anahola Beach Park (p96)
- Ha'ena Beach Park (p144)
- Hanalei Bay, at Black Pot Beach Park (Hanalei Pier) (p128)
- Kealia Beach Park (p96)
- Kekaha Beach Park (p222)
- Lydgate Beach Park (p66)
- Po'ipu Beach Park (p168)
- Salt Pond Beach Park (p205)

Diving

While Kaua'i waters cannot quite compare with the calm, clear waters off the Big Island's Kona Coast, diving is still excellent here. South Shore waters see the most diving activity, both from shore and dive boats.

Note that the closest hyperbaric chambers for recompression therapy are located on O'ahu. If you encounter trouble, call the **Coast Guard Rescue Center** (☎O'ahu 808-536-4336) in Honolulu. For members, **Divers Alert Network** (DAN; ☎emergency hotline 919-684-9111, info 800-446-2671; www.diversalertnetwork.org; annual membership from $35) gives advice on diving emergencies, insurance, decompression services, illness and injury.

Dive Sites

South Shore

General Store (60–90ft) Interesting lava formations, an 1892 shipwreck (mostly anchors), and loads of marine life, including boarfish, dolphins, sharks and mantas possible. The sea gets rough on this boat dive, so expect strong currents.

Harbor Ledges (60–70ft) An excellent beginner to intermediate dive, with lots of fish and sea turtles.

Stone House (40–60ft) Another good, shallow beginner dive, with good coral and octopuses.

Koloa Landing (5–45ft) Considered the best shore dive on the island, it's conveniently located and easy to enter, with a quick drop-off. At this year-round site, you'll see large schools of fish, eels and sea turtles.

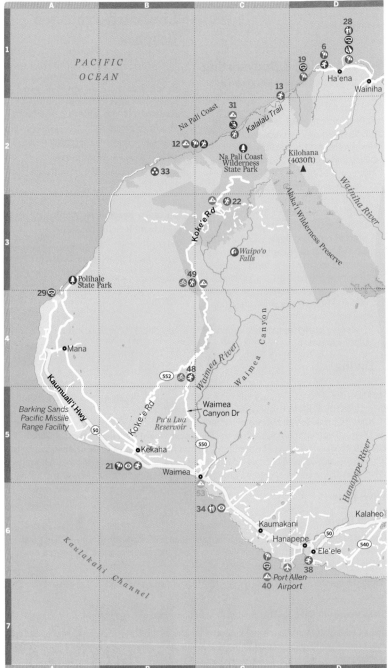

PACIFIC OCEAN

Na Pali Coast

Kalalau Trail

Na Pali Coast Wilderness State Park

Ha'ena

Wainiha

Wainiha River

Kilohana (4030ft)

Alaka'i Wilderness Preserve

Koke'e Rd

Waipo'o Falls

Polihale State Park

Mana

Kaumuali'i Hwy

Barking Sands Pacific Missile Range Facility

Koke'e Rd

Waimea River

Waimea Canyon

Pu'u Lua Reservoir

Waimea Canyon Dr

Kekaha

Waimea

Kaulakahi Channel

Kaumakani

Hanapepe

Kalaheo

'Ele'ele

Port Allen Airport

Hanapepe River

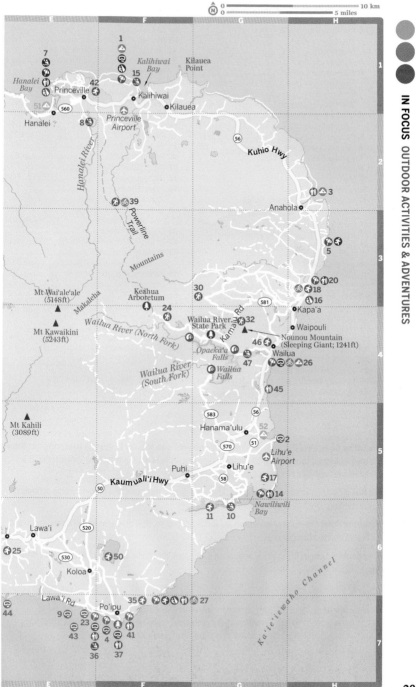

0   10 km
0   5 miles

Kalihiwai Bay
Kilauea Point
1
15
Kilauea
7
Hanalei Bay
42
Princeville
51   560
8
Hanalei
Princeville Airport

Kuhio Hwy
56

39
Powerline Trail

Mountains

3
Anahola
5

20
18
16

Mt Wai'ale'ale (5148ft)
Keahua Arboretum
30
581
Kapa'a

24
Wailua River (North Fork)
Waipouli

Mt Kawaikini (5243ft)
Makaleha
Wailua River State Park
Kamani Rd
32
Nounou Mountain (Sleeping Giant; 1241ft)
46
Opaeka'a Falls
47
Wailua
26

Wailua River (South Fork)
Wailua Falls
45

Mt Kahili (3089ft)
583
56
52
Hanama'ulu
2
570
51
Lihu'e Airport

Puhi
58
Lihu'e
17
14

Kaumuali'i Hwy
11   10
Nawiliwili Bay

Lawa'i
520
25
530
50
Koloa

Lawa'i Rd
35
27
44
Po'ipu
9
23
43
4   41
36   37

Kaieiewaho Channel

Kaua'i Outdoor Activities & Adventures

Sheraton Caverns (20–65ft) Kaua'i's overall top boat dive spot for beginners to experts has three partially collapsed lava tubes with shafts of glowing sunlight illuminating their dim interior. It's home to sea turtles, sharks, octopuses, mantas and more.

Ice Box (65–85ft) For intermediate and advanced divers, this coral reef presents large schools of fish, including boarfish, and occasional sharks.

Nukumoi Point (30–60ft) Also known as 'Tortugas', this shallow dive sees lots of *honu* (green sea turtles); open to all levels.

Brennecke's Ledge (65–85ft) Experienced divers look for sharks and squirrelfish as they drift over a large black coral shelf. Boat access only.

Lihu'e

Ahukini Landing (10–65ft) A shore dive for all levels, with the best area seaward from the jetty. Reef contains ordnance from WWII. Big rays, octopuses and lobster seen, and sometimes humpback whales during winter. Water conditions are often rough.

North Shore

Tunnels (5–65ft) Boating traffic is heavy here off Makua Beach, but the slowly appearing drop-off contains interesting tunnels. Poor visibility and high surf in winter.

Westside

Mana Crack (55–110ft) A miles-long ledge full of sharks, fish, sea turtles, dolphins and pristine coral. For experienced divers with a boat in summer.

Ni'ihau

Various sites (40–120ft) Huge lava formations, alluring wall dives, a plethora of marine life, and unlimited visibility lead insiders to call this the best diving in Hawaii. You'll see spinner dolphins, sharks and rays, rare reef fish and monk seals. It's for advanced divers only. The often-choppy crossing from Kaua'i takes at least two hours and is doable only from late spring to early autumn.

Fishing

Saltwater Fishing

Deep-sea fishing is fantastic off Kaua'i, which is surrounded by extremely deep waters quite close to shore. You can sail to depths of over 6000ft within an hour at trolling speed. The day's offshore catch includes giant marlin and tuna, plus midweight fish such as mahimahi and *ono* (wahoo). Inshore catches include *uku* (gray snapper), *ulua* (giant trevally), *kaku* (barracuda) and *kamanu* (rainbow runner).

Both shared and private charter boats usually depart from Nawiliwili Small Boat Harbor in Lihu'e, Port Allen Harbor in 'Ele'ele, Kikiaola Small Boat Harbor in Kekaha, or Lihi Boat Ramp in Kapa'a. Island policy is for the captain to share the catch at his discretion, a policy that seems lopsided at best. Those prone to seasickness need to take appropriate safeguards or think twice.

Deep-sea fishing

Na Pali Coast Sea Tours

Seeing the Na Pali Coast by sea is an unforgettable experience. It simply looks awesome: primordial valleys of green not only beckon you to explore, but to head back in time. Depending on your craft, you can paddle, snorkel, venture into sea caves or just kick back with a tropical drink, luxuriating in one of the world's great views. Assuming you can stomach the wave action, there's really no question of whether you should experience this Kaua'i highlight – the only question is how. Here's some help with sorting through the complexities.

BOAT TOURS

You have three types to choose from: catamarans (powered or sail), rafts (either Zodiacs or rigid-hulled inflatable boats) or kayaks.

Catamarans are the cushiest, offering smoother rides, ample shade, restrooms and crowd-pleasing amenities like on-board water slides and unlimited food and beverages. Some sport sails (and actually use them), while others are entirely motorized. If you've only sailed monohulls before, this is a far more stable and roomy experience.

Rafts are the thrillseeker's choice, bouncing along the water, entering caves (in mellower weather), and making beach landings, but most lack any shade, restrooms or comfy seating, so they're not for everyone (bad backs beware). The best rafts are rigid-hull inflatables, with hard bottoms that allow smoother rides (sit in back for less jostling). The largest may include a canopy and even a toilet.

Kayaks are for people who want a workout with their Na Pali Coast tour. They're of the sit-on-top variety, with seat backs and pedal rudders. You don't need to be a triathlete or kayaking expert to use one, but you should be in top physical condition.

DEPARTURE POINT

You can access the Na Pali Coast from the North Shore or from Westside. If you're visiting in the summer months, the North Shore – whether Hanalei or 'Anini – is definitely preferable, and the only option for kayaks, which paddle 17 miles from Ha'ena Beach Park to Polihale State Park. Kayak trips are organized by two outfitters in Hanalei.

Boat trips from Westside have to cover a lot of extra water before they reach the Na Pali Coast. As a result, they only get to see half the coastline. But in the winter months when waves are brutal on the North Shore, those tours stop running, leaving you no other choice. Westside tours depart from either Port Allen Harbor in 'Ele'ele or Kikiaola Small Boat Harbor in Kekaha. The latter is better, as it is closer to your destination, removing many miles of superfluous and potentially stomach-churning travel. However, winter weather still takes its toll, preventing landings at Nu'alolo Kai and limiting snorkeling opportunities.

PREPARATIONS

Book Na Pali Coast boat or kayak tours as early in your trip as possible (ideally before you arrive), as high surf or foul weather may cause cancellations. If you are prone to seasickness – a very real issue – inquire about sea conditions, take medication ahead of time and opt for the catamaran. Morning trips generally see the calmest seas.

Freshwater Fishing

Freshwater fishing – for largemouth and smallmouth bass, rainbow trout, the beautiful peacock bass and even bluegill – is much less well known, but nonetheless interesting. Kaua'i has a handful of rivers and 165 reservoirs ranging in size from 2 acres all the way up to the 1000-acre Waita Reservoir. Almost all were constructed as irrigation impoundments for pineapple and sugarcane fields and are privately owned, with introduced fish. To cast independently at regulated public fishing areas you'll need a freshwater license from the **Division of Aquatic Resources** (Map p44; ☎808-274-3344; www.dlnr.hawaii.gov/dar; Room 306, 3060 Eiwa St; 7-day tourist license $10). For a guided bass fishing trip, consider going out with expert bass fisherman Tom Christy, who has exclusive access to several impoundments; book his services through **Hawaii Fishing Adventures & Charters** (☎877-388-1376; www.sportfishhawaii.com/bassfishing.htm; half-/full-day trip from $265/375). Fishing for bass is productive all year, but April to August is best.

Kayaking

River Kayaking

With at least five rivers, including the only navigable one statewide, river kayaking is all the rage on Kaua'i. A guided paddling trip up the Wailua River, which includes a dip at a 100ft waterfall, is the classic. Due to the river's popularity, the county strictly regulates its use (eg no tours on Sundays).

If you're seeking a solitary nature experience, you should visit Kaua'i's other rivers, smaller, but perhaps more charming and leisurely. Hanalei River and Kalihiwai Stream are highly recommended. A handful of kayak tours navigate the Hule'ia River, which passes through the otherwise off-limits Hule'ia National Wildlife Refuge.

Most kayaking outfitters and tour companies are based in Wailua, Hanalei, Lihu'e or Po'ipu.

Sea Kayaking

Officially all first-time sea kayaking off Kaua'i must be done on a guided tour because of rough surf. Beginners can learn in Po'ipu and Hanalei, while the fit and ambitious can challenge themselves on the grueling 17-mile Na Pali Coast kayak trek, possible only between April and October.

Kitesurfing

Kitesurfing, also known as kiteboarding, is an emerging sport that combines surfing maneuvers, windsurfing speed and the aerial thrills of paragliding. The experience requires lessons (currently not available on Kaua'i), and no small amount of athleticism. Spectators can watch the action at Kapa'a Beach Park, Hanalei Bay and along the Maha'ulepu Coast.

Rafting

A raft is not just an inflatable boat – it's a sport. What else would you call bashing through waves and zipping in and out of sea caves? On Kaua'i, rafts are used mainly to see the Na Pali Coast, and either depart from Kikiaola Small Boat Harbor in Kekaha, or for a bumpier ride, Port Allen Harbor in 'Ele'ele. Seeing the Na Pali Coast by sea is one of Kaua'i's great outdoor experiences, and rafts let you get more close up and personal than catamarans. Riders should be good swimmers and not prone to seasickness.

Sailing

Given all of those Polynesian navigators, you might think that Kaua'i would be a great place to rent a sailboat. But the mighty Pacific is no Caribbean Sea, friendly to bare

boaters. The island's lack of harbors and anchorages, and the magnitude of the waves, particularly in winter, translates into no sailboat rentals. That does not mean there is no sailing to be had. There are several companies who will take you on a sailing (non-motorized) catamaran tour of the Na Pali Coast, and this is a wonderful experience, as long as your stomach agrees. Most catamaran tour companies are located at the Port Allen Marina Center in 'Ele'ele; book ahead.

Snorkeling

You shouldn't leave Kaua'i without having snorkeled. It's a wonderful entrée into a completely different, often beautiful world, almost anyone can do it, and it's dirt cheap. Rental equipment is freely available, but if you're passing through Lihu'e you can buy some for under $10 at big-box chain stores.

The South Shore has the most snorkeling locations around Po'ipu. If you're on the Westside, go to Salt Pond Beach Park, with its shallow waters. On the Eastside, choose Lydgate Beach Park, which has a protected lagoon perfect for kids. On the North Shore head to 'Anini Beach Park, Ke'e Beach or Makua (Tunnels) Beach, all of which offer spectacular settings both above and below the water, with the best conditions usually in summer. Snorkeling is also a key part of most Na Pali Coast boat tours.

Stand-Up Paddle Boarding

In the 1960s, Waikiki watermen developed stand-up paddle boarding (SUP) when teaching groups of beginning surfers. Standing on their boards, using a paddle to propel themselves, they could easily view their surroundings. In the early 2000s, SUP emerged as a global sport when big-name pros started doing it as a substitute when waves were flat. Companies that provide rentals and lessons have cropped up by beaches and rivers island-wide, including at Lihu'e's Kalapaki Beach, near Wailua on the Eastside, around Po'ipu on the South Shore and in Hanalei on the North Shore.

Stand-up paddle boarding

Surfing

Ever since the 1970s when surf bums flocked to the North Shore, Kaua'i has been known as a surf mecca. Today Hanalei remains a surf town, and many residents start or end their day catching waves. The best time of year for surfing depends on your skill level. For experienced surfers, the North Shore is terrific in winter, especially at Hanalei Bay, where winter waves average over 6ft (with 20ft or higher surf possible anytime). But nowadays North Shore breaks are crowded year-round, especially when the surf is under 6ft and attracts the masses (the bigger the waves, the smaller the crowd). The vibe in the local line-ups can be aggressive, with everyone trying to claim a piece of the action.

Kaua'i's Surf Beaches & Breaks

As a tourist in Hawaii, there are some places you go and there are some places you don't go. For many local families the beach parks are meeting places where generations gather to celebrate life under the sun. They're tied to these places by a sense of community and culture, and they aren't eager for outsiders to push them out. As a conscious traveler, it's important to understand this. Most folks who live in Hawaii are happy to share the spots that have become gentrified over the past 100 years, and usually will greet you with open arms – but they do reserve the right to protect some of their sacred surf grounds.

In the water, basic surf etiquette is vital. The person 'deepest,' or furthest outside, has the right of way. When somebody is already up and riding, don't take off on the wave in front of them. Also, remember you're a visitor out in the line-up, so don't expect to get every wave that comes your way. There's a definite pecking order and, frankly, as a tourist you're at the bottom. That said, usually if you give a wave, you'll get a wave in return. In general, be generous in the water, understand your place and surf with a smile, and you should be fine.

The Garden Isle is one of Hawaii's most challenging islands for surfers. On the North Shore, a heavy local vibe is pervasive. With the Princeville resort overlooking the break, residents may be a bit more understanding of out-of-towners in the water at **Hanalei Bay** than at other North Shore spots, but surfing with respect is a must. Between localism and the inaccessibility of the Na Pali Coast, not to mention a sizable tiger shark population, you may want to pass on surfing the North Shore.

As a general rule, surf tourism is relegated to the South Shore around Po'ipu. Chances are good that you'll be staying in this popular area anyway, which is perfect because there are some fun waves to be had there. Breaking best in the summer on south swells, spots like **BK's**, **Acid Drop** and **Centers** challenge even the most advanced surfers. First-timers can get their feet wet at **Inside Po'ipu** near the Sheraton resort. Only bodyboarding and bodysurfing are permitted at **Brennecke's Beach** – no stand-up surfing.

On the Eastside, **Unreals** breaks at Anahola Bay. It's a consistent right point that can work well on easterly wind swell, when *kona* (leeward) winds are offshore.

Surfline (www.surfline.com) reports current conditions at the island's best-known surf breaks.

The South Shore is best in summer. Hugely popular Po'ipu Beach Park gets crowded, while Shipwreck Beach and Maha'ulepu Beach draw only experts. Pakalas, also known as Infinities, near Waimea, is the Westside's hottest break, but it's for locals only and the unprotected western waters mean winter breaks are treacherous. Transitional swells happen on the Eastside, where surfers hit Kealia Beach Park and Lihu'e's Kalapaki Beach. Eastside swells often break on distant reefs and hence get blown out except during early-morning hours and *kona* (leeward) wind conditions. Check on current swells online or call the **surf hotline** (☎808-241-7873).

Surfing lessons and board rentals are available primarily in Hanalei and Po'ipu, as well as at Kalapaki Beach in Lihu'e.

Swimming

You can find protected swimming lagoons year-round at Lydgate Beach Park and Salt Pond Beach Park. Elsewhere, swimming is a seasonal sport. On the North Shore, swimming is lovely in summer, when waters are glassy at Hanalei Bay and Ke'e Beach. In winter, when giant swells pound the North Shore, head to the South Shore, especially Po'ipu Beach Park.

Lap swimmers who need lanes and walls can take advantage of the Olympic-sized YMCA pool in Lihu'e.

Ocean Safety

The Hawaiian Islands don't have a continental shelf. Consequently, the ocean doesn't roll up gently to their doorstep: it strikes them. Hard. This creates swimming conditions that are altogether different than those on the mainland. The ocean has a devastating power here, producing dangerous rip currents, rogue waves and undertows. For most visitors, the following warning applies: *you cannot think of swimming in Hawaii the way you think of swimming back home*. This is particularly true of Kaua'i, which has the highest per capita drowning rate of all of the main Hawaiian Islands. Between 2003 and 2012 there were 70 ocean drownings, over half of them tourists. That's about seven tourists a year, or one less than every two months.

To protect yourself, heed the basic warnings:

○ Never turn your back on the ocean.

○ Never swim alone. If you're an inexperienced swimmer, swim only at lifeguarded beaches. At beaches without lifeguards, swim only if (and where) locals are doing so.

○ Observe the surf awhile before entering. Look for recurring sets of waves, currents and other swimmers.

○ Observe the wind. Windy conditions increase ocean chop.

○ Don't walk on coastal rocks, where an unexpected wave can sweep you out. It's easy to misjudge the 'safe zone.'

○ Don't assume that water conditions are consistent in all regions.

There is, of course, no reason why you can't have a great time swimming on Kaua'i. Just use your head, and if that little voice is warning you about something, listen to it. For current information and more advice, read the ocean report and safety tips online at **Hawaii Beach Safety** (www.hawaiibeachsafety.com) and **Kaua'i Explorer** (www.kauaiexplorer.com).

Waterskiing & Wakeboarding

Waterskiing is not a major sport on Kaua'i, and only one company is permitted to tow skiers on the Wailua River: Kauai Water Ski Co (p71), based in Wailua. But the calm, freshwater river is a gentle place to learn. You can also try wakeboarding, the aquatic version of snowboarding, in which you're towed behind a boat on a single board.

Windsurfing

While Kaua'i lacks Maui's world-class wind-surfing beaches, it does have some decent sites. On the North Shore, 'Anini Beach Park, with calm, shallow, reef-protected waters, is ideal for beginners. Instructors use specialized jumbo boards that offer stability and small, lightweight sails. Book ahead for lessons with Windsurf Kaua'i (p116). More experienced folks can likely handle the North Shore's Makua (Tunnels) Beach or Kawailoa Bay on the South Shore.

Whale Watching

Each winter about 10,000 North Pacific humpback whales migrate to the shallow coastal waters off the Hawaiian Islands to breed, calve and nurse. Whale-watching boat tours are a hot-ticket item, especially during the peak migration season (January through March). Although it can't compete with the sheer number of whales spotted off Maui or the Big Island, Kaua'i still sees plenty of migratory whales, with some of its North Shore waters protected by the **Hawaiian Islands Humpback Whale National Marine Sanctuary** (www.hawaiihumpbackwhale.noaa.gov). Whale-watching boat tours depart mainly from Port Allen Harbor and Kikiaola Small Boat Harbor on the Westside.

On Land

Kaua'i boasts the greenest, steepest mountains and valleys found across the Hawaiian Islands, making for phenomenal hiking especially around Waimea Canyon and along the Na Pali Coast. And when your feet hurt, there's always that ATV, bicycle, golf cart, horse or zipline to ride.

ATV

Kaua'i has an endless number of dirt tracks, and large expanses of unpopulated private land. This makes it a beckoning playground for an all-terrain vehicle (ATV). If you've never driven one before, don't be cowed by the great big four-wheeled thing; it's a breeze, and loads of fun. Just be prepared to swallow a few bugs and get dirty.

Of the few companies that specialize in ATV tours, Kipu Ranch Adventures (p43) in Lihu'e is often recommended.

Cycling & Mountain Biking

Road Cycling

It's possible to ride along the belt highway in the Westside, South Shore and most of the Eastside, but there are no bike lanes, and road shoulders can be narrow or non-existent. Only experienced cyclists should consider cycling as transportation on Kaua'i.

Once the Eastside's coastal path, Ke Ala Hele Makalae, is completed, cycling from Lihu'e all the way to Anahola will be doable by the masses. For now, the path is used only recreationally in stretches near Lydgate Beach Park and from Kapa'a Beach Park north to Paliku (Donkey) Beach. Bear in mind that cyclists share the path with pedestrians.

Cycling the North Shore past Princeville is impossible along the narrow, cliffside highway. However, the Westside is a very different story. Cycling downhill on Hwy 550 from Waimea Canyon is so spectacular that it has been turned into a guided tour; book ahead with Outfitters Kauai (p42).

Mountain Biking

If you aren't afraid of mud and puddles, you can go wild on countless dirt roads and a few trails islandwide. The Powerline Trail is a decent, if potholed and muddy, option – and you can start from either Wailua or Princeville. The dirt roads near Poʻipu, above Mahaʻulepu Beach, are flat but nice and dry, and you're less likely to encounter rain showers there. For a solitary ride, your best bets are the hunter roads at Waimea Canyon State Park. For more information contact Na Ala Hele (p304) and Kauai Cycle (p81), an Eastside bike rental and repair shop with a knowledgeable crew.

Camping

Kauaʻi offers camping at all levels of roughin' it. Some campgrounds, such as ʻAnini Beach Park, are within view of houses; others, such as the campsite at Kalalau Beach, are miles from civilization. For camping supplies and rentals, the best rental source is Pedal 'n Paddle (p132) in Hanalei. You can also buy camping gear from some outdoor outfitters, such as Da Life (p57) at Kalapaki Beach, or from chain retailers like Kmart, Walmart, Costco and the Sports Authority, all in Lihuʻe.

State Parks

State-park campsites can be found at the following parks:

Na Pali Coast Wilderness State Park Camping at Hanakapiʻai and Kalalau Valleys requires an overnight hike.

Kokeʻe State Park Drive-up and hike-in camping.

Waimea Canyon State Park Hike-in camping only.

Permits are required from the Division of State Parks (p151), obtainable either in person in Lihuʻe or online at https://camping.ehawaii.gov up to a year in advance. Fees range from $18 to $30 per night (or $20 per person per night on the Na Pali Coast). Maximum-stay limits of three to five nights are enforced.

For backcountry camping on the Westside, the **Division of Forestry & Wildlife** (📞808-274-3433; www.dlnr.hawaii.gov/dofaw; Room 306, 3060 Eiwa St, Lihu'e; ⏱8am-3:30pm **Mon-Fri)** issues free permits for four sites in Waimea Canyon, three sites in and around Koke'e State Park, and the Waialae site near the Alaka'i Wilderness Preserve. Apply online or in person at the Lihu'e office.

County Parks

The county maintains seven campgrounds on Kaua'i, all of which have bathrooms, cold-water outdoor showers and picnic tables. Moving clockwise around the island, these are:

Ha'ena Beach Park (closed 10am Monday to noon Tuesday)

Black Pot Beach Park (Hanalei Pier) (open Friday and Saturday nights only)

'Anini Beach Park (closed 10am Tuesday to noon Wednesday)

Anahola Beach Park (closed 10am Thursday to noon Friday)

Hanama'ulu Beach Park (temporarily closed for camping at the time of research)

Salt Pond Beach Park (closed 10am Tuesday to noon Wednesday)

Lucy Wright Park (closed 10am Monday to noon Tuesday)

The best county campsites are the coastal parks at Ha'ena, Hanalei, Salt Pond Beach and the particularly secluded and idyllic 'Anini Beach. The parks at Lucy Wright, Anahola and Hanama'ulu tend to attract a rougher, shadier crowd and are not recommended for solo or female campers. Each campground is closed one day a week for cleaning and in order to prevent people from permanently squatting there.

Camping permits cost $3 per night per adult camper (children under 18 free) and are issued in person or by mail (at least one month in advance) by the **Division of Parks & Recreation** (Map p44; 📞808-241-4463; www.kauai.gov; Suite 105, Lihu'e Civic Center, 4444 Rice St, Lihu'e; ⏱8am-4pm Mon-Fri) in Lihu'e. For mail-in permits, only cashier's checks or money orders are accepted for payment. Permits can also be obtained at the following four satellite locations:

Hanapepe Recreation Center (📞808-335-3731; 4451 Puolo Rd; ⏱8am-noon Mon-Fri)

Kalaheo Neighborhood Center (Map p188; 📞808-332-9770; 4480 Papalina Rd, Kalaheo; ⏱noon-4pm Mon-Fri)

Kapa'a Neighborhood Center (Map p82; 📞808-822-1931; 4491 Kou St; ⏱10am-noon Mon, Wed & Fri, 8am-noon Tue & Thu)

Kilauea Neighborhood Center (Map p110; 📞808-828-1421; 2460 Keneke St; ⏱10am-noon Mon, Wed & Fri, 8am-4pm Tue & Thu)

Golf

Kaua'i has only nine golf courses, but there's something for every taste and budget. Pros and experts can try the St Regis' Makai Golf Club and world-class Prince Golf Course in Princeville, Kaua'i Lagoons Golf Club in Lihu'e and Po'ipu Bay Golf Course. Budget or novice players have the Puakea Golf Course and the Wailua Municipal Golf Course in Lihu'e, the latter considered among the nation's finest municipal courses, and dirt-cheap Kukuiolono Golf Course. To save on resort fees, golf in the afternoon for the 'twilight' rate.

Hiking

If you don't explore the island on foot, you're missing out on Kaua'i's finest (and free) terrestrial offerings. Hike up mountaintop wet forests, along steep coastal cliffs and down a colossal lava canyon – places you can't get to by car. Trails range from easy walks to precarious treks, catering to all skill levels. For the most variety, head to Waimea Canyon and Koke'e State Parks. Don't miss the Pihea Trail, which connects to the Alaka'i Swamp Trail, for a look at pristine native forest filled with singing birds, or trek the Awa'awapuhi Trail or Nualolo Trail for breathtaking views of the Na Pali cliffs.

Along the Na Pali Coast, the wilderness Kalalau Trail now attracts anyone with two legs – but only for the first section to Hanakapi'ai Beach. Eastside hikes head inland and upward, such as the Nounou Mountain Trails, which afford sweeping mountain-to-ocean views, and the Kuilau Ridge and Moalepe Trails. In addition to official trails, Kaua'i's vast coastline allows mesmerizing ocean walks, particularly along the cliffs of the Maha'ulepu Coast and the endless carpet of sand in remote Polihale State Park.

Guided Hikes

The Kaua'i chapter of the **Sierra Club** (www.hi.sierraclub.org/kauai; annual membership from $15) leads guided hikes ranging from beach clean-up walks to hardy day-long treks. With a suggested donation of only $5 per person for non-members, these outings are

Hiking Safety on Kaua'i

- Take enough water for your entire trip, especially the uphill return journey, and treat any water found along the trails.
- Pack first-aid supplies and snacks.
- Cell phones can be handy, but may lack reception in many remote areas (eg Koke'e State Park, Na Pali Coast).
- Wear appropriate footwear: while Chacos or Tevas are fine for easy coastal walks, bring hiking shoes or boots for major trails.
- Rain is always a factor, especially on the North Shore, at Koke'e State Park and in Waimea Canyon. Trails that are doable in dry weather can become precariously slippery with mud.
- Flash floods are real threats wherever there are stream or river crossings. Never cross a waterway when it's raining. River fords may quickly rise to impassable levels, preventing you from returning for hours or days.
- If possible, hike with a companion or at least tell someone your expected return time.
- Don't go off-trail or bushwhack new trails.
- Lava terrain is frequently eroded and can be unstable, especially along cliffs.
- Never go beyond fenced lookouts.
- Note the time of sunset and plan to return well before it's dark. Be aware that daylight will fade inside a canyon long before sundown.
- Most accidents occur not due to a trail's inherent slipperiness or steepness, but because hikers take unnecessary risks. Park and forestry officials have little patience for this, because it requires expensive rescue missions that jeopardize others' safety.

an extraordinary bargain. All hikers must sign a liability waiver, and those under age 18 must be accompanied by an adult. Advance registration may also be required; check the website in advance.

Kaua'i Nature Tours (p153) offers hiking tours all over the island. While they are expensive, they include guides who are full of endless tales, scientific facts and colorful historical and cultural information about the island.

Horseback Riding

Vast pastureland stretches from open coastal cliffs to jungly rainforests, providing ample terrain for horseback riding. A handful of stables offer tours, mainly for beginners and families. On the South Shore, CJM Country Stables (p177) rides along the Maha'ulepu Coast, while on the North Shore, Princeville Ranch Stables (p119), Silver Falls Ranch (p107) and Esprit De Corps Riding Academy (p107) traverse green pastures, ranch lands, streams and waterfalls.

Ziplining

Ziplines, which first appeared in Costa Rica, are now proliferating across Hawaii. But location matters – and Kaua'i's magnificent forests are hard to beat. This outdoor adventure requires neither skill nor training, but participants must meet minimum age and maximum weight restrictions. There are three outfits in Lihu'e to call on, and one each in Koloa and Princeville.

By Air

Seeing Kaua'i from the air is utterly unlike seeing it by land or by sea. It's a completely different story. In fact, it's the only way to see much of the island, the majority of which is privately owned. It's also a thrilling experience, one you might want to have at all costs (and it *will* cost). Helicopter tours are by far the most common, though not necessarily the best. To check any tour company's flight record, consult the **National Transport Safety Board** (www.ntsb.gov) accident database. Consider all options before making a decision.

Fixed-Wing Scenic Flights

With one exception, there seems to be no point in choosing a fixed-wing aircraft to tour Kaua'i, not when you can take a helicopter right to the cone of Mt Wai'ale'ale and hover there to your heart's content. The exception is an open-cockpit biplane, which flies so slowly it may as well be hovering. The combination of the romance of early aviation, the sheer sensation of the wind and roaring engine, and the emerald tropical island sliding below, not to mention sitting side-by-side in near embrace, makes this many a honeymooner's first choice. In fact, if it were up to passengers, biplanes would probably be as popular as helicopters on Kaua'i, but there's currently only one company that offers these scenic flights: AirVentures Hawaii (p45), based in Lihu'e.

Helicopter Tours

The most popular choice for seeing Kaua'i from the air is to take a helicopter ride. You'll have to decide what kind of aircraft you want to fly in, what kind of tour you want (some land in neat places), and whether you want the doors on or off (some passengers like the visibility, others don't like the exposure to wind and possibly rain). Most helicopter tour companies depart from the airports in Lihu'e, Princeville and Port Allen.

Lei

PAM MCLEAN / GETTY IMAGES

Fragrant and ephemeral, lei embody the beauty of nature and the embrace of the community, freely given and freely shared. Greetings. Love. Honor. Respect. Peace. Celebration. Spirituality. Good luck. Farewell. These beautiful garlands, handcrafted from fresh tropical flora, can signify all of these meanings, and more. Lei making is a sensuous and transitory art form, perfectly matched with the gentle character of these Polynesian islands.

The Art of the Lei

In choosing their materials, lei makers tell a story – since flowers and plants embody Hawaiian places and myths – and express emotions. They may use feathers, nuts, shells, seeds, seaweed, vines, leaves and fruit, in addition to more familiar fragrant flowers. Handmade lei are typically created by knotting, braiding, winding, stringing or sewing the raw natural materials together.

Worn daily, lei were integral to ancient Hawaiian society. In the islands' Polynesian past, lei were made part of sacred hula dances and given as special gifts to loved ones, healing medicine to the sick and offerings to the gods, all practices that continue in Hawaii today. So powerful a symbol were they that on ancient Hawaii's battlefields, the right lei could bring peace to warring armies.

Nowadays locals don lei for special events, such as weddings, birthdays, anniversaries, graduations and public ceremonies. In general, it's no longer common to make one's own lei, unless you're a devoted member of a hula *halau* (school). For ceremonial hula (as opposed to popular shows for entertainment), performers are often required to make their own lei, even gathering the raw materials by hand.

Modern Celebrations

For visitors to Hawaii, the tradition of giving and receiving lei dates back to the 19th-century steamships that first brought tourists to the islands. In the heyday of cruise-ship tourism, disembarking passengers were greeted by local vendors who would toss garlands around the necks of *malihini* (newcomers).

Lei in Print

Ka Lei: The Leis of Hawaii (Ku Pa'a Publishing, 1995) Written by Marie McDonald, a recognized *kupuna* (elder) from the Big Island, this is an in-depth look at the art of Hawaiian lei making before Western contact and during contemporary times.

Na Lei Makamae: The Treasured Lei (University of Hawai'i Press, 2003) This artful, beautiful blend of botany and culture by Marie McDonald and Paul Weissich surveys the Hawaiian flowers traditionally used in lei and their meaning and mythology.

The tradition of giving a kiss with a lei began during WWII, allegedly when a hula dancer at a USO club was dared by her friends to give a military serviceman a peck on the cheek when offering him a flower lei.

In 1927 the poet Don Blanding and Honolulu journalist Grace Tower Warren called for making May 1 a holiday to celebrate lei. The next year, Leonard and Ruth Hawk composed the popular tune 'May Day is Lei Day in Hawaii.' Every year, Lei Day is celebrated across the islands with Hawaiian music, hula dancing, parades, lei-making workshops and contests, and more fun.

Lei Etiquette

○ Don't wear a lei hanging directly down around your neck. Instead, drape a closed (circular) lei over your shoulders, making sure that equal lengths are hanging over your front and back.

○ When traditionally presenting a lei, bow your head slightly and raise the lei above your heart. Don't drape it with your own hands over the head of the recipient, as this isn't respectful; let them do it themselves.

○ Don't give a closed lei to a pregnant woman, as it may bring bad luck to the unborn child; choose an open (untied) lei or *haku* (head) lei instead.

○ Resist the temptation to wear a lei intended for someone else. It's bad luck.

○ Never refuse a lei, and don't take one off in the presence of the giver.

○ When you stop wearing your lei, don't throw it in the trash. Untie the string, remove the bow and return the lei's natural elements to the earth (eg scatter flowers in the sea, bury seeds or nuts) instead.

Shopping for Lei

A typical Hawaiian lei costs anywhere from $10 for a single strand of orchids or plumeria to thousands of dollars for a 100% genuine Ni'ihau shell lei necklace. Beware that some *kukui* (candlenut) and *puka* shell lei are just cheap (even plastic) imports.

When shopping for a lei, ask the florist or shopkeeper for advice about the most appropriate lei for the occasion (eg for a bride, pick a string of pearl-like *pikake* jasmine flowers), and indicate if you're giving the lei to a man or a woman. Of course, it's OK to buy a lei for yourself any time!

A unique lei tradition on the Garden Island, leathery *mokihana* berries that faintly smell of licorice are often woven with strands of glossy, green maile vines. *Mokihana* trees grow in the rain-soaked forests on the western slopes of mighty Mt Wai'ale'ale.

On Kaua'i, you can buy fresh lei at Flowers Forever (p55) in downtown Lihu'e. Does an airport lei greeting to surprise your *ipo* (sweetheart) sound like fun? Several companies offer this service, including **Greeters of Hawaii** (☎ from US mainland 800-366-8559, in Hawaii 888-523-4487; www.greetersofhawaii.com), which has been in the business of giving aloha since 1957.

Survival
Guide

Po'ipu Beach (p168)
GEORGE OZE/ALAMY ©

A-Z

Directory

●●●

Accommodations

REVIEWS

o Sleeping reviews are listed by author preference. We recommend accommodations that provide good value at various price points, but the bell curve applies: most recommendations are midrange properties.

o Rates are categorized for the cost of a high-season, double-occupancy room with private bathroom but no breakfast, unless otherwise specified. Rates do not include the 13.96% accommodations tax.

o Where a pool or air-conditioning is available, we include swimming ⓢ or air-conditioning ❄ icons.

o Wireless internet access is noted by the wi-fi icon ⓦ. If there are computer terminals,

we include the internet icon @. A fee for either may apply, especially at large hotels.

SEASONS & BOOKING

o Unless otherwise noted, all lodgings listed in this book are open year-round.

o At many hotels and condos, rates rise during the winter high season (mid-December through March), and during major holidays. Book months in advance for peak periods.

SMOKING

o Smoking rooms are increasingly rare, especially since a statewide ban on smoking in all public spaces.

HOTELS & RESORTS

o The difference between a hotel and a resort is the amenities, such as spas, pool complexes, multiple restaurants, and children's programs. Kaua'i resorts don't mess around: amenities are, if anything, over the top (have you seen a hotel with five poolside hot tubs?).

o Never pay 'rack rates,' which refer to the published highest annual rates. Major hotels deeply cut their rack rates to remain as close to capacity as possible. Rates fluctuate madly based on seasonal occupancy.

o Within a given hotel, rates depend mainly on the view. Ocean views cost 50% to 100% more than garden or mountain (or parking lot) views. Be aware that descriptors such as 'oceanfront' and 'oceanview' are used liberally, even when you may require a telescope to spot the surf.

o Check the hotel's website or discount online travel-booking sites for reduced rates.

B&BS & GUESTHOUSES

o B&Bs offer the chance to stay in a home-like environment in which getting to know the owner and other travelers may be part of the experience. They vary from spare bedrooms in family households to historic homes to pull-out-the-stops romantic hideaways. Some include a kitchenette, private access or other apartment amenities.

o B&Bs generally have a resident owner, typically a couple, and include breakfast. They are distinct from guesthouses, which are managed properties that may or may not include breakfast.

o Many B&Bs require a two- or three-night minimum stay (though some will waive this if you pay a higher one-night rate) and offer discounts for extended stays. Some exclude young children due to the impact on other guests. Rates typically cover two guests, with extra-person charges ranging from $10 to $35.

o For listings, see **Affordable Paradise** (www.affordable -paradise.com) and **Bed & Breakfast Hawaii** (www. bandb-hawaii.com).

Book Your Stay Online

For more accommodations reviews by Lonely Planet authors, check out www.lonelyplanet.com/ hotels. You'll find independent reviews, as well as recommendations on the best places to stay. Best of all, you can book online.

VACATION RENTALS

o Vacation rentals offer privacy, usually a kitchen (or kitchenette) and your own parking space, so you don't have to do the resort marathon. They can also be a real money-saver, as you don't have to eat out all the time. There is typically a separate cleaning fee. Make sure you know who to call if there is a problem, as many vacation rentals have nonresident owners.

o The best online sources for vacation rentals are **Vacation Rentals By Owner** (www. vrbo.com) and **Airbnb** (www. airbnb.com). **FlipKey** (www. flipkey.com) contains both agency and private listings.

o On paper, tourist accommodations on Kaua'i are only allowed in designated areas, such as Po'ipu, Princeville and Kapa'a. Local government hasn't always enforced this law, however, so there are lots of off-the-grid accommodations – and plenty of people staying at them. You don't need to worry about this unless there's a crackdown. If the situation changes, government-approved rentals have a TVR (Transit Vacation Rental) number.

CONDOMINIUMS

o Condos are individually owned apartments that include a kitchen(ette) and washer/ dryer, and are typically more spacious than hotel rooms. They are often rented out on behalf of absentee owners by on-site managers or rental agencies. Units may differ widely within a single complex.

Accommodations Prices

The following price ranges refer to a double room with private bath in high season. Unless otherwise stated, breakfast and taxes are not included.

$ less than $100
$$ $100 to $250
$$$ more than $250

o Most condo units have a multiday minimum stay, especially in high season, of three to seven days.

o The weekly rental rate is often six times the daily rate and the monthly rate three times the weekly. One-time cleaning fees average $75 to $150 for a studio or one-bedroom unit, depending on the length of stay.

o To save money, try booking condos directly with owners or the complex first, then go through island rental agencies.

o Do your own internet search for online condo rental classifieds at **Vacation Rentals by Owner** (www. vrbo.com) and **Airbnb** (www. airbnb.com).

CAMPING

o See p292-3 for details of campgrounds in Kaua'i's state and county parks and permit information.

Customs Regulations

Non-US citizens and permanent residents may import the following duty free:

o 1L of liquor (if you're over 21 years old)

o 200 cigarettes (one carton) or 100 non-Cuban cigars (if you're over 18 years old)

o $100 worth of gifts

Hawaii has strict restrictions against bringing in any fresh fruits and plants, to prevent entry of invasive species. The rabies-free state enforces strict pet quarantine laws. (For information on bringing service animals, see Travelers with Disabilities, p308) For complete details, contact the **Hawaiian Department of Agriculture** (☎ 808-483-7151; www.hdoa.hawaii.gov).

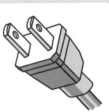

Electricity

120V/60Hz

120V/60Hz

Food

Restaurant reviews are listed by author preference within each price category (budget, midrange and top end), in the Eating section of each regional chapter. For more on local cuisine, see the Food & Drink chapter (p254).

Gay & Lesbian Travelers

Sexual preference on Kaua'i is basically a non-issue. The island culture here is very welcoming and diverse. Hawaii has strong legislation that protects minority groups, and there is also a constitutional guarantee of privacy regarding sexual behavior between consenting adults. The state also recently passed legislation giving same-sex couples the right to marry. That said, there's neither a gay scene nor public displays of affection on the island, as locals tend to keep their private lives to themselves.

These resources support gay visitors to Hawaii:

Pride Guide Hawaii (www. gogayhawaii.com) Gay friendly events, dining, shopping, weddings and more.

Pacific Ocean Holidays (📞 808-923-2400; www. gayhawaiivacations.com) Personalized vacation packages for gay and lesbian travelers.

Purple Roofs (www. purpleroofs.com) Online directory of LGBTQ-friendly accommodations.

Insurance

Worldwide travel insurance is available at www.lonelyplanet. com/travel_services. You can buy, extend and claim online anytime – even if you're already on the road.

International Travelers

VISAS

○ Rules for US entry keep changing. Confirm current visa and passport requirements for your country at the **US Department of State** (www. travel.state.gov) website.

○ Upon arriving in the US, all foreign visitors must have electronic (inkless) fingerprints and a digital photo taken, a process that takes under a minute. For more information, see the **US Department of Homeland Security** (www. dhs.gov) website.

CONSULATES

In the state of Hawaii, all foreign consulates are located on O'ahu, in Honolulu:

Australia (📞 808-529-8100; 1000 Bishop St)

Japan (📞 808-543-3111; 1742 Nu'uanu Ave)

Korea (📞 808-595-6109; 2756 Pali Hwy)

New Zealand (📞 808-595-2200; 3929 Old Pali Rd)

Internet Access

Wi-Fi Available at many accommodations, although a surprising number of larger hotels offer only wired in-room access. Most towns have at least one cafe with wi-fi.

Restaurant Prices
Price indicators are usually for the cost of a main dish; the price estimates do not include taxes, tips or beverages.

$ less than $12

$$ $12 to $30

$$$ more than $30

Public Libraries Island libraries (www.librarieshawaii.org) have free computer terminals (with a temporary non-resident library card, $10) and sometimes free wi-fi (no card required).

Free or Fee? Smaller accommodations (eg B&Bs) typically provide free wi-fi; larger hotels will often charge $12 to $15 per day for wired in-room access or wi-fi.

Reviews In this book, reviews with the 🛜 icon indicate that wi-fi is available; those with the @ icon indicate that computer terminals are available.

Language

Hawaii has two official languages: English and Hawaiian. There's also an unofficial vernacular, pidgin (also called Hawai'i Creole English), which has a laid-back, lilting accent and colorful vocabulary that permeates the official tongues. While the Hawaiian language's multisyllabic, vowel-heavy words may seem daunting, the pronunciation is actually quite straightforward.

The 'okina punctuation mark (') is the Hawaiian language's glottal stop, which determines the pronunciation and meaning of words. In this book, Hawai'i (with the 'okina) refers to the island of Hawai'i (the Big Island), to ancient Hawai'i and to the Kingdom of Hawai'i pre-statehood. Hawaii (without the 'okina) refers to the US territory that became a state in 1959.

Climate

Lihu'e

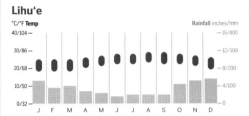

Princeville

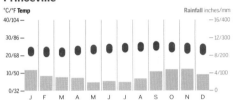

Koke'e State Park

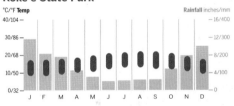

Legal Matters

○ You are entitled to an attorney from the moment that you are arrested. The **Hawaii State Bar Association** (📞808-537-9140) is one starting point to find an attorney. If you can't afford one, the state is obligated to provide one for free.

○ Driving with a blood alcohol level of 0.08% or higher constitutes driving under the influence (DUI), a serious offense that may incur heavy fines, a suspended driver's license, jail time and other penalties.

○ Possessing marijuana and nonprescription narcotics is illegal. Foreigners convicted of a drug offense face immediate deportation.

○ It's illegal to carry open containers of alcohol inside a motor vehicle, even if they're empty. Unless containers are still sealed and have never been opened, store them in the trunk.

○ Both hitchhiking and public nudity (eg at nude beaches) are illegal, but the laws are not always enforced.

Minimum Legal Age to...

- Drink alcohol – 21
- Buy tobacco – 18
- Vote in an election – 18
- Drive a car – 16

- Smoking cigarettes is prohibited in all public spaces, including airports, bars, restaurants and businesses.

Maps

Franko's Maps (www.frankosmaps.com) Outstanding full-color, fold-up, waterproof maps ($6 to $11) that pinpoint snorkeling, diving, surfing and kayaking spots and also identify tropical fish.

Kaua'i Island Atlas & Maps (www.envdhawaii.com) Like a land version of the Franko map, with all sorts of info on climate, geology and culture, along with town insets. Available ($10) at the Koke'e Museum.

Kaua'i: Island of Discovery Nice fold-out tourist freebie available from Kaua'i Visitors Bureau and at Lihu'e Airport. Identifies all locations used in feature films.

Na Ala Hele (http://hawaiitrails.ehawaii.gov) Detailed topographical trail maps for hikers and mountain bikers, online from the Division of Forestry & Wildlife.

US Geographical Survey (www.usgs.gov) Map geeks and backcountry hikers can download maps for free online, or order printed maps. Pay attention to topo map dates, since some were drawn decades ago.

Money

ATMs ATMs are available 24/7 at banks, supermarkets, convenience stores, shopping centers and gas stations. Expect a surcharge of about $3 per transaction, plus any fees charged by your home bank.

Checks Out-of-state personal checks are generally not accepted.

Credit Cards Major credit cards are widely accepted at larger businesses, and they're necessary to rent a car, order tickets by phone or book a hotel room. Note that smaller businesses such as B&Bs typically do not accept credit cards.

Moneychangers Outside of cities and larger towns, exchanging money may be impossible, so make sure you carry enough cash and/or a credit card.

Taxes Hawaii has a 4.17% state sales tax tacked onto virtually everything, including meals, groceries and car rentals (which also entail additional state and local tax surcharges). Lodging taxes total 13.96%.

Traveler's Checks Rather archaic nowadays, traveler's checks (in US dollars) are accepted only by larger tourist-oriented businesses, such as hotels, resorts and high-end restaurants.

TIPPING

Leaving no tip is rare and requires real cause.

Airport & hotel porters $2 per bag, minimum $5 per cart

Bartenders 15% to 20% per round, minimum $1 per drink

Housekeeping staff $2 to $4 daily, left under the card provided; more if you're messy

Parking valets At least $2 when handed back your car keys

Street Addresses

Street addresses on Kaua'i might seem long, but there's a pattern. The numerical prefix in street addresses along Kaua'i's highways (eg 3-4567 Kuhio Hwy) refers to one of five tax zones: 1 refers to Waimea and vicinity, including Ni'ihau; 2 is Koloa and Po'ipu; 3 is Lihu'e to the Wailua River; 4 is Kapa'a and Anahola; and 5 is the North Shore.

Restaurants 18% to 20%, unless gratuity is automatically included (common for groups of six or more)

Taxi drivers 10% to 15% of metered fare, rounded up to the next dollar

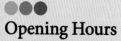

Opening Hours

Standard opening hours year-round are as follows:

Banks 8:30am to 4pm Monday to Friday, some to 6pm Friday and 9am to noon or 1pm Saturday

Bars 11am or noon to midnight daily

Businesses 8:30am to 4:30pm Monday to Friday, some post offices 9am to noon Saturday

Restaurants breakfast 6am to 10am, lunch 11:30am to 2pm, dinner 5pm to 9:30pm

Shops 9am to 5pm Monday to Saturday, some also noon to 5pm Sunday

Post

○ The **US postal service** (USPS; ☎800-275-8777; www.usps.com) delivers mail to and from Kaua'i. Service is reliable but slower than on the mainland. First-class airmail between Kaua'i and the mainland takes up to five days.

○ First-class letters up to 1oz (about 28g) cost 49¢ within the USA, and $1.15 to foreign countries.

○ You can receive mail c/o General Delivery at most post offices on Kaua'i, but you must first complete an application in person. Bring two forms of ID and your temporary local address. The accepted application is valid for 30 days; mail is held for up to 15 days. Some accommodations will also hold mail for incoming guests.

Kaua'i at the Movies

Kaua'i has an extraordinary cinematic history; when Hollywood wants paradise, this is their first stop. Below are some of the most popular movies filmed on the island. For a free map of more films and locations, stop by the Kaua'i Visitors Bureau (p57) in Lihu'e.

Pirates of the Caribbean 4 (2011)

Just Go with It (2011)

The Descendants (2011)

Soul Surfer (2011)

Avatar (2010)

High School Reunion Season 5 (2008)

Perfect Getaway (2008)

Tropic Thunder (2008)

Jurassic Park 3 (2001)

Manhunt (2001)

The Time Machine (2001)

Mighty Joe Young (1998)

George of the Jungle (1997)

The Lost World: Jurassic Park (1997)

Outbreak (1995)

Jurassic Park (1993)

Honeymoon in Vegas (1992)

Hook (1991)

Lord of the Flies (1990)

Throw Momma from the Train (1987)

The Thorn Birds (1983)

Raiders of the Lost Ark (1983)

Seven (1980)

Fantasy Island (1977)

Islands in the Stream (1977)

King Kong (1976)

Gilligan's Island (1964)

Blue Hawaii (1961)

South Pacific (1958)

Pagan Love Song (1950)

White Heat (1934)

Public Holidays

On the following national holidays, banks, schools and government offices (including post offices) close, and museums, transportation and other services operate on a Sunday schedule. Holidays falling on a weekend are usually observed the following Monday.

New Year's Day January 1

Martin Luther King Jr Day Third Monday in January

Presidents' Day Third Monday in February

Prince Kuhio Day March 26

Good Friday Friday before Easter Sunday in March/April

Memorial Day Last Monday in May

King Kamehameha Day June 11

Independence Day July 4

Statehood Day Third Friday in August

Labor Day First Monday in September

Columbus Day Second Monday in October

Veterans Day November 11

Thanksgiving Fourth Thursday in November

Christmas Day December 25

Safe Travel

Visitors who become accident or crime victims can contact the **Visitor Aloha Society** **of Hawaii** (VASH; ☎ 808-926-8274; www.visitoraloha societyofhawaii.org), a traveler's aid organization, for short-term assistance.

HIKING & SWIMMING

The major risks on Kaua'i lie here. See the boxes on Ocean Safety (p290) and Hiking Safety (p294) on Kaua'i.

THEFT & VIOLENCE

Kaua'i is a pretty quiet place and there's virtually no nightlife. Populated areas, such as towns and major sights, are relatively safe. Having said that, the island has its issues, like everywhere else.

○ There's a drug problem, generally involving ice (crystal methamphetamine) or *pakalolo* (marijuana), which fuels petty crime. Be on guard at deserted beaches and parks and at county campgrounds after dark.

○ Car break-ins occur mainly in remote areas, including campgrounds, and trailhead parking lots, but also at busy places like beach parking lots. Do not leave anything valuable in your parked car. If that's not possible, pack everything away out of sight, preferably in the trunk, *before* arriving at your destination.

○ There's a deep insider/outsider mentality, with racial overtones. Certain beaches, surf spots, swimming holes, and rural neighborhoods are unofficially considered locals only. In these places haole (white) tourists might encounter resentment or worse. The key is to avoid confrontation. Be careful in places where that bright new aloha shirt makes you stand out.

TRESPASSING

○ Heed *kapu* (no trespassing) signs on private property.

○ Like the rest of the USA, Hawaii does not have the open-access laws found in certain European countries.

TSUNAMI

During the 20th century, Kaua'i was hit by two major tsunamis. Both ravaged the North Shore, causing 14 deaths in 1946, and demolishing 75 homes and washing out six essential bridges in 1957. Today, new homes built in tsunami-prone areas (flood zones) must be built high off the ground.

○ If you're at the coast when a tsunami occurs, immediately head inland.

○ The front section of local telephone books has maps of areas susceptible to tsunamis and safety evacuation zones.

○ Kaua'i has four civil defense sirens that can be used to issue a tsunami warning.

Telephone

DIALING CODES

○ Domestic long-distance calls must be preceded by ☎1.

○ Toll-free numbers (area codes ☎800, ☎866, ☎877 or ☎888) must be preceded by ☎1.

○ For all Kaua'i calls, dial only the seven-digit local number. For inter-island calls, dial ☎1-808 and then the seven-digit number; long-distance charges apply.

- For direct international calls, dial 011 plus the country code, area code and local number. An exception is Canada, where you dial 1 plus the area code and local number, but international rates still apply.

- If you're calling from abroad, the US country code is 1.

CELL PHONES

- You need a multiband GSM phone to make calls in the USA. If your phone doesn't work here, you can pop in a US prepaid rechargeable SIM card (with an unlocked multiband phone) or buy an inexpensive prepaid phone.

- Verizon has the best cellular network across the state, but AT&T and Sprint have decent coverage. While coverage on Kaua'i is good in major towns, it's spotty or nonexistent in rural areas.

PAYPHONES & PHONE CARDS

- Although payphones are a dying breed, they are still found in shopping centers, beach parks and other public places. Local calls cost 50¢. Interisland calls are long-distance and more costly. Prepaid phone cards are sold at convenience stores, supermarkets and other locations.

Time

- Hawaii has its own time zone and does not observe Daylight Saving Time (DST) like most of the US mainland.

- During standard time (winter), Hawaii time differs

from Los Angeles by two hours, from New York by five hours, from London by 10 hours and from Tokyo by 19 hours. During daylight saving time (summer), the difference is one hour more for countries that observe it.

- In midwinter, the sun rises around 7am and sets around 6pm. In midsummer, it rises before 6am and sets after 7pm.

- Upon arrival, set your internal clock to 'island time,' meaning slow down!

Practicalities

- **Electricity** Voltage is 110/120V at 50/60Hz, with a standard US plug.

- **Laundry** Many condos, B&Bs, inns and vacation rentals include free or inexpensive use of washers and dryers; hotels typically offer coin-operated laundry facilities.

- **Newspapers & Magazines** *The Garden Island* (www.thegardenisland.com), Kaua'i's daily newspaper, the best source of current island events and issues; *Edible Hawaiian Islands* (www.ediblecommunities.com) is a quarterly food magazine; *101 Things to Do* (www.101thingstodo.com) and *This Week Kaua'i* (www.thisweekhawaii.com/kauai) are freebie tourist pamphlets handy for activities info and cost-cutting coupons.

- **Radio** KKCR 91.9FM (www.kkcr.org) is Kaua'i community radio – 100% volunteer-run, listener-supported and noncommercial. KIPL 88.9FM and KIPO 89.3FM are Hawaii Public Radio (www.hawaiipublicradio.org), broadcasting news, talk shows and jazz, blues, Hawaiian and world music. KITH 98.9FM has Hawaiian hits of the past 20 years, plus 'Jawaiian' reggae. KONG 93.5FM (www.kongradio.com) is a popular station playing mainstream US pop and contemporary island music. KTOH 99.9FM and KUAI 720AM (www.kuai720am.com) are country music stations.

- **TV** All the major US TV networks and cable channels are represented. KVIC, the Kaua'i Visitor Information Channel, is a televised loop of tourist information on channel 3.

- **Weights & Measures** Imperial (except 1 US gallon = 0.83 gallons).

Tourist Information

101 Things to Do (www.101thingstodo.com) Free publication describing major attractions.

Hawaii Visitors & Convention Bureau (800-464-2924; www.gohawaii.com) Handy for island hoppers.

Kaua'i Visitors Bureau (Map p44; 808-245-3971,

800-262-1400; www.gohawaii.com/kauai; Suite 101, 4334 Rice St, Lihu'e) A good starting point.

This Week (www.thisweekhawaii.com) Free publication with weekly events and handy maps.

Travelers with Disabilities

Accommodations Major hotels are equipped with elevators, phones with TDD (telecommunications device for the deaf) and wheelchair-accessible rooms (which must be reserved in advance). But B&Bs and smaller, older hotels are probably not.

General Information
The **Disability and Communication Access Board** (DCAB; ☎ 808-586-8121; www.health.hawaii.gov/dcab; room 101, 919 Ala Moana Blvd, Honolulu, O'ahu) also provides a tip sheet specifically for Kaua'i at www.health.hawaii.gov/dcab/community-resources/visitors.

Mobility There are currently no car rental agencies with lift-equipped vehicles. **Gammie HomeCare** (☎ 808-632-2333; www.gammie.com; 3206 Akahi St, Lihu'e; ⏰ 8:30am-5pm Mon-Fri) rents portable ramps, wheelchairs, hospital beds, walking aids and other medical equipment. **Wheelchair Getaways of Hawaii** (☎ 800-638-1912; www.wheelchairgetaways.com)

and **Wheelers Van Rentals** (☎ 800-456-1731; www.wheelersvanrentals.com) rent wheelchair-accessible vans. The Kaua'i Bus system is fully wheelchair-accessible. Kaua'i County provides an all-terrain wheelchair at lifeguard stations at some beach parks; call ☎ 808-241-4460 for more information..

Seeing-Eye & Guide Dogs
Mobility dogs are not subject to the general quarantine rules for pets if they meet the Department of Agriculture's minimum requirements; see http://hdoa.hawaii.gov/ai/aqs/animal-quarantine-information-page/guide-service-dogs-entering-hawaii for more details. All animals must enter the state via Honolulu International Airport.

Volunteering

For opportunities to volunteer on environmental projects, see p273.

Work

○ US citizens can legally work in Hawaii, but employment opportunities are limited. Short-term employment will probably mean entry-level jobs at tourist bars and restaurants. Specific outdoor skills (eg scuba diving) might land you a job with an activity outfitter or tour company.

○ Check the listings in newspaper classifieds and also **Kaua'i Craigslist** (http://honolulu.craigslist.org/kau).

Transport

Getting There & Away

Flights can be booked online at lonelyplanet.com/flights.

✈ AIR
Virtually all travelers to Kaua'i arrive by air, and the vast majority stop first at Honolulu International Airport. If you have a layover in Honolulu, make sure the ticket agent marks your baggage with Lihu'e (LIH) as the final destination.

US domestic and international airfares vary too much for generalizations about the cheapest carriers or months. But you can count on across-the-board fare hikes from mid-December to mid-March.

AIRPORTS
All commercial flights land in Lihu'e, mostly via Honolulu, which is 40 minutes away by air. Most commercial air tours depart from Lihu'e, but some use two other, smaller airports on the island: Port Allen Airport (Map p200) and Princeville Airport (off Map p118).

Lihu'e Airport (LIH; ☎ 808-274-3800; www.hawaii.gov/lih)

Honolulu International Airport (HNL; ☎ 808-836-6411; www.hawaii.gov/hnl)

Getting Around

TO/FROM THE AIRPORT

Almost all visitors to Kaua'i rent cars from the agencies located at Lihu'e Airport. Those foregoing rental cars can find taxis curbside outside the baggage-claim area. Average fares from Lihu'e Airport include Lihu'e ($9 to $13), Po'ipu ($42 to $53) and Princeville ($89 to $119).

৬⃝ BICYCLE

○ Kaua'i is compact enough for road cycling, but the going can be tough. Although the winter months are particularly wet, showers are common year-round. Dedicated bicycle lanes are generally rare, and roads can be narrow, winding and heavily trafficked. Riding along the North Shore is not possible.

○ A 16-mile coastal bicycle path (p87) from Lihu'e to Anahola is partly completed, but the path currently seems geared toward recreation rather than commuting.

○ Bicycle-rental shops are found in Waipouli (p81), Kapa'a (p86) and Po'ipu (p187). Riders under 16 years old must wear a helmet.

🚌 BUS

The county's **Kaua'i Bus** (☎ 808-246-8110; www.kauai.gov; 3220 Ho'olako St; one-way fare adult/senior & child 7-18yr $2/1) is fine for major stops, but routes and runs are limited. Buses operate approximately hourly on weekdays, with a reduced schedule on Saturdays, Sundays and holidays. Schedules are available online and at island businesses including Big Save, Kukui Grove Center and Safeway. Lihu'e is the hub. Buses are air-conditioned and equipped with bicycle racks and wheelchair ramps.

Some caveats: drivers will accept only the exact fare; a monthly pass costs $35; you can transport a folding baby stroller, bicycle, or bodyboard (but not a surfboard); stops are marked but sometimes hard to spot.

🚗 CAR & MOTORCYCLE

AUTOMOBILE ASSOCIATIONS

○ For 24-hour emergency roadside assistance, free maps and discounts on car rentals and accommodations, members are served by the **American Automobile Association** (AAA; ☎ 800-736-2886, emergency 800-222-4357; www.aaa.com), from its office in Honolulu.

○ AAA has reciprocal agreements with automobile associations in other countries, so bring your membership card from home.

DRIVING LICENSES

○ An international driving license, which must be obtained before you leave home, is necessary only if your country of origin is a non-English-speaking one.

○ You need a valid motorcycle license to rent one, but a standard driving license will suffice for mopeds. The minimum age for renting a motorcycle is 21; for a moped, it's 16.

FUEL & TOWING

○ With the exception of remote areas such as Waimea Canyon Rd and the North Shore beyond Princeville, fuel is available everywhere, but expect to pay 20% more than the mainland. Towing is also expensive and should

Climate Change & Travel

Every form of transport that relies on carbon-based fuel generates CO_2, the main cause of human-induced climate change. Modern travel is dependent on airplanes, which might use less fuel per kilometer per person than most cars but travel much greater distances. The altitude at which aircraft emit gases (including CO_2) and particles also contributes to their climate change impact. Many websites offer 'carbon calculators' that allow people to estimate the carbon emissions generated by their journey and, for those who wish to do so, to offset the impact of the greenhouse gases emitted with contributions to portfolios of climate-friendly initiatives throughout the world. Lonely Planet offsets the carbon footprint of all staff and author travel.

Road Distances & Times

Average driving distances and times from Lihu'e are listed below. Allow more time during morning and afternoon rush hours and on weekends.

DESTINATION	MILES	TIME
Anahola	14	25min
Hanalei	31	1hr
Hanapepe	16	30min
Kapa'a	8	15min
Ke'e Beach	40	1¼hr
Kilauea Lighthouse	25	40min
Po'ipu	10	20min
Port Allen	15	25min
Princeville	28	45min
Waimea	23	40min
Waimea Canyon	42	1½hr

be avoided at all costs. Fees start around $65, plus $6.50 per mile.

RENTAL

◦ Renting a car often costs more on Kaua'i than on the other major Hawaiian Islands. Normally, a rock-bottom economy car from a major rental company will cost you $200 per week, with rates doubling during the peak periods. Rental rates will generally include unlimited mileage.

◦ To minimize costs, comparison shop using travel websites. Differences of 50% between suppliers is not unheard of.

◦ Another strategy for cost saving is to use a purely local rental agency. These mom-and-pop firms, which generally operate from home, rent used vehicles that may be 10 years old, but can be had for $20 to $25 per day.

◦ For motorcycle rentals, the go-to place is Kaua'i Harley-Davidson (p58), which has a 20-bike fleet in Puhi, just outside Lihu'e. For mopeds, try Kaua'i Car & Scooter Rental (p58).

◦ If you want a 4WD for getting to some of the sights, rates average $70 to $120 per day (before taxes and fees). Agencies prohibit driving off-road, meaning that if you get stuck they'll slap a penalty on you.

RENTAL AGENCIES

Rent A Car Kauai (☎ 808-639-7149; www.rentacarkauai.com; Lihu'e) Great customer service and diligent maintenance makes this family firm the best choice. Cars are $25 per day for seven days, $20 thereafter. Free airport pick-up and drop-off.

Kauai Rent A Car (☎ 808-246-1881; www.kauairentacar.

com; Kapa'a) The Eastside option, with free airport pick-up and drop-off.

Kaua'i Car & Scooter Rental (☎ 808-245-7177; www.kauaiscooter.com; 3371 Wilcox Rd, Lihu'e; ⊙ 8am-6pm) If you can't find a car, there's always a scooter. There is a second location at 3414 Po'ipu Rd, Koloa.

Island Cars (☎ 808-246-6000, 800-246-6009; www.islandcars.net; 2983 Aukele St, Lihu'e) Offers consistently cheap rates, but car quality is less consistent.

ROAD CONDITIONS, HAZARDS & RULES

◦ Kaua'i remains very rural, with only one coastal highway connecting all major destinations. It's hard to get lost for long.

◦ Highway congestion has been lessened by road-widening, but there is still rush-hour traffic, especially between Lihu'e and Kapa'a. To help combat this, a 'contra-flow' lane is created from 5am to 10:30am weekdays on Kuhio Hwy (Hwy 56) in the Wailua area; this turns a northbound lane into a southbound lane by reversing the flow of traffic.

◦ Stay alert for one-lane-bridge crossings. Whenever there's no sign on one-lane stretches, downhill traffic must yield to uphill traffic.

◦ While drivers do tend to speed on highways, in-town driving is courteous and rather leisurely. Locals don't honk (unless a crash is imminent), they don't tailgate and they let faster cars pass. Do the same.

○ State law prohibits more than one rider per moped, as well as requiring that they be driven in single file at a maximum of 30mph. Also, mopeds are not to be driven on sidewalks or freeways, but rather on roads with lower speed limits or on the highway shoulder.

○ The state requires helmets only for motorcycle or moped/scooter riders under age 18. Rental agencies provide free helmets for all riders: use them.

HITCHHIKING

Hitchhiking is technically illegal statewide and hitchhiking anywhere is not without risks. Lonely Planet does not recommend it. Hitchers should size up each situation carefully before getting in cars, and women should be wary of hitching alone. People who do choose to hitchhike will be safer if they travel in pairs and let someone know where they are planning to go.

Hitchhiking is not a common practice among locals. You're most likely to find a ride along the North Shore.

TAXI

○ Taxis are not that common in rural Kaua'i. Companies include **Akiko's Taxi** (☏808-822-7588), in the Lihu'e–Kapa'a area; **North Shore Cab** (☏808-826-4118; www.northshorecab.com), based in Princeville; and **Southshore Cab** (☏808-742-1525) in Po'ipu.

○ Fares are based on mileage regardless of the number of passengers. Since cabs are often station wagons or minivans, they offer good value for groups. The standard flag-down fee is $3, plus 30¢ per one-eighth additional mile.

○ Cabs line up at the airport during normal business hours, but they don't run all night or cruise for passengers; for any rides outside a trip from the airport, you'll need to call ahead.

TOURS

Here, 'tours' refer to group sightseeing options. For activity tours (snorkeling cruises, ziplining adventures etc), see the Outdoor Activities & Adventures chapter (p280) for general information, and the regional chapters for details.

Bus tour companies generally offer whirlwind regional tours (eg Fern Grotto, Waimea Canyon,

North Shore) which only allow superficial 'stop-and-click' sightseeing. Forgo them unless you're a non-driver with no other option. Typical rates range from $60 to $100 for adults and $40 to $65 for children, depending on the tour itinerary. However, two major companies, **Gray Line Hawaii** (☏ 800-622-3011; www.polyad.com) and **Roberts Hawaii** (☏ 866-898-2519; www.robertshawaii.com) have recently started some interesting tours of Kaua'i film locations, of which there is an extraordinary number (see p297). Gray Line Hawaii's six-hour tour (adult/child 6-11yr $97/65) shows you the relevant film clip as you are looking at the real site. Roberts Hawaii (adult/child 4-11yr $95/47) does as well, and throws in lunch where *The Descendants* was filmed. Or see Maps (p304) if you want to lead your own tour.

Highway Nicknames

Locals call highways by nickname rather than by number. Here's a cheat sheet:

Hwy 50	Kaumuali'i Hwy
Hwy 51	Kapule Hwy
Hwy 56	Kuhio Hwy
Hwy 58	Nawiliwili Rd
Hwy 520	Maluhia Rd (Tree Tunnel) and Po'ipu Rd
Hwy 530	Koloa Rd
Hwy 540	Halewili Rd
Hwy 550	Waimea Canyon Dr/Koke'e Rd
Hwy 560	Kuhio Hwy (continuation of Hwy 56)
Hwy 570	Ahukini Rd
Hwy 580	Kuamo'o Rd
Hwy 581	Kamalu Rd and Olohena Rd
Hwy 583	Ma'alo Rd

Behind the Scenes

Author Thanks

Sara Benson

Thanks to Alex Howard for ace editorial problem-solving skills and project leadership, and to all of my Hawaii co-authors for their research tips and expert input. Thanks also to all of the travelers, locals and long-time residents who shared insider spots, savvy advice and more. Without Jai's help, this trip to Kaua'i would never have happened in the middle of two tropical storms – *shukriyaa*.

Acknowledgments

Climate map data adapted from Peel MC, Finlayson BL & McMahon TA (2007) 'Updated World Map of the Köppen-Geiger Climate Classification', Hydrology and Earth System Sciences, 11, 1633¬44.

Cover photographs
Front: Kalalau Valley, Koke'e State Park, Waimea Canyon, Dennis Frates/Alamy
Back: Makua (Tunnels) Beach, Ha'ena, Monica & Michael Sweet/Corbis

This Book

This 2nd edition of Lonely Planet's *Discover Kaua'i* w. written by Sara Benson. The previous edition was wri ten by Paul Stiles and E Clark Carroll. This guidebook was produced by the following:

Destination Editor Alexander Howard

Product Editors Briohny Hooper, Kate Mathews

Senior Cartographer Anthony Phelan

Book Designer Wendy Wright

Assisting Editors Carolyn Boicos, Paul Harding, Elizabeth Jones, Susan Paterson, Martine Power, Kirste Rawlings, Saralinda Turner

Cover Researcher Naomi Parker

Thanks to Sasha Baskett, Peter Cruttenden, Brendan Dempsey, Ryan Evans, Anna Harris, Kate James, Diana Saengkham, Lyahna Spencer, Tony Wheeler.

SEND US YOUR FEEDBACK

We love to hear from travelers – your comments kee us on our toes and help make our books better. Our well-traveled team reads every word on what you loved or loathed about this book. Although we cann reply individually to postal submissions, we always guarantee that your feedback goes straight to the appropriate authors, in time for the next edition. Each person who sends us information is thanked i the next edition, the most useful submissions are rewarded with a selection of digital PDF chapters.

Visit **lonelyplanet.com/contact** to submit you updates and suggestions or to ask for help. Our award-winning website also features inspirational travel stories, news and discussions.

Index